SLIPPERY NOODLES

SLIPPERY NOODLES

A Culinary History of China

Hsiang Ju Lin

PROSPECT BOOKS

2015

First published in 2015 in Great Britain and the United States
by Prospect Books,
26 Parke Road, London, SW13 9NG

BRITISH LIBRARY CATALOGUING IN PUBLICATION DATA:
A catalogue entry of this book is available from the British Library.

Typeset and designed by Rebecca Gillieron and Catheryn Kilgarriff in Adobe Garamond Pro.

The cover illustration is *Chinese at Breakfast, moveable chow shop, Canton* from Bridgeman Images.

ISBN 978-1-909248-37-3

Printed and bound by the Gutenberg Press, Malta.

Contents

Foreword

This is an account of how Chinese cooking evolved over two thousand years, written in an informal style for the general reader. Rich in detail, this book sets the story of Chinese cuisine against its changing culture. History comes to life as the individuals who contributed to the food culture enter the narrative. They came from different walks of life. Rich merchants, artists, street food vendors, peasants, housewives, and a few enterprising monks are a few of the figures. Practitioners of Chinese medicine routinely gave prescriptions that resembled recipes. There was the gourmet who insisted that he liked simple meals (although his cook might have thought otherwise). There were the gentlemen cooks – highly educated men with a deep and abiding interest in food, and wrote about it.

'Food and drink are not simple matters,' a gentleman cook wrote. The reader may come to share his view as he delves into the history of China's unique cuisine. The author evokes the taste of the foods: the lamb tartare that was an ancient delicacy, to the raw fish sliced at the table, the stir-fries, the 'mock' foods made to look and taste like something else. Menus from extraordinary banquets showed how styles of extreme dining changed across different periods of China's history.

In scope the book exceeds that of any other work on Chinese culinary history. Many of the excerpts from the literature have never been translated into English. For example it draws upon a cookbook written by a salt merchant of the eighteenth-nineteenth century, whose manuscript was did not appear in print until the 1980s. Notes at the end of each chapter provide the scholar with full references to its sources in traditional Chinese and pinyin – Chinese books, poetry, journals and records.

And I thank my publisher, Tom Jaine, for making the book happen.

Hsiang Ju Lin
December 2014

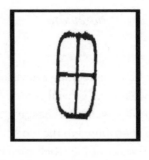

CHAPTER ONE

IN MEDIEVAL CHINA

'I hope that future readers will not laugh at me.' Jia Sixie

In the sixth century, a man named Jia Sixie wrote a book called *Essential Skills for Common Folk*. He gave us the earliest comprehensive look at Chinese cooking. At that time China was defined by the Yellow River region. With its source in the Tibetan plateau, the river flowed north and then made the first of three right angle turns – east, south and east – finally turning northeast to reach the Yellow Sea. Jia was a government official and a specialist in plant and soil cultivation. He worked in the provinces that bordered the lower reaches of the Yellow River. His outlook was unusual. The book was a manual for farmers, but it covered the culinary arts as well. To his mind the primary purpose of farming was to produce food, food preparation being the final step. 'From tilling and planting to making vinegar and condiments, whatever is part of the farmer's life, I have set it all down,' he wrote. 'I collected material from old books, recorded the oral traditions, and interviewed persons with relevant experience. I wrote this book for the younger generations in the family. I would not dare show it to men of learning. The language is straight and plain. Everything is exactly the way I heard it. I did not change a word,' he added, hoping future readers would not ridicule him.

Jia wrote his book just as the Northern Wei dynasty was drawing to a chaotic end. In 528 the emperor was poisoned by his mother in a power struggle. Six emperors succeeded him over the next five years. Northern Wei was one of several dynasties that coexisted in the fifth and sixth centuries. China was divided into numerous kingdoms, and peopled by individuals from different cultures, among them Chinese, Tibetan and central Asian. Some were nomads, others rooted to the land. Dynastic changes were frequent and boundaries between the kingdoms shifted with each change. A unit of measurement might have different values in different places. For example, a unit of capacity was 400 mL in Northern Wei; in other kingdoms it would be 300 mL, or 200 mL. Weights and measures might change within the same dynasty, affecting daily activities, creating havoc.

Around the time that Jia wrote his book, new cultural and religious elements penetrated China via the Silk Road, a web of routes connecting with central Asia. Buddhism had entered China via that route, and grottoes large and small were carved out of the rocks to house Buddhist figures. A contemporary of Jia wrote about the babble of strange tongues in what is modern-day Xian.

> *The bird flutters in distress.*
> *Foreign sounds rend the air.*
> *I know only our local tongue –*
> *How can I face these strangers?*

In those turbulent times common folk formed communities, seeking mutual protection. These communities had to be self-sufficient. Agriculture was basic to their survival, providing defenses against hunger and cold. To Jia's mind other activities were trivial. Flowers were pleasing to the eye, he said, but they do not bear fruit. So he documented everything that ordinary people did in connection with food.

Jia's directions were explicit and detailed, rather like those of a fussy aunt who would not only explain what to do, but what not do. He usually gave the amounts of each ingredient. (Definitions of units of weight, capacity and length are at the end of this book.) Jia sometimes indicated the time required for specific steps in food preparation. In the absence of kitchen timers, the intervals were expressed in terms of common experience. He and others after him used the following expressions to denote short and long time intervals: *the duration of a meal; the time required for cooking a meal; the time required for cooking 40 L of rice.* 'Butter is made by churning sour milk in an earthen jar with a long-handled paddle *for the duration of a meal*,' he wrote.

Jia's book was not the oldest Chinese book on cooking. Jia cited *Cui Hao's Food Classic* many times. Actually more is known about Cui Hao than Jia because he was a minister in the Northern Wei dynasty; Cui is in the history books. He came to write the book on food because of his mother, Madam Lu.

> During my childhood and youth I saw my women relatives carry out their duties — mostly preparing food and drink to serve the elders and to honor the ancestors. They personally performed these duties although there were servants. Then, a 10-year period of unrest and famine followed. They could not provide anything but gruel and vegetables to stave off hunger. My late mother had said, 'The younger generation knows nothing (about cooking).' So she dictated the book to me. Her gentle words are in the nine chapters.

Cui Hao's Food Classic was written a hundred years before Jia. That work was eventually lost to history, so one turns to Jia to learn how things were done in the sixth century.

NOTES

Except where noted, the translations are my own. I apologize for any errors they may contain.

The following sources were invaluable.

An Enumeration of Chinese Materia Medica (1980) by Shui-ying Hu. Hong Kong: The Chinese University Press ISBN 962-201-189-6

Science and Civilisation in China by J. Needham. Vol. 6, part 5: Fermentation and food science (2000) by H. T. Huang. Cambridge: Cambridge University Press. ISBN 521 65270 7 hardback (abbreviated SCC6-5)

Zhongguo pengren cidian 中國烹飪辭典 (1988) by Xiao Fan 蕭帆. Beijing: Zhongguo shangye chubanshe 中國商業出版社 ISBN 7-5044-1387-9

*Zhongguo pengren guji congkan*中國烹飪古籍叢刊. Beijing: Zhongguo shangye chubanshe 中國商業出版社 (abbreviated ZPGC). The ZPGC series consists of separate volumes with original texts edited, annotated, and rendered into modern Chinese.

The Electronic Version of *Wenyuange Siku Quanshu* 文淵閣四庫全書電子版. Portable hard disk version 1.0 (2010). Hong Kong: Digital Heritage Publishing Ltd (abbreviated SKQS). The electronic library includes a dictionary of old Chinese and search tool. Texts from SKQS are identified by square brackets [ ].

In Medieval China

Opening line and first quotation: [*Essential Skills for Common Folk* Qi min yao shu 齊民要術 by Jia Sixie 賈思勰 (6ᵗʰ c). Author's Introduction, pp. 6-7]
Background: *A History of Chinese Civilization* by Jacques Gernet (English edition, 1982) Cambridge University Press. ISBN 0-521-49781-7 paperback
End of Northern Wei dynasty: [*Zi zhi tong jian* 資治通鑑 by Sima Guang 司馬光 (1019-1086). Ch. 152, 155]
Units of capacity: *A Concise History of Ancient Chinese Measures and Weights, Zhongguo gu dai ji liang tu jian* 中國古代計量圖鑒 (2005) by Qiu Guangming 丘光明 (in Chinese and English) pp. 99-100
Strange tongues: *Changan ting bai she* 長安聽百舌 (first line 萬里風煙異) by Wei Ding 韋鼎 (515-593). [*Yi wen lei ju* 藝文類聚 ed. by Ouyang Xun 歐陽詢 (557-641), Ch. 92, p. 22]
Time intervals: (*duration of a meal*) Yi shi jiu 一食久; (*time required for cooking a meal*) yi chui jiu 一炊久; (*time required to cook 40 L rice*) chui yi dan mi qing 炊一石米頃. Examples: [*Qi min yao shu* 齊民要術 by Jia Sixie 賈思勰] Chapter: Part, page(s) are respectively abbreviated [9:80,20] [9:80,5] [8:77,30] without reference to Jia's book.
Churning butter: [6:57,21] An English translation is in SCC6-5, p. 253.

Social conditions: The times in which Cui Hao (and later Jia Sixie) lived are described in *Han ye ke lai* 寒夜客來 (2005) by Lu Yaodong 逯耀東; Beijing北京: Shenghuo dushi xinzhi chubanshe 生活讀書新知出版社 ISBN 7-108-02352-0. pp.82-89
Cui Hao's Food Classic: *Cui shi shi jing* 崔氏食經 by Cui Hao 崔浩 (d 450).
About Madam Lu: *[Ce Fu Yuan Gui* 冊府元龜 by Wang Qinruo 王欽若 (962-1025) and Yang Yi 楊億 (940-1020) Ch. 794, p. 14]

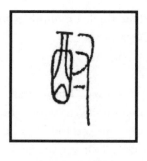

CHAPTER TWO

MAKING YEAST CAKES, MAKING WINE

'The master respectfully called upon the lords of the earth, the five deities of the east, south, west, north and center. He asked for their blessings. On this auspicious day in the seventh lunar month, hundreds or thousands of yeast cakes would be made.'

Making wine required two separate steps: the first was yeast cake production. Yeast was made during the summer and stored as dried cakes, remaining stable up to three years. The second step was fermentation of cereal grains. There were elements of mystery to both of these processes. Small wonder that the deities had to be invoked before the activities started.

Wine-making was a complicated process. Unlike the production of wine from grapes in which microbes on the fruit skin and in the air work their magic on sugar, grain-based wines derive their alcohol from starches — large molecules consisting of sugars linked to each other. Wines were made from cereal grains: sorghum, glutinous and non-glutinous rice or millet. The grain was cooked, altering the starches in ways that would allow the yeast cake to convert them into sugars. Yeast cakes were complex mixtures of yeast, fungi and starch-digesting enzymes. But this is a modern way of looking at the process. In depicting how rural communities made wine, Jia evoked the seasons, the people and the farm animals.

Yeast Cakes

There were two kinds of yeast cake. 'Magic yeast cakes consume five times more grain than the common variety,' Jia wrote. 'Beginners using magic yeast cakes may complain that the wine was too weak. That is because they do not use enough grain.' Jia included four ways to make magic yeast cakes. Three of them required building a special hut with a roof made of straw, not tile. Narrow trenches were dug in the floor of the hut allowing a person to enter the hut and to reach the yeast cakes that would be placed inside to mature.

Yeast cakes were made using 40 L of wheat in each form — steamed, toasted and raw. They were mixed and ground fine. Water was added to make the cakes that were packed in round metal moulds, about 14 cm in diameter and four cm high. Planks were placed on the moulds and the cakes were packed down by having the bigger boys stamp on them. Next, a hole was made in the centre of each cake, and they were spread out on the floor of the hut. Its single wooden door was sealed with mud. After seven days the cakes were turned and the door was sealed again. At the end of 14 days the cakes were stacked in a pile. After 21 days they were sun-dried, hung up by means of string passed through the hole in each cake.

In another method, steamed, toasted and raw wheat were used in the proportions of 3:2:1. This was apparently something animals liked, for Jia said, 'Keep the dogs and chickens away, or they will eat the cakes.' Small boys were recruited to shape these yeast cakes by hand, about 9 cm across and 6 cm thick.

Common Yeast Cakes

By contrast common yeast cakes were simpler to prepare, requiring only toasted wheat. 'To achieve an even golden colour, the grains are placed in a large wok over a fire, and stirred continuously by means of a long-handled paddle suspended with a rope hung on a wooden peg. Without this device the stirring would be have to stop from time to time (because the workers would tire),' Jia commented, 'and the toasting would be very uneven. The wheat is ground — but not too fine, otherwise the lees will not separate cleanly from the wine. Just enough water is added to make the ground wheat stick together, but not so much that the hands become sticky. Formed into a pile, the wheat is left overnight. The next morning it is pounded and packed into wooden moulds 30 cm square. Place planks on them and get some strong young fellows to stamp on them. The cakes should be five to six cm thick. Make a hole in each square.'

A few days earlier, mugwort had been collected and the leaves thoroughly sun-dried. Mugwort is an herb similar to wormwood (the plant added to flavour European beer). To mature, common yeast cakes were placed on beds of dried mugwort leaves and, covered with a thicker layer of the same. Left in a sealed hut for three weeks, the yeast cakes acquired colourful mouldy coats. After thorough sun-drying they were stacked up for later use.

Making Wine

With yeast cakes on hand, wine could be made at any time of the year. The water for making wine was usually collected months ahead of use. For example, water for spring wine was collected in November-December, when the mulberry leaves fell, and the water would begin to freeze. Magic yeast cakes were taken out, sun-dried, brushed clean, cleaved into smaller pieces and pounded in a pestle. Common yeast cakes were first scraped on all six sides and also around the hole in the middle, reducing its weight by one-third, and likewise pulverized.

Yeast was mixed with water. When large bubbles resembling fish eyes appeared, it was suitable for making wine. The exact process for making wine varied with the time of year, as Jia noted below in his meticulous way.

Sorghum Wine

Any kind of sorghum will do; but the red and white varieties are especially good. Make this at any season. Use six parts of sorghum for one part of common yeast cake. Magic yeast cake is much more powerful, so adjust accordingly. In spring and autumn, break the yeast cake into pieces; in winter, it has to be ground fine and sifted. Use three parts water for ten parts sorghum.

In spring and autumn, the yeast cake is soaked in cold water.

As it becomes active, strain it discarding the solids. In winter, warm the jar by steaming, and wrap straw around it. Make a paste from hot water and sorghum, and then let it cool; use this to soak the yeast. It will become active after standing overnight.

Now it is time to prepare the sorghum. Measure it out and divide it into three portions. Cook one portion and let it cool to body temperature, and then mix it with the active yeast suspension. Seal the jar with mud. In spring, let it stand one day; autumn, two days; winter, three days. Seal the jar with mud each time you examine the wine. When you see that the grain is digested, use the next portion. After the third portion is digested, seal the jar again and wait ten days for it to mature. Then, press it (to separate the wine from the lees).

The wine has a silvery sheen. In its taste one can find the bite of ginger, the fragrance of pepper, the sweetness of honey and some bitterness. It is sweet-smelling, strong, light and palatable, clearly superior to wines made with millet or husked sorghum.

Strong Wine

Most of Jia's recipes for alcoholic drinks used the word *jiu* for ordinary wine. Especially strong wine was called by a different name — *zhou*. There are only two recipes for the latter among dozens for *jiu*. The stronger drink was made from millet flour in contrast to the use of whole or broken grains (such as rice) used for *jiu*. Often, it was made at the beginning of the year for consumption during the summer because its fermentation took place over months as compared to days for ordinary wines.

Strong Millet Wine

It is best to use magic yeast cakes, prepared the usual way. The millet must be pounded, rinsed until the water is clear, and soaked overnight in water. The next morning, it is milled and winnowed. The flour must be as fine as that used to make puddings. Cook a small amount of the flour in water to make a thin paste. The rest of the flour is steamed and then partially cooled. Thoroughly mix in the soaked yeast. When the thin paste is at body temperature, add it to the jar and mix it with the cooked flour. You can use a bat to pound it. Put the entire mixture in an earthen jar, and seal it with mud. Whenever you find a crack in the mud seal, immediately seal it with fresh mud, so none of the gasses escape.

Make this at New Year. There will be heavy showers in spring. After they pass check the contents of the jar. If you see clear wine, it is drinkable but seal the jar again. By August-September the wine is really ready. Ladle out the wine but do not dip deep into the jar. Its colour is dark, like that of sesame oil.

Four liters of it will make 20 people drunk. Those used to drinking 4 L of ordinary wine can only drink 600 mL of this. If they drink twice that amount, they are beyond help and they will die. Before this fatal stage is reached a drunken person is unconscious, his body is on fire. He can be revived by pouring warm water over him. Pour it over his head and on his face. Soon he will be sitting up.

NOTES

Three sources: [*Qi min yao shu* 齊民要術 by Jia Sixie 賈思勰, ch. 7]
Qi min yao shu. Yin shi bu fen. 齊民要術. 飲食部份 by Jia Sixie 賈思勰, *ZPGC edition*, ed. by Shi Shenghan 石聲漢, 1984. Original text and translations into modern Chinese
SCC6-5, pp.168-181, gives an excellent, fuller version of the same material in English.
Invocation: Zhu qu wen 祝麴文 [7:64,6]
Lunar calendar: Since Chinese New Year invariably falls in January or February, the lunar month by the Western calendar will be one or two months later. The seventh lunar month would fall in August-September.
Magic yeast cakes: Shen qu 神麴 [7:64,5-10]; (strength) [7:64,8]
Wheat: Xiao mai 小麥, *Triticum aestivum;* (steamed) Zheng 蒸; (toasted) Chao 炒; (raw) Sheng 生
Common yeast cakes: Ben qu 笨麴 or Qu 麴 [7:66, 16-17]

HSIANG JU LIN

Mugwort: Ai 艾, *Artemisia vulgaris*

Water collection for wine-making [7:64,13]

Sorghum wine: Liang mi jiu 粱米酒 (Gao liang jiu 高粱酒) [7:66,21-22]

Sorghum: Gao liang 高粱, *Sorghum bicolor, Sorghum vulgare*

Alcoholic drinks: (wine) Jiu 酒; (strong wine) Zhou 酎

Strong millet wine: Ji mi zhou 稷米酎 [7:66,22-23]

Non-glutinous millet: Ji mi 稷米, a variety of broomcorn millet, *Panicum miliaceum*

Reviving the drunk [7:66,23]

CHAPTER THREE

YELLOW MOULD AND YELLOW COAT

Break chicken eggs into a shallow dish. Beat the whites and yolks together. Add some fermented black beans, salt and finely cut scallions. Scramble the eggs in sesame oil. This is quite fragrant.

The process of fermentation by means of the yellow moulds was perhaps beyond understanding, but the results were undeniable. A clear example was the transformation of the intractable soybean into a soft flavourful nugget, the fermented black bean that added taste to a host of foods, even scrambled eggs as Jia suggested. Furthermore, yellow moulds could prevent meat, fish, and vegetables from spoiling. In that process food changed in taste, texture and often colour as well.

Fermented Black Beans
These beans were of sufficient importance to be produced in large quantities. Air-borne spores were the sole source of the mould. They would feed on cooked unhulled soybeans. Jia provided two sets of directions, for the home and for large scale production. As in the production of yeast cakes, the latter entailed building a special hut.

Production of Fermented Black Beans

A straw-roofed hut was built to make fermented beans. Located in a shady place, its walls, window and small door were sealed with mud so that the wind, insects and rats could not get in. Each hut housed a pit 60-90 cm deep that would hold up to 800 L of beans. The minimum amount was 400 L because of the need to generate enough heat during the course of fermentation. Fermented soybeans should be made during the cooler months (because one could always raise the temperature). If the weather were too hot, the beans might spoil, turn mushy and smell bad. Not even the pigs or dogs would eat them.

Beans were boiled just until they were swollen, and would give a little when pinched. Drained and cooled outdoors, they were heaped in a conical pile inside the hut. Twice a day, someone would crawl into the hut and test the temperature of the pile by plunging his hand into it. If it felt as warm as his armpit, the beans on the outside were shifted to the center of the conical pile. After four or five such turns, a white mould would form. At this point the pile was shaped into a 60 cm-high cone with a flat top. As the probing of the temperature continued, the height of the pile was decreased by about 14 cm with each turn. Eventually the pile was covered all over with white mould. When that mould began to turn yellow, the pile was reduced to a height of nine cm and it was left undisturbed for three days.

The matted beans were cut into long strips separated by channels and smoothed down. When overgrown with yellow mould the strips were moved outdoors, and the mould was scattered to the winds by fanning. The beans were washed and rinsed to remove the mould so the product would not taste bitter. A thick layer of chaff was packed in the pit and its sides lined with mats. The beans were poured in, and someone got into the pit and stamped on them to pack them. After he climbed out, mats were laid on top of the beans and covered with more chaff. It would take about ten days in summer or 15 days in winter for the fermented beans to ripen. If left too long, the flavour was bitter; if not long enough, the colour was too pale and the flavour weak. When ripened, the beans were dried under the sun. They would be good for over a year.

The starting material was soybeans that might have skins of any colour; the finished product was invariably very dark, almost black, the result of fermentation and ripening. The product described above was unsalted. Jia did mention the use of salty fermented black beans in fish soups.

Soy Extract

Any mention of soybeans brings up the subject of soy sauce, the best known of fermented soybean products. All the ingredients for making soy sauce were present in Jia's time: beans, moulds, wheat flour and salt. Yet none of the procedures that he gave included the defining step for making soy sauce — fermentation of mouldy beans in copious amounts of brine. Jia described two products that come close to soy sauce as we know it. The more important liquid seasoning was soy extract, made by steeping fermented black beans in boiling water. 'Do not stir the beans or the broth will be cloudy,' Jia wrote. 'The broth should be the colour of amber. If it is too dark, it will be bitter.'

The number of recipes employing soy extract in Jia's book shows it was the principal liquid seasoning. A few examples describe how it was used.

For steaming lamb, pork, goose or duck, the seasoning was 3 parts lard plus 1 part soy extract (by volume) and 1 part tangerine peel.

Pork, lamb or fatty deer meat was cut into slivers the width of scallions and pan-fried, adding soy extract and salt. Leafy pickled vegetables cut into narrow strands 15 cm long were mixed in. Some pickle juice was added for sourness.

Beef, pig or lamb liver cut into 1.5 x 4.5 cm slices was marinated with soy extract, scallions, and salt, wrapped in caul fat and grilled.

Lamb large intestine was stuffed with minced lamb that had been with fine- cut scallions (white part), salt, soy extract, ginger and ground pepper. Tie two of these sausages together and grill them. 'Delicious,' Jia added.

Mix 200 mL each of wine, fish sauce, soy extract, and add about 100 mL each of ginger, scallions and tangerine peel to make a marinade. Clean a fat duck or a young goose, bone it and marinate slices of the meat for the time required to cook a meal, and then grill them.

Yellow Coat and Yellow Mould

Moulds were specially cultivated to act as fermenting agents, much like yeast cakes. The most important of these were called yellow coat and yellow mould. Yellow coat referred to the mould covering the wheat grains; yellow mould to that grown on wheat flour. They were instrumental in the making of condiments and sauces. The moulds grew from airborne spores landing on some form of cooked wheat, and the mouldy wheat was added to food that was to undergo fermentation. It is to Jia's credit that he recognized that fermentation was carried out by the moulds – not by the wheat or flour on which they grew. This point was made amply clear from the text below.

> Preparation of Yellow Coat and Yellow Mould
>
> Make yellow coat during July-August. Soak washed wheat grains in water until they turn sour, and then drain and steam them. Spread them out on a bamboo tray in a 6 cm-thick layer to cool. Cover them with reeds (cut the day before) to prevent water or dew from collecting on the grains. In about seven days when yellow coat has visibly grown all over the wheat grains, remove the reeds without disturbing the coat and sun-dry the yellow grains.
>
> Do not winnow the mouldy grains! The people of a certain prefecture winnow the mouldy grains in the wind. This is a big mistake. To obtain fermentation you must have the activity in the yellow coat. If you remove that by winnowing, the results will not be good.
>
> Make yellow mould between July and August. Mill the wheat grains, soak the flour in water and steam it. Cool and spread the flour evenly. Proceed as for making yellow coat. Of course you must not winnow (the mouldy flour) or you will lose its activity.

Bean Paste

The three principal fermenting agents yeast cakes, yellow coat and yellow mould were used singly or often in combination. According to one authority, microbial growth would have been suppressed under some of the conditions used in the course of processing, even as the substances that could break down proteins and starches retained their activities. In this manner many of the preserved foods acquired agreeable tastes and flavours and were made into condiments, sauces or liquid seasonings. The preparation of bean paste might serve as illustration. In the process described below that converts soybeans into a paste, cooked soybeans were mixed with two dry fermenting agents – yeast cake and yellow mould – and then mixed with brine. In the first phase yellow mould grew on the relatively dry beans. The addition of brine inhibited their further growth, and the lengthy incubation that followed improved the flavour of the mixture.

Preparation of Bean Paste

Black-skinned soybeans were steamed for half a day, the beans were then repacked in the steamer so the bottom ones were on top and they were steamed again until the next morning. After sun-drying the beans were steamed again and then pounded in a mortar and pestle. Some of the black skins were loosened and removed. After more steaming, sun-drying and pounding to loosen the black skins, light-coloured beans were steamed again for the duration of a meal and a final sun-drying, they were mixed with other ingredients. For every 12 L beans, 4 L each of yeast cake and yellow mould, 2 L salt and a bunch of wild fennel were used. All of the components had to be dry, or the beans would spoil. They were rubbed together until the hands hurt. Two large jars were packed full to the brim with the beans, and sealed with mud. It would take three to five weeks before the fermenting mixture contracted — pulling away from the sides of the jar and developing cracks on top — and was covered with yellow mould. Then the contents of the two jars were divided between three large jars so more yellow mould and brine could be added.

To every 400 L of fermenting beans, 12 L more of yellow mould was added. At dawn quantities of brine had been made and allowed to settle; 12 L salt was added to every 40 L of well water. Yellow mould was mixed with a small amount of clear brine, strained and mixed with the beans and more brine to obtain the consistency of gruel. The jars were placed in the sun to evaporate, and stirred daily for 10 days, scraping the bottom of the jars. Over the following 20 days they were stirred briefly once a day. Although the bean paste was edible then, it would be better after 100 days.

Bean paste had many uses. Most important, the paste was diluted with wine or broth, and filtered to make a liquid seasoning called clear bean sauce. This was the other sauce of Jia's time that invited comparison with soy sauce. At this point Jia inserted two recipes. Lamb á la *tartare* called for clear bean sauce. The first recipe consisted of raw lamb and raw pork fat marinated in clear bean sauce and then mixed with fresh ginger and raw eggs. The 'dry' version was a combination of the raw mixture with a portion of the same ingredients, previously cooked – certainly tamer but perhaps not as tasty.

Winter melons were packed in bean paste to preserve them. Bean paste was added to blood sausage as seasoning. It was added to elm nuts to make a condiment.

Fish Sauce

Fish sauce could be made in several ways, with and without fermenting agents. Jia included a recipe from an earlier cookbook. The minister's recipe called for dried anchovies, soaked and rinsed, leaving the scales untouched. To 4 L of the softened anchovies were added 1.6 L yeast cake, 400 mL of yellow mould, and 1 L of salt. The mixture ripened in a sealed jar over a period of two weeks. It had an extraordinary fragrance, the minister added.

Jia's fish sauce recipe called for yellow coat as the fermenting agent. Anchovies, mackerel or carp were incubated in a sealed jar placed in the sun. This product was diluted with wine for use as a seasoning.

So a small pig was butchered, split down its chest and belly so that it would lie flat. It was trimmed to an even thickness. A mixture of chopped pork and duck meat seasoned with fish sauce, tangerine peel and other aromatics was placed on top and smoothed out. A plank was placed on the pig and weighted down. Next morning the plank was removed. The pig was brushed with honey and slowly roasted, first turning gold, then red.

SLIPPERY NOODLES

Fermented Meat

The combination of yeast cake with a yellow mould was powerful. Applied to raw meat, it prevented spoilage and turned the meat into a paste that was the base of a sauce.

Preparation of Meat Sauce

To use beef, lamb, river deer, deer or rabbit meat the animals have to be freshly slaughtered. The bone and fat are removed and the meat chopped. Four L of prepared meat was thoroughly mixed with 2 L of yeast cake (pounded and sieved), 800 mL of salt and 400 mL of yellow mould, then sealed in an earthen jar and placed in the sun about two weeks. If there is no yeasty smell when you open the jar, it is done.

Buy a freshly killed pheasant and stew it until the meat falls to pieces. Use only the broth, let it cool and thin the fermented meat paste with it to make the sauce. If there is no pheasant, then use chicken broth; if there is no chicken broth, use wine.

Fermented Meat and Bones

'Donkey meat, horse meat or pork can be preserved in this manner. It is best made at New Year's. The preserved meat will be good straight through the summer. Coarsely chop the meat without removing the bones. Combine yeast cakes with a half-volume each of salt and moulded wheat (yellow coat). Mix it with the meat, pack the mixture into a jar and seal it with mud. Place the jar in the sun. It is ready in 14 days. Cook it before serving it. This can be used in place of meat sauce.'

Pickling Vegetables with Yellow Coat

According to Jia, turnip and mustard greens were harvested in November-December (mustard seeds were harvested in spring). The greens were pickled in the same manner. They were soaked in brine for three days and then they were placed in a large jar, in layers with the stalks laid in the same direction. In alternating layers the stalks faced opposite directions. Each layer was sprinkled with moulded wheat (previously sieved and pounded to a powder) and warm thin millet gruel was poured over it. Previously used brine was used to fill the jar to the top. With time the greens turned yellow.

Of course, most vegetables were pickled without the addition of fermenting agents, as we shall see in the next chapter. But Jia had said, the flavour of these pickled greens was excellent.

NOTES

Opening lines: (scrambled eggs) Chao ji zi fa 炒雞子法 [6:57,26]

Soybean: Jia uses the term bean (Dou 豆) to stand for soybean (Da dou 大豆, Huang dou 黃豆), *Glycine max*

Large scale production of fermented black beans: Zuo chi 作豉 [8:72,12-14]. See SCC6-5, pp. 337-338 for the full English translation. See also History of fermented black soybeans by W. Shurtleff and A. Aoyagi. <www.soyinfocenter.com/books/150>

Salty black beans: (watershield soup) Chun geng 蓴羹 [8:76,25]; (steamed fish) Chun zheng yu 純蒸魚 [8:78,32]

Soy extract preparation: Chi zhi 豉汁 (given under fish-watershield soup) Shi kuai yu chun geng 食膾魚蓴羹 [8:76,24-25]

Soy extract uses: (seasoning for steamed lamb, etc., given under steamed bear) Zheng xiong 蒸熊 [8:77,28]; (meat and pickles) Ju xiao 菹肖 [8:79,34]; (grilled liver) Gan zhi 肝炙 [9:80,2-3]; (stuffed intestines) Guan chang 灌腸 [9:80,3]; (grilled duck or goose) Nan zhi 腩炙 [9:80,5]

Fermenting agents: (yellow coat) Huang yi 黃衣, also called moulded wheat, Mai hun 麥䴷 [8:68,1]; (yellow mould) Huang zheng 黃蒸

Preparation of yellow coat: Zuo huang yi fa 作黃衣法 [8:68,1-2]

Preparation of yellow mould: Zuo huang zheng fa 作黃蒸法 [8:68,2]. See SCC6-5, pp. 335-336 for other English translations, and pp. 339-340 for discussion of microbial activities under different conditions.

Preparation of bean paste: Zuo jiang fa 作醬法 [8:70,3-5]. The full translation is in SCC6-5, pp.347-349. Wild fennel: Ju 蓾

Bean paste: Jiang 醬 or Dou jiang 豆醬; (clear bean sauce) Jiang qing 醬清; (lamb á la *tartare*, raw and dry) Sheng shan fa 生脠法 and Zuo zao shan 作燥脠 [8:70,7]; (melons) Zhong dong gua fa 種冬瓜法 [2:14,23]; (blood sausage) Yang pan chang ci hu 羊盤腸雌斛 [8:76,23-24]; (elm nut condiment) Yu zi jiang 榆子醬 [8:70,6]

Fish sauce: (the minister's recipe) Gan ji yu jiang fa 乾鱭魚醬法. The fish 鱭魚 is a species within genus *Coilia*, Grenadier anchovies. (Jia's recipe) Zuo yu jiang fa 作魚醬法 [8:70,6]

SLIPPERY NOODLES

Roast pig: Po zhi zhun fa 膊炙豚法 [9:80,3]

Preparation of meat sauce: (without bones) Rou jiang 肉醬 [8:70,5]. For a fuller version see SCC6-5, pp. 381-382

Fermented meat: (with bones) Zi rou 膟肉 [9:81,8]

Pickling vegetables: (harvesting) Zhong shu jie 種蜀芥 [3:23,10]; (pickling) Wu qing song kui shu jie xian ju fa 蕪菁菘葵蜀芥鹹葅法[9:88,25]. See SCC6-5, pp. 405-406 for a translation of the latter and discussion

Turnip: Wuqing 蕪菁, *Brassica rapa.* Cabbage: Song 菘 *Brassica campestris.* Chinese mallow: Kui 葵, *Malva verticillata.* White mustard: Shu jie 蜀芥 *Brassica hirta.*

CHAPTER FOUR

FOOD PRESERVATION

Slice deer meat into slabs about the size of one's palm. Air-dry them in a shady place. Taken with a little salt, this is as sweet and crisp as frozen snow.

Aside from fermentation, Jia described at least four other methods for preserving meat. Air-dried meat was prepared close to New Year's holiday, to take advantage of the cold and it would keep until the following summer. 'Use lean beef, lamb or deer because fatty meat does not keep long. The meat of cattle and lamb and especially the young that had died of starvation can also be used because it is very lean. Slice the meat, put it in cold water and rub it so the blood comes out. Soak it overnight in salt water with pepper in it. (Young lamb is not sliced — before soaking it is simply washed in warm water to remove the rank smell.) Dry the meat in the shade until it is barely moist. Pound the slices with a bat until they are firm but not mashed.'

Alternatively, meat was marinated before air-drying. When it was made at New Year's, Jia said, it was called 'chilblains meat' because the procedure involved much manipulation in the cold.

Savoury Dried Meat
'Several kinds of meats can be used: beef, lamb, deer meat, and pork from

wild pigs and domesticated pigs. Cut the meat into strips or slices, always with the grain. Make a broth with crushed beef or lamb bones, skim off the foam and let it settle. Use good fermented black beans and cook them with the broth until their flavour comes out. Discard the beans. Add a little salt, scallions, tangerine peel, ginger and Sichuan pepper, all pounded fine. Immerse the meat in the marinade and rub it in with the fingers. Taste it after three days. If the flavour is rich enough, take the strips out.

'String the meat up and hang them in the shade under the eaves on the north side of the house. When the strips are just damp, turn and press them between your fingers to firm them up. When the meat is completely dry, store them in an unused room. There must be no smoke in the air, or the meat will be bitter. Place the meat in paper bags (so the flies will not soil it) and hang them up.'

Meat Sealed in Mud

According to Jia's description no salt was used in this method of preservation. 'A butchered pig was hung overnight, or until no more moisture appeared.' It was cut into smaller pieces, as for roasting or grilling (that would include the loin of grown animals or the legs of younger ones). 'The meat was made into bundles with cogon grass or rice straw, thickly coated with mud and hung outdoors in the shade, facing north. Cracks that developed were sealed again with mud. This meat would keep until the following summer. It tastes like that from a freshly slaughtered animal.'

Immersion in Fat

One of Jia's recipes has a French counterpart — *confit de porc*. It utilizes rendered fat to prevent meat from contact with air and moisture. 'Raise a pig so it becomes big and fat, and slaughter it in the New Year. You cannot make this kind of pork with a two year-old pig because its meat is not so firm,' Jia wrote. 'Scald off the hair and hold the pig over a fire until the skin turns brown. Scrape the skin clean and remove the internal organs. Remove the belly fat, and render it. Cut the meat with the skin attached into large pieces. Cook them using just enough water to cover the meat. After all the water has evaporated, cook the pork in the fat using enough to cover the meat. For every 800 mL of fat, use 1.2 L wine and 1.2 L of salt. For best results, simmer it for half a day. Transfer the meat to an earthen jar. Enough rendered fat must be poured into the jar to submerge the pork.'

Immersion in Lees

Lees were the residue of whatever grain was used for making wine. Jia wrote, 'Mix water and lees to the consistency of gruel. Add plenty of salt. Place in it roasted or grilled meats and store in a cool place. This can be made in any season. The meat will keep for 10 days in summer.'

Preservation of Vegetables

One method of storing fresh vegetables consisted of burying them in the earth. 'Around October-December, chose a sunny corner of the garden, facing south, and dig a pit about 1.5 m deep. The fresh vegetables and earth are packed in alternating layers, to within 0.3 m of the top. Fill the space with earth and cover it with a thick layer of grain stalks. This way, the vegetables will last through the winter, and they will taste as fresh as in summer.' Turnip greens, cabbage, mallow and mustard greens could be preserved for days with strong brine. 'Pick the good plants and tie them in bundles with cattail stalks. Wash them in very strong brine and place them in the jar. If you wash them in plain water, they will rot,' Jia wrote. The brine wash water was allowed to settle, and the relatively clear portion poured into the jar completely immersing the vegetables. 'Do not stir the contents of the jar. These vegetables will retain their green colour.' They were used in two ways: the brine was washed out and they were cooked. 'They tasted like fresh vegetables,' Jia added. Otherwise the turnip greens and mustard greens were pickled with moulded wheat, as described in the previous chapter.

Cui Hao's Food Classic, written a century before Jia, was the source of several methods for preserving melons. Oriental pickling melons (that resemble cucumbers) were packed in a mixture of lees and salt. 'After three days take each one out, wipe it off and put it back in the lees. This prevents them from bruising. As with all melons, they will turn bad if bruised.' Cui added, 'It would be better to put the melons in cloth bags during the pickling process.'

'In Sichuan they have an excellent way.' Cui wrote. 'They cook rice gruel and add salt until it tastes just right. When the gruel is cold they put the gourds in it and seal the jar with mud.' Gruels made with a variety of starchy grains such as rice created good conditions for growth of some bacteria. They fed on starches, and in the absence of air produced enough lactic acid to turn many foods pleasantly sour.

Foods Preserved with Salt and Rice

'Such a technique was used to preserve raw carp:

Spring and autumn are the seasons to make preserved fish. Do not make it in winter, for it will not ripen in the cold. Do not make this in summer because fish easily spoils in the heat. Salt is indispensable: it promotes ripening, adds flavour and prevents the growth of maggots. Use fresh, large carp, over 45 cm long. They have tough skin and strong bones. Use lean fish. Fat ones do not keep as well.

1. Scale the fish and cut it into slices 3 x 6 cm and about 1.5 cm thick. These dimensions are approximate; do not follow them rigidly. If the slices are too thick, they are inedible. The outside becomes too sour while the center, near the bone, tastes raw and fishy. Leave some skin on each slice.

2. Soak the slices in water to rinse away the blood.

3. Sprinkle the slices of fish with salt, spread them on a bamboo rack and weight them down (even overnight) to expel liquid. Otherwise, the fish will spoil.

4. Cook non-glutinous rice. The cooked rice must be firm or the fish will spoil.

5. To the rice add whole cornelian cherries and finely cut tangerine peel — just enough for some fragrance. Add good wine (use 200 mL for every 4 L of the finished product); it will speed up the ripening process. Mix every together until the rice will stick to the fish.

6. Pack a jar with a layer of fish, then a layer of rice, and so on placing the fattier pieces of fish in the upper layers. (They should be eaten first because they will not keep as long.) Top off with a thick layer of rice.

7. Put eight layers of bamboo or cattail leaves over the top. Place a woven bamboo cover over the mouth of the jar . Place the jar indoors away from sunlight or fire. In winter cover the jar with grain stalks so it does not freeze.

8. The juices will be red at first; discard them. When the juices are pale and sour the fish is ripe.'

Preserved fish was added to a soup made with pork, lamb and beef. Beaten eggs were added to the boiling liquid; when the egg floated, the soup was done. The preserved fish added flavour. With another soup made simply with soy extract, preserved fish, a few stalks of scallion and beaten egg, guests were served only the broth and some of the egg.

The salt-and-rice method also was applied to meat. 'Use fatty pork. Singe the skin (to remove the hairs) and cut the piece into strips 15 cm wide. Boil the strips of pork until barely cooked, and let them cool. Slice into pieces through the skin. Mix cooked rice with salt and cornelian cherries. Pack a jar with alternating layers of meat and rice, seal the jar with mud and leave it in the sun for one month. Eat this with pickled garlic or ginger and vinegar, as you wish. Cooked with fish, it is excellent.'

Oak Bark Eggs

True to his aim of describing every step of food production from start to finish, Jia began his description of pickling duck eggs with the farm. 'Feed the ducks well. Keep the males away and each female can produce 100 eggs. 'Obtain bark from the Yuan tree.' According to a fourth-century scholar whom Jia quoted, 'This tree is large, like a chestnut. It is found in the South. Its bark is thick: its decoction is reddish; eggs and fruit can be stored in it.' So this preservation method was known at least two centuries before Jia. Modern annotators have identified the tree as an oak.

Jia continued: 'Wash, chop and boil the bark. For every 8 L of the decoction add 400 mL salt. When it has cooled pour the decoction into a large jar and immerse the eggs in it. (If the liquid is still warm the eggs will spoil.) If the salt concentration is right, the eggs will float. The eggs are ready in one month. Boil them first. Preserved eggs go well with wine or with meals.'

NOTES

Meat preservation by air-drying: (deer meat) Tian fei fu 甜肥脯; (plain dried meat) Bai fu 白脯; (savoury dried meat) Wu wei fu 五味脯, also called 'chilblains meat' Zhu fu 瘃脯[8:75,19-20]
Mud pack: Bao rou 苞肉 [9:81,9-10]. (cuts of meat for roasting or grilling) Bang zhi

SLIPPERY NOODLES

棒炙 [9:80,2].

Cogon grass: Mao jian 茅菅, *Imperata cylindrica,* used for thatching roofs or making mats, ropes.

Immersion in fat: Ao rou 奥肉 (9:81,9). The proportions of fat, wine and salt given in the ZPGC version (p.168) are 1:2:3.

Immersion in lees: Zao rou 糟肉 [9:81,9]

Preserved vegetables: (storage underground) Cang sheng cai fa 藏生菜法 [9:88,26-27]; (storage in brine) Wu qing song kui shu jie xian ju fa 蕪菁菘葵蜀芥鹹葅法 [9:88,25]

Cattail: Ruo 蒻 (genus *Typha*)

Pickling methods from 'Cui Hao's Food Classic' [9:88,28-29]: Shi jing cang yue gua fa <食經>藏越瓜法; (Sichuan pickles) Shi jing cang gua fa <食經>藏瓜法

Oriental pickling melon: Yue gua 越瓜(Cai gua 菜瓜, *Cucumis melo* var. *conomon*)

Preserved fish: Yu zha 魚鮓 [8:74,17-18]

Non-glutinous rice: Jing mi 秔米 (Geng mi 粳米, *Oryza sativa*]

Asian cornelian cherry: Zhu yu 茱萸 (Shan zhu yu 山茱萸, *Cornus officinalis*)

Preserved fish in soup [8:78,32]: (with meat) Zheng yu zha fa 胚魚鮓法; (without meat) Shi jing zheng zha fa <食經>胚鮓法

Preserved pork: Zuo zhu rou zha fa 作豬肉鮓法 [8:74,19]

Oak bark eggs: Zuo yuan zi fa 作杬子法 [6:60,28-29]

fourth-century scholar: Guo Pu 郭璞 (276-324) described the Yuan tree.

Classification: (Yuan tree) Yuan mu 杬木, a variety of oak, *Quercus.* In: *Qi min yao shu* 齊民要術 (1982) by Jia Sixie 賈思勰 , annotated by Miao Qiyu 繆啟愉. Beijing 北京: Nong ye chubanshe 農業出版社, p. 454.

CHAPTER FIVE

BREAD AND PASTA

Plant plenty of wheat. Its many varieties can be stored for a long time. Wheat provides food, but only after it is boiled or made into flour.

The boiled wheat that Jia speaks of had been used for centuries, but unlike millet, barley and rice, wheat was not easily cooked. It was preferably milled into flour that could be turned into bread or pasta. Leavened bread was known long before Jia, but he provided the earliest detailed description of its preparation. Two kinds of leavening agents were known. Jia included a method from *Cui Hao's Food Classic* — a sour rice gruel. 'Boil down 4 L of sour rice gruel to 2.8 L. Then add 400 mL of raw non-glutinous rice and cook it to make (more) gruel.' A part of this was used to leaven wheat flour. 'To raise 40 L flour in July-August, use 800 ml of the leaven; in winter, use twice as much.'

Fermenting white wine was required to make the other leavening agent. (The white wine was also used to cook dog meat that was made into a preserve with chicken eggs.) According to Jia, preparation of this wine began with hours-long boiling of water to lighten its colour. This was mixed with rice, broomcorn millet and common yeast cakes for the first round of fermentation.

Rice was added for the second round. During summer, these two steps were carried out at night when it was cooler. Thus the entire procedure took two whole days and nights to complete. 'The wine has a fragrance,' Jia wrote, 'and it is good for three to five days.'

To make leaven for bread, white wine was first mixed with rice gruel. Jia wrote, 'Make gruel with 3 L of rice. Mix it with about 2.6 L of white wine and leave it near the fire. When you see large bubbles resembling fish eyes appear, pour some of it through a piece of cloth and wring it out. Mix the clear liquid (the leaven) with 40 L wheat flour. When the dough rises, make the bread.' The raised dough was made into 'roast pasta,' a term still used today for baked or toasted leavened breads of almost any kind. They could be sweet or savoury, plain or with filling, round, triangular or rectangular in shape. Jia described oven-baked bread with a filling of lamb cooked with scallions and soy extract. Another kind of bread had bone marrow and honey worked into the dough. It was about 1 cm thick. Placed in the oven, it puffed up.

The raised dough could also be fried. 'Small pieces of raised dough are soaked in water and then drained on a lacquered plate. Transfer it onto your wrist. Do not add dry flour!' Jia cautioned. 'Tip it into hot fat and it will soon float. Tip it over with a stick, and when it floats again, quickly remove it from the fat. They are lovely. One side will be brown, the other side is paler. Be careful not to pierce the bun, it is the steam inside that keeps it soft.'

Pasta

Wheat flour pasta took many shapes. Pasta known as chess pieces was popular. Strips of dough the diameter of one's little finger were sliced into small rounds resembling the pieces used in the ancient chess game called Go. Steamed and cooled, chess piece pasta could be stored for 10 days in winter.

'Wheat flour rice' was simulated rice made with wheat flour dough. Dry flour was first steamed and then made into dough and cut into grain-size pieces. The mock rice was steamed, sieved, and steamed again.

The most interesting of the pasta was a kind that over the centuries came to be called 'slippery noodles.'

Pasta Made with Soaked Dough

'Shape the dough into pieces the size of a thumb: about 6 cm in length. Soak them in a dish of cold water. Then press each piece against the side of the dish until the dough is very thin and drop it into rapidly boiling water. When the pieces float, they are done — glistening white, delectable, slippery, truly extraordinary.'

Another recipe also called for soaking raw dough in cold water.

'Sift the flour through a piece of silk. Make a thick meat soup; when it has cooled mix it with the flour. Form the dough into a strand the thickness of a chopstick. Cut it into 30 cm lengths and soak them in water. Then press each strand until it is as thin as the leaf of chive, and cook them in boiling water.'

The long history of slippery noodles may have begun around this time. Only a few decades after Jia, these noodles were included among dozens of fancy dishes in a menu for a luxury-loving emperor. Although most people used the noodle dough made with water, the idea of making noodle dough with meat stock was not lost. For example, a sixteenth-century gourmet had noodles made with rich chicken stock instead of water.

Byproducts: Wheat Starch and Gluten
Two ingredients in the Chinese kitchen — wheat starch and the protein called gluten — were the keys to Jia's slippery noodle recipes. Wheat gluten and wheat starch may have been recognized as two different substances around Jia's time. Certainly two centuries after Jia, these two substances in wheat flour were intentionally separated from each other. A medical text described the procedure. 'Take 3 L of wheat. Adding water, grind it into flour. Work the flour and the water until a large wad is formed and then stop. Let the cloudy liquid settle, and strain the solids through a white silk bag.' The solids were starch granules, used for preparing a herbal sweetmeat. The wad was composed of gluten.

We now understand why Jia's noodles were slippery. Wheat starch is a thickener. Wheat flour dough placed in cold water released starch granules. As pieces of dough were pressed against the side of the container, more starch was washed out, but incompletely. Gluten had formed as a result of soaking flour in water. It was a cross-linked network of protein strands making the dough strong and elastic. Upon boiling the noodles, the residual wheat starch thickened. This was what made the noodles slippery.

SLIPPERY NOODLES

NOTES

Opening lines: [2:10,11]

Boiled wheat: Mai fan 麥飯 [Cai Zhonglang Ji 蔡中郎集 by Cai Yong 蔡邕 (133-192), Ch. 22, p. 40]

Leavening agents [9:82,11]：(sour leaven from *Cui Hao's Food Classic*) Shi jing yue zuo bing xiao fa <食經>曰作餅酵法; (white wine leaven) Zuo bai bing fa 作白餅法

Cooking dog meat: <Shi jing> yue zuo quan zhe fa <食經>曰作曰犬朕法 [9:81,10]

White wine: He dong yi jiu fa 河東頤白酒法 [7:66,19]. The yeast cakes called Yi qu 頤麴 were made in autumn, unlike common yeast cakes made in summer.

Broomcorn millet: Shu mi 黍米, *Panicum miliaceum*

Breads: (roast pasta with lamb filling) Zuo shao bing fa 作燒餅法[9:82, 11]. The term roast pasta is taken from SCC6-5, pp.470-475, on leavening and breads. (marrow bread) Sui bing fa 髓餅法 [9:82,12]; (fried bread) Bu tou 餢餘[9:82,13]

Pasta: (chess pieces) Qi zi mian 棊子麵 or Qie mian zhu 切麵粥[9:82,13-14]; (wheat flour rice) Shi jing yue zuo mian fan fa <食經>曰作麵飯法 [9:86,21]

Go chess game: Wei qi 圍棋

Soaked dough [9:82,13]: Shui hua mian 水滑麵 ; (original name,) Bo tun 餺飩; (dough made with meat broth) Yin shui bo tun 引水餺飩. See SCC6-5, pp. 480-483, for more about noodles

Emperor's menu: Slippery noodles were called Hua bing 滑餅 In: *The Food Classic*, Shi jing 食經 by Xie Feng 謝諷 (fl 605-616), Qing yi lu (yin shi bu fen) 清異錄 (飲食部份) by Tao Gu 陶穀(902-970); ed. by Li Yimin 李益民, Wang Minde 王明德, and Wang Zihui 王子輝 (ZPGC, 1985, p. 14)

The emperor: Sui Yangdi 隋煬帝 (r 605-616)

Sixteenth-century gourmet: Ji mian 雞麵 [Zhu yu shan fang 竹嶼山房 (1504) by Song Xu 宋詡, Song Gongwang 宋公望 and Song Maocheng 宋懋澄. Yang sheng bu er 養生部二 , part II ch. 2, p. 1]

Wheat byproducts: (wheat starch) Cheng fen 澄粉; (wheat gluten) Mian jin 麵筋. See SCC6-5, pp.498-499, for discussion

Prescription using wheat starch: [Xiao mai mian shi si wei jian 小麥麵 十四味煎 in Wai tai mi yao fang 外臺秘要方 (752) by Wang Dao 王燾 (670-755). Ch. 27, p.59]

CHAPTER SIX

MAKING MALTOSE SYRUP

A light rain overnight – at last Qingming is close!
Though the sun is pale, the greenhouse is bursting,
The fields bristle with beards of grain.
We have roasted the tea leaves.
Now we pour syrup on the puddings.
Our guests will have refreshments. This joy
That has neither scent nor sound is hard to name.

It may be difficult to grasp the fact that in medieval China people had over a millennium of recorded history to draw upon. The events celebrated by some yearly festivals were sometimes overlooked or nearly forgotten, having occurred so long ago. So it was with Cold Foods Day, commemorating an event that occurred nine centuries before Jia. Jia told the story of its origin. Cold Foods Day marked the death of a good man wronged by his ruler. To drive the man out of the mountains where he had fled, the forests were set on fire. The man was found burnt to death, his arms clasped around a tree. 'Many people still grieve for him,' Jia continued. 'So on this day no fires are lit. People cook something sweet and eat it cold.' Cold Foods Day fell on the day before Qingming, the festival that marked the arrival of spring and warmer weather. Families paid their respects at ancestral tombs. It was also the time for visiting friends and relatives where cold pastries and other treats had been readied. A barley pudding with maltose syrup poured over it was one of the holiday refreshments.

The preparations for making apricot barley pudding were extensive. New clay bowls with a capacity of 8 L were bought. But first, the iron cooking pots had to be seasoned to prevent foods cooked in it from darkening.

'Tightly tie stalks of the wormwood plant together and cut off both ends. Heat water in the pot and scrub it with the brush. Buy several slabs of fat pork with the skin on, about the size of one's hand. Rub the pot with it. Then scrub the pot with water; if the water turns inky, repeat the whole procedure as many times as necessary until the wash water is clear.'

'There are people who can make this pudding, so I set down their way of making it,' Jia wrote. Indeed his recipe for the pudding seems to have been patched together from several accounts. (I have tried to fill in some gaps.) 'To make apricot barley pudding,' Jia wrote. 'do not use barley planted in spring.' The variety of barley used for this pudding was planted in spring or autumn. 'A month before the holiday, the barley is winnowed and sorted into five or six groups according to size: the largest grains were the size of chick peas. Sun dry them thoroughly.'

To prepare the pudding: 'The seasoned pot was used to make gruel with the largest barley grains and then washed.'

Apricot stones were cracked. 'Apricot kernels, scalded to remove their skins, were ground. Water was added, and the mixture was wrung through a piece of silk to obtain the liquid — it should be pure and thick. The liquid was heated over a cow dung fire.' Cow dung used as fuel produced steady low heat. 'When the liquid was almost boiling, and wrinkles appeared on its surface, barley was added.' Probably the different sizes of barley were added in sequence, the larger grains before the smaller ones. 'The barley must be stirred without stop until it is thoroughly cooked and as soft like mud. Then, pour it into the new dishes.' As the pudding set extruded water seeped through the porous clay. 'Do not cover the dish. Do not move it! The colour of the pudding should resemble lard, the grains of barley like jade. Leave it until the 8th day of the 4th lunar month.

'If the pot were not properly seasoned, the pudding would be black. If the heat was too high, the pudding would burn and taste bitter. If the clay dish were old, the liquid in the pudding could not seep out. The dish must be uncovered, or the pudding will crack.'

Maltose Syrup

The syrup that went over the pudding was formed by the action of wheat sprouts on cooked rice. It converted the starches in glutinous rice into raw syrup that then was boiled down. Sprouting wheat was initially white and this was used to make 'white' syrup. When the sprouts turned green, they were compacted into cakes and dried. This kind of malt was used for 'black' syrup.

Black Maltose Syrup

Use cakes of green sprouted wheat. Pulverize them and use 4 L for every 40 L rice. The rice must be picked over dozens of times, washed, cooked and then spread out to cool. While the rice is still warm, thoroughly mix it with the malt. Place the mixture in an earthen jar with a closed bunghole. Smooth out the mixture, but do not pack it down. Cover the jar with a quilt to keep it warm. In winter, pack straw around the jar and leave it for a whole day. In summer, it will require half a day for the rice to be digested. When the layer of rice has diminished, stop.

Heat water to the fish-eyes stage and pour the near-boiling water into the jar to form a layer 30 cm deep. Mix thoroughly. Let it stand for *the duration of a meal.* Pull out the bung and collect the raw syrup.

Cook down the syrup in a pot fitted with a steamer rack. Every time the liquid comes to a boil add two more ladlefuls, and keep the fire low or the syrup will burn. Place the steamer rack on top to prevent the syrup from boiling over. When all of the raw syrup is in the pot and it is not boiling over, the rack can be removed. A man with a ladle must stir the syrup without stopping. When the syrup is done, the fire may be extinguished. When the syrup begins to cool, the stirring may be stopped and the ladle taken out.

The syrup for the pudding was thinned so 'its colour was red, its flavour pronounced.' The product could be cooked further for other uses, turning into a molasses-like substance that is still used today: for the pork filling in steamed buns, or for marinating meat to be grilled or roasted. The heavy syrup will stick to almost everything, including raw meat.

In antiquity it was written, 'When serving your elders, use honey, dates, chestnuts and maltose to sweeten the food.' Seven centuries before Jia, a queen upon reaching middle age had declared, 'Do not bother me with affairs of state. Let me fuss over my grandchildren and suck candy.' That was maltose, made into hard candy. By Jia's time these four substances were still the only sweeteners and only maltose was man-made.

NOTES

Opening poem: Nan ge zi 南歌子(first line 日薄花房綻) [*Dongpo Ci* 東坡詞 by Su Shi 蘇軾, p. 38] Su Shi, also known as Su Dongpo 蘇東坡 (1036-1101)
Cold Foods Day: Han shi jie 寒食節, the day preceding Qingming festival 清明節 commemorates the death of Jie Zitui 介子推 [9:85,17]
Seasoning the pot: Zhi fu ling bu yu fa 治釜令不渝法 [9:85,17-18]
Wormwood plant: brush made with stalks of Hao 蒿, a variety of *Artemisia*
Apricot barley pudding: Zhu xing lao zhou fa 煮杏酪粥法 [9:85,19-20]
Barley: Mai 麥 or Da mai 大麥, *Hordeum vulgare.* The Kuang mai 穬麥 variety with its many spikes is planted in spring and autumn [2:10,10-11]
Apricot: Xing 杏 *Prunus armeniaca;* (kernel) Xing ren 杏仁
Syrup: Zhu li fa 煮醴法 [9:85,18] refers to Zhu hei xing fa 煮黑餳法 [9:89,37]. The latter method is detailed under Zhu bai xing fa 煮白餳法 [9:89,36-37]. See SCC6.5, pp. 458-459 for further details.
Sweeteners: Nei ze 內則 in Li ji 禮記 (475-221 BCE). Sturgeon, Donald (ed.) 2011. Chinese Text Project. http://ctext.org (dates) Zao 棗 *Ziziphus jujube*; (chestnuts) Li 栗 *Castanea mollisima*; (maltose) I 飴; (honey) Mi 密
Hard candy: Words of Ming de ma huang hou 明德馬皇后 (first century) [*Gu wen ya zheng* 古文雅正 by Cai Shiyuan 蔡世遠 (1682-1733), Ch. 4, p. 8]

CHAPTER SEVEN

FOOD PREPARATION

Now's the time for water shield!
There are buckets of them for sale.
How to cook it? With perch, of course –
One that's three feet long.

Water shield is a wild plant that grows in the shallower parts of fresh water lakes. It may also be cultivated. Jia spoke of planting water shield in fish ponds or streams. Its reddish stems support broad, nearly round leaves. Like the lotus, its roots are embedded in mud; and its leaves shed water, allowing them to float on the water's surface. Unlike the lotus, the leaves and stems of water shield are edible. Jia said, 'Water shield is the best of vegetables to make soup. Use the stems in May or June when their leaves have not yet sprouted. A month or two later, the leaves will be fully grown, and they are silky.' Water shield and perch soup may appear in modern times in the course of a banquet. It was known several centuries before Jia, so it has a history of over two millennia.

To describe making the soup, Jia drew upon his own knowledge and that of the minister. 'Water shield leaves are left whole but blanched,' the minister wrote. Aside from perch, carp and culter - two fishes that were rather similar to each other - were used. To start the soup, 'Slices of carp are cut diagonally and placed in cold water with the water shield,' the minister said. Upon heating, the water shield released a clear jelly that thickened the soup. 'When the fish slices turn white, add one-tenth volume of cold water (to stop the cooking). Do not stir it too much, or the fish and vegetables will break up, making the soup cloudy,' Jia wrote, adding, 'The soup must taste of water shield. Do not add scallions, shallots, rice, pickles or vinegar.' Water shield soup was remarkable in its own right, but in Jia's day it must have been exceptional because many of their soups were thick, heavy and sour.

Soups

Even the simplest soup that Jia described was rich and heavy. It was made with sesame seeds, ground and boiled. Four litres were used to make less than a litre of soup and rice was added for thickening. Rice was commonly used in soups as thickener: in carp soup to make the fish silkier and in rabbit soup to make the stringy meat smoother.

Soups laced with vinegar were favored. Vinegars were made from a variety of cereal grains, fermented with yellow mould, moulded wheat, lees or other agents. Jia described over 20 ways of making vinegar. The various kinds of vinegar were dark in colour, deep and complex in flavour. Vinegar was added to soup at the last moment together with a little salt. The acidity lifted the flavour of soups.

A set of pig's feet meant the four feet from one pig. Three sets were used for a soup, boiled until the large bones could be removed. Vinegar was the perfect foil for the unctuous textures of pig's feet. Another sour soup was made with deer heads. They were cooked, boned and cut into pieces two fingers thick and were finished in a separately made pork stock that called for nearly a kg of pork for each head. Vinegar, salt and fermented black beans were added to taste.

One particular soup had all three attributes: it was heavy, thick and sour. Made with pork, lamb, taro (a starchy root) and rice, it was seasoned with soy extract and a generous amount of vinegar.

Cooking Methods: Boiling

There were only a handful of cooking methods in Jia's time. Besides boiling and steaming, there was the open fire for roasting and grilling. Nonetheless, a fair amount of effort went into food preparation, starting with the domestication of animals, particularly the pig, to provide food for man. 'The pig pen can be small, and it does not have to be particularly clean,' Jia wrote in his chapter on animal husbandry. 'It should provide the pigs with shelter from rain and snow.' Suckling pigs were used for food when they were only a few weeks old. If males reached the age of 60 days they were gelded. 'It makes the animal meaty, and its bones delicate.'

An immaculately clean suckling pig was the starting material for a dish of boiled pork.

'Thoroughly wash the suckling pig in warm water. If there are coarse hairs on the skin, use tweezers to pluck them out. Fine hairs must be shaved off. Rub the skin with sundew leaves, wash it and scrape it with a knife. Scrub the cooking pot so it will not darken the meat. Put the pig in a silk bag with small stones to weight it down. Boil it in a mixture of vinegar, flour and water. As foam appears, skim it off. When the vinegared water comes to a boil, immediately take the pig out and douse it with cold water. Rub the skin again with sundew leaves until it is immaculate.

'Make a thin paste with flour and water. Place the pig back in the bag, weighted down as before, and heat it in the watery paste, bringing it to a boil. Remove the foam. When the pig is thoroughly cooked, take it out and place it in a deep dish. Mix the thin paste with cold water. Pour the warm liquid over the pig. After a good soak, chop the pork into pieces and serve it. It is the colour of white jade. It glides down the throat.'

Steaming

Steaming food had several advantages over boiling. The water in the boiling pot may have been less than pristine, but the steam rising from it was pure. Rice was steamed, not boiled. Steamers were made as three-piece sets: a pot for boiling water, a steamer compartment with perforated bottom, and a close fitting lid. The pot might have three legs; it was a free-standing appliance that could be set over a fire. The steamer set remained in use for centuries, even after the kitchen stove came into use. For the latter, a round-bottomed pot without legs fit into a round opening on top of the stove.

SLIPPERY NOODLES

Steamed piglet must have been the centerpiece of many feasts in Jia's time.

'Choose a fat piglet, wash it well and then parboil it. Four hundred mL of raw, dry glutinous rice is soaked in strong soy extract, acquiring a golden colour; it is steamed until half-cooked and seasoned with more soy extract. Prepare 400 mL each of slivered ginger, tangerine peel and leaves and 1.6 L scallion stalks, cut into 9 cm lengths. Mix it with the rice. Place the pig and the rice in a crock, closely cover it and steam it for *the time required to cook two or three meals*. Add 1.2 L lard and 400 mL soy extract and steam it again.'

Roasting
'Select a fat suckling pig or a piglet — it can be either a female or a gelded male. Clean, scrape and shave the skin as described for Boiled Suckling Pig. Make a small slit in the abdomen and remove the innards. Stuff the pig with lemon grass and skewer it on a wooden stick. Roast the pig over a slow fire, turning it continuously. Paint the pig with clear wine but stop when the skin just turns colour. Smear it with a piece of fresh pork fat (if you do not have the fat use sesame oil). The skin will be the colour of amber or gold. The meat melts in the mouth like snow. The juices and fat run together.'

Grilling
Jia seemed to have tasted everything, from the cooks' best creations to some culinary blunders. Most of his admonitions on what not to do applied to the technique of grilling. 'Beef tenderloin is grilled on a stick, but *one side at a time*. It is sliced and served immediately before another side is grilled. If you waited for all four sides to be grilled,' Jia said, 'the meat would be tough and inedible.'

Meat was often marinated before grilling. 'Use beef, lamb or venison, and marinate them with crushed scallions, salt and soy extract but *not too long,* or the meat will be tough. Poke the fire and place the meat close to the hottest part. Turn the pieces continuously *but never lift it away from the heat*. The moment its colour changes, the meat is done, and it is juicy and tender.

'Beef omasum from an older animal is thick and luscious,' Jia wrote. 'Thread the pieces on a skewer, jam them together. Hold the skewer close to the fire. When the pieces on the outside split, slice and serve it immediately.

If you try to smooth out the leaves and skewer them neatly, or if the fire is *not hot enough,* or if you are constantly *moving the skewer,* the result is inedible.'

Food Service
Some works of art of sixth century China depict religious figures seated on benches or stools, with one foot on the ground. These were foreign postures because benches, sitting stools and chairs did not become standard pieces of furniture in China until centuries later. In the world that Jia lived in most people sat on mats laid on the floor. Esteemed persons might be seated in the centuries-old manner - on platforms raised just a few inches high. At meals, food was placed on low tables in front of them. Because people dined at separate tables food was served in individual portions.

Stewed Beef
'Boil a large piece of beef until it can be readily cut with a knife. Cut slabs about 10 cm square and half as thick. When it is time to serve it, add to the cooking broth: ginger, scallions, tangerine peel, celery and sand leeks, all chopped fine. Season it with salt and vinegar. Pour this broth into a separately prepared hot thick meat soup. Stirring to keep the solid ingredients from settling, ladle the near-boiling liquid into bowls. Place a slab of beef in each bowl. After a while the meat will swell and more hot soup can be added.'

Food was plated in small portions. 'Clams are grilled and served on the half shell on copper plates: six to a plate if large, eight if the clams are small. Oysters are prepared the same way, three to a plate.' Just two pieces of grilled fish were served in a bowl.

Grilled Fish
'This best is made with bream or culter. Carefully clean and scale the fish. Cut it into pieces about 3 cm square. Ginger, tangerine peel, pepper, scallions, celery, sand leeks, perilla and edible cornelian cherries are cut fine and mixed with the fish together with salt, fermented black beans and vinegar. It may be left overnight. When grilling the fish moisten it with coriander juice, and repeat when the fish looks dry. When done the fish has a reddish colour. Put two pieces in each bowl — never just a single piece.'

SLIPPERY NOODLES

Two persons might share one dish. Jia wrote: 'Fill a bowl half full of ginger, cut fine, with some of the honey water it was cooked in. Provide a single pair of chopsticks. This is for two people.' Probably the dish would be placed on a side table between them.

There was etiquette to food presentation that is no longer practiced in China. For example, if rice were used to thicken a soup, etiquette required that individual grains should not be seen. For a carp soup thickened with rice, Jia cautioned: 'Before you put the soup in the bowls, remove every rice grain from it. Otherwise it would be improper.'

Medieval Cooking

The trio of fermented black beans-scallions-salt appeared in many recipes in Jia's book including the scrambled eggs mentioned earlier. The word *an* described some dishes employing this particular combination of flavours.

An Chicken

'Mix salt, fermented black beans, scallion stalks (white part) split down the middle, with some toasted dry perilla. Place it in water with a whole chicken and boil it. When done, remove the chicken and the scallions. Strain the cooking liquid and let it settle. Slice the chicken in small pieces, plate it and pour some of the warm broth over it.'

An Fatback

'Boil fatback with salt and fermented black beans until cooked. Cut it into very thin slices about 3 by 7 cm, and place them into a fresh portion of water containing scallions, sand leeks, salt, soy extract, and some cut shallot leaves. The sand leeks and shallot leaves can be omitted.'

Dishes composed of fish and meat cooked together were called *zheng*, also an obsolete word. Jia applied it to soups using preserved fish such as carp fermented in rice. His recipe for 'Noblemen's Soup' was made with meat scraps left on the butcher block, some other kind of meat and preserved fish. Some say the soup originated as leftover food that noblemen would give to farmers working in the fields.

Perhaps more than at any other period in Chinese culinary history dishes were made by mixing different meats, as Jia showed. A sour soup was made with soft-shelled turtle, lamb and wine. In another recipe fowl was cooked with lamb. Five large ducks and six small ducks were cooked in wine; then it was made into a soup with about a kg of lamb, taro, rice and seasonings.

Another soup was made with a piece of fat duck, a piece of lamb with skin on and bone in, and some pork and then sweetened with honey. It was completed by the addition of lamb omasum (one of the animal's stomachs). By the time the soup was brought to a boil every one of the ingredients was perfectly cooked.

Fish and fowl were prepared together. Thin slices of raw culter were filled with a mixture of chopped boned roasted duckling, pickles, ginger, tangerine peel and garlic, seasoned with vinegar and fish sauce. They were rolled up, fastened on skewers and grilled.

Fish was combined with duck in another fashion. A whole culter 60 cm long was cleaned but not eviscerated. A slit was made along its back, and salt was rubbed in. Minced duck meat that had been mixed with seasonings was first cooked and then stuffed into the fish abdomen. With the opening fastened with skewers, the fish was grilled over a low fire until it was half-done. Then it was painted with vinegar, fish sauce and soy extract and finished on the grill. The combination of fish and duck appears to be unique to Jia's place and time.

NOTES

Opening poem: Ji shan xing 稽山行 (first line 稽山何巍巍) by Lu You 陸游 (1125-1209) [*Jian nan shi gao* 劍南詩槁 by Lu Ziju 陸子虡 and Lu You 陸游, Ch.65, p.1]
Water shield: Chun 蓴 *Brasenia shreberi;* (planting) Zong chun fa 種蓴法 [6:61,30]
Water shield-fish soup: (according to Jia) Kuai yu chun geng 膾魚蓴羹[8:76,24-25]; (according to the minister) Chun geng 蓴羹 [8:76,25-26]
Fish: Lu yu 鱸魚 is commonly translated perch, although both *Zhongguo pengren cidian* 中國烹飪辭典 and *Ci Hai* Dictionary 辭海 place it in genus *Lateolabrax,* Asian seabass. Carp varieties : (common carp) Li yu 鯉魚 *Cyprinus carpio;* (culter) Bai yu 白魚 *Chanodichthys erythropterus*
Sesame soup: Hu ma geng 胡麻羹 [8:76,23]
Rice as thickener: (carp soup) Li yu huo 鯉魚臛 [8:76,26]; (rabbit soup) Zuo tu geng

SLIPPERY NOODLES

fa 作兔羹法 [8:76,22]

Vinegar: Zuo cu 作酢 [8:71,8-12]

Sour soups: (pig's feet) Zhu ti suan geng 豬蹄酸羹 [8:76,22]; (deer heads) Jiang zhu fa羌煑法 [8:76,24]; (meat and taro): Shi jing zuo yu zi suan huo fa <食經>作芋子酸臛法 [8:76,21]

Raising pigs: Yang zhu養豬 [6:58,24]

Boiled suckling pig: Bai yao zhun fa 白瀹肫法 [8:79,35]

Sundew leaves: Mao gao 茅蒿, a variety of the carnivorous plant Sundew, *Drosera peltata*. *Drosera* leaves contain adhesive (Zhang, M., et al., Nanofibers and nanoparticles from the insect-capturing adhesive of the Sundew (*Drosera*) for cell attachment. Journal of Nanobiotechnology, 2010, 8:20)

Steamers and stoves: SCC6.5, pp. 67-68, 76-81

Steamed piglet: Zheng tun fa 蒸豚法 [8:77,28-29]

Glutinous grain: Shu mi 秫米 may be glutinous sorghum, glutinous millet or glutinous rice. In this context it is probably glutinous rice (usually called Nuo mi 糯米, *Oryza glutinosa*)

Aromatics: (ginger) Jiang薑, *Zingiber officinale*; (Mandarin orange, tangerine) Ju 橘, *Citrus reticulata*; (scallion, spring onion) Cong bai 蔥白, *Allium fistulosum*

Roast pig: Zhi zhu fa 炙豬法 [9:80,1-2]

Lemon grass: According to the ZPGC edition of Jia's book (p. 155), mao ru 茅茹 refers to xiang mao 香茅 lemon grass, *Cymbopogon citratus*

Grilling: (beef tenderloin) Bang zhi 棒炙[9:80:2]; (marinating meat) Nan zhi 腩炙 [9:80,2]; (beef omasum) Niu xian zhi 牛胘炙 [9:80,3]

Foreign postures: *China: Dawn of a Golden Ag*e, 200-750 AD, by James C.Y. Watt. New York: The Metropolitan Museum of Art (2004) p. 92, Fig. 99; p. 262, cat. no. 163.

Seating at meals: SCC6.5, pp.114-115

Stewed beef: Lan shu 爛熟. (celery) Hu qin 胡芹, *Apium graveolens* var. *dulce*; (sand leek) Xiao suan 小蒜, *Allium scorodoprasum*

Small servings: (clams) Zhi han 炙蚶 [9:80,7]; (oysters) Zhi li 炙蠣[9:80,8]

Grilled fish: Zhi yu 炙魚 [9:80,8]. (bream) Bian 鯿 *Megalobrama amblycephala*; (perilla) Su 蘇 *Perilla frutescens*; (edible cornelian cherry) Dang 欓, *Zanthoxylum ailanthoides*; (coriander) Xiang cai 香菜, *Coriandrum sativum*

Honeyed ginger: Mi jiang 密薑 [9:87,23-24]

Etiquette: (rice in carp soup) Li yu huo 鯉魚臛 [8:76,26]

Meat or fish cooked with scallions-fermented beans-salt: An 腤; (chicken) An ji 腤雞 [8:78,33]; (fatback) An bai rou 腤白肉[8:78,33]

Shallot leaves: Shallot stalks are composed of tightly furled leaves

Fish cooked with meat: Zheng 胚 or Zheng 鯖; (pork, lamb, beef) Zheng yu zha fa 胚魚鮓法 [8:78,32]; Shi jing zheng <食經>胚法 zha fa [8:78,32]

Noblemen's soup: Wu hou zheng fa五侯胚法 [8:78,32]; (origin) [*Tai ping guang ji* 太平廣記 by Li Fang 李昉 (925-996), Ch.234, p.4]

Mixed meats: (turtle, lamb) Zuo bie huo fa 作鱉臛法 [8:76,22]; (duck, lamb) Zuo ya huo 作鴨臛法 [8:76,22]; (duck, lamb, pork, lamb omasum) Yang jie jie fa 羊節解法[8:76,24]

Fish and fowl: (duck-fish rolls) Xian zhi 銜炙[9:80,4] ; (fish stuffed with duck) Niang zhi bai yu fa 釀炙白魚法[9:80,5]

CHAPTER EIGHT

LOOKING BACK TO ANCIENT TIMES

The ancient kings had no palaces. In winter they lived in caves; in summer, in huts made of branches. Without fire, they lived on fruits; they drank the blood of birds and beasts and ate the meat without removing the feathers or hair. With fire, they could bake, boil, grill and roast food, and make wine and sauces. With fire, kings could feed the living and honour the dead.

Prior to the appearance of Jia's book, information on food and cooking was patchy. Going back a thousand years to the sixth century BC, we find ourselves in the time of Confucius. Unlikely as it may seem, some Confucian classics contained information on food and cooking. Confucius edited a few of the books. Others were added and codified in the centuries following his death. They were annotated by many scholars, clarifying ancient words and syntax. Although history and legend may have merged in some parts, as in the passage above, the Confucian classics covered almost every aspect of human activity from the rearing of children to funeral rites. Naturally, they touched upon care and feeding. A few lines from a chapter titled 'The Pattern of the Family' provide a sketch of family life.

Children had no set bedtimes, nor did they have fixed mealtimes.

At the age of seven, boys and girls did not sit together, nor did they take their meals together.

At the age of ten, a girl would be instructed in doing women's work such as overseeing the food used in sacrifices. That meant providing wines and sauces, filling bamboo dishes with fruits and nuts, and setting out dishes of preserved meats and pickled vegetables.

When a girl married, she and her husband would wait upon his parents at meals. After the elders had finished they ate the leftovers. When she herself was widowed, her eldest son waited upon her.

The Daily Fare

'Soup and grains were used by all, whether nobility or common folk, without distinction.' Soups, especially meat soups, were important. The ancients had three words that stood for thick beef soup, thick lamb soup and thick pork soup where it took two or three words to name soups made with fowl or vegetables. Jia used another word denoting thick meat soup. There are no special words to identify thick or thin vegetable soups.

Eight kinds of cooked grain were named in 'The Pattern of the Family': non-glutinous millet, glutinous millet, rice, common millet, white millet, yellow millet, late-harvested rice, early-harvested millet. The statement that food and grains were used by all without distinction was not exactly true.

Higher ranking officials usually had meat with their meals – either jerky or some other kind of preserved meat. Lower-ranking officers had no meat, nor did they have a choice of two soups to go with the rice or millet.

But meals for old folks were not as spare.

Among common folk, old people had food 'with fats and oils to enrich the food, and fresh or dried food smoothly coated with (thickeners from the Corydalis plant, day lily, white elm and elm tree.' The thickeners were prepared from roots of the flowering plants and the inner bark of certain elms.

'A dozen elms may have similar leaves but their bark and wood may be different. Some varieties of elm do not have slippery barks. The bark of the white elm is collected in March-April. Its rough outer layer is ground off, revealing the slippery white bark underneath. In times of famine, farmers used to make a powder with it, for food.'

Herbs used to flavour food varied with the seasons. In spring mincemeat was flavoured with scallions; in autumn mustard was used. For pork, chives were used in spring, and in autumn there was knotweed, a bitter and peppery leaf. Plums were used year-round in soups, meat and fowl. It was said, 'As starter is to wine, so are salt and plums to soup.'

Table Manners

Dining etiquette was set out in a Confucian text about rules of propriety. 'There is a set way of presenting a meal. Fresh meat with bones is placed on the diner's left, sliced meat on the right. Cooked grain is placed to his left and soup on the right. Vinegar and sauces are placed closest to him, the roast and minced meats further away. A side dish of scallions is placed at one end, wines and drinks on the right.

'(As a guest) do not wad the rice into a ball. Do not try to put back the grains sticking to your fingers. Do not slurp when you eat. Do not smack your lips. Do not crunch the bones. Do not return the uneaten fish or meats to the common dish. Do not feed the bones to the dogs.

'Do not snatch the food. Do not spread out the rice (to cool it, as if you were anxious to eat. Do not eat millet with your chopsticks; use the spoon. Do not gulp the soup. Do not season the soup. Do not pick your teeth.' If a guest adds seasoning to the soup, the host would say, "This food is very poorly cooked!" If the guest uses lots of condiments, the host would say, "I am sorry the food is not tasty." Fresh meats are juicy and can be chewed. Dried meats must first be torn to small pieces. Roasted meats are taken in small pieces, not swallowed whole.'

Sacrificial Ceremonies

'Everyone eats and drinks, but only a few appreciate flavour,' Confucius said in discussing why so few people practiced his philosophy. These words can be interpreted differently. Perhaps gourmets were scarce in those times because dried, pickled fish, meat and vegetables could only go so far to please the palate. It is possible this was one reason why much was made of the ceremonies at which animals were sacrificed: they provided fresh meat.

An account of the ceremony at which animals were slaughtered is given in *Ceremonial Usages*. 'The ceremony begins with invocations to honour the dead and secure the blessing of Heaven.' An ancient poem revealed that the sacrificial killing was performed with a knife that tinkled as it was wielded, because bells, made in the shape of a mythical bird resembling the phoenix, were tied to it.

> *To our ancestors we offer*
> *Clear wine and a red bull.*
> *Under the tinkling knife*
> *The beast is shorn of its hair.*
> *We take the fat and collect its blood.*

The blood with the hair or feathers (of the victim) is presented. The flesh, uncooked, is set on stands. The bones with the flesh on them are sodden and rush mats and coarse cloths are placed underneath. Robes of dyed silk are put on. Sweet and clear wines are offered. By tradition coloured water is included to commemorate the times when there was no wine.

Sacrificial meats, roasted and grilled, are brought out. The ruler and his consort take turns in presenting these foods at the altar. The ruler might offer one kind of roasted meat, his consort another kind. Having completed the service, they retire. The sacrificed animals are carved up and cooked, adding to the pots the half-raw pieces offered at the ceremony. All the vessels are filled (with meat), including the square or round baskets, bamboo splint-baskets, stemmed platters, and small tripods usually employed for soup. After benedictions and blessings, the ceremony comes to a close.

NOTES

Sources: *Xian Qin peng ren shi liao xuan zhu* 先秦烹飪史料選注 (ZPGC, 1987) *Duan ju shi san jing jing wen* 斷句十三經經文(abbrev. DJ13) (1965 Taipei: Taiwan Kaiming Book Co. 台灣開明書店 Sturgeon Donald (ed.) 2011. Chinese Text Project (abbrev. ctext). http://ctext.org

About the texts: According to the above-named ZPGC, *Liji* 禮記 was edited in the pre-Qin era (before 2nd-1st c BCE). It was a collection of works from about the Spring

SLIPPERY NOODLES

and Autumn period (8ᵗʰ-5ᵗʰ c BCE). Among these works was *Liji* 禮記, edited by Confucius (551-479 BCE)

Translations: The excerpts from *Liji* and the poem from *Shi jing* are in my words; they are based on translations by James Legge (1815-1897) and translations into modern Chinese in the ZPGC publication cited above.

Opening quotation: (DJ13) Li yun 禮運 in *Liji* 禮記, p.44; (ctext) *Liji* 禮記, Li yun 禮運, para 6, tr. J. Legge.

Bedtimes: (DJ13) *Liji* 禮記, p. 54; (ctext) *Liji* 禮記, Nei ze 內則, para 7, tr. J. Legge.

Age seven: (DJ13) *Liji* 禮記, p. 58; (ctext) *Liji* 禮記, Nei ze 內則, para 77, tr. J. Legge.

Age ten: (DJ13) *Liji* 禮記, p. 59; (ctext) *Liji* 禮記, Nei ze 內則, para 81, tr. J. Legge.

Married: (DJ13) *Liji* 禮記, p. 54; (ctext) *Liji* 禮記, Nei ze 內則, para 11, tr. J. Legge.

Soup and grains: (DJ13) *Liji* 禮記, p. 56; (ctext) *Liji* 禮記, Nei ze, 內則, para 45, tr. J. Legge.

Soup vocabulary: (thick beef soup) xin 腥; (thick lamb soup) xun 臐; (thick pork soup) xiao 膮; (thick meat soup) huo 臛

Foods rich and smooth: (DJ13) *Liji* 禮記, p. 55; (ctext) *Liji* 禮記, Nei ze 內則, para 4, tr. J. Legge

Source of thickeners: (corydalis) Jin 菫, genus *Corydalis*; (daylily) xuan cao 萱草, *Hemerocallis fulva*; (varieties of elm) fen 枌, yu 榆, *Ulmus pumila*. [*Ben cao gang mu* 本草綱目 by Li Shizhen 李時珍 (1518-1593). Corydalis: Ch. 26, p.64; day lily: Ch. 26, pp.20-22; elm bark: Ch. 35, part 2, pp. 33-34]

Seasoning: (DJ13) *Liji* 禮記, p. 44; (ctext) *Liji* 禮記, Li yun 禮運, para 6, tr. J. Legge.

Flavourings: (scallions , spring onions) Cong 蔥, *Allium fistulosum*; (mustard seeds) Jie 芥, *Brassica juncea*; Chinese leeks, chives) Jiu 韭 *Allium tuberosum*; (knotweed) Liao 蓼 *Polygonum hydropiper*; (plum) Mei 梅, *Prunus mume*

Salt and plums: (DJ13) Shang shu 尚書, p. 15; (ctext) Shang Shu 尚書, Charge to Yue III 說命下, para. 7, tr. J. Legge.

Table manners: (DJ13) *Liji* 禮記, p. 3; (ctext) *Liji* 禮記, Qu li I 曲禮, para 45, tr. J. Legge

'Everyone eats: (DJ13) Liji 禮記, p. 107; (ctext) *Liji* 禮記, Zong yong 中庸, para 4, tr. J. Legge

Ceremonial usages: (DJ13) Liji 禮記, p. 44; (ctext) *Liji* 禮記, Li yun 禮運, para 7, 8 , tr. J. Legge.

Tinkling knife: Xin nan shan 信南山 in *Xian Qin peng ren shi liao xuan zhu* 先秦烹飪史料選注 (ZPGC, 1987). (ctext) *Shi jing* 詩經 Xiao ya 小雅.

CHAPTER NINE

FOOD ADMINISTRATION IN THE ROYAL PALACE

First Month (early February):
Wild geese fly north, going home.
Fish swim up to the ice.
Ponds begin to melt.
Farmers rush to clear the fields.
At dusk Orion is in the south.
We see the Dipper, its handle pointing down.
Second month (early March):
Millet must be planted now.
We offer sturgeon at the altar.
Stealthily we scoop larvae from ant nests
To make condiments for offerings.
Young lambs must be weaned
In time for the summer sacrifice.
Third month (early April):
High officials receive gifts of ice.
Women pick mulberry leaves for the silkworms.

SLIPPERY NOODLES

The constellation of three stars has disappeared.
That does not mean that it has died –
Are there not times when you do not see me?
Fourth month (early June):
The apricot tree is bearing fruit.
The Pleiades appear: At dusk we see
The brightest southern star, Centaurus.

These excerpts are from an ancient farmer's calendar, a remarkable work from Confucian literature. The movements of the stars across the heavens were recorded so accurately, they enabled dating of the calendar to about 350 BCE. The farmer's calendar referred to the sacrificial offerings made throughout the year, and to the harvesting of plums and peaches for the ceremonies. It mentioned the annual ice distribution, an event that occurred only in the palace. These observations dovetailed with those given in a very different piece of Confucian literature from the same era. The topic of this chapter is a document with the imposing title, *Celestial Ministry* that detailed staffing of the royal palace. In the bureaucracy the officers at the very top — the administrator general and the two palace administrators — were not directly concerned with food. That was left to dozens of units making up the food administration.

High-ranking noblemen headed many units within the food administration, assisted by nobles of lesser rank. Below the nobles were commoners who might work as managers, store-keepers, scribes and many minor staff. Below them were numerous 'servants' largely recruited by corvée. Thus the vast bureaucracy came to include turtle catchers, pickle makers, doctors and veterinarians, chefs and cooks, and eunuchs who supervised women staff. The duties and the staffing of each unit were set out.

Food Administrator

Duties: To oversee food and drink for the emperor, empress and crown prince. Their fare consists of the six grains, the six drinks, 120 fine dishes, the eight delicacies and 120 kinds of condiments and pickles. On days when domestic animals (oxen, pig, lamb, horse, dog, chicken) are slaughtered a meal will consist of 12 tripods each with an accompanying platter (of food). The administrator will act as steward, presenting a dish and tasting it. Only then will the emperor eat. Music is played when food is served and the table is cleared. The emperor does not take full meals when there is a funeral, famine or some other calamity. At those times he eats sparingly. When he conducts rites the food administrator assists him.

Staff: 14 noblemen, 2 senior staff, 4 secretaries, 12 minor staff, 120 servants

Butcher

Duties: To supply the six wild animals (moose, deer, muntjac, wolf, pig and rabbit), the six fowl (goose, partridge, quail, pheasant, turtledove, squab) in all their variety.

The animals may be live, dead or freshly slaughtered. Their meat may be made into jerky. The butcher will provide the finest meats for the royal family. He will prepare offerings with the meat of wild beasts, if requested; these offerings will be cooked in traditional ways. In spring, young lamb or a small pig is cooked in fragrant fat (beef suet). In summer dried fish is cooked in pungent (dog) fat. In autumn rank (chicken) fat is used for venison, and in winter birds are cooked in rich (lamb) fat.

The accounts are done at the end of the year omitting the expenses for the royal family's provisions.

Staff: 12 noblemen, 2 senior staff, 4 secretaries, 12 minor staff and 40 servants.

Inner Court Chef

Duties: In charge of preparing the royal family's food, from cutting and cooking to seasoning. When the emperor conducts a sacrifice, the chef will fill tripods and platters with the meats; he will choose the condiments. He must also prepare the dried meats, with and without bones, the sacrificial soup, fatty meat and bones and the dried fish that the emperor enjoys. He serves the queen and crown prince as well. He must reject the ox that cries in the night, its flavour will be off; the lamb whose coat is cold and odorous; the dog whose legs are reddish; it will taste rank. The fowl that does not chirp, the pig that has gone blind, the horse whose back has darkened — their flesh is inedible.

At sacrificial rites he must carve up and cook the animals, even as drinking and eating go on. He must prepare the sacrificial soup and the different dried meats, the fish and fowl.

Staff: 12 noblemen, 2 senior staff, 4 secretaries, 10 minor staff and 100 servants.

Outer Court Chef

Duties: In charge of sacrificial offerings for the outer palace; they will consist of dried meat slices and strips, and dried meat without bones. The chef will set them out on tripods and platters. His other duties are to provide guests with supper and breakfast, to feed the elderly, the orphans and those in service, to set out the tripods at lesser funeral services.

Staff: 12 noblemen, 2 senior staff, 4 secretaries, 10 minor staff and 100 servants.

Cooks

In antiquity, enormous metal tripods were used as cooking vessels. A team of cooks was required to handle them.

Duties: To assist the inner and outer court chefs in preparing soups in large tripods or pots. One must know the amounts of water, heat and time to use. Two kinds of meat soups are served at sacrificial ceremonies: made with salt and vegetables, or without.

Staff: 4 noblemen, 1 senior staff, 2 secretaries, 5 minor staff and 50 servants.

Procurement of Food

Much of the food for the emperor was produced on his land. Thus he participated once a year in a ceremony on his land. As recorded elsewhere, 'At the start of spring the emperor personally worked in the fields, ploughing three rows. Three dukes plowed five rows, and other noblemen nine rows. The common folk numbering 300 plowed 500 acres.'

Farm Manager

Duties: In charge of cultivating the emperor's land; to harvest millet, and to provide mugwort, wild fruits and gourds for ceremonial offerings. The manager will stand in for the emperor in ceremonies where no animal is sacrificed, and at funerals.

Should a fire break out, those with the emperor's surname bear the guilt and are put to death. Their servants are sent to work under the inner and outer court chefs.

Staff: 2 noblemen, 1 senior staff, 2 secretaries, 30 minor staff and 300 servants.

Hunter-Trapper

Duties: To net land animals and identify them by name; in winter, the wolf; in summer, the elk; other animals in other seasons. To prepare nets for trapping. Live and dead, animals are required for ceremonial offerings and at funerals. Some animal parts go to the jerky maker. Skin, fur, tendons and horns are sent to the palace's Jade House (a unit that made jewellery and household items from different materials).

Staff: 12 noblemen, 2 senior staff, 4 secretaries, 4 minor staff and 40 servants.

Jerky Maker

Duties: In charge of making dried meat; to convert the hunter-trapper's catch into dried meat slices, cured meat and so forth; to provide jerky for all occasions.

Staff: 4 noblemen, 2 senior staff, 2 secretaries and 20 servants.

Fishermen

Duties: In charge of maintaining the fish traps in winter, of presenting the emperor with sturgeon, in spring. He will supply fresh and dried fish to the emperor, and fish for ceremonial occasions. To handle all matters relating to fish, including sending thebby-products to Jade House.

Staff: 6 noblemen, 2 senior staff, 4 secretaries, 30 minor staff and 300 servants.

Turtle Catcher

Duties: To catch animals with shells and other creatures that lie hidden: turtles and bivalves in spring, tortoises and fish in autumn; to supply the condiment makers with oysters, shellfish and larvae.

Staff: 4 noblemen, 2 senior staff, 2 secretaries and 16 servants.

Wine Administration

Wine Manager

Duties: To furnish appropriate wines for the royal family, for ceremonial rites, forguests and so forth. The wine manager makes ready the five (incompletely) fermented wines that are variously foamy, thick and sweet, cloudy, red, and clear. He is to dispense the three fully fermented wines that have been separated from the lees: one wine that is made overnight and two that take months to produce. He will also dispense the four drinks — the cloudy-sweet wine that is filtered and diluted, a healthful wine made from rice gruel, tart wine and sweet millet wine. All these wines must be served at the correct strength and consistency.

Staff: 12 noblemen, 2 senior staff, 8 secretaries, 8 minor staff and 80 servants.

The wine manager was also the administrative head of the ice collection team known as ice man, the sections that made wine, beverages, condiments and pickles, the unit that prepared salt; and the offering bearers. The ice man's job description provides a link to the farmer's calendar, also known as the Hsia calendar. Commentaries agree that ice-cutting could only have occurred in the 12th month of the Hsia calendar, January — not the 12th month of another calendar in use at this period. That would have fallen in November and there would have been no ice.

Ice Man

Duties: In charge of all matters related to ice. In the 12th month ice is cut, three times more than will be used. In spring the ice is supplied in large vessels to the inner and outer court chefs and to the wine and beverage makers. Ice is also supplied for ceremonial rites, guests and at important funerals (for the body of the deceased). In summer there is the annual ice distribution to palace officials. The ice house is cleaned in autumn.

Staff: 2 noblemen, 2 senior staff, 2 secretaries, 8 minor staff and 80 servants.

Staffing Arrangements

Every unit discussed so far was entirely staffed by men. Women were employed in other sections and their roles as artisans were acknowledged. Because men were excluded from these units, eunuchs took the place of noblemen as supervisors.

Wine Makers

Duties: In charge of the five fermenting wines and three wines, Married women are recruited for wine production. To handle all matters pertaining to wines.

Staff: 10 eunuchs, 30 women wine makers, 300 women servants.

A commentary provided more information: 'The women recruited to this unit all had experience in wine-making. These married women made the wines.'

Beverage Makers

Duties: In charge of preparing the royal family's six drinks: water, a tart starch-based beverage, sweet wine, a cold beverage, medicinal wine and fermented rice gruel. Such beverages are offered to guests. This unit is under the wine administration.

Staff: 5 eunuchs, 15 women beverage makers, 150 women servants.

Condiment Makers

Duties: In charge of the four groups of stemmed dishes. For breakfast: salt-preserved chives, thin and thick condiments, sweet flag root, moose condiment with bones, salt-preserved turnips, bear condiment with bones, salt-preserved water shield, muntjac condiment with bones.

At meals, salt-preserved mallow, wasp condiment, omasum, bee condiment, oyster condiment, pork shoulder, fish condiment. Additional dishes: salt preserved celery, rabbit condiment, cattail stem, thick and thin condiments, salt-preserved young bamboo shoots, goose condiment, salt-preserved bamboo shoots, fish condiment. Additionally, gruel and rice.

At rites, funerals and for guests, special offerings are presented in stemmed dishes. Delicacies prepared in the inner court are served to the royal family. When the emperor presides at a ceremony, 60 jars of condiment are set out, with the five partially fermented wines, seven condiments, seven kinds of salt-preserved vegetables and three kinds of condiments with bones. For guests, 50 jars of condiments are served. Condiments are provided for all occasions.

Staff: 1 eunuch, 20 women condiment makers, 40 women servants.

Pickle Makers

Duties: In charge of the five incompletely fermented wines and seven pickles for rites; to serve guests with pickles and sauces; to set out 50 jars of pickles and wines when the emperor conducts a rite; to provide the queen and crown prince with sauces, wines and pickles; to provide 50 jars of pickles and wines and to guests; to provide pickles for every occasion.

Staff: 2 eunuchs, 20 women pickle makers, 40 women servants.

This description suggests some overlapping of duties among units. As an annotator wrote, 'Condiments and pickles should be one unit, but they divided it into two. The food administrator had most of the stemmed platters and dishes, but the pickle makers had the jars and all were needed for the ceremonies. It was the food administrator and condiment makers who filled the stemmed dishes with wine and pickles — not the pickle makers. When the emperor performed rites, 60 jars each came from the condiment and pickle makers. So, the food administrator could present 120 jars on those occasions.'

Salt Unit

Duties: In charge of all matters related to salt. Bitter salt and loose salt are provided at ceremonies. Guests receive carved salt figurines and loose salt, To undertake all work including boiling of brine.

Staff: 2 eunuchs, 20 women salt processors, 40 women servants

Offering Bearers

The offering bearers took as the name of their office the stemmed bamboo dishes that held preserved fruit and dried meats.

Duties: In charge of the four groups of offerings made in rites conducted by the emperor and empress. Morning offerings consisted of toasted wheat, toasted hemp seed, rice, millet, carved salt tigers, sliced fish, smoked river fish and smoked ocean fish. Dates, chestnuts, peaches, prunes and hazelnuts formed the second group; with caltrop, foxnut, chestnuts and jerky as the third offering. The fourth group consists of two steamed delicacies, one made with non-glutinous rice and ground soybeans, another made with glutinous rice and and millet.

Staff: 1 eunuch, 10 women offering bearers, 20 women servants.

Medical Administration

Doctors were also on the staff, headed by a medical administrator who was assisted by two nutritionists, eight general practitioners, eight specialists who treated ulcers, trauma, fractures and other conditions, and four veterinarians. They were all noblemen.

Medical Administrator

Duties: In charge of all medical matters, from handling poisons to managing the medical services; to direct patients to the appropriate specialist. At year's end, he will review and grade each each doctor's performance.

Staff: 6 noblemen, 2 senior staff, 2 secretaries and 20 servants.

The nutritionists' duties were traditional, following the principles of medicine established in ancient times. In fact, the words originally came from the classics. 'Grain is favoured in spring, soups in summer, sauces in autumn and wine in winter. Tastes change with the seasons: favour the sour in spring, bitter in summer, peppery in autumn and salty in winter. And make the foods easy to swallow and sweet. Beef goes well with glutinous rice, non-glutinous millet with mutton, glutinous millet with pork, common millet with dog, wheat with wild goose and wild rice with fish.' In addition, the nutritionists must oversee the choice of the emperor's drinks, his 100 fine foods, 100 condiments and the eight delicacies.

SLIPPERY NOODLES

NOTES

Opening lines: Excerpts from *Xia xiao zheng* 夏小正, an ancient farmer's calendar in *Da Dai Li Ji* 大戴禮記, a work edited by Da Dai 大戴 (Dai De 戴德, 2nd-1st c BCE). It was one of the four classics in which rituals of the Zhou dynasty (18th-3rd c BCE) were recorded, the first three being *Liji* 禮記, *Zhou li* 周禮 and *Yili* 儀禮.

Sources: Sturgeon, Donald (ed.) 2011. Chinese Text Project http://ctext.org *Da Dai Li Ji* 大戴禮記 [Xia xiao zheng Dai shi zhuan 夏小正戴氏傳 annotated by Fu Songqing 傅崧卿 (Song 宋 dynasty]

Dating the calendar: Chatley, H. The date of the Hsia calendar *Hsia Hsiao Cheng. J. Royal Asiatic Society.* 1938;523-533

Science and Civilisation in China by J. Needham, *Vol. 3: Mathematics and the sciences of the heavens and earth* (1959), with Wang Ling. Cambridge: Cambridge University Press, pp. 194-196

Celestial ministry: Tian guan zhong zai 天官冢宰. 'Celestial Ministry of State' is the first of six chapters in *Zhou li* 周禮 (Rites of Zhou, 5th-3rd c BCE). They describe the organization of ministries of state, education, society, army, justice and public works. The ministries were given prefixes: heaven, earth and the four seasons.

Sources: *Duan ju shi san jing jing wen* 斷句十三經經文 (1965) Taipei: Taiwan Kaiming Book Co. 台灣開明書店. *Zhou li* 周禮, pp. 1-13

Sturgeon, Donald (ed.) 2011. Chinese Text Project. http://ctext.org Tian guan zhong zai 天官冢宰

Xian Qin peng ren shi liao xuan zhu 先秦烹飪史料選注 (ZPGC, 1987), pp. 57-85 (excerpts translated into modern Chinese)

Biot, Edouard. *Le Tcheou-li, ou Rites de Tcheou. Tome I.* (1851) Paris: Bibliotheque Nationale. (French translation)

[*Zhou li quan jing shi yuan* 周禮全經釋原 by Ke Shangqian 柯尚遷 (Ming 明 dynasty), Ch. 3, pp. 1-42] (explanation and clarification)

Organization: (administrator general) Da zai 大宰; (palace administrators) Gong zheng 宮正; (food administrator) Shan fu 膳夫

Food preparation: (butcher) Pao ren 庖人; (inner court chef) Nei yong 內饔; (outer court chef) Wai yong 外饔; (cooks) Peng ren 烹人

Wild animals: (moose, elk) Mi 麋, *Alces alces*; (deer) Lu 鹿, *Cervus sika*; (muntjac) Jun 麕, *Muntiacus reevesi*

Traditional ways: The pairing of meat from one animal with the fat of a different one was given in 'The Pattern of the Family.' (DJ13) *Liji* 禮記, p. 56; (ctext) *Liji* 禮記, Nei ze, 內則, para 37, tr. J. Legge.

Sacrificial meats and fish: (dried meat strips) Xiu 脩; (sacrificial soup) Xing 刑 or

Xing geng 鉶羹; (boneless dried meat, large pieces of fish) Hu 膴; (animal or fowl, halved) Pan gu 胖骨; (dried fish) Xiu 鱐; (dried meat slices, jerky) Fu 脯; (dried or salted meat) Xi 腊

Tripod soups: (meat soup, with salt and vegetables) Xing geng 鉶羹; (plain meat soup) Tai geng 太羹

Ploughing fields: [*Zhou li zhu shu* 周禮注疏 by Lu Deming 陸德明, Jia Gongyan 賈公彥 and Zheng Xuan 鄭玄(127-200 CE), Ch. 4, p. 21] The acreage for the area given in Mu 畝 is guesswork.

Food procurement: (farm manager) Dian shi 甸師

Hunter-trapper: Shou ren 獸人. Jade House: Yu fu 玉府; (ctext) Tian guan zhong zai 天官冢宰, para 33, 115

Jerky maker: La ren 臘人

Fishermen: Yu ren 漁人. Fish traps consisted of nets strung under bridges built on stone embankments. According to SKQS, Wei 鮪 is Xun 鱏, sturgeon, family *Acipenseridae*.

Turtle catcher: Bie ren 鱉人

Wine manager: Jiu zheng 酒正. More information on the eight items below is given in SCC6.5, pp.164-165

Fermenting liquids: 1. Fa qi 泛齊 (foamy) 2. Li qi 醴齊 (thick, sweet) 3. Ang qi 盎齊 (pale, cloudy) 4. Ti qi 緹齊 (orange-red) 5. Chen qi 沈齊 (clear liquid overlying lees) Finished, filtered wines: 6. Shi jiu 事酒 (quick fermentation) 7. Xi jiu 昔酒 (3 months' fermentation) 8. Qing jiu 清酒 (6 months' fermentation)

Four drinks: (No. 2 above, diluted) Qing 清; (medicinal) Yi 醫; (tart wine) Jiang 漿; (wine or thin gruel)Yi 酏

Ice man: Ling ren 凌人

No ice: The first month of the Zhou 周 calendar preceded that of the Hsia calendar by about two months. *Chinese History: A Manual* by Endymion Wilkinson (2000). Harvard-Yenching Institute Monograph Series, 52. pp. 170-172

[*Zhou li zhu shu* 周禮注疏 by Lu Deming 陸德明, Jia Gongyan賈公彥 and Zheng Xuan 鄭玄, Ch. 3, p. 5; Ch. 5, p.27]

Wine and beverage makers: Jiu ren 酒人, Jiang ren 漿人

Married women: [*Zhou li quan jing shi yuan* 周禮全經釋原 by Ke Shangqian 柯尚遷, Ch. 3, p. 33]

Condiment makers: Hai ren 醢人

Vegetables: (sweet flag, root) Chang ben 菖本, *Acorus calamus*; (another name for water shield) Mao 茆; (mallow) Kui 葵, *Malva verticillata*; (Cattail, stem) Shen pu 深浦, genus *Typha*; (young bamboo shoots) Tai 箈; (bamboo shoots) Sun 筍, genus *Phyllostachys*

SLIPPERY NOODLES

Pickle makers: Xi ren 醯人

Annotator: [*Zhou li quan jing shi yuan* 周禮全經釋原 by Ke Shangqian 柯尚遷, Ch. 3, p. 40]

Salt unit: Yan ren 鹽人. Different kinds of salt are discussed under 'Medicines: Animal, Plant and Mineral.'

Offering bearers: Bian ren 籩人

Offerings: Feng 麷 (pronunciation according to the given ZPGC source), toasted wheat. Fen 蕡, toasted hemp seed, *Cannabis sativa*. Definitions given in [Yi li zhu su 儀禮主疏 by Lu Deming 陸德明, Jia Gongyan 賈公彥 and Zheng Xuan 鄭玄, Ch. 17, p. 9]. (rice) Bai 白; (millet) Hei 黑; (carved salt figurine) Xing yan 形鹽; (smoked river fish) Bao yu 鮑魚; (smoked ocean fish) Su 鱐; (hazelnut) Zhen 榛 *Corylus heterophylla*; (water caltrop) Ling 菱, *Trapa natans;* (foxnut) Qian 芡, *Euryale ferox*.

Steamed puddings: (made with soybean and non-glutinous rice) Qu er 糗餌; (made with glutinous rice) Fen ci 粉餈. [Zhou li quan jing shi yuan 周禮全經釋原 by Ke Shangqian 柯尚遷, Ch. 3, p. 37]

Medical administration: (administrator) Yi shi醫師; (nutritionists) Shi yi 食醫; (general practitioners) Ji yi疾醫; (specialists) Yang yi 瘍醫; (veterinarians) Shou yi 獸醫

Nutritionists' duties: The first four sentences are identical to (DJ13) *Liji* 禮記, p. 56; (ctext) *Liji* 禮記, Nei ze, 內則, para 34-36, tr. J. Legge.

Grains: (glutinous rice) Tu 稌; (wild rice) Gu 菰, *Zizania canduciflora*

CHAPTER TEN

THE EIGHT DELICACIES IN ANTIQUITY

Mats are laid down for the feast,
Tables are set out, and attendants eagerly serve.
Guests and host exchange many toasts.
The host rinses his cup, the guests set theirs down.
Thick and thin condiments are brought in —
Grilled meats and roasts, excellent filets,
Beef tongue and beef omasum —
All to the sound of drums and music!

The term 'eight delicacies' has been used for over two millenia to identify the most wonderful foods. The dishes so named changed significantly over the centuries, expressing different styles of cooking in each period. In antiquity, meat and fat were delicacies. They were listed in *The Pattern of the Family*.

1. Smothered Rice: fried meat paste put on top of rice, with fat poured over.

2. A similar dish made with millet.

3. The Bake: A young pig is stuffed with dates, coated with mud and straw and baked. The hard clay is broken off. Crisp rich crackling is stripped

from the meat, mixed with ground rice (to coat the meat). The pig is fried in sufficient oil to cover, then placed in a tripod with some perilla. The tripod is set in a large cauldron of water; in this fashion the pig is steamed for three days and nights without stopping, taking care that water does not go into the tripod. The pork is seasoned with thick meat paste and vinegar.

4. Pounded Delicacy. Use meat from cattle, sheep, moose, deer and muntjac. Use only meat near the spine — the loin. Take equal parts of the meat from the five animals and pound them flat. Remove the tendons and silver skin. The meat is cooked and then trimmed.

5. Marinated Delicacy. Use beef from a freshly slaughtered animal. Slice it thin, cutting across the grain. Soak the meat slices in good wine, overnight. Eat it with meat paste or vinegar and plum sauce.

6. Pan-fried Meat, made with any one of the five meats. Remove the sinews and silver skin. Lay the meat on reed mats and sprinkle it with cinnamon, ginger and salt. The meat can be eaten after it has dried. If moist meat is wanted, pan-fry the seasoned meat (without drying it) with some meat paste.

7. Rice Dumplings. Chop fine equal amounts of beef, mutton and pork, and mix with twice as much (cooked) rice. Form them into cakes and fry them.

8. Liver and Fat. Wrap a dog's liver in caul fat. Wet it and roast it until charred. Do not season the fat with knotweed. Make rice water with rice grains. Dice fat that is taken from the wolf's chest. Add it (and the liver) to the rice gruel.

This was the summit of cooking in antiquity. Four ways of cooking were mentioned: baking (3), roasting (8), steaming (3) and frying (1, 2, 7). Meat was also eaten raw (5, 6).

Flavours

It seems that thick meat paste was a prop of ancient cookery, used in the kitchen as seasoning or diluted to make thick and thin sauces for the table, as in the opening poem. Five of the eight delicacies called for the meat paste in one form or another (1-3, 5, 6). A commentary to the classics described how meat paste was made. 'Meat was sliced and dried, broken into smaller pieces, mixed with yeast cake and salt, moistened with wine and then packed in a jar that remained sealed for 100 days.' The ancient recipe resembled

Jia Sixie's methods for preparation of meat sauce in its use of salt and yeast cake. However, Jia used raw (not dried) meat, no wine, and fermentation was carried out for two weeks.

Fat was an important flavouring used in ancient cookery. Grains were enhanced by fat, and had a better mouth-feel, and it provided distinctive flavours depending on the source — dog, beef, lamb, fox or pork. Speaking of the first two delicacies, a commentator wrote, 'The flavour (of the rice and millet) might be too bland, so rich fat must be poured over all and allowed to soak in.' Like this gentleman, one can almost taste the foods of antiquity.

NOTES

Opening poem: 'Xing wei' 行葦 (2nd verse) from *Shi jing* 詩經 (10th-9th c BCE). (DJ13) Mao shi 毛詩, p. 69; (ctext) *Shi jing* 詩經, Da ya 大雅, Sheng min zhi shen 生民之什, Xing wei 行葦

Eight delicacies: Ba zhen 八珍 (DJ13) *Liji* 禮記, p. 57. (ctext) *Liji* 禮記, Nei ze, 內則, para 50-56, tr. J. Legge

Smothered rice: Zhun ao 淳熬; (similar millet dish) Zhun mu 淳母

The Bake: Pao tun 炮; (herbs related to perilla) Xiang 蘻

Pounded delicacy: Dao zhen 擣珍

Marinated delicacy): Zi 漬; (plum sauce) Yi 醷

Pan-fried meat: Ao 熬; (cinnamon) Gui 桂, *Cinnamomum cassia*

Rice dumplings: San 糝

Liver and fat: Gan liao 肝膋

Meat paste and derived sauces: (meat paste or thick sauce) Hai 醢; (thin sauce) Tan 醓

Making meat paste: [*Zhou li zhu shu* 周禮注疏 by Lu Deming 陸德明, Jia Gongyan 賈公彥 and Zheng Xuan 鄭玄 (127-200 CE), Ch. 6, p. 1] compared to Jia's method, Rou jiang 肉醬 [8:70,5].

Adding fat to grain: [*Li ji zhu shu* 禮記註疏 by Kong Yingjian 孔穎建, Lu Deming 陸德明 and Zheng Xuan 鄭玄. Ch. 28, p.19]

CHAPTER ELEVEN

TURNING POINT

Meat might be cooked a long time — but it must not fall apart. Food may be sweet but it must not be cloying; sour but not harsh; peppery hot, but not in excess; bland but not thin; fatty without being greasy.

Tastes had changed by the time unification of China was achieved by the first emperor of Qin, a few centuries later. Historians consider the Qin emperor's reign (221 BCE to 210 BCE) as the watershed between ancient and medieval China. The same might be said of its gastronomy. The opening sentences are from a voluminous work about government, society, and many other subjects written by a large number of scholars and historians who were under the benefaction of the Qin minister by the name of Lu Buwei. Collectively the chapters presented a philosophy of government. In one chapter of Lu's book the art of cooking was expounded. The opening sentences summarized in a nutshell the goals of the Chinese cook. They may have also hinted at how an emperor should govern his people: setting a goal to reach, but not going beyond. This was not the only time the culinary approach was applied to governing. The philosopher Laotse had said, 'Govern a large country as you would cook small fish.' He meant, handle them with the lightest of touches.

A commentator explained: 'Do not keep turning (the fish). Leave them alone. An impatient cook can ruin food. The ruler of a large country must be calm.' The ability to bridge two vastly different topics revealed the way Lu's mind worked. He was a man of extraordinary deviousness, a business man turned politician. He assembled thinkers, scholars and writers around him. At one time, he had 3,000 house-guests and 10,000 servants. He was skilled in manipulating princes, kings and high-born ladies. Some think that that he was the Qin emperor's biological father because he handed over one of his concubines (who was pregnant) to the future emperor's nominal father. The politics of his time were exceptional; so were the remarks on cooking in his book.

He attributed many comments to Yi Yin in whom the arts of cooking and of governing were embodied. According to popular legend he was the cook who became prime minister. This story has been questioned, but the fact that Yi Yin was a powerful minister in the Shang dynasty cannot be denied. As the story goes, Yi Yin was an orphan raised by cooks. He became a splendid cook and in that capacity he was hired by a ruler. Yi Yin did not want to remain always a cook, so he took the opportunity while serving the ruler at meal times to expound his political strategy. In one such conversation, Yi Yin discusses the importance of timing in politics and in cooking.

The ruler asked Yi Yin, 'Is the strategy feasible?'

Yi Yin replied, 'You now rule a small country. The conditions are not right. When you become emperor — that will be the time.' 'For what wondrous changes take place in the cooking pot! Every time the pot is brought to the boil the food undergoes a change. The cook uses water, fuel and fire. Sometimes he uses a hot flame, sometimes low heat. He achieves balance between the sour, salty, bitter, hot and sweet. Each cook will add the seasonings in a different order. The amounts are minute, the results subtly different. I find it difficult to express. It is like an arrow hitting its mark.

'There are three kinds of animals. Those that swim taste fishy; those that devour other creatures smell of blood; those that graze smell of lamb. They may be repugnant, but the cook can turn rank and odorous flesh into delicious meat. The choicest meats are orangutan lips, roasted badger, swallow's rump, knuckles, yak tail and elephant (trunk).'

There followed a lyrical passage, in which real and mythical places were mentioned. For example, 'Phoenix eggs are found in the Flowing Sands, south of Red Mountain.' The phoenix is a fabled bird. According to the commentator Gao You, Flowing Sands was a real place, about 300 km west of Dunhuang, a city on the northern Silk Road; and Red Mountain lies south of Flowing Sands.

'The best fish are found in Dongting Lake. The red turtle with six feet and scaly skin lives in waters nearby. There are flying fish; they look like carp with wings and at night they fly into the Eastern Sea. Among vegetables, the clover fern that grows on Kunlun mountain is the best. The longevity tree is found on Kunlun, and eating its fruit is said to confer immortality. In the southeast the Che and Xuan trees have edible leaves; the Jia tree in the south has jade-green leaves that also are edible. Rue, the fragrant-smelling, bitter-tasting herb, is found in the south as are chive flowers (that were made into a condiment, in the royal palace). There, water celery grows, and a flower that blooms in deep pools. There is ginger and cinnamon in the southern interior. Bamboo shoots come from the south. Lumps of salt are found in Daxia lake in the northwest. In the west, there is a condiment made with sturgeon, a jade-coloured distilled drink, and eggs large as an urn.

'Xuan mountain grows the best grains. Buzhou in the northwest of Kunlun has millet, south of Kunlun there is non-glutinous millet of both common and black varieties. As for water, that at Sanwei is like dew; Kunlun has its springs; water from the high mountains of the west flows through Jizhou, that claims to be the origin of all springs. The best of fruits is that of the cherry apple tree that grows on Kunlun. All the emperors ate the many kinds of fruits. East of Kunlun the smoke tree bears sweet fruit. Oranges grow on the river banks and pumelos elsewhere. By the Han River is the lichen that grows on rocks.

'These things will come to you when you become the emperor.'

Yi Yin lived in the sixteenth century BCE. Some of his views, as set out in Lu's book, seem advanced for the era he lived in. The opening sentences, also attributed to Yi Yin described food prepared with subtlety. The cuisine was sophisticated. The cooks were skilled in manipulating heat, timing and seasonings. They could turn the rank meats into delicious food. Orangutan lips and elephant were mentioned as fine foods; these items were very different from the eight delicacies of antiquity. In the hands of skilled cooks, the lips, knuckles and trunk could be transformed into food that would please gourmets. They favoured richly flavoured morsels with just the right combination of cartilaginous and smooth textures. Orangutan lips and elephant trunk would eventually appear among the eight delicacies of later dynasties.

The observed differences between the style of food preparation attributed to Yi Yin in Lu's book and that of ancient times call for comparison of Lu's version with Yi Yin's original text. Of course, the latter no longer exists. Gao You, the gentleman who annotated Lu's book about four centuries after it was completed, provided a clue that may unravel the mystery. In his preface to *The Annals of Lu Buwei*, Gao You wrote:

> My family had a copy (of Lu's annals). I investigated and found
> it greatly surpassed the minor works among philosophers. The
> text had suffered lacunae and errors, and worse, minor scholars
> had made changes and corrections based on their own ideas.

The length of the book that Gao You annotated was one-third longer than the current text. So parts of Lu's book had been changed before and after it was annotated by Gao You. It is possible that the writer under Lu's patronage put his own ideas into the chapter, adding contemporary (third century BC) aspects of cooking and of the enjoyment of food.

The cuisine was moving in a new direction. Because the turning point remains obscure the chapter in Lu's book will have to serve. The nameless writer was pointing to horizons beyond the boundaries of China. In a century or so, a few brave men left the known world, entering foreign lands to its West.

NOTES

Opening quotation: *The Annals of Lu Buwei* [Lüshi chun qiu 呂氏春秋 by Lu Buwei 呂不韋 (290-235 BCE), annotated by Gao You 髙誘 (E. Han dynsty, 25-220), Ch.14, pp. 4-9] The quotations are from the section titled 'Fundamental Tastes' (Ben wei 本味)

Philosopher's advice: Zhi da guo ruo peng xiao xian 治大國若烹小鮮 (Laotse 老子, 6th c BCE) [*Laozi dao de jing* 老子道德經, commentary by He Shanggong 何上公

SLIPPERY NOODLES

(E. Han dynasty, 25-220). Part 2, p. 30]

Biography of Lu Buwei: [*Shi Ji* 史記 by Ssu-ma Ch'ien 司馬遷 (145-86 BCE). Ch. 85] (English translation) *Records of the Grand Historian: Qin Dynasty* (1995) by Burton Watson. New York: Columbia University Press

Biography of Yi Yin: [*Shang shi* 尚史 by Li Kai. Ch. 24, pp. 11-18]

Story questioned: [*Meng zi ji shu* 孟子集疏 by Cai Mo 蔡模, Ch. 9, p. 13]

Food items: (orangutang) Xing xing 猩猩, genus *Pongo*; (badger) Huan huan 獾獾, *Meles meles*; (swallow's rump) Yan zi cui 鷰之翠; (knuckle, wrist) Wan 掔 or Wan 腕; (yak) Mao 旄, *Bos grunnien;*

Elephant: Xiang 象, family *Elephantidae*. The text did not specify which part of the elephant was eaten. Although oxtail and deer tail were delicacies, that could not be said of elephant tail. Finally a commentator said, 'Of all parts of the elephant, the only delicious part is the nose (trunk); roasted, it is crisp and sweet.' In: *Lüshi chun qiu ben wei pian* 呂氏春秋本味篇, by Wang Liqi 王利器, Wang Zhenmin 王贞珉, and Qiu Pangtong 邱庞同. ZPGC (1984) p. 49

Kunlun mountains: The author seems to use Kunlun 崑崙 in both the mythical and the geographical sense. The mythical Kunlun has no known location, and is the site of wondrous plants and creatures. The vast Kunlun mountain range skirts the southern border of Taklamakan Desert. See next two entries.

Clover fern: Ping 蘋, *Marsilia quadrifolia*, is identified by the commentator Gao You as growing on the real Kunlun mountain, whose height is about 4000 km

Longevity tree: The same commentator writes that this tree, Shou mu 壽木 grows on Kunlun mountain, most probably the mythical one.

Animals: (ray or skate) Yao 鰩; (sturgeon) Tan wei 鱣鮪

Plants: (rue) Yun 芸, *Ruta graveolens*; (water-celery) Shui qin (水)芹, *Oenantha javanica*; (bamboo shoots) Jun 菌; (grain) He 禾; (millet) Su 粟; (non-glutinous millet) Ji 穄; (black, non-glutinous millet) Ju 秬; (sand cherry-apple tree) Sha tang 沙棠: (smoke-tree) Lu 櫨, genus *Cotinus coggygria*; (orange) Ju 橘, *Citrus sinensis*; (pomelo) You 柚, *Citrus grandis*; (rock lichen) Shi er 石耳, *Umbillicaria esculenta*

The Annals of Lu Buwei by John Knoblock and Jeffrey Riegel (2000) Stanford: Stanford University Press. The Gao You *Preface* to the *Lüshi chunqiu*. Pp. 671-672. (English translation). [*Lüshi chun qiu* 呂氏春秋 by Luu Buwei 呂不韋 annotated by Gao You 高誘. Original preface, Yuan xu 原序, p. 2]

CHAPTER TWELVE

FOREIGN THINGS

This morning it rained — the air is not so dusty.
I see the willows at the hostel are fresh and green.
Have another cup of wine, sir.
West of Yang Pass, you will not find friends.

Yang Pass was one of the few outposts in the immense desert located in northwest China. The pass was a gateway to regions further west, across the fearsome Taklamakan desert and on to central Asia. Around the year 139 BCE under orders from the emperor, a man named Zhang Qian set out with about a hundred men to negotiate a treaty with one of the lesser tribes in the west. The aim was to neutralize the fierce Xiongnu, a tribe that was based north of the desert. The Xiongnu were nomads, belligerent, often clashing with Chinese and with other foreign tribes. To carry out his mission Zhang would have to skirt the northern boundary of the desert and cross a mountain range at its western end, a journey of about 5000 km. Zhang did all this and more.

Accompanying Zhang was a slave, a barbarian. On his outward journey Zhang was captured and imprisoned by the Xiongnu. During this period he married a foreign woman and they had a son. After 10 years of imprisonment Zhang was able to escape with his family and the slave. He had kept his credentials, and he proceeded to complete his mission. The journey would take him to Ferghana, reached only after crossing formidable mountains. He achieved his objective, travelling through Transoxiana, and then north to meet the long sought-after tribal ruler in Sogdiana. The latter was indifferent to the idea of a treaty.

Zhang continued his travels, south to Bactria, observing everything around him, and inquiring about neighbouring kingdoms: Parthia, Mesopotamia and India. On his return journey Zhang was captured and imprisoned again, finally returning to the capital after 13 years. He had lost all his men except the slave. The emperor honored Zhang and conferred an official title on the slave. Undaunted, Zhang undertook other missions for the emperor. As a man 'he was mighty, generous to others and trusting; the barbarians liked him.' Zhang's last expedition was to liaise with barbarian tribes in the northwest.

But it was his journey to central Asia that was historic. He reported what he had seen and heard to the emperor, giving a view of the west from China almost to the Mediterranean.

'The kingdom of Dayuan (Ferghana) ties about 4000 km directly west of our country. The people plant rice and wheat. They make grape wine. Altogether they have about 10,000 people in about 70 towns. Their soldiers ride, shooting with bow and arrows. They have many fine horses, said to be bred from horses that live in the high mountains, so they are called 'heavenly horses.'

'Transoxiana is 800-1200 km to the west. It is inhabited by nomadic people like the Xiongnu. Once proud, with ten to 20 thousand archers, they were known as the Great Yuezhi and lived near Dunhuang. But after the Xiongnu killed their king and used his skull as drinking cup, these people fled, retreating west. They re- established their court north of the Oxus River. Some of their tribe were left behind; they are known as the lesser ones.

'Parthia is even further west. It is much like Ferghana with its wheat, rice and grape wine. It is a large country with several hundred towns. It also borders the Oxus River. People use wagons and boats to reach neighbouring countries. Their coins are made of silver, showing a likeness of the king. When a king dies, the coins are replaced with those bearing the new king's image.

'Mesopotamia is close to the Western Sea, to the west of Parthia. The climate is hot and humid, the people live by farming, and great birds produce eggs as large as urns. The people are numerous, and Parthia lays claim to some of them.

'Bactria is 800 km to the southwest of Ferghana, which it resembles. It lies south of the Oxus River. They have only a few minor chieftains. Their soldiers fear combat, but they are good traders. The population of Bactria is large, exceeding a million. The capital is called Bactra and its markets sell everything. I saw bamboo canes and Sichuan fabrics there. How did they arrive? I inquired. The Bactrian replied, "India lies several thousand km southeast. The people there are much like us, and it is warm and humid. There, they ride to battle on elephants, and there is a great river." Zhang observed: Bactria lies southwest of China; India is southeast of Bactria yet it has Chinese goods. Sichuan cannot be far away.

'In this manner the emperor learned about Ferghana, Bactria and Parthia. They were large countries. They coveted Chinese things and wished to trade with China. They had neither silk nor lacquer, nor did they know how to cast metal.' Zhang journeyed along routes that came to be known as the northern Silk Road. This was to be the one of the routes that over the next millennium connected central Asia to China, on which diplomats, monks and traders travelled.

The Appellation 'Hu'

Foreigners looked distinctly different from Chinese. They had 'deep-set eyes, and were hairy.' Parthian coins showed rulers with curly hair and curly beards, large eyes and prominent noses. Foreigners from different parts did not resemble each other. The Xiongnu barbarian was 'short, with a stocky body, and a very large round head, broad face, prominent cheekbones, wide nostrils, a fairly bushy mustache and no beard save for a tuft of stiff hair on the chin. The head is usually shaved, except for a tuft on top.' Despite obvious differences, the Chinese used one word for all of them: *Hu*. It described non-Chinese peoples to the north and west of China. It is telling that when in the third century a Chinese woman poet married one of these foreigners and had two children by him, she referred to them as her Hu sons.

The term Hu was also given to objects that came to China from central Asia or generally, from foreign lands west of China. There was an emperor of the second century who was enamoured of all things Hu. 'He loved Hu attire, Hu tents, Hu 'beds', Hu seats, Hu food, Hu harps, Hu pipes and Hu dancing. A Hu bed was a folding chair, allowing a person to sit with knees bent and both feet on the floor. Some Hu beds were stools; others had high backs and armrests. He also loved Hu cake, a baked flatbread covered with sesame seeds.

Many foodstuffs may have originated in Europe, the Mediterranean or India but because they were transmitted to China via common routes, they acquired the prefix Hu. Carrots originated in Europe, were cultivated in central Asia and did not arrive in China until the thirteenth century. A book of that period has an illustration of the familiar large round radish of China. The slender carrot is shown next to it, dubbed 'Hu radish,' a name retained to this day.

Black pepper originating in India was known as Hu pepper. Walnuts were called Hu peaches. Cucumbers were Hu gourds. Hu celery grew on dry land, as opposed to Chinese water celery that grew in shallow waters; Jia Sixie described a salad made with Hu celery. Coriander was known as Hu parsley, among several names. Additionally there is the ambiguous term *Hu ma* that stood for any one of three different plants, sesame, flax and hemp, all of which produce oil-rich seeds.

Other plants notably chives and some varieties of peas and beans also came from the West. Their early Chinese names bearing the designation Hu have largely been replaced.

Novel Plants

Of course, not every plant brought from the west received the Hu appellation. Alfalfa and grape were among the first of plants brought from the west, for 'People drink wine and horses eat alfalfa. Foreign visitors saw these plants flourishing on the palace grounds.'

> *Beyond Yang Pass there was only sand and dust.*
> *Geese were seen in spring, but few people.*
> *Now the heavenly horses have alfalfa,*
> *And grape vines have taken root.*

Pomegranate followed several centuries later, but none of these three plants received the designation Hu. Long pepper was a spice that originated in India but entered China via the same route, retaining its Indian name; in Sanskrit it is called *pippal*, in Chinese *pipo*. Spinach came from Nepal probably before eighth century. In China it was called by its Nepalese name, *boleng*. As time went by this was shortened to *bo*, except in some provinces such as Fujian where it is still called by its full, foreign name (pronounced in Fujian dialect): *boleng* vegetable.

The almond tree was well established in China by the Tang dynasty. A ninth century scholar spoke of it as: 'The flat peach comes from Podan, in Persia. The large tree has leaves like that of the peach tree and produces white blossoms. The fruit pulp is bitter, acrid and inedible. Its stone is large like that of the peach but flat. The kernel inside is sweet and considered a delicacy in the western regions.' Unfortunately the almond was identified by the word for apricot and the ambiguity was compounded by calling apricot kernels and almond kernels by the same term.

Reception

Pepper and coriander were taken up. Walnuts came to be used as a pastry filling. Chinese hands did not take to the art of making grape wine and though it was popular in some quarters, grape wine could never compete with wines made with grains. The grape was still considered exotic in the sixth century when a conversation between five men went like this.

A (to B and C): 'I finally had the chance to eat some grapes. They were tasty.' D: 'What were they like?' E: 'Like soft dates.' A (to E): 'I think that you have never tasted them — you might as well have said they taste like lychees.' B: 'Once, at summer's end I got drunk and woke up with a hangover. I crushed a few grapes in water and ate them — they were sweet but not overly so, tart but not vinegary. My mouth waters when I recall it.' C: 'Zhang Qian brought grapes from Ferghana. There are three kinds: yellow, white and black. In the west they make grape wine, and bring it as tribute. Near our capital city, there are over eight acres of grape vines.' D: 'Are they like oranges and pomelos?' A: 'Juicier, but not as fragrant.' C (to D): 'Words are not enough. Just put one in your mouth and eat it.'

SLIPPERY NOODLES

Imported Technologies

Foreign contacts also brought new food technologies to China, the most important dealing with the production of granulated cane sugar (to be discussed later), and butter. The techniques for making butter and clarified butter probably came by the same route as Buddhist monks, for these dairy products were often linked to Buddhist literature. 'Milk is transformed into sour milk, which in turn is transformed into butter; raw butter is cooked and transformed into clarified butter.' This series of transformations was an analogy to the successive stages of Buddhist enlightenment, clarified butter representing the ultimate stage.

The introduction of butter-making was successful; it was used in both cooking and baking. By the eleventh century, butter was often presented to officials from those seeking favours.

A Gift of Butter

The visitor at the gate called out, 'Here! Here!
I personally prepared these 60 kilograms of butter.
I hurried here to His Excellency's residence —
Hoping to see him return in his elegant carriage.'
'Do not bother,' the gatekeeper said.
'Others before you came with larger amounts of butter.
Yesterday one gift came in a lacquer bucket.
Now you show up late with a small amount,
And it is only wrapped in coloured paper.'
Shamed, the visitor vowed to be the best next year.

But one must pause now and resume the narrative of how Chinese cooking developed after Jia.

NOTES

Poem: Song *Yuan er shi Anxi* 送元二使安西 and both by Wang Wei 王維 (699-759) [W*en yuan ying hua* 文苑英華 ed. Li Fang 李昉, Ch. 299, 10] Yang Pass (Yang guan 陽關) and the town of Anxi (安西) are both located near Dunhuang

The emperor: Han Wudi 漢武帝 (r 141-87 BCE)

The envoy: Zhang Qian 張騫 (d 113 BCE)

A nomadic tribe: Xiongnu 匈奴

First mission: *Through the Jade Gate to Rome,* by John E. Hill (2009). John E. Hill. Pp. 575-586

Zhang's travels, various impressions: [Shi Ji 史記 by Sima Qian 司馬遷, Ch. 123, pp.1-10, 18] *Records of the Grand Historian: Han Dynasty II* (1993) by Burton Watson. Columbia University Press, pp. 231-252 (English translation)

Ferghana: Dayuan 大宛, situated in a valley that crosses present-day Tajikstan, Kyrgistan and Uzbekistan

Transoxiana: Da Yuezhi 大月氏, in Kazakstan

Sogdiana: Kang Ju 康居, in Uzbekistan

Bactria: Daxia 大夏, in present-day Afghanistan

Parthia: Anxi 安息, located in present-day Iran

Mesopotamia: Tiaoji 條枝, in Iraq

India: Shendu 身毒

Oxus River: (Amu Darya) Gui shui 媯水; source, Pamir mountains

Bactra: Lanshi cheng 藍市城

'Short and stocky': Léon Wieger, quoted in *The Empire of the Steppes* (1970) by René Grousset, tr. Naomi Walford. New Brunswick: Rutgers University Press, p. 21

Hu sons: Hu jia shi ba pai 胡笳十八拍 by Cai Yan 蔡琰 (177?-239?) [*Gu yue yuan* 古樂苑 ed. Mei Dingzuo 梅鼎祚 Ch. 31, p.12]

All things Hu: Emperor Han Lingdi 漢靈帝 (r 168-188) [*Hou Han shu* 後漢書 by Sima Biao 司馬彪 (W. Jin dynasty, 265-316). Ch. 23, p. 8] (Hu beds) (Hu tents): *Hu chuang* 胡床, Hu zhang 胡帳 (Zhang wo 帳幄) [*Shi wu ji yuan* 事務紀原 by Gao Cheng 高承, Ch. 8, pp. 4-5]

Hu cake: Hu bing 胡餅

Carrot: (Hu radish) Hu luo bo 胡蘿蔔, *Daucus carota. Yin shan zheng yao* 飲膳正要 (1330) by Husihui 忽思慧 (fl 1315-1330). (1989) Shanghai上海: Shanghai shu dian 上海書店. Illustrations, p. 161.

Sino-Iranica (1919) by Berthold Laufer (1874-1934). Publication 201, Anthropological Series, vol. XV, no.3, Chicago: Field Museum of Natural History (abbrev. SIBL) pp. 451-454

SLIPPERY NOODLES

Black pepper: Hu jiao 胡椒, *Piper nigrum*. SIBL 374-375

Walnut: Hu tao 胡桃 (or He tao 核桃) *Juglans regia*. SIBL 254-275

Cucumber: Hu gua 胡瓜 (or Huang gua 黃瓜) *Cucumis sativus*. SIBL 300-301

Dryland celery: Hu qin 胡芹 *Apium graveolens*. Hu celery salad [9:88,32]

Coriander: Hu sui 胡荽 *Coriandrum sativum*. SIBL 297-299

Ambiguity: Hu ma 胡麻 may mean sesame (*Sesamum indicum*), flax (linseed, *Linum usitatissumum*), or hemp (genus *Cannabis*)

Chives, peas and beans: SIBL 302-304, 305-308

Alfafa: Mu xu 苜蓿, *Medicago sativa*. SIBL 208-219

Grape: Pu tao (as given below, 浦陶) 葡萄, *Vitis vinifera*. SIBL 220-245

'People drink': [Shi Ji 史記 by Sima Qian 司馬遷, Ch. 123, pp. 17-18]

Poem: Song Liu sizhi fu Anxi 送劉司直赴安西 by Wang Wei 王維 [*Wen yuan ying hua* 文苑英華 ed. Li Fang 李昉, Ch. 299, 10]

Pomegranate: Shi liu 石榴, *Punica granatum*. SIBL 276-287

Long pepper: Pi bo 畢撥, *Piper longum*. SIBL 374-375

Spinach: Bo leng 菠棱, *Spinacia oleracea*. SIBL 392-398.

Almond: Xing 杏 or Xing ren 杏仁. SIBL 405-409

Flat peach (almond): [You yang za zu 酉陽雜俎 by Duan Chengshi 段成式 (d 863), Ch. 18, p. 11]

Ambiguity: (fruit) Xing 杏 may mean apricot, *Prunus armeniaca,* or almond, *Prunus amygdalus*. (kernel) Xing ren 杏仁 may mean apricot kernel or the almond, which is a kernel

Five men: [You yang za zu 酉陽雜俎 by Duan Chengshi 段成式, Ch. 18, p. 6] (A) Geng Xin 庚信 (531-581); (B) Wei Zhaoshi 魏肇師; (C) Wei Jin 尉瑾 (550-571); (D) Chen Zhao 陳昭 (ninth century); (E) Xu Jinfang 徐君房 (Qin dynasty, 221-207 BCE). The imaginary conversation was a literarary maneuver, also used elsewhere in Duan's book.

Milk to butter: (Buddhist text) *Tian tai si jiao yi* 天台四教儀 by Di Guan 諦觀 (d 571?) in: Dazheng xin xiu Dazheng cang jing 大正 新脩大正藏經 vol. 46, no. 1931

A gift of butter: *Niu su hang* 牛蘇行 by Jiang Duanyou 江端友 (fl 1099) [*Song shi ji shi* 宋詩紀事 by Li E 厲鶚. Ch. 33, pp. 55-56]

CHAPTER THIRTEEN

FOOD CULTURE

Food and drink are not simple matters.

Following the turmoil of Jia's time came a period of prosperity and relative stability that lasted for a few decades. In this short span of time China was unified once again, setting the foundation for a flowering of its culture. The first emperor of the Sui dynasty extended the borders by conquering the kingdom then ruling central China. China's coastline now ran past the mouth of the Yangtse River down to Guangdong. He centralized administration and created a scheme for civil service examinations that was to last many centuries. He standardized weights and measures, and introduced the 'large' and 'small' systems (shown in table at the end of this book). He planned a canal system with three arms that would link the two great rivers. The first arm would stretch east from Xian to the Yellow River and the central plain. From that central point, the second arm would extend southeast to the Yangtse River, and the third arm would reach north to Beijing.

His son, the second emperor, is despised by many because he was a tyrant. He completed the canal system envisioned by his father at a frightful human cost. 'By imperial edict, all men between 15 and 50 years of age were conscripted; they numbered 3.6 million. Additionally the very young, the old and women were recruited, making a total of 5.4 million labourers (to work on the northern canal).' He also can be recognized for his achievements. He fortified sections of the Great Wall, rebuilt two capital cities and numerous Buddhist temples and palaces. He is also remembered for his extravagant style of living.

The Emperor's Tour

In the year 605, the second emperor of Sui went on an inspection trip of the newly completed portion of the southern arm of the Grand Canal. At that time the southern terminus was located at Yangzhou, about 1000 km from the old capital city of Xian. The canal was about 70 m wide. The imperial avenue lined with willow trees ran beside it. Approaching Yangzhou the emperor was presented with the local specialty, pickled crabs. They were probably much like those described by Jia.

> Preserved Crabs
>
> In October-November, get female crabs and put them in water immediately (female crabs have large round abdomens, while those of male crabs are long and narrow). Do not hurt them and do not let them die. By the next day, they are clean. Put the live crabs in thin maltose syrup overnight. Then place the crabs in brine and seal the jar with mud. After 20 days, remove the crabs and put minced ginger in the abdominal cavities. Place them in a jar, and pour enough knotweed extract to cover them. A jar will hold 100 crabs.

For the emperor, each crab was decorated with cut-outs made with gold-coloured paper. He received 2000 of these crabs. Considering the size of his entourage that was not too many.

The emperor arrived in October. A fleet of boats was constructed for the emperor's tour. The imperial dragon boat had four decks, the top one consisting of four halls for holding audiences and for worship. The next two decks housed 120 luxuriously fitted rooms. The lowest deck was for amenities. There were in addition three-decker boats that were essentially floating palaces. For the horses, there were boats fitted with wide doors. With princes, princesses, courtiers and officials, monks, nuns, Taoist priests and guests on board, the boats numbered in the thousands, stretching over 100 km. Tens of thousands of people on shore were required to tow them. Moreover, the people living near the canal were required to provide food for this floating city. The common people caught birds, beasts and fish with traps and nets until the woods, waters and land were nearly bare.

The Emperor's Menu

The second Sui emperor's food administrator wrote a book titled *The Food Classic*. Only a small fragment is extant, a list of 53 items from a menu. The items (detailed under Notes) fall into different groups, revealing something about the gastronomy of seventh century China.

There were a number of dishes made with raw fish or raw meat. When on his tour down the canal the second emperor was presented with river perch he remarked, 'The flavour of the southeast is to be found in the jade of the fish and the gold of the relish.' He was speaking of sliced raw fish mixed with slivers of tangerine peel, a popular southern dish. Raw fish was served with great style. Much skill was required to slice the fish. The chef showed off his skills by slicing raw fish at the table with two knives.

Swiftly he wields the knives right and left.
Snow-white slices drift down on the golden plate.

The fish course was named 'Flying Phoenixes' because bells made in the shape of phoenixes were tied to the knives in the manner used in antiquity for animal sacrifices. Now the bells tinkled as raw fish was sliced to paper thinness.

Among the soups one was clear, six were thick. Their ingredients were now more refined. One soup was made with partridges, another with turtle. Steamed bear and lamb and roasted meats were carry-overs from earlier times. Additionally there were dishes made different ways: dainty meat cakes, goose terrine, duck prepared with its own fat, and chicken cut so fine it resembled a heap of threads. This was food intended to be picked up by chopsticks made of precious stuff such as ivory or rhinoceros horn.

Two of the menu items are of particular interest. The first was described by a word (*ding*) that meant food for display, probably a kind of pastry. The second item was a food sculpture, a model of a platform or an altar that was made with flour. 'Look but do not eat' items may be a kind of food that is unique to China. They were usually pastries or fruit, presented on fancy dishes. A few centuries later, display tables bearing dozens of such items might be set out at a banquet to show the lavishness of the occasion.

Clearly, the emperor's menu showed new ways of regarding food.

Food and Art

In the centuries following the Sui dynasty, painting and poetry flourished. New notions and ideas about the art of eating also took shape. The remark that opens this chapter — that food and drink are not simple matters — was written by a scholar; he meant that it was a worthy subject of study. Some cooks expressed this interest in their own way. A Buddhist nun created a form of food display, using food to simulate paintings.

The eighth century poet-painter Wang Wei was the inspiration for her food tableaus, a practice that persists to the present day. Wang wrote 20 quatrains about his home.

> *I see no one in these mountains,*
> *Yet I hear human voices.*
> *Light that entered the dark forest*
> *Shines in the dank moss.*

> *My new home lies in the hollow.*
> *The old willow mutters,*
> *'Who is this person?*
> *I much prefer the former one.'*

Being an artist Wang made paintings to go with the poetry. Although Wang's paintings were lost he had another kind of legacy. The Buddhist nun cleverly created a food tableau that she called 'The Poet's Home,' depicting 20 sites. She used perch forcemeat, preserved meat, meat paste and an assortment of fresh and pickled vegetables, fruit and food colouring to portray scenes that the poet had made famous. Comparable food constructions can be found in other cultures, such as miniature buildings and objects that are made with sugar or marzipan. The nun's creation went a little beyond that; it was best enjoyed by those who were familiar with the poet's work. It was food made to please the literati.

Many elements of society would contribute to the food culture that began in the Sui dynasty, only a few decades after Jia. They included the literati, officials, connoisseurs, the rich and the poor, Northerners, Southerners and foreigners, farmers, peasants, doctors, business men, monks, housewives, and cooks. Food culture took many forms, among them prodigious drinking sessions; banquets with guests stupefied by food and drink; ostentatious display; street food; frugal home meals; or elegant home meals; tea, dim sum and much more.

NOTES

Opening quotation: *Xing yuan lu* 醒園錄 by Li Huanan 李化南 (mid 18ᵗʰ c), ed. by Hou Hanchu 候漢初, and Xiong Sizhi 熊四智 (ZPGC, 1984) pp. 2, 5

The first and second emperors: Sui Wendi 隋文帝 (r 581-604), Sui Yangdi 隋煬帝 (r 605-616)

First emperor's accomplishments: *The Sui Dynasty* (1978) by Arthur E. Wright. New York: Alfred E. Knopf, (territorial expansion) pp. 139-156; (civil service reform) pp. 90-103; (canal system) pp.177-180.

'Large' and 'small' measures: *A Concise History of Ancient Chinese Measures and Weights*, *Zhongguo gu dai ji liang tu jian* 中國古代計量圖鑒 (2005) by Qiu Guangming 丘光明 (in Chinese and English), p. 102

Human cost: *Kai he ji* 開河記 (Tang dynasty, anonymous) [Shuo fu 說郛 ed. Tao Zongyi 陶宗儀, ch. 110b, pp.14-15]

Emperor's tour: [*Zi zhi tong jian* 資治通鑑 by Sima Guang 司馬光 (1019-1086), ch. 180, 21-24]

[*Sui shu* 隋書 (636) by Wei Zheng 魏徵, ch.3, pp.6-8]

Preserved crabs: Cang xie fa 藏蟹法 [8:70,7] Crabs for the emperor: [*Li dai shi hua* 歷代詩話 ed. by Wu Jingbiao 吳景旭, ch. 61, pp.13-14]

The Food Classic: *Shi jing* 食經 by Xie Feng 謝諷 [*Qing yi lu* 清異錄 by Tao Gu 陶穀 (902?-970), ch. 2, pp. 64-66] Further source: Qing yi lu. Yin shi bufen 清異錄。飲食部份 by Tao Gu 陶穀, edited by Li Yimin 林益民, Wang Mingde 王明德 and Wang Zihui 王子輝, ZPGC 1985, pp.13-16 . Hereafter abbreviated TG-ZPGC, page(s)

SLIPPERY NOODLES

Raw fish: ('Flying Phoenixes') Fei luan kuai 飛鸞膾；魚膾永加王特封, 加料鹽花魚屑

Raw lamb:天真羊膾, 北齊武威王生羊膾, 刀羊皮雅膾

Raw meat: 爽酒十樣卷生, 咄嗟膾, 專門膾, 天孫膾

Soups: (partridge) 香翠鶉羹, (turtle) 金丸玉菜膼鱉; (lamb) 細供沒忽羊羹, (fish) 剪雲析魚羹; (other) 折箸羹, 十二香點膼；春香泛湯

Steamed meat: (lamb) 露漿山子羊蒸, (bear) 白消熊

Grilled or roasted food: (lamb) 烙羊成美公, 高細浮動羊；(other) 乾炙滿天星, 龍鬚炙, 金裝韭黃艾炙

Meat dishes: (meat cakes) 急成小餤, 朱衣餤; (lamb roll) 修羊寶卷; (goose terrine) 花折鵝糕; (duck fat) 交加鴨脂; (chicken slivers) 剔縷雞; (other) 連珠起肉

Pasta, rice: (slippery noodles) 滑餅; (pasta with broth) 湯裝浮萍麵, 楊花泛湯糝餅; (rice) 越國公碎金飯, 新治月華飯；(other) 象牙䭀, 恬乳花面英

Bread, pastry: 雲頭對爐餅, 金碎香餅子, 乾坤奕餅, 含漿餅, 紫龍糕, 添酥冷白寒具

Preserved food and condiments: (crab) 藏蟹含春侯; (meat) 無憂腊; (condiments) 魚羊仙料, 千日醬, 加乳腐

Display items: (pastry) Jun zi ding 君子飣; (food sculpture) cuo gao qiao zhuang tan yang bing 撮高巧裝壇樣餅

Unidentified: 虞公斷醒酢，暗裝籠味

Poem: 'Guan da yu ge' 觀打魚歌 [*Jiu jia ji zhu Du sh*i九家集注杜詩 by Du Fu 杜甫 (712-770) ch. 10, pp. 9-10)

Poet's home: Lu chai 鹿柴; Meng cheng ao 孟城坳 by Wang Wei 王維 [*Tang ren wan shou jue ju xuan* 唐人萬首絕句選 ed. by Wang Shizhen 王士禎, ch. 1, pp. 4-5]

Food art: Wang chuan xiao yang 輞川小樣 (TG - ZPGC, pp. 4-5)

91

CHAPTER FOURTEEN

THE FLAMING TAIL BANQUET

I found a 'Flaming Tail' banquet menu among old books kept by the family. I made a few notes on the more interesting items.

In the Tang dynasty men who were appointed to high office by the emperor were often obliged to express their gratitude by giving a flaming tail feast. According to one legend, a Yellow River carp fought its way through the rapids called the Dragon's Gate. Emerging upstream, lightning struck its tail and set it on fire, transforming the fish into a dragon. This was possibly an oblique reference to the emperor, often represented by the mythical animal. The opening words refer to a banquet held in the year 709 on the occasion of an official's promotion to a high post. His family kept the menu that a writer came across over two centuries later. He added notes on each of the 58 items in this feast of long ago.

The diners would probably have been seated on benches around tables that were the same height as the benches. They were served by food bearers, girls with rouged cheeks, red lips and carefully coiffed hair, wearing flowing kimono-like garments. Each held a platter of food.

SLIPPERY NOODLES

The Flaming Tail Banquet

Menu
1 Golden Butter Cakes - Steamed pastry
2 Thorn Apple Pastry - Filled, shaped like the spiky round fruit and baked
3 Black Sesame Pastry - Made with butter, honey and flour, and fried
4 Red Cakes - Made with butter dyed red
5 Brahmin Cakes - Steamed pastry probably made with leavened dough
6 Queen's Rice - Yellow rice topped with many ingredients (named for the folk goddess Queen Mother of the West)
7 Seven-Tiered Pastry - Dough folded, cut and shaped like a flower
8 Golden Bells - Toasted butter pastry shaped like bells
9 Grilled Shrimp - Made with fresh shrimp
10 Beef Intestines - Sausages stuffed with lamb marrow
11 Varieties of Wonton - Flower-shaped wonton with 24 different fillings
 (cooked at the table)
12 Slippery Noodles - Made in various shapes (cooked at the table)
13 Air-dried Meat - Preserved meat pounded thin
14 Sweet Pastry Puffs - Fried multi-layered dough
15 Clam Soup - A thick soup served at room temperature
16 Tangan Cake Flower - shaped cake (Tangan, a city in Sichuan)
17 Gold and Silver Rolls - Rolls filled with crabmeat and crab roe
18 Pastry Lamps - Steamed pastry made in the shape of oil lamps
19 Crystal Cakes - Translucent glutinous flour pastries with date filling
20 Petal Cakes - Made from two kinds of pastry dough
21 Jade Cakes - Peppermint-flavoured moulded cakes
22 Palace Chess Pieces - Boiled coin-shaped pasta
23 Longevity Rice - Gruel Porridge made with health-promoting
 ingredients
24 Oyster Mushroom Buns Flavoured with mixed spices
25 Honey Dumplings - Spicy glutinous rice dumplings dyed red
26 Sweet Snow - Crisp pastry toasted with honey
27 Octagonal Cakes - A moulded Cold Foods Day pastry
28 The Musical Troupe - Steamed pastries depicting the 70-member
 ensemble

29 White Dragon Soup - Thick soup made with perch

30 Golden Chestnuts - Steamed pastry made with fish roe

31 Phoenix Eggs - Immature chicken eggs prepared with swim bladder

32 Lamb Omasum - The leaves cut into long strips

33 Instant Sauce - Raw fish and lamb pounded together

34 Whole Fish - Marinated in milk

35 Clove-scented Slices - Salted raw fish or meat seasoned with oil of cloves

36 Chicken with Onions - Steamed with vinegar

37 Wuxing Carp - Specialty of Wuxing, a city in Zhejiang province

38 Xijiang Meatballs - Specialty of a region west of Guangdong

39 Whole Roasted Lamb - Eating lamb was believed to ward off calamity

40 Roast Tongue - 300 slices of roasted lamb tongue and deer tongue

41 The Eight Fairies - A goose, boned and cut into eight pieces

42 Snow Cherries - Frog's legs coated with soybean starch, fried

43 Fairy Chicken - Slices of chicken cooked in milk

44 Crisp Mixed Meat - Deer meat and chicken coated with rice flour, fried

45 Steamed Bear - Preserved bear's paw or preserved bear meat

46 Mao Soup - Mao is one of 12 animal symbols in the calendar. It stands
for rabbit; this is rabbit soup.

47 Cold Jellied Soup - Made with leopard cat meat

48 'Chopstick' Partridge - Grilled or fried partridge, cut into chopstick-
thin strips

49 Steamed Donkey - Donkey meat preserved in rice wine lees

50 Veal in Clear Broth - Cooked 'in water' (without sauce)

51 Five Raw Meats - Slices of lamb, pig, beef, bear and deer

52 Lamb Mixed Grill - Lamb offal and meat coated with soybean flour,
grilled

53 Assorted Fried Food - Ingredients sliced thin, deep-fried

54 Multicolour Cakes - For display: coloured dough in fancy shapes

55 Sliced Sausage - Made of meaty joints, sliced thin, served cold

56 Brown Turtle - In clear broth with lamb fat and duck egg yolks

57 Liver Cold Cuts - Cooked with rose petals, slivered and piled high

58 Meat Balls in Broth - Large meat balls

SLIPPERY NOODLES

Display Items

With much to choose from, it is best to begin with the inedible, or at least those items intended primarily for show. No. 28, the Musical Troupe was a tableau formed with pastries fashioned to represent the 70 lady musicians and singers, costumed as fairies. Although each piece had a vegetarian filling, the pastries were probably more to be admired than consumed.

Multicolour Cakes (no. 54) represented a class of food that was edible but not meant to be eaten; they were simply set out and used again on another occasion. (The term for these display items also came to mean plagiarism, which likewise denotes re-use though of a different kind.) They were made with many pieces of vividly coloured dough individually wrapped with caul fat that were pressed into intricately carved wooden moulds. Such pastries have been unearthed in the Chinese tombs of the Tang dynasty at Astana cemetery on the Silk Road.

Butter Pastry and Fancy Cakes

Pastry making had come into its own. The homely pastries described by Jia now appeared in more stylish forms. On this occasion glutinous rice dumplings were dyed red (no. 25). Buns for Cold Foods Day appeared as octagonal pastries (no. 27).

Several kinds of pastry were made with butter incorporated in the dough (no. 1, 3, 8). Jia had used butter. He put it into some vegetarian dishes, but did not use it in pastry. One might look to India, where there was the practice of using clarified butter in pastry. Brahmin was the old name for India, and Brahmin Cakes (no. 5) may have been a butter pastry.

There are about a dozen other fancy cakes that showed the pastry chef's skill. Sweet Pastry Puffs (no. 14) were made in two steps. Glutinous rice flour was mixed with water, sugar, leavened with fermenting wine, rolled out thin, dried on a griddle and then air-dried. It was then fried in lard and sprinkled with crushed sesame seeds. Miniature objects such as oil lamps (no. 18) and bells (no. 8) were made with pastry. Faux chestnuts were fashioned from small pieces of steamed dough topped with fish roe (no. 30).

Jade Cakes (no. 21) were flavoured with peppermint, an indigenous plant whose flavour was extracted by distillation, probably with a steamer holding the leaves, covered with a piece of silk spread with bean starch. Volatile essences carried up by steam were trapped in the starch.

Food as Entertainment

The feast began with pastries and eventually progressed to meat, with diversions in between. Two courses were cooked at the table (no. 11, 12), wonton and noodles. The basic shape of the wonton was a half-moon, and the filling was usually meat. At this banquet wontons not only came with different fillings but in different shapes. Slippery noodles were usually ribbon-like but here they were shaped like flowers or ducks. A few minutes of boiling in stock and they were ready.

One course might have caught a little attention. Phoenix Eggs (no. 31) were unlaid immature eggs often found in older hens. They appear to consist of yolk, and they lack the white and shell found in mature eggs. In this feast they were cooked with silvery swim bladders that are found in carp and yellow croaker.

Jia spoke of cooking lamb omasum (the third stomach or 'hundred leaves') in stews or soups. In another demonstration of knife skills, omasum was cleverly sliced into foot-long lengths (no. 32).

No. 33-35 consisted of raw fish and raw meat. No. 33 was raw lamb and raw fish pounded together. No. 34 was a whole fish brought to the table (and sliced). The fish had been soaked in milk that could have come from a cow, mare, ewe or yak. It is possible that the milk was used to cleanse the fish of blood and then discarded. No. 34 is noteworthy because there are no similar dishes in Chinese cuisine from this or any other period. Another course of raw flesh followed, fragrant with scent of cloves (no. 35).

Exotic Meats

This would not be a Chinese feast without the inclusion of some rare foods. Bear meat and paws were usually preserved during the winter months. Turning hard and dry, they had to be steamed for hours to make them edible (no. 45). Chinese chefs routinely face the challenge of turning difficult ingredients into something not only edible but delicious. Confronting bear meat or paws, a chef might think of the Duke Ling who in the year 607 BCE killed his cook because the bear paws were not sufficiently tender. 'Because his cook had not done bears' paws thoroughly, (the Duke) put him to death, and made some of his women carry his body past the court in a basket.' The general opinion of the Duke was that he was not a gentleman.

Jellied consommé, finely chopped, was a cold soup made with the meat of the Asian leopard cat (no. 47). This cat is the wild ancestor of the Bengal cat. In antiquity the leopard cat's patterned coat was used to make fur coats for the nobility.

> In the days of the first month, they go after badgers,
> And take foxes and wild cats,
> To make furs for our young princes.

Cats have not found much favour in Chinese cooking. However, leopard cat still is prepared in the two southern provinces of Guangdong and Guangxi. Its meat was traditionally made into soups.

The donkey was a beast of burden on the Silk Road. It eventually became a source of meat. Jia had described preserving donkey meat by fermentation. At the banquet, guests were served donkey meat steamed until very soft with rice wine lees (no. 49). In later times many other ways were found to prepare donkey meat, most of them requiring long slow cooking. Even now there are shops and restaurants that specialize in donkey meat.

A clear turtle soup was presented as the banquet neared its end. Turtle has always been prized for its delicate flesh, especially for the 'skirt,' the soft tissue around the shell. The flavour is rich but its flesh lacks fat, so for this feast turtle was cooked with lamb fat and egg yolks (No. 56).

NOTES

Opening quotation and source: (TG - ZPGC edition, pp. 5-13)
Additional sources: [*Qing yi lu* 清異錄 by Tao Gu 陶穀, ch. 2, pp. 62-64]
Wang gu de zhi wei 往古的滋味 (2006) by Wang Renxiang 王仁湘. Jinan 濟南: Shandong huabao chubanshe 山東畫報出版社. pp. 238-243
Banquet in the year 709: (host) Wei Juyuan 韋巨源 (631-710), a high official of the Tang dynasty in the time of Empress Wu Zetian 武則天
No. 2: Man tuo 曼陀 (also called Man tuo lo 曼陀羅) thorn apple, *Datura metel*
No. 5: (Brahmin cakes) Polomen qing gao mian 婆羅門輕高面

No. 11: (wonton cooked at the table) Sheng jin er shi si qi hun tun 生進二十四氣餛飩

No. 12: (noodles cooked at the table) Sheng jin ya hua tang bing 生進鴨花湯餅. In the Tang dynasty, slippery noodles were called Tang bing 湯餅 [*Gui tian lu* 歸天錄 by Ouyang Xiu 歐陽修 (1007-1072), ch. 2, p. 9]

No. 21: Yu lu tuan 玉露團. Peppermint distillate (Long nao bo he 龍腦薄荷, *Mentha arvensis*) is called Yu lu shuang 玉露霜. An apparatus for its preparation is shown in [*Zun sheng ba jian* 遵生八箋 by Gao Lian 高濂 (1527-1620), ch. 13, p. 22]

No. 24: Tian hua bi luo 天花鏪鑼. (oyster mushroom) Tian hua 天花, *Pleurotus ostreatus*

No. 28: (musical troupe) Su zheng yin sheng bu 素蒸音聲部

No. 31: (immature chicken eggs) Feng huang tai 鳳凰胎

No. 33: (raw fish and lamb sauce) Gun shun jiang 逡巡醬

No. 34: (milk-soaked fish) Ru niang yu 乳釀魚

No. 35: (clove-scented slices) Ding zi xiang lin kuai 丁子香淋膾; (clove) Ding xiang 丁香, *Eugenia caryophyllata*

No. 47: (jellied consommé) Qing liang huo sui 請涼臛碎 (leopard cat) Bao mao 豹貓 or Li 狸 *Prionailurus bengalensis*

No. 49: (donkey) Nuan han hua niang luu zheng 暖寒花釀驢蒸

No. 54: (multicolour cakes) Hong luo ding 紅羅飣

(meanings) '飳飣 ..fruit, etc. arranged for show, not meant to be eaten; to plagiarize.' (Entry 6483 in *Mathews' Chinese–English Dictionary*, revised American edition. Cambridge: Harvard University Press

(Tang dynasty cakes) *Wang gu de zi wei* 往古的滋味(2006) by Wang Renxiang 王仁湘 Jinan 濟南: Shandong huabao chubanshe 山東劃報出版社. p. 293

Duke Ling: (DJ13) 春秋左傳, p .75. 'The Chun Tsew, with the Tso Chuen', in *The Chinese Classics* by James Legge, Vol. 5, Part I (1872), p. 290.

Leopard cat: *Zhongguo pengren cidian* 中國烹飪辭典 (1988) by Xiao Fan 蕭帆. Beijing: Zhongguo shangye chubanshe 中國商業出版社. pp. 29-30

Fur coats: (DJ13) Mao shi 毛詩, p. 38; (ctext) Shi jing 詩經, Guo feng 國風, Qi yue 七月 para 4, tr. J. Legge

CHAPTER FIFTEEN

FOOD AND MEDICINE

A doctor must first understand the origin of a patient's sickness to know how to attack it, and treat it with food. If that fails, use medicine. Medicines are strong, like armed soldiers. Much of the time they are quite unsuitable. While combating sickness they attack everything using excessive force.

In ancient times strong-tasting medicines were thought to be most effective in combating sickness. Medicines that tasted bitter, peppery, sour or acrid were favored over mild-tasting ones. 'Unless the medicine makes the patient dizzy, nauseated or faint, he might not recover.' No wonder, then, that foods were the preferred remedies. The opening lines were by Sun Simiao, a seventh century physician and author of two voluminous medical books. The outlook voiced by Sun echoed long-held views on the importance of food therapy in treating patients. It so profoundly influenced the practice of traditional medicine that it seemed a physician would have to know both medicine and food. The adage that 'medicine and food have a common origin' was true enough, for in traditional medicine almost all of the materials came from plants and animals.

Food and medicine could be used for a common objective – to restore or maintain health. Given the fact that most people are born healthy and possess *qi*, the vital force that is common to all living things, the duty of the physician was to help them maintain that force, mainly by means of nutrition.

Taste and Nature of Foods

How then did the physician prescribe food? The classification system was based on a food's 'taste.' Most food items were thought to possess one or two of the five tastes: sweet, salty, sour, bitter or hot (peppery). The 'sweet' group was by far the largest of the five. It included sugar cane and fruits, but sweet did not always mean sugary. It also included foods that were relatively bland compared to those that were peppery, bitter, salty or sour. Most fish and grains were classified as sweet. Beef was considered sweet.

The second aspect of a food was its nature, described by any one or two of five words: cold, warm and hot, toxic or non-toxic, neutral. Cold, warm and hot did not refer to temperature of the food but to the effects it produced on the human body. Wine's nature was 'extremely hot and very toxic.' Wine was hot not because it was drunk warm, but because it made the drinker feel hot. Tea, always taken hot, was 'cold' and non-toxic because drinking it cooled the body.

Sun described the taste and nature of about 150 foods. Each part of a plant — flower, fruit, seed, leaf, stem or root — could differ from another part in taste or nature. For example, the green leaves and seeds of the scallion were peppery and their nature was warm, but the white part of the stalk was neutral. Apricots were sour; its kernel was toxic. Each part of an animal — skin, fat, meat or bone, head, heart, lungs, stomach, kidney and intestines, ears, hoofs or any other feature — could possess a different nature. According to Sun, pork was peppery and its nature, neutral, but pig's testicles were sweet in taste and warm in nature. To Sun, the taste of lamb meat was bitter and sweet. A nutritionist who was Sun's disciple was of the opinion that lamb meat was warming, but its liver was cold in nature and lamb bones were hot. These classifications, made by individuals, were subjective but there was a degree of concordance among them.

Nutritionists and physicians used these classifications as guidelines in diet therapy for patients with different disorders. According to Sun, patients with heart disease were to avoid salty foods; they were to take foods deemed bitter

SLIPPERY NOODLES

(sweet, sour or peppery foods could be substituted). Those with lung diseases were to avoid taking the bitter, and choose peppery foods (or something sweet, salty or sour). The guidelines remain unchanged into the sixteenth century when they were stated in the standard reference to medicinal materials.

Prescriptions

'Women's disorders are ten times more difficult to treat than their husbands',' Sun wrote. He devoted many chapters in his books to women's health. For women three months' pregnant who were alternately tearful, sad, angry and happy (among several other complaints), Sun prescribed a rooster soup cooked with medicinal ingredients. The recipe illustrates several points. Two systems of measurements were used, the 'large' and the 'small.' Users of the Song dynasty edition of Sun's works were alerted. 'The units of weight are *jin* and *liang*, the units of volume *sheng* and *ho*, the units of length *chi* and *cun*. Everyone who prepares medicines must know this. In the Sui dynasty there was the large *sheng* and the small *sheng*, causing much confusion. Master Sun was born at the end of the Sui dynasty and died in the Tang dynasty. He used the Sui system of measurements. In the year 682, the Tang dynasty adopted the Sui system. Therefore, in this book three small *liang* equal one large *liang*, and three small *sheng* make one large *sheng*. '

The small scale was used to weigh out medicinal ingredients and precious metals. The large scale was for general use, large units of volume being used for water.

In making medicinal soups large amounts of liquid were typically reduced to smaller volumes. In the recipe below, a rooster was boiled with 7.8 L water until the liquid volume was reduced by half. It was reduced further in the step of boiling the medicinal ingredients.

The third feature was the informed choice of meat (or fish) to make the soup base. According to Sun, both taste of black and red roosters was sweet, their natures warm (in contrast to the white rooster, whose meat was sour). The physician's judgement was also essential in choosing the kind of remedy to use. The medicinal substances in rooster soup were almost uniformly sweet in taste and non-toxic in nature. Nine of these ingredients were plant materials. The tenth was donkey hide glue, a substance that will be detailed in a later chapter. This was a gentle tonic, not strong medicine.

Rooster Soup

One rooster, cleaned as usual and cut up

13 g each of raw ginger, paishu root, baical skullcap root

100 mL mondo grass root (previously boiled, soaked and pounded)

26 g each of peony root, licorice root, ginseng, China root, donkey hide glue

12 dates, crushed

Boil the rooster in 7.8 L water, reducing the volume to half. Remove the chicken. All the other ingredients (except the donkey hide glue that is reserved), are broken into small pieces added to the soup and boiled. Take half of the liquid, add to it 600 mL wine with the donkey hide glue and heat all together. Take 600 mLof the soup per day in three doses.

Sun prescribed a foxglove decoction for women after childbirth who wished to regain their former looks, 'to be fair-skinned and plump' as he put it. Chinese foxglove is one of the most-used ingredients in traditional medicine. The root of this flowering plant is used either raw or cooked. Cooked foxglove root is obtained from pharmacies. They are large black nuggets, somewhat resembling truffles in appearance. Its colour and intriguing texture is the result of labour-intensive processes. To obtain foxglove juice the root was simply pounded. The juice was taken raw or boiled to extract its essence.

Foxglove Decoction

2 L Foxglove juice

440 g Lamb fat

1 L Ginger juice

L Honey

Egg

Wine

Reduce the foxglove juice to half its volume by boiling. Add the lamb fat and again reduce it to half-volume. Add the ginger juice and reduce the liquid. Transfer it to a copper pot and cook it with honey until syrup forms. This is taken with one large raw egg mixed with warm wine, three times a day.

Sun prescribed substances rich in calcium for nursing mothers. This is of interest because changes in calcium metabolism are now known to occur in lactation. One prescription consisted simply of water in which crushed gypsum (calcium sulfate) was boiled and then strained out. Twelve of the 20 other prescriptions to induce lactation called for stalactite (a type of limestone with calcium carbonate as its principal component). Pieces of stalactite were brewed with herbs, such as globethistle root, an ingredient that was thought to induce lactation.

Carp Soup

One crucian carp about 20 cm long

110 g pork fat

26 g each of stalactite and globethistle root

2.4 L wine

Do not wash the fish or the fat. Chop up the stalactite and globethistle root.

Cook all four ingredients in the wine. When the fish is done the medicine also will be ready. Discard the solids, let the liquid cool down and divide it into five doses.

Food or Medicine?

The tenet that food was medicine did not mean that pharmacists were cooks. Pharmacists were more educated and knowledgeable than cooks. They were quicker to see applications for new substances. Foreign spices were included in many prescriptions preceding their use in the kitchen. Pharmacies were equipped with heavy mortar and pestles to pound minerals, giant cleavers mounted on stands to shave hard roots like ginseng, and balances to weigh out the lightest of materials, such as dried flowers or leaves. Pharmacists' kitchens were equipped with huge stoves, large clay and copper pots in which large volumes of liquid could be boiled down. Herbal brews could take hours to cook and some of their smells were pungent and pervasive.

On the other hand, many foods prescribed in traditional medicine were prepared in the home, where cooks made them more palatable. Exquisite soups were created, incorporating some ingredients of traditional medicine with fish, meat or fowl. For example, a soup was prepared with carp stuffed with lotus seeds and glutinous rice; it was both soothing and nourishing. Beef was cooked with black pepper and star anise (for their warming qualities) and presented with thick slices of the meat in clear broth. Another was a golden soup made with chicken steamed for several hours with ginseng and donkey hide glue. Such soups were made by professional cooks, not pharmacists. Unlike many of the bitter and pungent brews pharmacists cooked up, one could not say if this was food or medicine. It was both.

NOTES

Opening lines: [*Bei ji qian jin yao fang* 備急千金要方 by Sun Simiao 孫思邈 (581-682), ed. by Lin Yi 林億 and Gao Baoheng 高保衡 (Song dynasty 10th - 13th c). Ch. 79, p. 2]

Dizzy, faint: Ruo yao fu ming xuan, jue ji fu chou 若藥弗瞑眩，厥疾弗瘳 (my translation) (DJ13) *Shang shu* 商書, p. 15; (ctext) *Shang shu* 商書, Charge to Yue I 說命上, para 3 tr. J. Legge

Sun's two books: The first, titled *Invaluable Prescriptions Beiji qianjin yao fang* 備急千金要方, was completed in 652. Its 30 chapters dealt with various disorders affecting men, women and children; food therapy, Shi zhi食治; maintaining health, Yang sheng養性; treating debility, Ping xiu 平脉; acupuncture and moxibustion, Zhenjiu 針灸. The second book titled *Supplementary Remedies Qian jin yi fang* 千金翼方, appeared in 682. Both books contained prescriptions. The SKQS edition referenced above consisted of excerpts from both books.

Food and medicine: *Zhongguo chu yi da guan* 中國廚藝文化大觀 (1992) ed. by Xu Zhiming 徐智明. Beijing: Zhongguo guoji guangbo chubanshe 中國國際廣播出版社. pp. 236-240

Common origin: Yi shi tong yuan 醫食同源

Vital force: Qi 氣. *Classified Dictionary of Traditional Chinese Medicine* 新編漢英中醫藥分類詞典 (2002) by Zhu-Fan Xie 謝竹藩. Beijing 北京: Foreign Languages Press 外語出版社. p. 49

Five tastes (Wei 味): (sour) Ssuan 酸, (salty) Xian 鹹, (peppery hot) La 辣, (bitter) Ku 苦, (sweet) Gan 甘

Five natures: (Xing 性) are (cold) Liang 涼, (warm) Wen 溫, (hot) Re 熱, (toxic) Du 毒 or (non-toxic) Wu du 無毒, (neutral) Ping 平

Characterization of foods: [*Bei ji qian jin yao fang* 備急千金要方 by Sun Simiao 孫

SLIPPERY NOODLES

思邈, ed. by Lin Yi 林億 and Gao Baoheng 高保衡, Ch. 79, pp. 3-5] Abbreviated [SS: Chapter, page(s)]

Qian jin shi zi 千金食治 by Sun Simiao 孫思邈, annotated by Wu Shouzu 吳受琚. (ZPGC edition, 1985, pp. 15-17). The text corresponds to that in Ch. 79 and 80 of the previous reference, with punctuation and footnotes.

Taste and nature: (wine) Jiu 酒 [SS:80,5]; (tea) Ming ye 茗葉 [SS:79,19]; (scallion) Cong 蔥 [SS:79,15]; (apricot kernel) Xing he ren 杏核仁, (apricot, the fruit) Xing shi 杏實[SS:79,10]; (pork) Tun rou 豚肉 [SS:80,11]; (pig testicles) Tun luan 豚卵; (lamb meat) Yang rou羊肉 [SS:80,8]

Sun's disciple: *Shi liao ben cao* 食療本草 (1984) by Meng Shen 孟詵 (621?-713?) and Zhang Dingzhuan

張鼎撰 Beijing北京: Ren min wei sheng chubanshe 人民衛生出版社, pp. 59-60.

Guidelines: [SS:79,5] *[Ben cao gang mu* 本草綱目 by Li Shizhen 李時珍(1518-1593), ch. 1b, p. 14]

Women's disorders: [SS:2,1]

Large and small scales: (Guide to users of the book) [SS: Fan li 凡例, p.1]

Rooster soup: Xiong ji tang fa 雄雞湯法 [SS:2:21-22]

Common ingredients: (raw ginger) Sheng jiang 生薑; (jujube) Da zao 大棗, *Zizyphus jujuba*

Medicinal ingredients: (paishu root) Bai shu白术, *Atractylodes macrocephala*; (baical skullcup root) Huang qin 黃芩, *Scutalaria baicalensis*; (mondo grass root) Mai men dong 麥門冬, *Ophiopogon japonicus*; (peony root) Shao yao 芍藥, *Paeonia lactiflora*; (licorice root) Gan cao 甘草, *Glycyrrhiza uralensis*; (ginseng root) Ren shen 人參 *Panax ginseng*; (China root) Fu ling 茯苓, *Poria cocos*; (donkey hide glue) Ah jiao 阿膠, *Gelatinum Asini;* (Chinese foxglove root) Di huang 地黃, *Rehmannia glutinosa;* (gypsum) Shi gao 石膏; (stalactite) Shi Zong ru 石鐘乳, *Stalactitum;* (globethistle root) Lou lu 漏蘆, *Rhaponticum uniflorum*

About Chinese foxglove: [Ben cao gang mu 本草綱目 by Li Shizhen 李時珍, ch. 16, pp. 1-11]

Foxglove decoction: Di huang yang zhi jian 地黃羊脂煎 [SS:4,3-4]

Calcium: Abrams, S.A. Editorial: 'Bone turnover during lactation – Can calcium supplementation make a difference?' J. Clin. Endo. Metab. 1998;83:1056-1058

Boiled gypsum: Shi gao tang石膏湯 [SS:3,30-31]

Formulas to induce lactation: [SS:3,29-33]

Carp soup: Ji yu tang 鯽魚湯 [SS:3,31]. Globethistle root: (also called Fei lian 飛廉) [SS:15,54-55]

Nourishing soups: Carp soup with lotus seeds and glutinous rice 蓮子糯米燉鯉魚;

Beef soup with star anise 茴香牛肉湯; Steamed chicken soup with ginseng 參膠燉烏骨雞. *Guangdong liang tang: zi bu pian* 廣東靚湯:滋補篇(2007) by He Guoliang 何國樑. Guangzhou 廣州: Guangzhou chubanshe 廣州出版社

CHAPTER SIXTEEN

THE BOOK OF TEA

If one is hot and thirsty, in low spirits, suffering from headache or blurred vision, or weak and aching all over, take four or five sips of tea. It is as good as clarified butter or a liqueur.

Lu Yu put these words in the first chapter of *The Book of Tea*, hailed as a classic in his lifetime and to this day. It seems an odd way to introduce the beverage known for its pure taste and mild fragrance. Why would Lu Yu compare tea to clarified butter? It probably had something to do with his upbringing in a monastery, for he was raised by Buddhist monks. In the Buddhist setting, clarified butter was regarded as superior food. The poem by Du Fu (a contemporary of Lu Yu) titled *In Dayun Temple with Abbot Zan* suggested as much.

> *I cross the great courtyard.*
> *Doors open, closing behind me.*
> *A bell sounds for meals —*
> *Clarified butter for nourishment,*
> *Food and drink for strength.*

My friend greets me, smiling.
He asks for a poem.

Lu Yu's life started in a monastery, but he would become a sometime actor, a friend of poets and artists, and eventually acclaimed as 'the saint of tea.' Lu Yu had been abandoned as a baby. A monk from Jinling temple (located in Hubei, in central China) found him on a river bank. The monastery took him in. The boy had no name. He acquired one from a phrase in an ancient book, 'Geese approach land; their feathers are made into ornaments.' The words land and feather were taken as his surname and first name.

Lu Yu loved to study. He was mischievous and disobedient. After a falling out with his mentor, young Lu Yu ran away from the monastery and joined a troupe of actors. He was clever, humourous and quick-witted, plain-looking — even ugly — and he stammered. (Some say he made the most of these defects by playing the buffoon.)

At age 27 he began to take an interest in literature, immersing himself in ancient poetry and song. Alone, he would go to wild places, intoning ancient poems, roaming, crying bitterly until the night turned pitch black and he was spent. Then he would go home.

This was but one aspect of Lu Yu's personality. Another was his fascination with tea. There was almost no end to the varieties of tea. Each region or central and southern China produced its own tea. The differences in the taste derived from the tea trees and the manner in which their leaves were processed. Lu Yu would sometimes go into the mountains and pick tea leaves. He also made friends among the literati. Among them was Huang Furan, a noted poet. Huang, nearly 20 years Lu's senior, may not have been up to that activity.

Picking tea leaves is not like picking beans.
The cliffs are steep, tier upon tier.
Before the sun is overhead
The basket is full, the breezes hot.
There is the old path to the temple,
Yet he will stay with the mountain folk —
To learn when the four-leaved Paris blooms!

SLIPPERY NOODLES

When he was about 40 years of age Lu Yu was able to set down in writing his knowledge of tea. Although he was the author of numerous other works that were unrelated to tea, he is recognized only for *The Book of Tea*. The first chapter was about the origins of tea, the implements for harvesting and processing, and tea production. Tea paraphernalia — the articles used in the formal process of brewing and drinking tea — was the subject of the second chapter. Chapter three dealt with brewing tea, drinking tea, tea history, tea-producing places, and various settings for drinking tea. It was a very short book. 'This will fit on a length of silk, or on four or six scrolls,' Lu Yu wrote.

Tea, its Origins and Production
'Tea is a beautiful tree that grows in the south. It can reach a height of 12 feet,' Lu Yu said. The tea plant was indigenous to southern China, an evergreen. Cultivated tea bushes were grown waist-high for easier harvesting.

'Leaves are plucked over a span of three months, beginning in March-April. Each tip consists of the furled bud or shoot and its neighbouring leaves. Do not harvest the tea on rainy days, nor when the sky is overcast. On sunny days pluck the tips and steam them, pound them and pack them into moulds. Dry the blocks over a fire, then string them up (to dry fully) and wrap them. There are seven steps from plucking the leaves to wrapping the bricks of tea.

'Some people think that shiny, black, smooth and flat tea bricks are the best, other kinds being inferior. Other people believe that wrinkled, rough-looking yellow tea bricks are the best. By these criteria any kind of tea could be the best. The brick of tea will look shiny if gum is exuded. If gum remains in the leaves the brick will have wrinkled surfaces. If it is night when the tea is processed it will turn black; bricks made earlier in the day are yellow. If the tea is weighted down after steaming, the leaves will be smooth, if not, they will be crumpled.

'Tea is like any other plant. Only your palate can tell if it is good or bad.'

Tea Paraphernalia
Making the beverage required a set of 25 tea articles. 'If you are in the city or at a nobleman's residence, Lu Yu said, to lack even one of these articles would

be a disaster.'

1.Wind Stove - Tripod with vents, for heating water

2.Basket - For fuel, usually charcoal

3. Poker - Length 36 cm, with a six-cornered head

4. Metal Tongs - Length 47 cm, with smooth tips

5, 6. Pot and Trivet - The pot was made of iron, porcelain or silver

7, 8. Bamboo Tongs, Paper Bag - For roasting and holding tea leaves

9.Grinder - Wheel-and-groove model, with feather brush

10. Sieve and box - To collect and store tea powder

11. Measuring Spoon - Made of metal, bamboo or sea shell

12, 13.Tank and Strainer - For fresh water, capacity 6 L

14. Ladle - Made from wood or from a gourd

15. Bamboo Chopsticks - To whisk tea powder with water

16. Salt Container - Porcelain shaker with slatted bamboo lid

17. Jar - For boiled water, capacity 1.2 L

18, 19. Bowls with Basket - Set of 10 bowls

20, 21. Brush and Basin - For washing bowls, basin capacity 4.8 L

22. Waste Bin - Capacity 3 L

23.Towels- Two, made of coarse cloth, length 72 cm

24, 25. Cabinet, Tray - To hold various articles

Each of the 25 items had exact specifications. For example, the 'wind stove' (item 1) used to heat water resembled an ancient bronze tripod (though much smaller). It had figures and inscriptions on each of the three legs. With three vents to increase air intake, the stove was designed to bring water to a quick boil.

The pot (item 5) used with this stove could be made of iron or earthenware, but Lu added, 'It is extravagant but elegant to boil water in a silver pot. The silver can always be recovered when the pot becomes unusable.'The pair of bamboo tongs (item 7) used to grasp a piece of brick tea for roasting was made by splitting a 36 cm length of fresh young bamboo down to the node. The cut bamboo imparted an agreeable aroma to the tea. Roasted tea leaves were placed in a bag made of heavy white rattan paper (item 8) to prevent the fragrance from escaping.

Roasted leaves were pulverized in the grinder (item 9) and then passed through a sieve fitted with a silk-lined box made of woven bamboo (item 10). The mouth of the box was 14 cm in diameter; the box was 11 cm high, large enough to hold the measuring spoon (item 11), its size 'one square inch' (3.6 cm square). 'The size of the spoon must be accurate,' Lu wrote. 'To brew tea the rule is, use one square inch spoonful for 600 mL water. Use less if you want it weaker, more if you like it stronger. So you must use the standard measure.' Items 12-17 were needed for brewing tea. The chopsticks (item 15) were 36 cm long, silver-tipped at both ends. The jar (item 17) in which tea was whisked with water was made of porcelain or clay.

Tea bowls (item 18) were either white Xing ware or celadon Yue ware. Celadon was a muted shade, a colour between green, blue, cream and gray. Xing porcelain was produced in northern China, Yue ware in southern China.

'Xing cannot compare with Yue. If Xing is silver, Yue is jade. If Xing is snow, Yue is ice. In white Xing ware, tea appears tinged with red. In Yue ware, tea appears green, which is suitable. Tea bowls of different colours are made in other places. In yellow bowls tea looks purple. In brown bowls it appears black, which is totally unsuitable for tea.'

Tea, Water and Fuel
The substances for brewing tea were simple: tea leaves, water, and fuel. According to Lu Yu, the formal way of preparing tea called for powdered tea, not tea leaves. Because tea leaves cannot be ground to a powder unless they are very dry, brick tea was broken to small pieces before roasting. 'Do not use the wind stove to roast tea, its heat is too intense and uneven,' Lu Yu cautioned. The preparation of tea began with roasting tea over a gentle fire.

> The heat must be even. Holding the tea near the fire with tongs turn it this way and that. When the outer leaves curl like shrimp shells, move the piece of tea 18 cm away from the heat. When the leaves loosen bring it closer to the fire again, driving out all the moisture.

Lu Yu considered mountain water to be the best for tea; second, water from the river; third, well water. River and well water were strained (items 12 and 13).

> Select a mountain spring with water flowing gently over some rocks. Do not collect it from a waterfall or rapid currents; drinking too much of that gives people diseases of the throat. Nor should you use water that collects in a gully; it stays there from summer to first frost, harboring who knows what creatures? River water fed by small fresh streams should be fetched from afar. If you must use well water, fetch it from a well from which water is frequently drawn.

To fuel the wind stove, Lu Yu said, 'Use charcoal; next best is hard wood such as mulberry. Wood such as cypress is unsuitable because it contains aromatic oils. A connoisseur of water concurred. 'Smoke is to be avoided. A piece of burning wood can fill the room with smoke, not to speak of the water. With that water, how can you have tea?'

The manner in heat, water and tea interacted was to Lu Yu's way of thinking, vital. Boiling the water was a three-stage process that had to be watched so each step of brewing tea could be performed at the right moment.

'At the first stage, large bubbles resembling fish eyes formed at the sides of the pot while the pot emitted a low hum. At this stage the water volume was adjusted (say, to 600 mL). Add a little salt (item 16) and taste it. Salt should improve the taste of water without introducing another flavour.'

The connoisseur spoke of 'undercooked water — the kindling has just caught fire and the water has just begun to boil (stage one). If the tea is hastily thrown in at this point, the water is like a child trying to do a man's job. Very difficult!' This was the reason for adding the tea at stage two.

'At the second stage, chains of bubbles like strings of pearls formed on the sides of the pot. A ladleful of the near-boiling water was placed in the jar. A measured amount of tea powder was added, whisked with the chopsticks and then added back to the pot.'

However, the connoisseur continued, 'Water boiled too long is like a hoary old man. Would you ask him to use a bow and arrow, or to walk with manly strides over long distances?'

In a short while the water was at a rolling boil (stage three) and froth rose to the top. Light froth was called 'blossoms' resembling flower petals that float on a pond. Thicker froth was called 'foam' and the thickest kind of froth was named 'buns' (suggesting fluffy steamed cakes).

Finally, the tea was poured making sure that froth was distributed to each bowl.

'Tea must be drunk hot, with froth on top. As the tea cools the froth disperses. The flavour remains. Tea picked early in the season (known as *cha*) is spare: its flavour lies hidden. After taking half a bowl of this tea, it might seem thin. Take more: the colour is pale yellow, its fragrance intensifies, its taste becomes sweet. Another variety of tea called *Jia* is bitter without the sweetness. *Chuan* tea that is picked late in the season might taste bitter at the first sip, but like *cha* turns sweet as you swallow it. That is tea.

Drinking Tea in the Wild

It was the height of elegance to make tea from powdered tea leaves in the prescribed manner with the correct utensils, but tea could also be enjoyed in informal settings. Lu Yu devoted a section to strategies whereby tea-making could be simplified. Much of tea paraphernalia could be dispensed with in the wild. 'If among the pines and rocks, you can make a fire with dry wood you will not need the wind stove, basket for fuel, poker, metal tongs, trivet, etc. (items 1-4, 6-8). If you find water near a mountain stream, you will not need the water tank, strainer or wash basin (items 12, 13, 21). If there are less than five persons, the tea can simply be crushed and you will not need the sieve or measuring spoon (items 10, 11).

'If you have clambered up a cliff by means of some vines, and are roasting tea in a mountain cave, or are just sharing some tea wrapped in paper, you do not need the grinder (item 9), nor will you need the ladle, chopsticks, salt, jar, the set of porcelain bowls or brush to wash them with (items 14-20). Nor will you need the tray for holding utensils (25).'

Tea Games

Lu Yu compared the froth floating on the tea bowl to clouds against the sky, among other things. The froth was an integral part of the drink (rather like foam on a cappuccino). Indeed, some tea masters could make the foam into shapes resembling animals, insects, fish, flowers and plants. This was called a tea show. Others might form words with the froth; with one word floating in a bowl, four bowls could form a line of poetry. It was in such an atmosphere that a person might form a tea club with his colleagues, who would take turns bringing different teas to be sampled. If the tea was a disappointment, the individual would be penalized.

Drinking tea could be an occasion for composing poetry. The compositions might even take a fanciful form such as a seven-word pyramid. The top line consisted of a single word. The six lines below it were composed of two halves, each with one more word than the one above.

Tea,
Sweet leaf, small buds.
Poet and monk, both crave tea.
Toast the leaves well, pound and sift them.
The tea powder is steeped, thick froth rims the cup.
Drink tea with the bright moon, or the red clouds at dawn.
Drink tea and you will not tire. Drink tea when you are very drunk.

So a group of friends might pass the afternoon in the shade of a bamboo grove, drinking and talking until 'the sun's rays slanted and cicadas began to sing.'

About Tea

Tea was a southern drink. Its ability to keep people awake was well known. A century before Lu Yu, rice gruel cooked with tea leaves was known to interfere with sleep. Tea was used to rouse those who had fallen into a drunken stupor. Monks drank tea to stay awake during hours of meditation. Several monasteries grew their own tea, and they played a role in spreading the popularity of the southern drink to northern China.

For northerners whose regular beverage was sour milk, tea would have presented quite a change. To northerners, tea was considered 'second to milk.' Lu Yu told the story of the scholar posted to the south. He became fond of local items such as tea, and the famous soup made with water shield. Upon returning home he enjoyed drinking sour milk and eating lamb again. When asked how tea compared to milk, he replied like a cosmopolitan. 'Tea is not inferior to sour milk.'

There were several styles of preparing tea. Lu Yu said of these practices, 'People have been drinking tea since ancient times. There is coarse tea, loose tea, ground tea, brick tea. They hack away at it, boil it, roast it and pound it. They pack it in jars and bottles, flood it with hot water and call it tea. They may add scallions, ginger, dates, tangerine peel, cornelian cherry, peppermint and so forth. They will boil it for a long time, and are proud that it is thick and smooth. They will have boiled away all the foam. The tea is like the water in gutters or canals. Alas, this is common practice.'

Lu Yu favored the unadulterated drink. In its pristine form, the first sensation is fragrance rising from the cup as it is brought to the lips. The initial taste may be slightly bitter. Then sweetness is perceived; it is not sugary but something deeper and milder. This is followed by a display of flavours that is unique to each kind of tea. The tea is swallowed, the throat relaxes, and the stomach feels a kind of warmth. The mouth having been cleansed, a second sip brings a different display of flavours. Another sip — soon the mind is at ease, and one's humour improves.

NOTES

Opening quotation: [*Cha jing* 茶經 by Lu Yu 陸羽 (733-804). Ch. 1, pp.1-2] Hereafter abbreviated [LY:chapter, page(s)]
Monastery: *Da yun si Zan gong fang* 大雲寺贊公房 by Du Fu 杜甫 [Du shi xiang zhu 杜詩詳注 ed. Qiu Zhao-ao 仇兆鰲. Ch. 4, pp. 60-61]
Lu Yu's biography: [*Xin Tang shu* 新唐書, ch.196. pp. 20-21] *Zhongguo wenxuejia da cidian* 中國文學家大辭典 (1934) ed. Tan Zhengbi 譚正壁. Shanghai上海: Guangming shu ju 光明書局. Entry 1415.
Lu Yu's name: (DJ13) Zhou Yi 周易, p. 18: (ctext): Zhou yi 周易, Yi jing 易經, Jian 漸, para 7
Picking tea: *Song Lu Hongzhan qi xia si cai cha* 送陸鴻漸棲霞寺採茶 by Huang Furan 皇甫冉 (717-770) [*Yu ding quan Tang shi* 御定全唐詩; ch. 249, pp. 1, 11] (four-leaved Paris) Wang sun cao 王孫草, *Paris tetraphylla*
The Book of Tea: a short book [LY:3,14]; harvesting [LY:1,4];; tea paraphernalia [LY:2,1-8], incomplete set [LY:3,14]; roasting tea [LY:3,1]; brewing tea, froth [LY:3,1-3]; informal settings [LY:3,14]; tea compared to milk [LY:3,11]; styles of preparing tea

[LY: 3,3-4]

Reference in English to *The Book of Tea:* (tea processing) SCC6-5, pp. 519-523; (tea drinking) SCC6-5, pp. 555-562

Tea nomenclature: Cha 茶 may refer to tea in general, the tea plant, *Camellia sinensis*, its leaves or the beverage; in a narrower sense the word means tea harvested early. She 蔎 was the southern name for Cha. Late-harvested tea was called Chuan 荈 or Ming茗; Ming can also mean tea buds. Jia 檟 was a variety of tea, usually considered bitter-tasting. [LY:1,1][LY:3,3]

Tea bowls: Xing ware 邢瓷; Yue ware 越瓷

Connoisseur: (*Sixteen Ways to Boil Water*) *Shi liu tang* 十六湯 by Su Yu 蘇虞 (Tang dynasty, 618-907) in (TG-ZPGC, pp.111-117).

Tea shows: Sheng cheng zhan 生成盞 and Cha bai xi 茶百戲 (TG-ZPGC edition, pp. 124-125)

Pyramid poem: 'Cha' 茶 by Yuan Zhen 元稹 (779-831) [Bai xiang shan shi ji 白香山詩集 Ch 40, p. 6]

The sun's rays...: Yu Zhao Ju cha yan 與趙莒茶宴 by Qian Qi 錢起 (710-782) [*Qian Zongwen ji* 錢仲文集. Ch.10, p.7]

Rice gruel tea: *Shi liao ben cao* 食療本草 (1984) by Meng Shen 孟詵 and Zhang Dingzhuan 張鼎撰. Beijing 北京: Ren min wei sheng chubanshe 人民衛生出版社. p. 25

CHAPTER SEVENTEEN

CANE SUGAR TECHNOLOGY

(New item) Granulated sugar, sweet, cooling, non-toxic; made from cane juice in Sichuan, the western regions and the Yangtse delta.
(New item) Hard honey, sweet, cooling, non-toxic; small cakes made of granulated sugar, buffalo milk and rice flour. Those made in the western and Yangtse regions are better than the Sichuan product.

—The New Pharmacopoeia

Traditionally, pharmaceutical reference books were handed down from one generation to the next. From time to time they were updated, and editors would identify new entries in the latest edition. *The New Pharmacopoeia,* completed in the year 659 and the first such book to be commissioned by an emperor, called attention to the fact that granulated sugar was made in China.

This was something new. Sugar cane had been cultivated in China since antiquity. People drank its very sweet juice, obtained by crushing the long stalks, or chewed the raw, peeled cane like a piece of fruit. Sugar cane juice also was made into syrup and used as a condiment, as mentioned in a poem from the third century BCE.

With the thick soup, sour and bitter,
Came hefty beef shanks from fat cattle,
Turtle and roast lamb with cane syrup,
Braised goose, wild duck and wild crane.

'Granulated sugar and hard honey are gifts from far-away countries.' As late as the second century CE, granulated sugar was an imported commodity. And it remained so until the early part of the seventh century when a Tang dynasty emperor was presented with granulated sugar as part of tribute from the western regions. The general reaction at court was, 'What is this?' Impressed when told it was made from cane juice, the emperor had the perspicacity to send an envoy to the kingdom of Magadha (in central India) to learn how granulated sugar was produced. The technology was passed to Chinese sugar cane farmers.

Granulated sugar was first produced in China within 30 years of the Tang emperor's accession to the throne in 627. The product probably resembled today's brown sugar, consisting of small crystals with residual molasses. By the tenth century there were factories producing granulated sugar and thick syrups, located mostly in the Yangtse delta. But the workers would still drink raw cane juice, on the sly, for refreshment.

The cakes called hard honey that were made with sugar, rice flour and buffalo milk soon dropped out of sight. Hard honey came to mean cane sugar refined by any process. 'The best quality hard honey comes from Sichuan and from Persia. It is white and fine, made with milk,' a 7th nutritionist wrote. Milk had been used in sugar refining in India and Persia. The nutritionist gave a recipe for lozenges, to be taken after meals as a digestive, made with hard honey — meaning granulated sugar — mixed with dates and the seeds of a prickly plant called Chinese teasel. The physician Sun Simiao included granulated sugar and its synonyms in a list of medicinal ingredients. So, practioners of traditional medicine employed granulated sugar, perhaps even before cooks used it in the kitchen.

Giant Sugar Crystals
The premier product of the sugar industry was rock sugar (also called rock candy), hard translucent crystals whose size was measured in centimeters.

118

SLIPPERY NOODLES

After the Emperor's envoy to India brought back the process for making granulated sugar, the art of making very large sugar crystals was transmitted to China by a Buddhist monk in the latter half of the eighth century. He happened to arrive in a part of Sichuan province where sugar cane flourished, but farmers had no success making crystalline cane sugar. The monk, who travelled about on a white donkey, taught the farmers the art of making very large cane sugar crystals. People came to believe the monk was the stuff of legend, and his white donkey actually a tiger, and a temple was built where the monk's thatched house once stood.

That region of Sichuan was also the home of Wang Zhuo, author of two books on poetry and more importantly of *The Rock Candy Book*, that described in detail how the giant crystals were made.

> The cane is harvested over two months, beginning November-December. It is peeled, and then cut into coin-sized pieces. This step requires 10 to 20 men — two men to peel the cane for the one who cuts it. The pieces of cane go into the roller, and then they are pounded. The crushed cane is placed in a steamer. When it comes out of the steamer it goes into the press to squeeze out the sugar water. The syrup is heated, and then steamed until 70% done. It is poured into large earthen jars. (Fresh water can be added to the pressed canes that are pressed again. Very sour vinegar is made from the liquid obtained in the second pressing.)
>
> After three days, the syrup is heated until 90% done. It becomes thick like malt sugar. If heated too much at this point, it becomes granular sugar. Bamboo sticks are then arranged around the inside of large jars. The syrup is poured in and the jars are covered. This is how rock sugar is made.
>
> Two days later, fine sand-like crystals appear on the surface of the syrup. By New Year's time, small pieces of sugar will have formed, and millet-sized grains may have crystallized around the bamboo sticks. Slowly, they grow to the size of beans. They might resemble knuckles, or landscaping rockery. By June-July, it is time to remove the crystallized sugar from the jars. They

will not grow any larger as spring runs into summer. We may even remove them a month earlier; if left too long, the crystals would dissolve. The crystals formed around the bamboo sticks are left under the hot sun for several days, until all the syrup has dripped off and the crystals are dry and hard. The crystals on the inside surface of the jars, resembling stalactites, are left in place. Instead, the jars are sun-dried. Pieces of sugar prized off with a metal tool are called 'mirrors.' Sugar crystals formed in the same jar may have different shapes and colours. The best quality resembles rockery — the kind that represent mountains in alandscaped garden. Next best are the crystals grown on the sticks; next, the mirrors, then, small lumps and the least-wanted, small crystals called 'sand.' The best colour is deep violet, followed by deep amber, light yellow and white. The largest pieces may weigh six to 12 kg. Heavier pieces may form but there will be sand in the center of the crystals.

It takes almost a year and a half from planting the cane to collecting the sugar crystals. When you finally open the jars, there may only a few hundred grams of rock sugar, or you might get several kilograms. If you get over 60 kg, you are rich. If the syrup failed to crystallize, you can always sell it to customers for making into their own granular sugar.

Rock sugar was so valued it became a gift item. In anticipation of tasting it, a recipient wrote in a thank-you poem, 'My tongue flicks out so far it almost touches my nose.'

Sugar Confections

The creator of the confection called ambrosia was born in 953, and his recipe survived unchanged well into the twentieth century. Ambrosia was made with a variety of starchy roots — lotus root, water caltrop, taro, water chestnuts, arrowhead root, foxnut seed and lily bulbs — mixed with sugar and honey. The sugar complemented the crunchy, soft and crisp textures of the starchy roots and bulbs. Honey bound the ingredients together.

SLIPPERY NOODLES

Ambrosia

Peel and steam the roots until very soft. Put them outdoors to dry a little, and then pound them in a mortar. Add Sichuan (cane) sugar, some honey and pound it some more. Shape it into balls, let them cool completely and then cut them into smaller pieces. Use quite a lot of sugar, but not too much honey or it becomes too soft.

A method of sugar refining practiced in the Ming dynasty consisted of purifying sugar with milk. 'This is a secret recipe from the royal kitchen. They make all their sweet confections from this sugar syrup.'

Purified Cane Syrup

Mix six kg of sugar with some water. Over a low heat bring it to a boil in a wok. Slowly add milk diluted with water (or use egg white mixed with water). When the syrup comes to a boil, extinguish the fire and let the covered wok stand for *the duration of a meal.* Then, uncover the pot and light the fire under one side of the wok. When the syrup on the heated side comes to a boil pour a little milk on it. Soon the impurities will collect on the bubbles. Using a slotted spoon, skim them off. (To prevent scorching apply a wet brush to that side of the wok.) Repeat this step.

On the third boil, increase the heat; add water to the bubbles which will push the milk to one side. After *the duration of a meal* skim off the dark foam. You might see some white crystals. Strain the syrup through a piece of cotton.

A confection called 'silk nests' was made with this syrup. It was quite unforgettable because it would shatter at the first bite. After the Ming dynasty fell no one made them, because those former workers in the royal kitchen had retired to Buddhist retreats.

Silk Nests

Smear a stone slab with sesame oil, and sprinkle flour over it. Heat sugar syrup until it spins a thread. After a while, pour it on the slab and cut it in half. Twist each half, turn and draw it out. Let it cool until it stiffens a bit, then pull, stretch and fold it repeatedly. The colour lightens. If the sugar gets too stiff, bring it near the fire. Stretch it several dozen times, and double the loop on the slab. Two persons on opposite sides will stretch and fold the sugar ribbons that will be thin as silk strands. Cut the strands and coil them to make little nests.

A street vendor would make candy animals by blowing air into wads of caramel. The sugar blower's activities always drew an audience of children and adults. A mixture of maltose syrup, granulated sugar and oil was cooked in a copper pot until it could spin a thread. A piece of caramel was made into a wad. The vendor poked one finger into it, swiftly pinched together the open end and pulled it, forming a thin hollow tube whose tip he placed in his mouth. Then he blew slowly and steadily, making a balloon. In less than a minute the sugar blower would have fashioned an animal, perhaps a dragon, or a rabbit or a mouse with a head, a tail and feet or claws on an artfully shaped body. By that time, the candy had cooled and hardened. Two painted dots for the eyes completed the wonderful creation. A child could buy it for a few coins. Sugar animals were brittle and fragile. This was not high art, but what joy it brought to countless children!

NOTES

Opening quotation: (*New Pharmacopoeia*) *Xin xiu ben cao* 新修本草 by Su Jing 蘇敬 (fl 659). Shanghai 上海: Shanghai gu ji chubanshe 上海古籍出版社, 1981). Facsimile of ten extant chapters, handwritten, without pagination, from a copy obtained from Japan around 750.

The New Pharmacopoeia: The book was commissioned in 652 and completed in 659 during the reign of emperor Gaozong 唐高宗 (r 650-683). [*Yu hai* 玉海 by Wang Yinglin 王應麟 (1223-1296), ch. 56, p. 10]

Cane syrup: *Zhao hun* 招魂 by Song Yu 宋玉 (Third century BCE) [*Xue lin* 學林 by

Wang Guanguo 王觀國 (Song dynasty), ch. 6, p. 34]

Far-away countries: *Chi bian* 七辨 by Zhang Heng 張衡 (78-139) [*Ge zhi jing yuan* 格致鏡原 by Chen Yuanlong 陳元龍, ch. 23, pp.15-16]

The emperor: Tang Taizong 唐太宗 (r 627-649)

Acquiring cane sugar technology: [*Ge zhi jing yuan* 格致鏡原 by Chen Yuanlong 陳元龍, ch. 23, p.16]

Sugar cane products: (cane juice syrup) Zhe jiang 蔗漿 or 柘漿; (granulated sugar) Sha tang 沙糖 or Sha yi 沙飴; (hard honey) Shi mi 石蜜. This term was ambiguous. During the seventh century, it could refer to pastries made with cane sugar as in the opening quotation, or to granulated sugar. (rock sugar, rock candy) Tang shuang 糖霜 or Tang bing 糖冰

Drinking cane juice on the sly: *Qing hui zhe* 青灰蔗 in (TG-ZPGC, p. 131)

Hard honey from Persia: *Shi liao ben cao* 食療本草 by Meng Shen 孟詵, p. 44. Sugar lozenges with Chinese teasel, *Ju sheng* 巨勝, *Dipsacus chinensis*, p. 45

Milk in sugar refining: *Science and Civilisation in China Vol. 6, part 3:* 'Agro-Industries and Forestry' by J. Needham, C. Daniels and N.K. Menzies (1996). Cambridge: Cambridge University Press, pp. 349-350

Sugar in traditional medicine: [SS:1,40]

The Rock Candy Book: [*Tang shuang pu* 糖霜譜 by Wang Zhuo 王灼 (fl 1162), pp. 1-2, 5-7]

Thank-you poem: Da Zizhou Yong Xi zhang lao ji tang shuang 答梓州雍熙長老寄糖霜 by Wang Tingjian 黃庭堅 (1045-1105) [*Yu ding pei wen qi song wu shi xuan* 御定佩文齊詠物詩選 by Wang Bin 汪霦 and Zhang Yushu 張玉書, ch 255, p. 1]

Ambrosia: Yun ying mien 雲英麵, recipe of Zheng Wenpao 鄭文寶 (953-1013) in (TG-ZPGC pp. 146-147)

Ingredients: (lotus root) Lian ou 蓮藕, *Nelumbo nucifera*; (taro) Yu tou 芋頭, *Colocasia esculenta*; (Chinese water chestnut) Bi qi 荸薺, *Eleocharus tuberosa*; (arrowhead root) Ci gu 慈菇, *Sagittaria sagittifolia*; (foxnut seed) Ji tou 雞頭 or Qian 芡, *Euryale ferox*; (lily bulb) Bai ho 百合, *Lilium brownii*

Purified cane syrup, silk nests: Qi tang lu fa 起糖滷法, Wo si fang 窩絲方 [*Zun sheng ba jian* 遵生八箋 by Gao Lian 高濂, ch. 13, pp. 1-2, 4]

Old palace employees: [*Xi he ci hua* 西河詞話 by Mao Qiling 毛奇齡 (1617-1716), ch. 2, p. 1]

Sugar blowing: Chui tang ren 吹糖人 by Ren Zhaoyu 任兆毓 www.xinghua.gov.cn

CHAPTER EIGHTEEN

SOUTHERN BORDERS

To a Friend Departing for the South
I bid you goodbye with a sigh and a frown.
The south is remote, with marshes and vast oceans.
Hanoi is at the border. Java lies beyond the seas.
Every day, the glaring sun, at night the foliage grows.
Few natives live to old age in those pestilential lands.
Savages in bright turbans and sarongs are hard to tame.
Warships churn the waters even as foreign wagons roll.
Olive trees bear sour fruit, sugar palm sago is bitter.
Large junks, all booms and masts, return from the seas.
Men in boats beat copper drums to appease river spirits.
Seasons are uniform: there is no frost and no winter.
Deadly plants thrive. Snakes and crocodiles lie in the mist.
Yellow clouds and dark rain will come before the typhoon.
Prisoners shuffle along the roads, while officials deliberate.
Heed my words: be correct and do not be tempted.
We of the north and these southerners have different customs.

SLIPPERY NOODLES

In the latter half of the ninth century, the Tang dynasty emperor appointed a man named Liu Xun to the post of sub-prefect in the city of Canton. Canton (present-day Guangzhou) was an important trading centre in southern China, part of a region divided into several prefectures. The city of Hanoi was in North Vietnam, at that time the southernmost prefecture of China. The opening poem was written at least four decades before Liu was posted to Canton. He might have seen it. It expressed the generally held view that the south was at the fringe of civilization, inhabited by savages. The south was where prisoners were sent and where officials who had fallen out of favour were exiled. Those appointed to posts in the south deserved sympathy.

Impressions

Liu took up his post in Canton. Mountains set close to the sea separated central China from the south. What they lacked in height was made up in depth and breadth, preventing icy winds from going south, trapping summer's heat in the Yangtse valley. While central China endured harsh winters and sweltering summers, the south enjoyed a subtropical climate. Date palms from Persia that had been transported by sea grew in the port city of Canton. 'I tasted a Persian date in a foreigner's home,' Liu wrote. 'Its colour was like that of granulated sugar. The pit had rounded ends, unlike Chinese dates that have pointed ones.' He pocketed it to plant in his garden.

As the poet said, the sky turned different colours before a typhoon. 'Clouds over the southern seas are deceiving. When patches of different colours appear, a typhoon is brewing. Suddenly there is thunder and lightning…the wind is violent, wrecking houses, striking trees, blowing roof tiles about like plates,' Liu wrote.

He saw crocodiles. 'They are the colour of mud, with four feet and a tail, like alligators. They move quickly, their mouths full of teeth, like saws. Deer on the river banks may be attacked by a swarm of alligators. When I see so many all together, I dare not approach. It is their lair.'

Some of the natives were savages, as the poet had said. Yet Liu noted, 'The barbarian tribes of southern China have metal drums. The drumhead is round, 72 cm in diameter with an hour-glass shaped frame decorated with animals, fish, plants and flowers. The thickness of the frame is 7 mm. The sounds produced on these drums are much like those from wooden-frame drums with animal skin drumheads.'

There were indeed ocean-going junks. Liu wrote, 'Merchant ships are constructed without any nails. To bind the beams, natives use fibres of the sugar palm that expand and strengthen in salt water. They resemble horse hair. Fabric is made out of these fibres. To make waterproof seals on the ships, they use olive sugar, a paste made with sap from the Chinese olive tree, its bark and leaves. Olive sugar resembles maltose syrup but it dries to lacquer-like hardness.'

It was a strange land. There was a wild climbing vine with yellow blossoms. In humans a leaf or two from the plant resulted in death within hours; yet sheep grew fat munching on its sprouts. There was a spot northwest of Canton where lychees ripened in late spring, two months earlier than elsewhere. Liu attributed this phenomenon to the proximity of a volcano. Violet quartz crystals were found with five sides instead of the usual six. 'As medicine,' Liu recorded, 'an infusion of these crystals is warming, non-toxic, and twice as efficacious as the white quartz found up north.'

In a certain location, 'there is a mountain with some coal deposits. Once a year the people like to go there with some food and prepare a meal on the spot. When the coal fire is very hot, they cook raw fish, onions, chives and pickles on it. The food cooks very fast, it may even boil.' Liu said. 'I have some friends and relatives in the south. They have attended these gatherings many times and they always have severe indigestion afterwards. I think there is poison in the coal that goes into the fire.'

With his tour of duty completed, Liu returned to the capital, but he found it lacking in peace and quiet. Contrary to the poet's warnings, he was beguiled by the south. He returned to live in the prefecture where he had served. There, Liu wrote a book that gave glimpses of the lands beyond the broad span of mountains.

The Seacoast

Perhaps one of the reasons Liu was fond of the south was its abundance of seafood. He observed some rocks at the edge of the sea that seemed to grow, forming crags and precipices. Actually they were oysters, large and small. 'Marinate large oysters and roast them. If they are small, fry them.'

Southerners were fond of shrimp, Liu noted. They would sprinkle vinegar sauce on live shrimp and quickly cover the dish. As chopped herbs sizzled in a hot pan, the cover was lifted. The shrimp jumped into the pan to escape the vinegar. 'Some boors like this. They think it is something special.' Liu remarked.

Southerners were also fond of jellyfish. 'It may be as big as a hat, or small as a bowl. It has 'feet' resembling strands of cotton, and no mouth or eyes,' Liu recorded, obviously unfamiliar with this creature. 'Clean it thoroughly with plant ashes, sprinkle it with sesame oil and wash it again until it resembles crystal or purple jade. Boil it with pepper and cinnamon, or cardamom and ginger, and then slice and fry it. Other ways to prepare jellyfish are to mix the slices with meat, peppery spices and vinegar, or with shrimp and vinegar. Shrimp is a closer match to jellyfish and the better choice.'

Cuttlefish was known as the black bandit for snatching its prey and squirting black ink. 'It has but one light bone, no scales, and four 'feet.' At high tide it grasps a rock with its two long feet and floats near the water's surface. When small fish and shrimp come by, it squirts sticky saliva, captures and eats them. Around Canton fisherman sometimes would net big ones. Fried cuttlefish is crisp and delicious. Cantonese serve it with vinegar and ginger slivers (a combination traditionally used for crab). Or they may salt the cuttlefish to dehydrate it, and eat it like a piece of dried meat.' The Cantonese seemed to have a heightened sense of taste. 'The crab claw's meat and shell taste of the sea. The Cantonese boil the claws in fresh water. When they drink, they may suck a claw for its salty juices. Some crabs have tomalley that resembles butter. They simply cook it in the shell with a little seasoning. There is also red crab tomalley that is like chicken or duck egg yolk. They put some cooked crabmeat in the shell with the tomalley, and mix it all with some fine cooked noodles. Exquisite.'

In spring 'jumping' fry were found along parts of the coastline. Fry could be any kind of young fish; here, it was the flathead mullet. 'Fishermen can see them coming from the distance like a cloud two to three hundred paces wide. Nets are not used. They scramble to position their boats in front of the oncoming fish. Frightened, the fry jump into the boat. The boat must not be positioned in the densest part, for with so many jumping in the boat would sink, so you can imagine how many fish there were!' Liu wrote. 'The young mullet could be split open, sprinkled with a little salt and a few drops of vinegar and eaten raw, with wine.' Pomfret was another salt water fish. Its body was shaped like a disk, a smooth silvery skin covering thick white flesh and only a few bones. After it was steamed with ginger and scallions on top of rice the bones were so soft, people could eat them. Dogs under the table, waiting in vain for fish bones, would doze off.

The Land

Liu visited a snake farm inland, where pythons were raised for their bile or gall bladders, items used in traditional medicine. 'Every year on the 5th day of the 5th lunar month, they take a snake out of the cage. By means of many canes they pin it to the ground, exposing the belly. They cut it open and extract the gall bladder that was the size of a duck egg. After draining the bile they might sew up the opening and either put the snake back in its cage or release it into the wild.' Elephants used to roam southern China. Liu spoke of tribal leaders who had performing elephants at their banquets. 'When the music started an actor entered leading an elephant by a golden bridle, its body covered with a brocade mantle. It knelt, pranced, and wagged its head and tail much like a dancing horse.' In the mountains, many families kept elephants to do the heavy work, the way cattle and horses were used elsewhere. Tame elephants were not used as food. But since antiquity elephant trunk was known as a delicacy. 'Natives capture them for the trunk that was both fatty and crisp when roasted or grilled,' Liu wrote. Another writer had sampled this delicacy. 'Its tastes like pork,' he said.

By the ninth century Canton had overtaken other southern cities as a trading centre. Nonetheless, Hanoi was still the premier city of North Vietnam, exhibiting a somewhat different culture. Travelling to this prefecture outside his jurisdiction, Liu had noted that sounds of the gourd mouth organ could be heard in Hanoi. It was a musical instrument used by several hill tribes, constructed with bamboo pipes of different lengths, fitted with free reeds. 'The music of the pipes was harmonious; the sound and pitch of each one was pure and clear.' In Hanoi, peacocks were raised; fans were made with their green and golden feathers.

'People in Hanoi entertained for business purposes, or perhaps to impress guests with their importance. Banquets usually began with a soup made with lamb, deer, chicken and pork (including the bones) all cooked together in one pot. The soup was strained and brought to the table in a tureen with a large ladle made of silver and horn. The host was the first to drink from the ladle, tipping it until the rim touched his nose. One by one his guests would drink the soup in the same manner. Then the feast could begin.'

Some guests might invoke the classics when pickled ant eggs were served, for in antiquity they were made into condiments. The flavour was strong, tasting like meat. This was something that ordinary people had no chance to taste. 'To obtain ant egg condiment you must know an official, or be related to one,' Liu wrote.

Water buffalo was another choice item. Roasted or grilled, the meat often made one feel bloated, so it was customary for local people to take the so-called 'magic condiment' before consuming the meat. It was made of the contents of buffalo stomach and intestines — digested grass — mixed with salt, sour milk, cinnamon and ginger. Visitors from the north all wanted to taste water buffalo, but to their discomfort they often failed to take magic condiment.

Southern Fruits

Liu described some fruits he had not seen before. 'The coconut tree bears fruit as large as bowls. The outer skin is rough and hard, about 1 cm thick. The inside resembles a container made of white gold. Astonishing! It holds a milky liquid that is quite refreshing to drink.' He had also never seen longan and lychee trees because they did not grow in northern climates.

Liu saw citron in its native habitat. This fruit grew in several shapes, one resembling a very large lemon, with a peel that might be green or yellow. 'In northern China, citron was displayed in the homes of the rich as an exotic fruit,' Liu noted. In its place of origin, the fragrance of the peel was more pronounced, the colours more vivid. 'Its peel could be carved with elegant designs, the exposed white pith rubbed with rouge and the whole fruit soaked in honey.' Citron was but one among a wide variety of citrus fruits.

Pomelo was a large pear-shaped fruit. Its thick skin was tough, as were the membranes separating the sections. Oddly the pulp was at its sweetest when the membranes were paper-dry. Best known was the mandarin orange (tangerine) whose aromatic peel enhanced the flavour of many foods. Tiny orange berries were said to have medicinal properties. Its glossy leaves were parched and taken in wine. Southerners would soak orange berries in honey and eat them, skin and all. Grafting and cultivation in different locales produced many other citrus varieties.

Chinese hickory nuts grew here as they did in central China. Almonds were definitely of foreign origin, variously said to come from Sumatra, Persia, and Hindu Kush (the land between present-day Afghanistan and Pakistan). Betel palm was native to the south. Betel nuts were cooked with sugar or honey. (The nut was also taken raw as a stimulant, wrapped in betel leaf with a dab of lime and chewed.)

Of all the fruits in the south, there were two that were outstanding, lychee and longan. Their trees were much alike, with heavy clusters of fruit hanging from thin twigs. Their fruits were the size of grapes. Encased in a hard-shelled globe, the pulp was pale and translucent and it held a large smooth nut. 'Just when the lychee harvest ends, longan ripens, as big as bullets. It is almost too sweet. Many say the lychee cannot compare. There is some truth to that,' said a visitor. These were some of the delights the south offered that the north could never produce. Lychee and longan grew only in a few warm and humid localities — in the south and in Sichuan. They could not be transported any distance. The poet Bo Juyi who wrote the opening poem was at one time banished to a remote part of Sichuan that he loathed (he compared the natives to wild apes) but he seemed to like the lychees.

'Here, lychee grows near the gorges, round as knobs, with leaves like those of the cassia tree and blossoms resembling those of the tangerine. Like grapes lychee ripens in summer. It has a pit like that of the loquat, a shell resembling red silk and inner membranes thin as raw silk. The pulp is white as ice or snow; the juices sweet and tart like wine or whey.

'Once plucked, the colour (of the shell) changes in a day, the fragrance of the pulp in two days, its taste changes within three days. By the fourth or fifth day, everything is gone.'

Perhaps this is why even now, when the fruit is in season, one tends to buy too much of it, and to eat too many at one sitting. But now, even as it was then, one must enjoy the moment.

SLIPPERY NOODLES

NOTES

Opening poem: *Song ke chun yiu Lingnan* 送客春遊嶺南 [*Bo shi chang qing ji* 白氏長慶集 by Bo Juyi 白居易 (772-846), ch. 17, pp. 4-5]

Hanoi: (old name) Jiaozhi 交趾; it may refer to the city or the prefecture it is in.

Sources: [*Lingpiao lu yi* 嶺表錄異 by Liu Xun 劉恂 (9th-10th c)] hereafter abbreviated with chapter and pages [LX:chapter,page(s)]. This book is known by five other titles: *Ling biao lu* 嶺表錄, *Ling biao ji* 嶺表記, *Ling biao yi lu* 嶺表異錄, *Ling biao lu yi ji* 嶺表錄異記 and *Ling nan lu yi*嶺南錄異.

[*Bei hu lu* 北戶錄 by Duan Gonglu 段公路 (fl 860-871)] hereafter abbreviated with chapter and pages [DG:chapter, page(s)].

The emperor: Tang Zhaozong 唐昭宗 (r 889-904)

Impressions: (Persian dates) Po si zhao 波斯棗 [LX:2,5-6]; (typhoons) Ju feng 颶風 [LX:1,1;2,1]; (crocodiles) E yu 鱷魚 [LX:1,7]; (savages) Mang yi 蠻夷 and (bronze drums) Tong gu 銅鼓 [LX:1,2-3]; (merchant ships) Jia ren chuan 賈人船 [LX:1,2]; (sugar palm) Guang lang 桄榔, *Arenga pinnata* [LX:2,4]; (olive sugar) Gan lan tang 橄欖糖; (Chinese olive) Gan lan 橄欖, *Canarium album* [LX:2,7]; (litchees) Li zhi 荔枝, *Litchi sinensis* [LX:2,1]; (purple quartz) Zi shi ying 紫石英 [LX:2,1]; (coal) Jiao shi 焦石 or 樵石 [LX:2,2]

Climbing vine: Hu wan cao 胡蔓草, genus *Gelsemium* [LX:2,4]. C. Rujjanawate, D. Kanjanapothi and A. Panthong. Pharmacological effect and toxicity of alkaloids from *Gelsemium elegans* Benth. J. Ethnopharm. (2003) 89:91-95

The seacoast: (oysters) Hao 蠔 or Mu li 牡蠣 [LX:2,10]; (shrimp) Xia 蝦 [LX:2,20]; (jellyfish) Shui mu 水母, *Rhopilema esculentum* [LX:1,8-9]; (cuttlefish) Wu zei yu 烏賊魚, order *Sepida* [LX: 1,5]; (salt water crabs) Shui xie 水蟹 [LX:2,9-10]; (horseshoe crabs) Hou yu 鱟魚, [LX:1,5]; ('jumping' fish fry) Tiao ting 跳艇, (flathead mullet) Zi yu 鯔魚, *Mugil cephalus* [LX:1,2]; (pomfret) Chang yu 鱠魚or 鯧魚, *Pampus argenteus* [LX:2,9]

The land: (python bile) Ran she dan 蚺蛇膽[LX3:9-10]; (performing elephants) Wu xiang 舞象 [LX:1,10]; (tame elephants) Yang xiang 養象 [LX:3,7]; [elephant trunk] Xiang bi 象鼻 [LX:1,10][DG:2,7-8]; (gourd pipes) Hulu sheng 葫蘆笙 [LX:2,2]; (peacocks) [LX:3,6]; (banquets) [LX:1,11]; (ant egg condiment) Yi luan jiang 蟻卵醬 [LX:1,4]; (water buffalo) Shui niu 水牛; (magic condiment) Sheng ji 聖虀 [LX:1,11]

Southern fruits: (coconut) Ye zi 椰子, *Cocos nucifera* [LX:2,7]; (longan) Long yan 龍眼 or Yi zhi 益智, *Euphoria longan* [DG:2,16] (citron) Xiang yuan 香櫞, *Citrus medica* [LX:2,7]; (orange berry) Shan xiao ju 山小橘, *Glycosmis citrifolia*; variety through grafting [DG:3,3].

Nuts: (Chinese hickory) Shan hu tao 山胡桃 or Shan he tao 山核桃, *Carya*

131

cathayyensis [DG:3,4; (almonds) Pian he tao 偏核桃, *Prunus amygdalus*; (betel palm)
Bing lang 檳榔, *Arecha catechu* [DG:2,16]

'Almost too sweet': [DG:3,1]

The poet's comments: (wild apes) Zi Jiangzhou zhi Zhongzhou 自江州至忠州
[Bai shi chang qing ji 白氏長慶集, by Bo Juyi 白居易, ch. 11, p. 2]. (translation)
Translations from the Chinese (1971) by Arthur Waley. Vintage Books, p. 215

Lychees :Mu lian li zhi tu 木蓮荔支圖 by Bo Juyi 白居易 [*Ji mu yuan hai* 記纂淵
海 by Pan Zimu 潘自牧, ch.92, p. 3]

CHAPTER NINETEEN

IN THE CAPITAL CITY

South of the palace grounds, there are covered walkways on either side for about 200 paces. There used to be street vendors here. Now the royal avenue has been closed off with black lacquered posts. The trees on either side of the brick-lined gullies are peach, plum, pear and apricot. In spring, their blossoms formed a kind of tapestry.

We come to a bridge. Here are ordinary homes, Che's Coal Shop, Zhang's Wines, a steamed bun shop, Li's Incense store, Grandmother's Meat Cakes, Li's Eatery. Turning west we cross another bridge. One of the city's best wine stores is here. It has lamb wine for 81 coppers a bottle, next to shops selling lamb rice and cooked lamb. Further down the street are several brothels. West of the royal avenue are more steamed bun shops, soup shops, tea shops and restaurants.

Reading *Reminiscences of the Eastern Capital* is like taking a stroll about the capital with its author. The memoir is precise in its description of the city, and alive with detail. Kaifeng, the capital of the Song dynasty, had the imperial palace at its centre, surrounded by the old city. The old city wall was rectangular, with three gates to the outer city on each side. The outer city wall was over 20 km in circumference, with many more gates and three-storied gate towers that overlooked the countryside. Red gates straddled canals and rivers, with walkways on either side for pedestrians. They were fitted with iron gratings that could be lowered into the water.

Eleven bridges spanned one of the rivers that flowed through the city; thirteen bridges crossed another. There was a wooden bridge built without pillars, arched like a rainbow. Large boats passed under it, bringing supplies to the capital. Another bridge near the palace was entirely made of stone — pillars, balustrades and roadway; even the river banks nearby were faced with carved stone. It was for carts and carriages. By day only flat boats could pass under that bridge; iron chains barred the way at night.

A stroll though the outer city could be unsettling. The walls separating the city from the countryside were thick. They were huge buildings in themselves. Armed soldiers were stationed every 200 paces inside the perimeter. Defenses and fortifications were in plain sight. Splendid as it was, the imperial city was threatened by foreign tribes in the north who had for decades made hostile moves against the Song.

The author of *Reminiscences* had lived in the city for more than two decades, since 1103. 'I lived the life of a playboy, and I did not tire of it. One morning there was gunfire, and soldiers everywhere. That was in 1126. The next year I left the city and fled south.' The Jurchen, invaders from the north, captured the city whose defenses had been weakened by fire bombs hurled over the outer city wall. The victors destroyed the capital. The reminiscences of Kaifeng would bring a smile and a nod to many readers, but they were scenes of a city that had vanished.

Urban Scenes

By the twelfth century, Kaifeng had a population of over half a million people, making it one of the largest cities of its time. With the royal family in residence, the city housed officials, administrators and government bureaux. The city attracted visitors from afar, the south, and the inland provinces. Its streets offered a show that dazzled the city's residents and visitors. The huge Xiangguo temple housed hundreds of statues and a relic — Buddha's tooth. On its grounds stood twin pagodas faced with glazed tiles. On occasion hundreds gathered there, and the temple prepared vegetarian food for them. The gold and silver exchange building was impressive, especially when one learned of the astonishing amounts of money being traded within. Fire stations were located at several points in the city, with soldiers manning its watchtowers by day and patrolling the streets at night. The 'devil's market' opened for business in the small hours of the night, a trading place for second-hand clothes, books, paintings and bric-a-brac. It would close promptly when the sky brightened. Brothels were clustered on two side streets named East and West Chicken Alley (chicken being a pun on the word for prostitute). Another street was lined with herbal medicine shops, including one that specialized in remedies for mouth, teeth and throat. Medical doctors, pediatricians and gynecologists were close by.

Daybreak
At the crack of dawn, drum towers signalled the fifth and final night watch. Gongs and wooden clappers in the monasteries sounded, rousing those who had to beg alms, to hasten to court or go to the city. The city's gates, wells and bridges were already open.

A small boy in front of a calabash soup store had the job of calling out to passersby. 'Breakfast inside! Stuffed lungs and stir-fried lungs!' Lanterns lit up the restaurants. Candles were for sale, only 20 coppers with breakfast — rice and dim sum — thrown in. They also sold tonics and hot water for morning ablutions, until dawn.

Hundreds of sheep and pigs were brought into the city, destined to be slaughtered. At the meat market, butchers would cut the meat into chunks or slices, or mince it for customers. What they could not sell during the day, they sold to street vendors at night. Wheat flour to be sold by the sackful was hauled in by cart drawn by donkey or some other beast of burden. Adding to the din, vendors sold tonics, drinks and snacks by a bridge near the royal avenue.

Fish were sold every morning near three of the outer city gates. Strung together with willow branches they splashed in shallow tubs of water. In winter, frozen fish from the Yellow River were brought to market. They were called 'passenger fish' because they arrived in carts.

There was brisk business in stores that sold oil cakes for breakfast (oil cakes were pieces of leavened dough pierced with holes and fried). At Hu bakeries, bread was made at wooden benches, with men rolling out dough, cutting and shaping it, adding different flavourings. By the fifth watch the clatter of metal pans was heard all over the city as breads and pastries were shoved into ovens. A few bakeries had as many as 50 ovens on their premises.

Quick Meals

Small eateries were everywhere. For those who wanted only a quick meal, small shops offered a variety of thick soups, Hu bread with fatback, lamb or ribs; baked marinated lamb, noodles with raw lamb, and the pasta called 'chess pieces' served cold; or hot baked rice and noodles. Sichuan food shops served noodles, a variety of fried meats and rice. Southern food shops offered fish dumplings and rice with fried fish. Like some other eateries they offered noodles flavoured with foxglove tree bark, a medicinal ingredient.

Calabash soup stores sold more than soup. Their entrances were festooned with red and green bunting and hung with pieces of pork and lamb as welcome signs. These stores offered better service. Each customer could specify exactly what he wanted — lean meat, fat meat, hot, warm or cold and so on. The hapless waiter would bring them, balancing as many as 20 bowls on his arms.

Vegetarian eateries sold food like that in temples: different kinds of noodles with vegetables and pickles, rice wrapped in lotus leaves, all kinds of rice, or plain rice with salted vegetables, radishes and such.

Wine Taxes and Yeast Sales

Government control of wine production and yeast sales had been in place for over a century. They applied to wineries all over China. In the 1070s, wine tax revenues from the eastern capital exceeded that from any other place (a city in Sichuan placed second). The government also had exclusive control over yeast supplies. Seventy two establishments in the capital city were permitted to make wine and sell it to the public because they bought yeast for this purpose from the government. Each of these 72 wine shops could call itself an 'established house' while other wine shops called 'bottom stores' could only sell wine made by others that was generally of an inferior quality.

Restaurants

Because drink was inevitably linked to food, restaurants were attached to established houses and bottom stores. In the lesser establishments, waitresses in white and blue aprons, with their hair done up in coils, poured tea and wine. A customer dropping in, seeing youths drinking. might consider engaging a prostitute, or striking up a conversation with a waitress or a singer, giving her money. In these restaurants low-class prostitutes appeared uninvited; they were given a little cash and sent away. Vendors moved among the tables passing out fruit or snacks whether the customers wanted them or not, collecting a few coins later. Such people were almost impossible to avoid except in a few restaurants where the above-mentioned kinds of people were not allowed inside the door.

In high-class restaurants, the wine was always choice, the pickles were superior. The menu might read like this:

Two thick soups — Partridge Soup — Clear Abalone Broth
Thick Soup with Crisp Ingredients — Kidneys Cooked Two Ways
Shrimp Mushrooms — Chicken Mushrooms
Thick Soup — Noodle Rings
Jade Chess Piece Pasta — Mock Pufferfish — Pickled Vegetables
Mandarin Fish — Mock Turtle — Abalone Dumplings
Abalone Soup — Shark Rugae — Twice-Cooked Freshwater Fish
Mock Clams — Fatback with Bread — Sliced Meat — Hu Bread —
Soup — Steamed Lamb — Lamb 'Horns' — Kidneys
Steamed Duck with Goose — Pork Slices with Kidneys
Roast Breast — Roast Duck — Grilled Beef Omasum on Skewers
Braised Head of Lamb — Roasted Lamb and Head of Lamb
Skewered Duck and Goose — Skewered Chicken — Skewered Rabbit
Stir-fried Rabbit — Rabbit Showered with Onions — Mock Wild Fox
Golden Threads — Tripe Soup — Thick Tripe Soup
Mock Roast — River Deer
Fried Partridge — Stir-fried Lung
Stir-fried Clams — Stir-fried Crabs — Boiled Crabs
Raw Crab with Wine — Ginger & Tangerine Peel

Several items in the menu are incomprehensible to the modern reader. Still, the menu illustrates three features of an evolving cuisine. First, the term 'stir-fried' had come to describe a certain way of preparing food, like roasting or steaming. That word had appeared in earlier texts. Jia Sixie scrambled eggs by 'stir-frying' them in sesame oil with scallions and fermented black beans. In his time, 'stir-fry' usually meant to toast in a pan, without oil. For example, one step in making magic yeast cakes that was to 'stir-fry wheat until it was golden but not burnt.' The physician Sun Simiao used the word in the same sense. Fresh ginger was pan-toasted 'until it was dry and nearly burnt.' Soy beans were pan-toasted 'until they stopped hissing.' In the twelfth century guests viewing the menu above could expect stir-fried dishes to consist of food that had been carefully sliced, perhaps coated with thickener, seasoned and cooked quickly with hot oil in a pan. It was a versatile technique applicable to many different foods: rabbit, lung, seafood.

If cooking is the art of fooling the palate, what better test for a cook than to make one thing taste like another? Mock foods were popular. For example, a non-poisonous fish had been substituted for the toxic pufferfish. It was a conversation piece. A guest might mention the seventh century nutritionist who warned, 'Do not eat this fish. When angry it puffs up with gases. The poison in its liver will kill a man. Reed roots cut up and boiled are a remedy.' Did this ancient remedy work? A diner wondered. Another guest answered by quoting a few lines by a poet (who in fact had died in Kaifeng only a few decades earlier).

> *They all said it is delicious beyond words.*
> *Who could have known? Now he's dead as can be.*

Third, some interesting delicacies appeared. In an earlier period shark and abalone were known by the same name, although their differences were recognized. In the early twelfth century interest in shark as food was confined to its meat and some internal organs; shark's fins and shark skin did not become important until later. One dish on this menu was composed of shark rugae, a particular kind of stomach lining. In an empty stomach the lining lay in long, deep, orderly folds. It could expand like a balloon when food entered the stomach. This was an excellent choice for those who liked omasum, tripe and kidneys.

At the second-class restaurants that were linked to the wine industry food service was informal.

SLIPPERY NOODLES

Food was prepared at any time and could be ordered from outside: grilled chicken, braised duck, lamb's foot, lamb's head, crisp tendons, ginger shrimp, wine shrimp, deer's foot, dried deer meat, sea food, fruit, lettuce, bamboo shoots. Here were small boys in white jackets and scarves, selling spicy pickles from white crocks. Others offered dried fruits, gingko, chestnuts, fresh pears, dried pears, dates; hoops of dried dates, pears and peaches; Chinese apple stuffed with dark plums; plums stuffed with cherries; fried pears, different varieties of pears, pomegranates; Sichuan milk candy, carved sugar lions, rock sugar; olives, varieties of tangerines, longan and lychees, lotus root, sugar cane, dried Chinese apple, dried banana; the seeds of the fruit called 'human face' (because its large seed kernel appeared to have eyes, nose and mouth); hazelnuts, torreya nuts; and other items. Different kinds of buns with lamb filling, pork or lamb in lotus leaf wrappers, roast meats, dried meats, preserved fish and so forth could also be ordered from outside.

At the third-class stores they sold cheap snacks: 'fried fish, duck eggs, stir-fried chicken or rabbit, fried meat, plum juice, soup made with blood, noodle soup and so forth. Each portion cost only 15 coppers.' 'The one feature common to all these kinds of restaurants was their layout. The courtyard was surrounded by small rooms, screened by bamboos, foliage and flowers. With the screens lowered, guests were ensured of privacy when with prostitutes, amidst the laughter and singing.'

Night Life
'Entrances to leading restaurants were always festooned, and only customers were allowed in. Small rooms were on either side of the courtyard, a hundred paces from the entrance. At night the lights were dazzling. Hundreds of heavily made-up prostitutes would be milling about the courtyard, calling loudly to the guests.' The establishment of which the author spoke was located near many shops, connecting to the two Chicken Alleys. Around 1120, a few of these buildings rose to the height of three to five stories, and the upper floors were connected by passageways and bridges. 'Looking up, the lights on the balcony of the restaurant were dazzling. They shone on its carved railings, and on the silk panels and pearly beads covering the doors.' The rooms bordering the verandas that looked down on an inner courtyard had screened windows and curtained doors.

HSIANG JU LIN

The songs and dances were lewd,
Wine quickly changed my mood.
In my youth I lived only for pleasure,
Racing up lantern-bright stairs in the dark of night.

A Night Market

To reach the night market, leave the old city via the central gate on the south wall. Cross one of the 11 bridges that span the river, then one of the 13 bridges that cross another waterway. Walk south to the night market. You will come across a street stall with meat grilling over embers, and some badger and wild fox jerky. Two stalls sell buns with fillings of goose, duck, chicken, rabbit, tripe, lung or fresh water eel, chicken skin and offal — no more than 15 coppers a piece. The Cao family in their place might be frying lamb, large intestine or jerky; or in winter, they fry once-frozen fish heads. They fry thin slices of meat seasoned with ginger and fermented black beans; viscera and 'red threads' (made of blood and flour); slices of sheep's head and chopped pig's feet, with radishes pickled with ginger.

In summer there were cold drinks flavoured with ground sesame and sugar, sugar sticks; dumplings with snow; dumplings with translucent wrappers; tart quince prepared either as a salty drink or with some medicinal herbs; dumplings with foxnut flour and sugar filling; cold drinks made with mung beans, licorice and snow; lychee jam; salty picked cabbage; dried apricots; tender ginger; asparagus lettuce; mustard pickle, and a kind of pasta. The vendors packed candied fruit and candied lychees, perilla jam, plums and oranges in red baskets.

In winter there was rabbit, first stewed and then roasted; belly pork, wild duck, sliced raw fish; fried dumplings; pig viscera.

So it went on until the third watch, around midnight. And so it continued night and day until the capital city was destroyed.

SLIPPERY NOODLES

NOTES

Opening paragraphs: *Reminiscences of the Eastern Capital* [*Dong jing meng hua lu* 東京夢華錄 by Meng Yuanlao 孟元老 (fl 1126-1147), ch. 2, pp. 1- 2] References to this source are hereafter abbreviated [MY: chapter, page(s)]

Eastern capital: Dong jing 東京, also known as Kaifeng 開封 or Bianjing 汴京, was the only capital of the Song dynasty until its fall in 1126.

The city: (plan) Wai cheng 外城, He dao 河道 [MY:1,1-4]

The author: [MY: preface]

Invaders: (the Jurchen) Nu zhen 女真, a foreign people based in Manchuria, later known as the Manchus

Urban scenes: (temple) Xiang guo si wan zing jiao yi 相國寺萬姓交易[MY:3,3-4]; (gold and silver exchange) Jin yin jiao yi suo 金銀交易所 [MY:2,5]; (fire prevention) Fang huo 防火 [MY:3,8]; ('devil's market') Gui shi zi 鬼市子 [MY:2,6]; (chicken alley) Ji er xiang 雞兒巷 [MY:2,7]; (pharmacies) Yi pu 醫鋪 [MY:3,1]

Daybreak: Tian xiao zhu ren ru shi 天曉諸人入市 [MY:3,8-9]; (meat market) Rou hang 肉行 [MY:4,6]; (fish market) Yu hang 魚行 [MY:4,7]; (bakeries) Bing dian 餅店 [MY:4,6-7]

Quick meals: Shi dian 食店 [MY:4, 5-6]; (foxglove tree bark) Tong pi 桐皮, *Paulownia fortunei*

Wine taxes and yeast sales: (before 1077) [*Wen xian tong kao* 文獻通考 by Ma Duanlin 馬端臨 (1254-1324), ch. 17, p. 14] [*Song shi* 宋史 by Tuoketuo 托克托(1314-1355), ch. 185, pp. 6-7]

Wine stores: (established house) Zheng dian 正店; (bottom stores) Jiao dian 腳店 [MY:2,8]

Restaurants: [MY:2,8-10]

Stir-fry: Chao 炒; Jia's scrambled eggs [6:57,26], yeast cakes [7:64,5]; Sun Simiao [SS;37,3][SS:42,8]

Pufferfish: Ho tun 河魨 or He zhu 河豚, family *Tetradontidae*. (seventh century nutritionist) *Shi liao ben cao* 食療本草 (1984) by Meng Shen 孟詵 and Zhang Dingzhuan 張鼎撰. Beijing北京: Ren min wei sheng chubanshe 人民衛生出版社. p. 102. ('Pufferfish poem') 'Fan rao zhou zuo zhong ke shi he tun yu' 范饒州坐中客語食河豚魚 [*Wan ling ji* 宛陵集 by Mei Yaochen 梅堯臣 (1002-1060), ch. 5, pp.7-8]

Shark or abalone: Jue ming 決明; (differences recognized by Chen Canqui 陳藏器, eighth century) [*Ben cao gang mu* 本草綱目 by Li Shizhen 李時珍(1518-1593), ch. 44, p. 42 annotation] (abalone, modern name) Bao yu 鮑魚 genus *Haliotis*; (shark) Sha yu 沙魚;

141

Rugae: (stomach lining) cheng chang 襯腸

Food items: (lettuce) Wo ju 萵苣, *lactuca sativa*; (gingko) Yin xing 銀杏 or Bai guo 白果, *Ginkgo biloba*; (Chinese apple) Lin qin 林檎, *Malus asiatica*; (milk candy) Sichuan ru tang 四川乳糖; (seed of 'human face' fruit) Ren mian zi 人面子, *Dracontomelon duperreanum Pierre*; (torreya nut) Fei zi 榧子, *Torreya grandis*

Night life: Jiu lou 酒樓 [MY:2,7]

The songs: Bian jing ji shi 汴京紀事 [*Pingshan ji* 屏山集 by Liu Zihui 劉子翬 (1101-1147) and Liu Ping 劉玶, ch. 18, p. 3]

Night market: Zhou qiao ye shi 州橋夜市 [MY: 2,4-5]; (gate and bridges) [MY:1, 2-3]; (asparagus lettuce) Wo ju sun 萵苣笋, *Lactuca sativa, var. augustana*

CHAPTER TWENTY

VAST APPETITES

Hills beyond verdant hills, villa upon villa,
The music never ceases on West Lake.
People are giddy with warm intoxicating breezes,
And they will turn Hangzhou into Kaifeng.

With the north taken by the Jurchen, the Song dynasty rulers renamed their empire Southern Song. The territory it covered was still vast, larger than any of its bordering states including that of the Jurchen. It extended from the Yangtze River to Vietnam. Set on West Lake and rimmed by low hills, the city of Hangzhou was made capital of Southern Song. The city flourished, striving to emulate the style of the old capital city. So strong was the desire to recapture the spirit of Kaifeng, a chronicler of Hangzhou life during the Southern Song period titled his work *A Dream of Kaifeng*. He adopted the distinctive narrative style of *Reminiscences of the Eastern Capital*. Some selections in the previous chapter show how lists were employed to create virtual descriptions of different venues. Night markets were described by itemizing the foods. Restaurant menus seemed to have been copied word for word. The imitator likewise copied entire restaurant menus. He listed the 22 kinds of vegetarian dim sum in one shop. Daily life in Hangzhou was pictured with a list of the sundry goods and services supplied by street peddlers and hawkers; it was four pages long. Another writer used the same narrative style. Street food was described by a list of 41 kinds of cooked food; 42 kinds of sweets and fruit; 17 varieties of pickled vegetable, 7 kinds of rice gruel; 17 kinds of cold drinks; 19 varieties of cakes and 52 kinds of steamed bread and pastry — each item identified by name.

The imitators made their point: Hangzhou was the new Kaifeng. It had acquired the hedonism as well as its urban vitality. Restaurants, eateries, teahouses and wine shops sprang up in the city, catering to every segment of society. For example, some teahouses were for the idle, some for the rich, and there were teahouses that gentlemen did not frequent and other teahouses for gentlemen who sought the company of prostitutes. The populace had a vast appetite for alcoholic drinks in the new capital, as in the old one. 'Everyone drank, in huge quantities. The daily wine tax revenues were in the hundreds of thousands,' a writer recalled, listing over 50 of the best wines for sale.

The General's Banquet

On a night in November 1151, barely two decades after Hangzhou was made the capital, one of the most famous banquets in history took place. The host was a Song general who had fought the Jurchen since Kaifeng fell. He was one of the three great generals of Southern Song. Now 65 years of age, he had earned the many honours and titles conferred upon him. On this night he hosted a feast for the first emperor of the Southern Song dynasty, once a young contender for the throne, now in the 24th year of his reign.

It was a grand occasion. One has only the banquet menu to read, because there is no record of the wines consumed. The banquet was divided into several parts. It started easily enough, with eight kinds of fresh fruit.

Citron - Mandarin Orange - Pomegranate - Orange
White Pear - Snow Pear - Two Varieties of Quince

Twelve kinds of dried fruits and nuts formed the second group of refreshments.

SLIPPERY NOODLES

Dried Lychee ~ Dried Longan ~Fragrant Lotus Root
Torreya Nuts ~ Hazelnuts ~ Pine Nuts
Dried Gingko ~ Slices of Pear ~ Preserved Dates
Lotus Seeds ~ Chinese Apple ~ Steamed Dates

The third group was not intended for consumption. The custom of presenting display pieces that had been part of the Flaming Tail banquet, in the previous dynasty, had been taken further. On this occasion the display consisted of aromatic herbs, seeds, flowers and roots used in traditional medicine.

Fragrant Yellow Chrysanthemums ~ Licorice Flowers~ Cinnabar Balls
Field Mint ~ Costus Root ~ Cloves ~Rangoon Creeper Seeds
Cardamom Flowers ~ Osmanthus Flowers ~ Paishu and Ginseng

Three groups of appetizers followed that were in turn sweet, sour and salty. Fruits and vegetables had been intricately carved or fashioned into stylized leaves and flowers and soaked in honey or sugar syrup.

Carved Plums ~ Bamboo Shoots ~ Winter Melon ~ Quince,
Green Plums ~Ginger & Orange

A dozen fruits and flowers came next. Spicy, tart and salty, they bridged the preceding sweets and the savoury appetizers that were to follow.

Spicy Quince ~ Peppered Plums ~ Spicy Wisteria Flowers
Spiced Cherries ~ Daylilies ~ Perilla-flavoured Crabapple ~ Grapes
Plums with Ginger ~ Two Kinds of Plum ~Pastry ~ Marinated Ginger

Cunningly chosen, the savoury items were mostly the kind commonly sold in the city. Some street foods had acquired nicknames. In the vernacular, 'threads' or 'strings' referred to shreds of flavourful preserved meat. Thin strips of dried meat were called 'abacus sticks' because they looked like the rods on which the beads were strung. 'Tree barks' were pieces of preserved meat resembling thorny spikes of the honey locust tree. 'Shadow puppets' were dried slices of fish or meat fixed on skewers, resembling leather puppets that animated shadow plays.

> 'Strings' ~ 'Tree Barbs' ~ Dried Shrimp ~ Dried Meat ~ Preserved
> Meat ~ Breast (of Pork or Lamb) ~ Freshly Sliced Raw Fish ~Pickles
> ~ Meat with Fermented Black Beans ~ Meat Cooked with Wine and
> Vinegar

Whole fresh fruits followed, many obtained from distant places.

> Imported Grapes ~ Almonds ~ Fresh Kumquats
> Fresh Coconut ~ Small Olives ~ Mandarin Oranges

Cut fresh fruit was offered.

> Sugar Cane ~ Persimmons ~ Slices of Orange ~ Green Oranges
> Golden Kumquats ~ Red Bayberries ~ Guangdong Sour Oranges

Sugar-coated fruits were presented before the meal began.

> Three Kinds of Lychee ~ Pastries ~ Sugar-coated Peach Slices
> Crisp Walnuts ~ Sugar-Coated Date Balls
> Sugar-coated Pear Slices ~ Spicy Grapes
> Sugar-Coated Pine Nuts ~ Rock Sugar Miniatures
> White Sugar-Coated Peach Slices

A writer of the tenth century had said, 'How many flavours can one get from the season's fruits? Fruit lasts at most nine days, but one can use honey, sugar, salt and spices, or ferment the fruit, sun-dry it and cook it as one pleases.' As was the custom, various kinds of fruit were served as foil for the effects of drink.

Drink and Food

The banquet began with 15 entrées, designed to complement the wines. Each course consisted of two dishes, interesting but not arresting, the seasoning kept light. The first course was steamed eggs and sliced kidneys. The second course was grilled chunks of lamb on skewers, accompanied by a thick soup, the first of many.

1. Steamed Quail Eggs	Scored and Sliced Kidney
2. Breast of Lamb (on skewers)	Thick Soup with Crisp Ingredients

The food was not meant to be filling, or the guests would stop drinking. There were just a few bites of lamb tongue, omasum and the feet of suckling pigs.

3. Lamb Tongue (on skewers)	Diced Omasum
4. Suckling Pig Feet (on skewers)	Thick Soup of Quail Eggs

Crunchy omasum and tripe provided different textures.

5. Thin-sliced Omasum	Fried Tripe

The tone of the dinner was elevated as shark was presented in two forms: thin slices served raw, matched to a soup made with the inner lining of its stomach.

6. Thin-sliced Shark	Soup of Stir-fried Shark Rugae

Stir-fried eel and crab introduced a change of pace. The flavour of eel was subtle and sweet; it was bolstered by the complex taste and textures of crab. The soup was made with fat goose cooked with the feet of suckling pigs.

7. Eel Stir-fried with Horseshoe Crab	Soup of Goose and Suckling Pig Feet

Almost everything on this menu could have been ordered in one of the first-class restaurants in the city. Maybe so, but tastes are not described in words. This was better. Crab shells had been filled with crabmeat combined with mandarin orange peel. 'A touch of yellow on the shell, to take with sips of wine.'

8. Crab Stuffed with Orange
   Soup of Lean Breast Meat
9. Shrimp with Pig's Feet
   Stir-Fried Eel, Southern Style

Large lakes near Hangzhou provided a variety of delicious crabs. The 10th course was raw crab lightly seasoned, mixed with tomalley and served in its shell. It was a little something to take as the wine continued to flow. To offset the vast amounts of drink, a sip of crab broth, probably a little salty, would settle the stomach.

10. Seasoned Crabmeat in its Shell
    Mock Clams (made with fish)
11. Choice Delicacies
    Clear Crab Broth

The chefs demonstrated their skills with jellied meat and mock food.

12. Quail in Jelly
    Mock Scallops (made with pig skin)

Once again, a matched pair: shrimp and shrimp soup.

13. Shrimp with Orange
    Soup with Fish and Shrimp

To keep the guests more or less sober, they now were offered heavier soups to settle the stomach. The chef was unafraid to serve the emperor food that common people ate. He served up a thick soup with flour dumplings (called 'cocoons' because they resembled silkworm cases) that was often sold by street vendors. Another soup contained pasta made with lamb's blood and flour, a popular food item in Hangzhou. Refreshing tidbits of cold jellyfish and raw clams accompanied these thick, hot soups. This brought to a close one phase of the banquet.

14. Sliced Jellyfish	'Cocoon' Dumpling Soup
15. Raw Clams	Blood Pasta Soup

Persuasion

Hosts sometimes expressed their hospitality by encouraging or 'persuading' the guests to drink. Food was a tactic to keep them drinking. With the 15 courses completed, a light interlude followed. Five entrées were served with two kinds of steamed bread.

Stir-fried Kidneys	Grilled Omasum	Grilled Quail
Pan-Fried Chicken		Pan-Fried Rabbit

Fruit was presented to signal a break.

The chef's recommendations were the ultimate means of persuasion. This may have been the best part of the feast: the freshest of seafood served raw; or barely grilled but still juicy; or stir-fried for a few seconds, silky oysters, tripe that crunched between the teeth.

Scallops with Tripe	Raw Scallops	Grilled Skewered Crab
Sea Snails Stir-fried with Ginger and Vinegar		Sea Snails with Tripe
Stewed Oysters	Oysters Stir-fried with Tripe	

Comments

The general's feast may be compared to the Flaming Tail banquets that were held in the Tang dynasty. They were likewise for the emperor. The Flaming Tail banquet was a lavish affair with many different courses. The general's banquet achieved elegance because in its way, the menu was spare. The chef had selected the freshest and best of ingredients. Clams, crabs and scallops that could be taken raw were served raw. In his hands stir-frying was an art. The entire process might take no more than a minute or two: a fiercely hot wok, a splash of oil, the sizzle when the ingredients are added, often a momentary ball of fire, a few tosses of the wok, a splash of seasoning and it was done.

The banquet was memorable even in its day. 'How recklessly the rich waste food! I remember the general's feast for the emperor — the fifteen courses, and all the dishes that followed,' a courtier wrote. Yet the style was appropriate for the grand occasion.

According to the same courtier, food prepared for the imperial family was no less sophisticated. The imperial style might be exemplified by a pair of lambs cooked in wine, the taste bolstered with spices and herbs. Yet the cooks knew the grand style should not be displayed every day. Food had to be interesting. A palace cook might prepare fish swim bladder in a peppery soup. The swim bladder was a curious organ, possessed only by some fish like the croaker (filled with gas it enabled the fish to croak).

Then again, the cook might prepare a relatively new food item, bean curd, in a manner that he thought suitable to the palatial surroundings. Bean curd was heated in a thickened rich stock and garnished with the most expensive ingredients. Some might say this presentation was entirely out of keeping with bean curd's lowly origins. Yet the expanding food culture had room for every conceivable style.

NOTES

Opening poem: *Ti Linan di* 題臨安邸 by Lin Sheng 林升 (fl 1174-1189) [*Song shi ji shi* 宋詩記事 by Li E 厲鶚, ch. 56, p. 18]. Linan was an old name for Hangzhou.
A Dream of Kaifeng: Liang 梁 was another name for Kaifeng. [Meng Liang lu 夢梁錄 by Wu Zimou
吳自牧(fl 1270); (restaurants, menu) Fen cha jiu dian 分茶酒店 ch. 16, pp. 4-8; (dim sum) Dian xin 點心, ch. 16, pp. 12-13; (sundries) Zhu se za mai 諸色雜賣, ch. 13, pp. 11-14]
Another writer: [*Wulin jiu shi* 武林舊事 by Zhou Mi 周密 (1232-1298); (food) Shi shi 市食 ch. 6, pp. 8-13; (wines, taxes) Zhu se ming jiu 諸色名酒, ch. 6, pp. 13-15]
The general: Zhang Jun 張俊(1086-1154)
The emperor: Song Gaozong 宋高宗 (r 1127-1162)
General's banquet: *Gaozong xing Zhang fu jie ci lue* 高宗幸張府節次略 by Zhou Mi 周密 [*Shuo fu* 說郛 ed. by Tao Zongyi 陶宗儀, ch. 53b, pp. 28-33]
Fresh fruits: (citron) Xiang yuan 香圓, *Citrus medica*; (tangerine) Zhen gan 眞柑; (pomegranate) Shi liu 石榴, *Punica granatum*; (orange) Cheng zi 橙子, *Citrus sinensis*; (white pear) E li 鵝梨, *Pyrus bretschneideri*; (snow pear) Ru li 乳梨, *Pyrus*

nivalis; (varieties of quince) Ming zha 榠楂 and Hua mu gua 花木瓜, variously given as *Pseudocydonia sinensis* or *Chaenomeles sinensis*

Nuts and dried fruits: (preserved lotus root) Xiang lian 香蓮; (torreya nut) Fei zi 榧子, *Torreya grandis*; (hazelnut) Zhen zi 榛子, *Corylus heterophylla*; (pine nut) Song zi 松子, *Pinus koraiensis, P. armandii*; (gingko) Yin xing 銀杏, *Gingko biloba*; (dried pears) 梨肉; (dried Chinese date, or jujube) 棗圈, *Ziziphus jujuba*; (lotus seeds) Lian zi rou 蓮子肉, *Nelumbo nucifera*; (Chinese apple) Lin qin xuan 林檎旋, genus *Malus*; (steamed dates) Da zheng zao 大蒸棗

Aromatic herbs: (chrysanthemums) Nao zi hua er 腦子花兒; (licorice flowers) Gan cao hua er 甘草花兒, *Glycyrrhiza uralensis*; (cinnabar) Zhu sha yuan zi 硃砂圓子; (field mint) Lung nao bo ho 龍腦薄荷, *Mentha arvensis*; (costus) Mu xiang 木香, *Saussurea costus*; (cloves) Ding xiang 丁香, *Syzygium aromaticum*; (Rangoon creeper) Shi jun zi 史君子, *Quisqualis indica;* (cardamom flower) Suo sha hua er 縮砂花兒, *Amomum xanthoides*; (osmanthus flower) Gong gui hua er 宮桂花兒, *Osmanthus fragrans*; (paishu) Bai shu 白术, *Atractylodes macrosephala*;(ginseng) Ren shen 人參, *Panax ginseng*

Carved fruit: (plum) Mei 梅, *Prunus mume*; (pear) Hong xiao er 紅消兒; (winter melon) Dong gua 冬瓜, *Benincasa hispida;* (green plum) Qing mei 青梅

Spicy-tart-salty: (spicy quince) Xiang yao mu gua 香藥木瓜 ; (peppered plums) Jiao mei 椒梅; (wisteria flowers) Xiang yao teng hua 香藥藤花, *Wisteria sinensis*; (spicy cherries) Qi xiang ying tao 砌香櫻桃, *Prunus pseudocerasus*; (daylily) Qi xiang xuan cao fu er 砌香萱草拂兒; (perilla-flavoured crabapple) Zhi su nai xiang 紫蘇奈香, *Prunus salicyna*; (grapes) Qi xiang pu tao 砌香蒲萄, genus *Vitis*; (ginger-flavoured plums) Jiang si mei 薑絲梅; (plum pastries) Mei rou bing er 梅肉餅兒, Zha si mei bing er 雜思梅餅兒; (marinated ginger) Shui hong jiang 水紅薑

Nicknames: ('threads,' 'strings') Xian 線; ('abacus sticks') Suan tiao 算條; ('tree barbs') Zao jia qian 皂莢鋌 (Chinese honey locust tree, Zao jiao 皂角, *Gleditsia sinensis*); ('shadow puppets') Ying xi 影戲 [*Wulin jiu shi* 武林舊事 by Zhou Mi 周密, ch. 6, p.11]

Savoury snacks: ('threads') Xian rou tiao zi 線肉條子; ('tree barbs') zao jiao ting zi 皂角鋌子, (dried shrimp) Xia la 鰕臘; (dried meat) Yun meng ba er 雲夢㸚兒; (preserved meat) Rou la 肉臘; (breast meat) Nai fang 妳房; (fresh-sliced seafood) Xuan xian 旋鮮; (meat with fermented black beans) Jin shan xian chi 金山鹹豉; (meat prepared with wine and vinegar) Jiu cu rou 酒醋肉; (pickles) Rou gua ji 肉瓜虀

Fresh fruit: (unidentified) Dong feng er 楝蜂兒; (foreign grapes) Pan pu tao 畨蒲萄; Ba lan 巴欖 almond [SIBL 406, 408]; (kumquat) Zi da jin ju, 子大金橘, *Fortunella margarita*; (coconut) Xin ye zi xiang ya ban 新椰子象牙板, *Cocos nucifera*; (olive)

151

Xiao gan lan 小橄欖, *Olea europaea*; (mandarin orange) Yu gan zi 榆柑子, *Citrus nobilis*

Cut fruit: (sugar cane) Gan zhe 甘蔗, genus *Saccharum*; (persimmon) Hong shi 紅柿, *Diospyros kaki*; (sliced orange) Qie cheng zi 切根(橙)子; (green orange) Lu ju 綠橘; (golden kumquats) Jin Ju 金橘; (red bayberry) Zhen yang mei 蔵楊梅, *Myrica rubra*; (unidentified) Xin luo ge 新羅葛;(unidentified) Qie mi dian 切蜜簟; (Guangdong sour oranges) Yi mu zi 切宜母子

Sugar-coated fruit: (lychee pastries) Li zhi gan lu bing 荔枝甘露餅, Li zhi liao hua 荔枝蓼花, Li zhi hao lang jun 荔枝好郎君; (sugar coated peach slices) Lung chan tao tiao 龍纏桃條; (crisp walnuts) Su Hu tao 酥胡桃; (sugar-coated dates) Chan zao tuan 纏棗圈; (sugar-coated pear slices) Chan li rou 纏梨肉; (spicy grapes) Xiang yao pu tao 香藥蒲萄; (sugar-coated pine nuts) Chan song zi 纏松子; (rock sugar-coated lotus seeds) Tang shuang yu feng er 糖霜玉蜂兒; (white sugar-coated peach slices) Bai chan tao tiao 白纏桃條

Fruits: (TG-ZPGC edition, p. 144)

Touch of yellow: Ding gong mo song you mou 丁公 默送蝤蛑 [*Dongpo quan ji* 東坡全集 by Su Dongpo 蘇東坡, ch. 11, p.6]

'Cocoon' dumpling soup: Er se jian er tang 二色蠒兒羹. [*Meng Liang lu* 夢梁錄 by Wu Zimou 吳自牧, ch. 13, p. 14] Blood pasta soup: Xue fen geng 血粉羹 was sold in breakfast shops [Meng Liang lu 夢梁錄 by Wu Zimou 吳自牧, ch. 13, pp. 7-8]

Chef's choices: (scallop) Jiang yao 江蟯; (swimming crab) You mou 蝤蛑, family *Portunidae*; (snails) Xiang lei 香螺; (oyster) Mu li 牡蠣. Ingredients in two dishes are unidentified: Jiang suan jia gong chuan 薑酸假公權 and (Zhang?) ju zha du 蟑蚷煠肚

Courtier's comments: Yu shi pi 玉食批 (S. Song dynasty 1127-1279) [*Shuo fu* 說郛 ed. by Tao Zongyi 陶宗儀, ch. 95a, pp. 14-15]

CHAPTER TWENTY-ONE

BEAN CURD

Tofu Poem
Alone at dawn I face the mill,
Pushing and pulling the endless wheel.
It crushes the beans, they tumble out.
I look up, watching for him to return.

An innovation is usually linked to the time it was introduced, first depicted or cited. But China's culinary history is fragmented and disorderly. Being the 'first' to achieve anything in a setting so far-flung and diverse may be a dubious distinction. The interval between invention and general acceptance often took centuries. No one can be certain when bean curd (*tofu*) was invented. Some say it was around the second century BCE; this might be legend or fact. I think it is legend because many have looked for references to bean curd in the millennium that followed, and nothing has been turned up.

An equally important question can be answered: when did this innovation gain popularity? Making bean curd is a complicated process. It was usually something bought at the market. The gourmet Yuan Mei said with pride, 'At home we are self-sufficient. We have everything, apart from bean curd and fresh meat that we must buy outside.' Given this circumstance, the interval between the invention and general acceptance of bean curd could have been relatively short.

By the tenth century, bean curd could be bought at markets. A scholar of that time had noted, 'When meat was withheld, bean curd was sold in the markets. Local folk called it cut-up lamb.' The preface to the opening poem said, 'The old man who was expecting his errant son's return was named Wang, age 86. He was illiterate. He lived in Jizhou in Suichuan district (in the province of Jiangxi, central China). In the period 990-1003, bean curd was sold in that village.'

Making Bean Curd

To bring fresh bean curd to the market in the morning still warm and fragrant in the wooden frames, it had to be made in the very early hours of the day. The entire process was lengthy and labour-intensive. However the poet Su Dongpo put it simply, 'Beans are cooked to make 'milk', milk congeals to form bean curd.' Soy beans were soaked ahead of time and then ground and strained, producing white liquid called 'milk' that was then boiled. A coagulant was added; it might be vinegar, alum, or the magnesium- and calcium-rich liquor left from crystallization of sea salt (called *nigari* in Japan). The half-set curd was poured into a cloth-lined wooden frame, and weighted down with a heavy wooden cover. The finished product typically bore the imprint of the cloth lining. It had a special fragrance that lasted only a few hours.

Not Just Food

Bean curd products were used for several purposes unrelated to food. In the making of sachets for perfuming clothes, dried herbs were first steamed with a sprinkling of wine and then steamed with soybean milk. These steps probably prevented crumbling or fragmentation of the plant material. The preparation of rosewood chips for flower censers likewise called for steaming the chips in soybean milk.

Pharmacists used bean curd as a carrier for preparing semi-precious stones. For example, pearls that were used in a prescription for chest ailments were first placed inside a cake of bean curd which was then boiled. The curd and pearls were then ground together and mixed with other ingredients, among them gold leaf, ox or buffalo gallstones and camphor. To prepare a tonic, amber was similarly put in a piece of bean curd, boiled five times and ground before mixing with frankincense, myrrh and calomel, among other substances.

A Versatile Food

As food, bean curd seemed to be adaptable to any circumstance. Bean curd was at one time eaten like gluten, dipped in honey. By the thirteenth century bean curd soup and fried bean curd were sold in the food and wine shops of Hangzhou. Bean curd required no chewing, so it was perfect for those who lacked a full complement of teeth. The opening poem was only one of many inspired by the humble food.

Tofu Poem

Man must have meat as he ages. But to a toothless old man, meat of any kind is not soft enough. Bean curd is truly the food for old people.

Beans grow on southern hillsides,
Ground in heavy mills,
Coarse meal turns into white milk.
Soft as butter, sweet as honey,
Bean curd glides down the throat.

In the family, it was enjoyed by both young and old. Bean curd was cheap and nutritious. A modern writer recalled his childhood in a household of eight persons headed by his grandmother, who cooked every meal. They were not rich.

'Grandmother's cooking was made up mostly of vegetables and bean curd. She stewed bean curd with soy sauce, to which she might add tiny dried shrimp or even some bamboo shoots. To vary the flavour of bean curd, she might add beans or fresh chopped vegetables that had been briefly salted, rinsed and then squeezed out. She would reheat left-over vegetables with bean curd, adding some fresh vegetables, a dish that I rather liked because it was better than bean curd cooked with only fresh vegetables.

'Stuffed bean curd made a strong impression on me. Each square of bean curd was cut diagonally. To make a pocket a horizontal slit was made in the long side of the triangle, and seasoned pork was stuffed into it. The bean curd was fried on both sides until nice and golden, and then finished with some soy sauce.'

Exquisite Bean Curd

The reader can best understand bean curd's appeal by turning to the recipes of Yuan Mei. One must skip ahead several hundred years to enter Yuan Mei's world. Many of Yuan Mei's bean curd recipes came from his friends. Bean curd easily absorbed flavours of other ingredients, so it was cooked in the finest of stocks; it could be combined with a host of other ingredients; and its texture could be altered.

> Mr. Yang's Bean Curd was made with blanched soft bean curd and slices of giant abalone cooked in chicken soup. It was finished with some mushrooms and spicy rice wine. The abalone must be sliced very thin, and the chicken soup must be rich.
>
> Mr. Jiang's Bean Curd employed dried shrimp for their exceptional flavour. Remove the outer parts of bean curd and slice each cake into 16 pieces. Dry them a bit and fry them in near-smoking lard. Add a pinch of salt, then turn the slices over. Add a teacupful of sweet wine and 120 large dried shrimp (or 300 small shrimp). Let it stew for two hours, add a small cupful of soy sauce and bring it to a boil, add a little sugar and bring it to a boil. Then add 120 pieces of scallions cut into about 1.8 cm lengths.
>
> Mr. Zhang's Bean Curd was made with bean curd were filled with some finely chopped dried shrimp and simply fried.
>
> Mr. Qing's Bean Curd was similar to the above, but made with softened fermented black beans as the filling.
>
> Prefect Wang's Bean Curd recipe was a gift from the Qing emperor Kangxi to a high official, who gave the imperial chef a thousand taels of silver for the recipe. Prefect Wang's grandfather was one of the official's followers; that is how he got the recipe. Cut tender bean curd into small bits and mix

it with bits of mushroom, pine nuts, watermelon seed kernels, chicken and ham. Drop all the ingredients into boiling chicken stock and cook it until just done. Take the soup with a spoon, not chopsticks.

Frozen Bean Curd (Yuan Mei's recipe) is made with firm bean curd. Let cakes of bean curd freeze overnight and cut them into cubes. Freezing creates many small holes in the curd so it resembles a beehive. Stew pieces of bean curd and the usual ingredients in stock with chicken, ham and fresh meat. Just before serving, remove all the meat, leaving only mushrooms and bamboo shoots.

Bean curd cooked for a long time also acquires the beehive appearance. So use soft bean curd for stir-frying, and old, firmer bean curd for stewing. In summer we cook bean curd with mushrooms. It is delicious. We do not add meat stock because it spoils the fresh taste.

Fermented Bean Curd

Just as milk can be transformed into a wide variety of cheeses by fermentation, bean curd was likewise converted into different products. There are probably as many kinds of fermented bean curds as there are cheeses but they can be grouped simply according to colour: white, red and black. Fermented white and red bean curd were used in cooking, adding their distinctive flavours to make mouth-watering dishes with pig's knuckles or belly pork, or even lending plain bean curd or vegetables their inimitable flavours. They were also used at the table as condiments. White fermented bean curds were the largest group. The finished products were small soft beige-coloured blocks stored in oil, or in a thick liquid that resembled the curd. Just a dab of the curd on the tongue delighted the palate. With its creamy texture and intriguing taste, it was the perfect complement to rice gruel.

Red fermented bean curds were prepared employing a mould that made a brilliant red pigment. These red curds were a specialty of the southern province of Fujian. The complex floral flavour improved the taste of rich meats. For example red condiment was mixed into the filling for barbecued pork buns.

A seventeenth-century cookbook described the making of the white and red condiments by techniques used respectively in central and southern China.

Its author was from central China. His account of how Fujian red fermented bean curd was made was confusingly interspersed with comments how the white curd was made in his native province of Zhejiang. Common to the two methods was the initial process of firming up the bean curd either by weighting it to expel the moisture, wrapping the pieces in absorbent paper or applying ashes, followed by steaming the pieces of curd.

The two-step procedure followed that was different for red and white curds. Step 1 was mould growth: long filaments formed fuzzy coats on the curd. Step 2 was fermentation in a briny liquid. (Some of the various moulds active in these steps are given under Notes.) Depending on how these two steps were carried out and whether the red mould was employed, the product was either red or white. The procedures following the initial process are given below, separately.

Fujian Fermented Red Bean Curd
Step 1: The steamed curd is set outdoors to dry in the breeze. The white moulds that forms on the curd is wiped off; in time it would turn turn black or pale red. Step 2: For every 10 L of curd, mix together 1.8 kg soy sauce, 600 g salt, 300 g red rice mould, plus fennel, ground Sichuan pepper and licorice, and wine. Add this mixture to the bean curd and seal the jar with mud.

White Fermented Bean Curd
Step 1: While the steamed curd is still hot, place the pieces on rice stalks, and covered them with rice chaff. When the white mould has formed in 5-6 days, press it into the curd for better flavour. Step 2: Rub salt into each piece of curd and lay them in a basin, alternating layers of curd and salt. Brine is formed. By day sun-dry the curd; put them back in the brine at night. This is repeated until all the brine is used up. Place the curd in a jar, add wine and seal the jar.

In the course of the second fermentation, the beany flavour would be lost. Complex tastes would develop, often modified by other added flavourings such as ginger, star anise, mixed spices, sugar, sesame oil and hot red peppers. The fermented curds would be ready in a month, but it was best to wait half a year.

A Street Food

Some people reserved their enthusiasm for smelly bean curd. Bean curd in its usual form was known over the centuries by several fancy names, but this particular kind of bean curd has never been called anything but 'smelly' or 'stinky.' In the same seventeenth-century cookbook there is another recipe for tofu that calls for 'making it smelly' and then frying the curd in near-boiling oil. 'Its flavour is wonderful,' the author said. The sentiment is shared by many.

Smelly bean is prepared from bean curd that has undergone fermentation in brine. There are many ways of preparing this product. The brine may contain some raw vegetables such as bamboo shoots, cabbage or mustard green. Over a period of days or months, the curd becomes spongy. Even to some of its fans, the smell could be compared to strong cheese that has gone bad. The curd itself might retain its original pale colour inside the fuzzy black coat of mould but with some methods of preparation the inside of the curd may turn dark grey, almost black. Of course, the furry mould was washed off before the curd was deep-fried.

Deep-fried smelly bean curd was usually sold by street vendors. There was never any need to ask where he was. The pungent smells drew customers from the surrounding streets. The vendor would appear around four o'clock in the afternoon, just when some people were ready for a snack. He would arrive, bearing a split bamboo pole on his shoulders, a small stove and cabinet hung at each end. He set up his portable kitchen. The vendor poured oil into a wok and heated it (he also brought his own fuel). The wok had a metal collar around it for draining the fried curd.

An early customer would wait impatiently for the oil to heat. When the first pieces were fried until crusty and golden, the customer added a little of the salty and spicy sauces that were placed on top of the cabinet. When he bit into the juicy interior all his senses of taste and smell were engaged. It was as if nothing else in the world existed. When he had finished eating he dropped a few coins into a hollow in the bamboo pole. The vendor would continue to fry the bean curd until the last piece was gone.

NOTES

Opening poem: Doufu shi 豆腐詩 [*Yin ju tong yi* 隱居通議 by Liu Xuan 劉壎 (b 1240), ch. 10, p. 11]

Self-sufficient: *Sui yuan yi shi* 隨園軼事 (1935) by Yuan Mei 袁枚 (1716-1798). Shanghai 上海: Da da tushu gong ying she 大達圖書供應社, p. 80

Cut-up lamb: Xiao zai yang 小宰羊 in (TG-ZPGC, p.12) Making bean curd: SCC6-5, p. 303

Not just food: [*Chen shi xiang pu* 陳氏香譜 by Chen Jing 陳敬 (Song dynasty 960-1279), (sachets) ch. 3, p. 38; (rosewood) ch. 1, pp. 31-32]

Pharmaceutical uses: (pearls)

Sheng ji zong lu zuan yao 聖濟總錄纂要 by Cheng Lin 程林 and Zhao Ji 趙佶 (1082-1135), ch. 9, p. 19] (amber) [*Ren zhai zhi zhi* 仁齋直指 by Yang Shiying 楊士瀛 (S. Song dynasty 1127-1279) and Zhu Chongzheng 朱崇正 (Ming dynasty, 1368-1644), ch. 20, p. 32]

Dipped in honey: [*Lao shue an bi ji* 老學庵筆記 by Lu You 陸游 (1125-1210, ch. 7, p. 4]

In Hangzhou: [*Meng Liang lu* 夢梁錄 by Wu Zimou 吳自牧, ch. 16, p. 4]

Tofu poem: *Doufu shi* 豆腐詩 in [*Gui chao gao* 龜剿稿 by Xie Yingfang 謝應芳 (1295?-1392?), ch. 17, pp. 74-75]

Grandmother's bean curd: *Tan chi* 談吃 (2006) by Zhang Zhenmei 張振楣. Harbin 哈尔滨: Beifang chubanshe 北方出版社, ISBN 7-5317-2020-5 pp. 66-67

Exquisite bean curd: *Sui yuan shi dan* 隨園食單 (2006) by Yuan Mei 袁枚. Beijing 北京: Zhongguo fang zhi chubanshe 中國織出版社, ISBN 7-5064-4028-8 pp.112-116

Spicy rice wine: Zao you 糟油, sweet rice wine with cloves, cinnamon, Solomon's seal (*Polygonatum odoratum*), angelica and 20 other spices.

Qing emperor: Kangxi 康熙 (r 1622-1722)

Fermented tofu: SCC6-5, pp. 325-328

Online source: *History of Traditional Fermented Soyfoods* by William Shurtleff and Akiko Auyagi http://www.soyinfocenter.com/HSS/fermented_tofu1.php

seventeenth century cookbook: (Fujian fermented bean curd) *Jian fu ru* 建腐乳 in *Shi xian hong mi* 食憲鴻秘 by Zhu Yizun 朱彝尊 (1629-1709), annotated by Qiu Pangtong 邱龐同 (ZPGC, 1985), pp. 61-62

White moulds: Gen mei jun 根黴菌, *Rhizopus chinensis* (a fungus with root like filaments); Mao mei 毛黴, *Mucor sufu* (a fungus lacking such filaments)

Red rice mould: (rice coated with a red mould) Hong qu mi 紅麴米; (red mould) Hong qu jun 红麴菌, *Monascus purpureus*

SLIPPERY NOODLES

Smelly bean curd: Dou fu fu 豆腐脯 in *Shi xian hong mi* 食憲鴻秘 by Zhu Yizun
朱彝尊, annotated by Qiu Pangtong 邱龐同 (ZPGC, 1985), p. 64

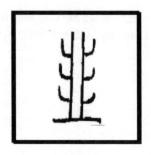

CHAPTER TWENTY-TWO

VEGETARIANS

I saw the animal alive; I cannot bear to see it dead.
I heard its cries; I cannot bear to eat its flesh.

'A gentleman will not step into the kitchen.' A gentleman would not go near anything bloody, and the kitchen was where fish and fowl were killed. These were age-old sentiments, reinforced by the introduction of Buddhism in China. The earliest Buddhist monks were accustomed to 'beg' for their daily food, as Buddha had done. It was common practice for monks to eat whatever was placed in their alms bowls. Although monastic vows did not specify the eating of meatless food, Buddhism forbade the killing of animals for food. It also forbade drinking wine. As centuries passed, rules were often bent.

The man who took the throne in the year 502 was the founder of the Liang dynasty. He had strong Buddhist leanings. He was known for his frugal habits: a vegetarian, shunning fish and meat, taking only one meal a day of vegetable soup and coarse rice. In 527, at the age of 63 he would take the vows of the Buddhist monk. A decade earlier, in the summer of 517 the emperor had issued an edict banning animal sacrifices at the temples, declaring them devilish. He declared that instead temple offerings would consist of flour (bread), vegetables and fruits

Because he saw that Buddhist dietary rules were being violated, the emperor addressed a gathering of 1448 monks and nuns on June 26, 517. 'Respected monks and nuns, learned masters and abbots,' the emperor said, 'the conduct of Buddhist practices should be left to monks, not to the laity. However the scriptures say Buddhist practices are entrusted to the emperor. So I must speak.'

He spoke of the ways in which monks and nuns violated the rule against killing animals for food. 'They might be unrepentant after punishment for such an act. They might declare 'I obey the rules' and eat meat and fish in secret. They might eat meat and fish, saying 'I did not kill it myself' or 'I paid money for it' but paying for meat is the same as butchering the animal. To deceive laymen, a monk might declare 'I am an ascetic; I diligently perform acts of virtue' and then go somewhere to have a drink. Senior monks are known to enjoy wine and meat in the monastery.'

His lengthy declaration banned them from taking meat and wine, on pain of banishment from the sect and rejoining lay society. The emperor stated his philosophy. 'The owl snatches the rat; jackals and wild dogs tear at meat. Man is the wisest of all animals, he is superior to them. He possesses innate kindness. He must not behave like a rank, odorous animal with an urge to kill.'

As for adhering to a vegetarian diet, the emperor said, 'Monks and nuns must have faith. If it is not strong enough they find it difficult. With enough faith, vegetables taste better than manna.'

Vegetarian Food for Common Folk

The emperor's ban was to have wide-reaching effects. One effect was to popularize vegetarianism among people. The Buddhist injunction not to kill animals for food was readily understood, and lay persons could share the compassion for living creatures. Jia's book appeared about two decades after the emperor's ban. It had a chapter on vegetarian cooking, with 11 recipes. Among the directions for making thick vegetable soups, a condiment made with oil and fermented black beans, and rice prepared with fermented black beans was a dish of slippery noodles.

Buttered Slippery Noodles and Rice
Boil 8 L of slippery noodles in 40 L water. Toast 1.2 L of rice
until brown, and boil them with the noodles. Strain everything
through a cloth. Add 400 mL butter; if there is no butter use
800 mL vegetable oil.

Notably, some of the vegetarian dishes contained meat.

Boiled Calabash
Five layers of food are cooked in a copper pot. Cabbage, mallow,
turnips, chives and Chinese spinach form the bottom layer,
topped with slices of boiled pork or lamb; the middle layer is
cucumber or winter melon. The fourth layer is calabash; the top
layer, scallions and fermented black beans.

To Cook Mushrooms
Mushrooms are also called 'chicken of the earth.' They are best
when the white caps just open, revealing the dark underside. If
you have gathered many mushrooms and are thinking of saving
them for the winter, wash them in salt water and dry them in
the sun, facing north.
To cook the mushrooms, first blanch them. Then cook them
with scallions and sesame oil or butter, fermented black beans,
salt and pepper. Mushrooms also go well with fatty lamb, chicken
or pork. If you add meat you can omit the butter. First boil the
meat, slice it and place the slices on top of the mushrooms as
in the calabash recipe above, without the vegetables of course.

'To cook mushrooms or calabash one can add meat or keep it all
vegetarian,' Jia added. 'They are generally considered vegetarian which is why
I have included them in this chapter.' Jia's comments foreshadowed a liberal
attitude toward the inclusion of meat in vegetarian diets.

SLIPPERY NOODLES

Monastery Food

Another effect of the emperor's ban was to improve the food in some monasteries. There was a cook, a monk, so clever he could make dozens of vegetarian dishes using simply gourds, and make each one taste different. In time, certain monasteries would be known for their vegetarian specialties, such as crusty rice with tiny mushrooms, or tender pastries. But some monasteries went their own way. A temple near the capital city of Kaifeng had a cook, also a monk, whose roast pig was so delicious guests at a single table would consume several kilograms of it. People called the temple Roast Pig Court.

A Parallel Cuisine

For many people, the resolve to forego meat and fish was compromised by the desire to taste them. As could be seen from restaurant menus of Kaifeng and Hangzhou, mock foods were popular. They came in many guises — mock turtle, mock scallops, mock wild fox and mock river deer. The cooks used one meat for another (for example, the head of a black lamb to make mock turtle soup). It was but a further step for these cooks to create an array of vegetarian dishes that resembled meat, fish and fowl.

A parallel cuisine developed that mimicked almost all the dishes of traditional cooking using vegetarian ingredients. In the thirteenth century a vegetarian restaurant in Hangzhou that kept to Buddhist dietary rules offered an extensive menu: 'fried eel with noodles,' 'fried puffer fish,' 'a pair of fish,' 'horseshoe crab steamed with lamb,' 'fried bones,' 'fowl on skewers,' 'lamb hoofs' and 'kidneys.' There was also mock lamb offal, mock donkey offal, mock intestine, mock snakehead (a fish) and mock roast duck.

To produce faux food one must know the look, texture and taste of the original. It is a kind of art, exemplified by a recipe for spare ribs in a modern vegetarian cookbook. It called for not only fake meat but fake bone. Lotus root was as rigid as raw carrot and it could be trimmed to resemble bone. Coated with a paste of glutinous rice and wheat flours it would stick when inserted into pieces of gluten, the fake meat. Furthermore, the paste formed a coating that would become crusty when the fake ribs were deep-fried.

There is more than one way to achieve a certain result. According to *The Complete Household Manager*, written during the thirteenth-fourteenth century, faux fried bones were made with milk curds, formed by the addition of a sour liquid (the fermentation product of flour mixed with raw vegetables) to boiled sour milk. The knobby pieces of curd were bony-looking. Coated with seasoned bean flour and wheat flour, they were steamed, cut and deep-fried.

Gluten was the most important stand-in for animal parts. The chapter on vegetarian cooking in *The Complete Household Manager* illustrated how it was used to mimic meat or fish.

Vegetarian lung: Cut cooked gluten to resemble pieces of lung, flavour them with spices. Coat them with bean flour, boil them and serve with the liquid.

Mock eel: Boil some finely cut noodles, rinse them in water and reserve. Boil gluten, coat it with bean flour, and sprinkle with some coloured water (to mimic the colour of eel skin); boil the gluten and cut it fine. Add some condiment and pickle juice and pour it over the noodles.

Grilled meat on skewers: Briefly fry pieces of gluten, add sauce, vinegar, scallions sour milk, etc. and marinate the gluten in it. Fix the pieces on skewers and grill them, painting the gluten with the marinade.

Mock raw fish: Make thin slices of gluten, and sandwich them between thin sheets of 'skin' (made of sweet potato flour or bean flour). Steam them and make thin slices.Cut into slivers, mushrooms, bamboo shoots, turnips, ginger, vegetables and 'skin' that has been dyed red. Season with vinegar and garnish the dish with coriander leaves..

Other foods were faked with jelly made from konjac, a large tuber. Brown konjac jelly was simply cut into strips to simulate jellyfish. There was no mention in *The Complete Household Manager* of some soy bean products that are extensively used in modern vegetarian cooking. Mock ham is made with soy milk skin (the film formed on heated soy milk) that is seasoned, rolled tightly and steamed. Vegetarian chicken is a standard item, made with multiple layers of soy milk skin, seasoned and compressed. Sliced, the cross-section reveals a pattern of fibres resembling that of chicken breast.

Real Meat
Mock foods were one feature that differentiated Chinese vegetarian cooking from its counterparts in other cultures. The presence of real meat in 'vegetarian'

dishes was another. The anomaly in Jia's vegetarian recipes was underscored in *The Complete Household Manager*. Among the 37 vegetarian recipes were six made with animal products. Pig's skin was made into a jelly and cleverly named 'Crystal Meats.' Another was raw lamb, sliced and mixed with bear fat, a combination that pleased the Chinese gourmets.

Mock stir-fried eel was made with lamb. The simulation could be considered successful if one set aside the basic idea underlying vegetarianism. Raw meat pounded to sausage consistency could assume the eel's smooth texture. Raw lamb was pounded, steamed and cut into slivers. Just as with authentic eel, the slivers were stir-fried with black fungus and seasoned with vinegar.

'The Eight Immortals' was a sumptuous dish served with three condiments: mustard, vinegar and a garlic-sour milk sauce. One of the ingredients was shark rugae. It must have added an interesting texture to this extraordinary mélange. 'Cut cooked chicken into slivers. Blanch the rugae and cut it into slivers. If you have no sheep tripe to be cut into fine slivers, use cooked shrimp. Cut sheep omasum into thin slivers, slice some lamb tongue, add slivered marinated ginger, and cut-cut bamboo shoots and lotus root.'

The Eccentric

Some people did not take vegetarian cooking too seriously. There was a gentleman whose outlook on meatless food was the motive behind a little joke he played on his guests. On one occasion he gave them a 20-course meal that consisted mostly of soupy dishes made with grains, vegetables, fruits and nuts. Astonished, a guest asked, 'How did this come about? The smells of smoke and fat are noticeably missing from this food.'

The host, who was a poet, replied, 'I wrote a 16-word verse for each of the 20 courses to enjoy with the food. The first five courses invoke the classics. They are the most important. In case you want to reproduce this meal, you do not have to provide all 20 courses, just five will do. If you can provide some of the last 15 items, fine; if not, never mind.' *The Book of Poetry* speaks of plucking wild clover-ferns. *The Book of Rites* mentions vegetable offerings at the sacrifices. Wild plants were presented to the highest officials, or offered to the spirits. Who says they cannot be served to one's own guests?

HSIANG JU LIN

A Plain Meal

1. Beans (bean curd strips, boiled and seasoned)
'Eat beans, drink water,' so the Rites say.
Only clear water reveals a pool's true depth.
2. Vegetable Soup (all produce from the garden can be made into soups)
Gourds and soups were offered to the spirits.
Guests will receive the same, with due respect.
3. Glutinous Rice Cakes (steamed rice flour puddings, sprinkled with sugar)
The ladies hold dishes of cakes and puddings,
They are getting hungry, awaiting the Gentleman's arrival.
4. Chives (spring chives)
The Odes say: chives were offered at sacrifices.
The ancients must have found their smell agreeable.
5. The Gift of Wheat ('butterfly' noodles, made with wheat flour and water)
6. Yams (the common yam, cooked, sliced, soaked in honey)
7. Lychees (dried Lychee meats, boiled with water)
8. Biscuits (sprinkled with salt and pepper)
9. Silver Pickles (yellow pickled vegetables mixed with ginger and pepper)
10. Dumplings (sugar-filled sorghum flour dumplings in soup)
11. Bamboo Shoots (cooked in soup with pickled vegetables)
12. Lotus Root (raw or cooked, arranged on a dish)
13. Daikon Soup (can be made like thick taro soup)
14. Chestnuts (steamed, doused with honey)
15. Taro (simmered, sliced)
16. Wolfberries (can be added to cakes, pastries or soup)
17. Shepherd's Purse ('Heaven's gift to the mountain-dweller')
18. Mung Bean Flour (made into a thick soup, with ginger)
19. Purple Mushrooms (the kind that grows on trees is best)
20. White Rice (pour good soup over it)
I hear rice being washed and steamed: so-so, foo-foo!
I ask for nothing more than plain white rice.

SLIPPERY NOODLES

The host had given the occasion an elegant veneer, invoking antiquity and the Confucian classics. The first verse referred to the *Book of Rites*, the second cited the *Analects of Confucius*; the third referred to the lady basket bearers of the Celestial Ministry; the fourth and twentieth verses were from odes in the *Book of Poetry*.

'I cannot help but smile,' the eccentric wrote. His guests had proven him right. He had made a mockery of vegetarian food, for the meal was hard to enjoy. 'The guests were not pleased but once past the gate they began to roar with laughter. They laugh at me and I laugh at them. If by some chance this menu were made public the laughter would be endless.'

Such was the makeup of Chinese vegetarian cooking in the centuries following the emperor's ban. Like the cuisine itself, it would undergo further changes.

NOTES

Opening words and first quotation: (DJ13) Mencius 孟子, p. 3; (ctext) Mengzi 孟子, Liang Hui Wang I 梁惠王上

The emperor: Liang Wudi 梁武帝 (r 502-549)

About the emperor: [*Zi zhi tong jian* 資治通鑑 by Sima Guang 司馬光(1019-1086)] Hereafter abbreviated with chapter and pages [SG:chapter,page(s)]. Temple sacrifices [SG:148,25-26]; monastic vows [SG:151,16]; frugal habits [SG, 159,10-11]

Gathering of 1448: *Guang hong ming ji* 廣弘明集 by Shi Daoxuan 釋道宣 (596-667), ch. 26, p. 29

The ban: *Duan jiu rou wen* 斷酒肉文 by Xiao Yan 蕭衍 (Liang Wudi 梁武帝) [*Han Wei liu chao bai san jia ji* 漢魏六朝百三家集 by Zhang Pu 張溥, ch. 80, pp.128-147] ('The owl') ch. 80, p. 136; ('better than manna') ch. 80, p. 145

Jia's recipes: (buttered slippery noodles) Su tuo fan 酥托飯 [9:87, 23]; su 酥 was an alternate word for butter, su 酥; tuo 托 or bu tuo 不托 was an alternate name for bo tun 餺飥 (slippery noodles); (boiled calabash) Fou gua hu fa 瓠瓜瓠法 [9:87,24]; (mushrooms) Fou jun fa 瓠菌法 [9:87,24]

Roast Pig Court: *Hua man lu* 劃墁錄 by Zhang Shunming 張舜明 (N. Song dynasty 960-1126) [*Shuo fu* 說郛 ed. by Tao Zongyi 陶宗儀, ch. 18a, p.21]

Thirteenth century vegetarian restaurant: [*Meng liang lu* 夢梁錄 by Wu Zimu 吳自牧, ch. 16, pp. 11-12]

Modern vegetarian cookbook: *Su cai shi pu da quan* 素菜食譜大全 (1970) by Zhao

169

Zhenxian 趙振羨. Hong Kong 香港: Wei Tung Book Store 匯通書店. (vegetarian spare ribs) Su sheng pai gu 素生炒排骨, pp. 50-51; (vegetarian ham) Su xiang huo tui 蘇香火腿 pp.63-64; (vegetarian chicken) Su ji zhi fa 素雞製法, p. 13

The Complete Household Manager: Ju jia bi yong shi lei quan ji 居家必用事類全集 (Yuan dynasty 1260-1368). Beijing 北京: Shu mu wen xian chubanshe 書目文獻 出版社. Hereafter abbreviated with location and page number(s): (JJBY, section, page(s))

Faux fried bones: (milk curds) gan ru tuan 乾乳團 (JJBY, Geng ji 庚集, p. 164); (mock fried bones) Zha gu tou 煠骨頭 (JJBY,Geng ji 庚集, p. 163)

Gluten: (vegetarian stuffed lung) Su guan fei 素灌肺 (JJBY, Geng ji 庚集, p. 162); Chao shan ru ji tao 炒鱔乳齏淘 (JJBY, Geng ji 庚集, p. 162); Ji fu 炙脯 (JJBY, Geng ji 庚集, p. 163); Jia yu kuai 假魚膾 (JJBY, Geng ji 庚集, p. 164)

Konjac: Ju ruo 蒟蒻, *Amorphophallus kionjac*; (mock jellyfish) Jia shui mu xian 假水 母線 (JJBY, Geng ji 庚集, p. 164)

Real meat: (pig skin jelly) Shui jing leng tao kuai水晶冷淘膾；(lamb with bear fat) Cao jia sheng hong 曹家生紅；(mock stir-fried eel) Jia chao shan 假炒鱔; (eight immortals) Ju ba xian 聚八仙 (JJBY, Geng ji 庚集, p. 162)

The eccentric: *Shu shi pu* 蔬食譜 by Chen Dasou 陳達叟 (twelfth-thirteenth century) *[Shuo fu* 說郛 ed. by Tao Zongyi 陶宗儀; ch. 106a, pp. 5-8)

Classical references: *1. Chuo shu yin shui* 啜菽飲水 (DJ13) Liji 禮記, p. 19; (ctext) Liji 禮記, Tan gong II, 檀弓下, para 172. 20. Shi zi sou sou, Zheng zi fu fu 釋之叟 叟烝之浮浮 (DJ13) 毛詩, p. 69; (ctext) *Shi jing* 詩經, Da ya 大雅, Sheng min zhi shen 生民之什, Sheng min 生民

Menu items: 6. Yams,Yu yan 玉延：(Chinese yam) Shan yao 山藥, *Discorea opposita* 16. Wolfberry, Cai ji采杞: Gou ji 枸杞, *Lyceum chinense* 17. Shepherd's purse, Gan ji 甘薺: Ji cai 薺菜, *Capsella bursa-pastoris* 18. Mung bean flour, Lu fen 菉粉: (mungbean) Lu dou菉豆 or 綠豆, *Phaseolus mungo* 19. Mushroom: Zi zhi 紫芝, *Ganoderma japonicum*

CHAPTER TWENTY-THREE

GENTLEMEN COOKS

On a summer's day I take my guests by boat to see the lotus pond. They pick lotus leaves to tie around the wine jars, and a few more for wrapping the seasoned fish. The sun is blazing, the breezes stifling. By the time we have circled the pond, the fish is cooked and we can smell the wine. It is perfect.

This description of an outing is from a thirteenth-century cookbook by a man named Lin Hong, of whom little is known except that one of his forbears was a recluse. The man had refused to become an official and chose to live in the mountains near Hangzhou, with his books as company, and 'the plum tree his wife, the cranes his children.' He never left the mountains for 20 years. Such a life style and the poetry he wrote eventually earned him recognition from two successive emperors. Most probably the recluse was the inspiration for Lin Hong's cookbook, *The Mountain-Dweller's Fare*.

'Often guests arrive in the morning,' he wrote. 'We first give them some wonton made with Chinese cedrela. Not only is this good for them, but it saves us from having to cook breakfast.' The fragrant leaves of the large tree were edible, and its roots were used in traditional medicine. Lin Hong lived in the mountains. In that setting many cooking ingredients were derived from plants and tubers. The water chestnut was 'sun-dried, and ground. Like the mung bean the starch settles in water and is collected. Water chestnut starch is sweet and smooth, quite different from other starches.' Mung bean starch had many uses. It was often made into sheets of dough, steamed and used as wrappers. Transparent noodles would be made from mung bean flour. Chinese yams were abundant in the area around Hangzhou. They resembled potatoes and 'grew as large as a man's hand', Lin wrote, 'its small flowers are white and furled like small dates, its leaves green. In summer they thrive in brown soil. The tubers are dug up summer and autumn, the whiter the better. Soak them overnight in water with some alum. In the morning wash off the sticky liquid, thoroughly dry them. Mill them into flour. Starch granules are separated from the flour and made into noodles. The starch is poured in a section of bamboo containing some vinegar water. Rinse the noodles to remove the sourness, and boil them as usual. Yams can also be eaten boiled, peeled, sprinkled with some salt or dipped in honey.'

Literary Notes

Lin Hong adopted a lifestyle described by the phrase 'coarse tea and plain rice,' meaning to choose the plain and simple over the ornate and expensive. Lin may have adopted the rural life style, but he was not a peasant. He was one of the first of the gentlemen cooks, highly educated men who on occasion would turn their literary talents to the description of food and drink. Their principal occupation may have that of a civil servant, poet, merchant, artist, or essayist. They cultivated the enjoyment of home, gardens and food. When writing about food and drink, some (like Lin Hong) did not leave behind their scholarship.

Orange Stuffed with Crab

Use a large orange with the stem attached. Cut off the top, remove the pulp leaving behind a little juice, and then fill it with crabmeat and tomalley. Put the top back and steam the orange over a mixture of wine, vinegar and water. Serve it with a little vinegar and salt.

SLIPPERY NOODLES

'This reminds me of lines in the poem in praise of crabs:

The colour yellow is sublime, it occupies the core and extends to the limbs. It is beautiful indeed!

'Actually these words are in *The Book of Changes*. They were embodied in the crab, and now in the orange stuffed with crab.'

Lin Hong assumed the reader was familiar with *The Book of Changes*, the Confucian classic of divination based on 64 hexagrams. The poem referred to the passage in that book explaining the earth hexagram, in which yellow symbolized wisdom. The full passage read: 'The gentleman being yellow at his core knows all. Superior to others, his strength radiates from the core to his limbs; it shows in his conduct; it is beautiful indeed.' The contents of the crab shell are yellow; man has limbs but the crab has even more limbs, so the crab could be said to embody the superior man. To some of the literati the taste of crab may have been enhanced by this link to the classics.

Lin Hong often presented his recipes with a few lines of poetry (often his own) or an anecdote. There was a dish made with lotus seed pods. With the seed head contents scooped out, the pods were empty shells. Fresh mandarin fish, seasoned with spices, some sauce and wine was placed in the shells and steamed. 'I once tasted this at a dinner given by Mr. Li and I composed a poem. Mr. Li liked the poem so much he sent me an ink stone and some fine inksticks.'

The lotus pod in her finery asked,
Why do we make such a fine pair?
The fish replied: Beneath the flowery lake
I twist and turn, like a dragon.

In the Mountains
'My wife cooked a cabbage soup. We thought it was very good,' Lin wrote. His friend Mr. Zheng had a suggestion. 'Mix dill seed, fennel, ginger and ground pepper and put them in a gourd. When you stir-fry blanched vegetables in oil, do not add water. Simply add some sauce and spices and immediately

cover the pan. The fragrance will drift into the mountains.'

Lin once went to a scenic mountainous region in the south to visit a friend. 'It was snowing. Someone caught a rabbit but there was no cook to prepare it. Our friend said, here in the mountains they simply cut the rabbit meat into thin slices, and marinate it for a while in wine, sauce and Sichuan peppercorns. Everyone in our party did as he suggested. We put a brazier on the table, put a pot half-filled with water on it and waited for it to boil. Then each person got a pair of chopsticks. He would immerse it in the boiling liquid for a few seconds, and then dip it into a sauce mixed to his liking. It was not just a simple way to have a meal. Around the table, we shared a kind of enthusiasm.

'Five or six years later, I happened to be in the capital and had hot pot in a friend's home. Suddenly I was reminded of the hot pot in the wintry forest. That was in another world.'

It is perhaps a Chinese characteristic to ascribe different tastes to some features of the natural world. Lin Hong had a recipe for Stone Soup. 'Find a brook with clear water. Pick 10 to 20 small white stones that have some moss attached. Also collect some of the water and boil the stones in it. It tastes sweet as snails. Perhaps, you will also get a hint of the stones.' To the mountain-dweller, the appearance of fiddlehead ferns meant spring. Lin Hong wrote: 'A fine soup could be made using only bamboo shoots and fiddlehead ferns from the mountain.' It seemed to bring to life a certain poem.

> The mountain-dweller sent ferns and shoots.
> I persuaded cook to make the soup
> And I personally fed the kitchen fire.
> Let me bring this soup back to court
> And let those meat-eaters taste this.

Innovations

Lin Hong's book was in some ways a landmark in the history of Chinese cooking. It was probably the first to mention two soybean products: bean curd and soy sauce. He made a thick soup with bean curd and hibiscus flowers and called it 'Rosy Clouds' because it reminded him of the sky after a snowfall. Lin was a great admirer of the poet Su Dongpo who was another gentleman cook. So he prepared Dongpo bean curd, just a simple dish of fried bean curd.

Soy sauce must have been something of a novelty in Lin's time. He used soy sauce mainly as a dressing for vegetables such as chives, or the tender leaves of the day-lily, or a mixture of mushrooms, bamboo shoots and wolfberries. He noted that soy sauce was used in the imperial kitchen to season dumplings. Lin Hong did not cook with soy sauce; for cooking he used 'sauce,' a term that Jia had used for bean paste, but was applied to other seasonings. 'Sauce' could have meant fermented beans in brine, a kind of seasoning known in Lin Hong's time.

The technique of stir-frying was sufficiently novel for Lin Hong to include in his book. It was a new technique and Lin had some misgivings.

'When the poet Li Bo wrote "A flask of fine wine on the table, and the golden chicken on a plate," the chicken was scalded and all the pin feathers were removed. It was boiled in water with sesame oil, salt, scallions and pepper until done, then chopped. The juices were served separately, sometimes mixed with a little wine.

'With this new method the food is stir-fried. The mountain-dweller has doubts about that. He fears the true flavour will be lost.'

No water was used when vegetables were stir-fried. This was an innovation, as Lin noted in his recipe for stir-frying vegetables with spices. 'I recently heard from the general, a friend of mine. He is particularly fond of braised vegetables. He said, 'Do not add water when stir-frying vegetables. Wait until the juices are released, then add the seasoning, cover the wok and cook until done.' He swears the fragrance surpasses that of the best meat.' Stir-frying was the key to blending many different ingredients while retaining their distinctive features. Lin described how vegetarian mock fried meat was made in the Wu family. First, gourd was fried in pork fat until it softened, mimicking the texture of fatty pork. Gluten was deep-fried to mimic lean pork. The illusion was completed when the two ingredients were stir-fried together with scallions, Sichuan pepper oil and wine. Lin Hong said, 'It not only looks like meat, it smells and tastes like meat.'

NOTES

The Mountain Dweller's Fare: This work appears in three collections, two of which I have compared. The first is the ZPGC edition edited by Wu Ke 烏克 (ZPGC, 1985). The second is the SKQS version [*Shuo fu* 說郛 ed. Tao Zongyi 陶宗儀] abbreviated [TZ:chapter, page(s)]. When the texts differ the chosen source is marked with an asterisk.

Opening lines: *Bi tong jiu* 碧筒酒. *Shan jia qing gong* 山家清供 by Lin Hong 林洪. (ZPGC, 1985) p. 96.

Lin Hong's ancestor: Lin Bu 林逋, also referred to as He jing xian sheng 和靖先生 (967-1028). *Zhongguo wen xue jia da cidian* 中國文學家大辭典 (1934) ed. Tan Zhengbi 譚正璧. Shanghai上海: Guangming shu ju 光明書局. Entry 1955. (biography) [*Song shi* 宋史 by Tuoketuo 托克托, ch. 457, pp. 19-20]

'Plum tree': [*Song shi chao* 宋詩鈔 by Wu Zizhen 吳之振, ch. 13, p. 1]

The emperors: *Song Zhenzong* 宋真宗 (r 998-1022); *Song Renzong* 宋仁宗 (r 1023-1063)

Wonton for guests: Chun gen hun tun 椿根餛飩 *[TZ:74a,7-8]. (Chinese cedrela): Xiang chun 香椿, *Toona sinensis*

Water chestnut: Bi chi 荸薺, *Eliocharis dulcis*; (water chestnut flour) Bi chi fen 荸薺粉 [TZ:74a,14]

Mung bean: Lu dou 綠豆, *Vigna radiate*; (Mung bean flour) Lu dou fen 綠豆粉 or Zhen fen 真粉 [TZ:74a,15]

Yam noodles: *Shan jia qing gong* 山家清供 by Lin Hong 林洪. (ZPGC, 1985) pp. 78-79.

Coarse tea and plain rice: Cu cha dan fan 粗茶淡飯 [*Shan gu ji* 山谷集 by Huang Tingjian 黃庭堅 (N. Song, 960-1126), ch. 8, p. 6]

Orange stuffed with crab: Xie niang deng 蟹釀橙 [TZ:74a,19]

In praise of crabs: *Zan xie* 贊蟹 by Wei Zhen 韋稹 (1158-1234) [TZ:74a,19]

The Book of Changes: (earth hexagram) Kun 坤. (DJ13) *Zhou yi* 周易 p.3; (ctext) *Zhou Yi* 周易, Yi jing 易經, Kun 坤, para 13

Lotus and fish: Lian fang yu bao 蓮房魚包 [TZ:74a,19]

Cabbage soup: Man shan xiang 滿山香 *Shan jia qing gong 山家清供 by Lin Hong 林洪. (ZPGC, 1985) pp. 86-88

Hot pot: Pu xia gong 撲霞供 [TZ:74a,16-17]

Stone soup: Bai shi geng 白石羹 *Shan jia qing gong 山家清供 by Lin Hong 林洪. (ZPGC, 1985) p. 65

Fiddlehead fern: Jue cai 蕨菜, an edible variety of bracken (*Pteridium aquilinum*).

(poem) Chen de shan jia sun jue chun 趁得山家筍蕨春 by Xu Fei 許棐 (fl 1239) in [TZ:74a,16]

Bean curd: (rosy clouds soup) Xue xia geng 雪霞羹

Su Dongpo's bean curd: Dongpo dou fu東坡豆腐 [TZ:74a,34]

Soy sauce: The term Jiang you 醬油 appears in *Shan jia qing gong* 山家清供 by Lin Hong 林洪. ZPGC, 1985); (with chives) Liu ye jiu 柳葉韭 (pp. 34-35); (dressing for salads) Shan jia san cui 山家三脆 (pp. 66-67); Wang you ji 忘憂虀 (pp. 98-99); (brake fern dumplings) Shan hai dou 山海兜 (p. 47)

'Sauce': The term Jiang 醬 appears in *Shan jia qing gong* 山家清供 by Lin Hong 林洪. ZPGC, 1985 in the following recipes. (snow pea leaves) Yuan xiu cai 元修菜 (pp. 37-38); (hot pot) Ba xia gong 拔霞供 (pp. 48-49); (fish in lotus pods) Lian fang yu bao 蓮房魚包 (pp. 55-56); (roast duck) Yuan ying zhi 鴛鴦炙 (pp. 81-82); (vegetable wonton) Sun jue hun tun 筍蕨餛飩 (pp. 82-83); (vegetables) Man shan xiang 滿山香 (pp. 86-88); (meat dumplings) Sheng rou jiao 勝肉餃 (pp. 96-97); (preserved burdock) Niu bang fu 牛蒡脯 (p. 104)

Stir-frying: (chicken) Huang jin ji 黃金雞 [TZ:74a,6]; (mock fried meat) Jia jian rou 假煎肉 [TZ:74a,75-77]

CHAPTER TWENTY-FOUR

MADAME WU'S HOME COOKING

Use flour to clean pig tripe, and sugar to clean other innards.
Season bamboo shoots with a little salt and peppermint.
A drop or two of oil rubbed on a fish reduces spattering.
Cook meat with one or two mulberry seeds to make it tender.
Meat cooked with vinegar will last 10 days during the summer.
Do not cook meat over a mulberry wood fire.
Put a bag of charred peas in the wine jar if the wine has soured.

These kitchen tips are from a book written by a woman known only as Madame Wu. She was from an area southwest of Shanghai. She had not much in common with gentlemen cooks. Her book, probably written around the same time as Lin Hong's, was about preserving fruits, vegetables and meats for the home, making good food and sweet pastries. It was a straightforward cookbook with no scholarly asides. It employed some culinary innovations mentioned by Lin Hong, namely soy sauce and stir-frying. (Oddly, bean curd was not mentioned.) Her ways of food preparation were meticulous. She specified how certain ingredients should be cut, because that affected the texture. Her methods were based on observation — how the ingredients looked at a certain stage of preparation. Madame Wu must have derived much pleasure from cooking.

Old Methods, New Ways

The large crocks of bean paste that Jia had described were still used to store raw food, but the selection of foods so preserved was distinctly different: whole fruits such as pears and Buddha's hand (a variety of citron that resembled a hand with many outstretched fingers); citron peel and tangerine peel; chewy gluten, crunchy rock fungus. Their flavours improved with storage in bean paste.

In the lengthy development of soy sauce that was finally developed three centuries later, yellow coat beans, so useful in Jia's time, were fermented in brine and spices were added to it. This was unlikely to be the soy sauce that Madame employed in a few recipes, because it was called yellow coat bean sauce.

'At dawn: in 20 bowls of boiling water dissolve 1.6 kg good quality salt. Let it cool and settle. Place in a large jar: 6.3 kg of good quality yellow coat beans and 10 bowls of sweet rice wine, add and mix in the cooled salt water. Place the jar in the sun for 49 days. Mix 40 g each of star anise and fennel, 20 g each of cardamom, cinnamon, sandalwood, tangerine peel, Sichuan peppercorns and 315 g of dried ginger slivers and almonds. Add the mixture to the jar. Leave it in the sun for two more days, with occasional stirring. Place it in small earthen jars. It will be ready in one year. Dip meat in this sauce.'

'Abacus sticks,' a popular snack in Hangzhou, were a form of preserved meat. Madame Wu made them, laying 10 cm long strips of pork in parallel, rubbing them with a mixture of sugar, Sichuan pepper and cardamom, sun-drying the seasoned meat and steaming it. Granulated sugar was no longer a rarity. It provided a new method for preserving food. 'Use 32 kg large eggplants. Leave the stems on and cut each eggplant lengthwise into six segments. Sprinkle them with 40 g of salt, and then blanch them. Drain off liquid. Add peppermint and fennel, two kg of sugar, half a wine cup of vinegar and leave it for three days. Liquid will form; remove the eggplant and sun-dry the pieces. Soak the eggplant in the liquid again and sun-dry it, as many times as necessary to use up all the liquid.'

Pickles

Pickles were not just a side dish; they were ingredients of many main dishes. Madame Wu's pickles were worthy of attention. They were made by a variety of methods, the simplest of which was applied to bamboo shoots and chives.

Sun-dried Bamboo Shoots

Peel raw bamboo shoots and slice them. Blanch them in salted water and then sun-dry them. To use soften the slices by soaking in water used for washing raw rice.

Salt-cured Chives

Chives are best before the frost, plump, with no yellow tips. Wash them well, let them dry, spread them on a dish, sprinkle evenly with salt; and repeat the layering and salting. After a day or two during which the chives are turned several times, put them in a crock, adding the brine that has formed. A little sesame oil poured over the top makes it better.
Wine dregs were another pickling agent.

Eggplant Pickled in Lees

For 2.2 kg eggplant, use 2.6 kg lees and 470 g salt mixed with 2- 3 bowls of river water. How sweet the eggplant — it requires no cooking at all!

Ginger Pickled in Lees

Use 440 g ginger that is not washed but rubbed clean with a dry cloth. Do not pierce the peel. Partially sun-dry it, and then pack it in a crock with 440g lees and 140 g salt.

Melons Preserved with Yellow Coat Beans

Apply 110 g salt to 440 g melons; after briny juices form, mix in 440 g beans. Stir the mixture twice a day for 49 days and store it in a jar.

SLIPPERY NOODLES

Stuffed Cucumbers

Use large firm cucumbers, sliced in half, with the seeds scooped out. Rub them with salt to draw out the water. Cut fresh ginger, tangerine peel, peppermint and purple perilla into slivers, and mix them with fennel, toasted cardamom and some granulated sugar. Stuff the cucumbers with the mixture, tie the two halves together with string and put them in the sauce crock. After five or six days, take them out and sun-dry them. Then slice them and sun-dry them again.

Madame Wu famously mixed slippery noodles with six kinds of pickled vegetables. The noodles were simply pieces of boiled dough that Jia had described how to make. She coated the noodles with rich sesame seed paste and almond paste, added the chives and the silvery slices of bamboo shoots. She mixed the noodles with eggplant and ginger redolent of wine, crisp pieces of melon and spicy cucumber. 'Adding some fried meat makes it even better,' she suggested. Fried meat was unnecessary but if added, they introduced a different note. This became the classic recipe for slippery noodles, appearing virtually unchanged in cookbooks of the fourteenth, sixteenth and eighteenth centuries.

The recipe for making slippery noodle dough showed insight. She sensed that as the dough was soaked in water, it was changing. She wrote, the dough is manipulated only after 'the flour has fully developed its character.' In more prosaic terms, she waited until gluten had formed in the dough.

Techniques

To Madame Wu, a plain dish of stir-fried cabbage meant that the whole vegetable first had to be blanched until half-done, in order to remove the sharpness of the raw vegetable. Then, it was cut fine and stir-fried in a little oil. After plating it she added a little vinegar. She had a keen sense of timing — how quickly flavours could change! 'Wait a few moments before eating it,' she said, knowing that in those few moments the sweet juices of the cabbage would mingle with the vinegar.

To make crispy-skinned chicken, she used a very high heat. She stir-fried chicken pieces in a little oil, adding vinegar, wine and a little salt. Each piece curled up 'like a spindle' as the liquid evaporated. The addition and evaporation of vinegar and wine was repeated several times until the chicken skin was crusty.

Madame Wu had a singular way of preparing meat. She rubbed soy sauce into thinly sliced raw meat and wiped off the excess. Then she stir-fried the meat in a red hot wok for a few seconds until it just turned white, effectively sealing the bloody juices in the meat. At this point she cut the meat into thin slivers and mixed them with eight other ingredients (pickled melon, pickled radishes, leeks, two varieties of cardamom, Sichuan pepper, tangerine peel, sesame oil). Vinegar was added at the last moment; it was meant to stimulate the palate, not to overwhelm the food.

She had a light touch. To make a salad, she first heated Sichuan peppercorns in sesame oil to bring out the flavour, and let it cool. 'To blanch cabbage, bean sprouts and celery, drop them into boiling water and then plunge them into cold water to keep them green and crisp. Just before serving blot off the water. Mix the oil with soy sauce, vinegar and sugar. Do not add it until last minute and do not stir too much.' This kind of finesse was rare.

Pastry

Cookies called 'thin crisps' could be traced to the eleventh century. Madame Wu made them with white granulated sugar, oil, flour in the proportion of 1:1:4, with water, some butter, salt and pepper. The dough was rolled thin, cut into rounds, sprinkled with sesame seeds, and baked in the oven.

An excellent confection was made by simply combining butter, flour and sugar syrup. Madame Wu was particular, not only about using fresh butter for pastry. 'To prepare flour for sweet pastry,' she wrote, 'Sift it three times, heat it in a large wok, stirring with a wooden paddle. Turn it out on the table, beat it and sift it again.' With this flour she made a kind of biscuit using clarified butter and sugar syrup.

Butter Biscuits

Melt butter in a small pan and strain it through a fine mesh cloth. Add just enough flour so the mixture neither to thin nor too crumbly. Stir it over heat with a small paddle until the flour is cooked. Meanwhile, heat sugar until it spins a thread.

Carefully pour it into the butter-flour mixture and beat until smooth. Turn it out on the board. Roll it out and cut it into elephant eye (diamond) shapes.

Postscript

As far as one knows, Madame Wu was an ordinary woman. She was not well connected, nor did she have literary accomplishments that would have helped to perpetuate her name. Her cookbook survived because in the first instance, it was included in a fourteenth- century anthology, with her name as author. Her book received further accolades of sorts; it was plagiarized at least twice. With identical names and wording, many of Madame Wu's recipes reappeared in another book by a gentleman cook. In the sixteenth century, a playwright copied most of her book without attribution. In this roundabout way Madame Wu's excellent cookbook reached a wide audience, for the playwright's work was popular and his book was reprinted several times.

NOTES

Opening lines: (Kitchen tips) Zhi shi you fa 治食有法 [TZ:95a,24] Source: *Zhong kui lu* 中饋錄 by Wu shi 吳氏 (Madame Wu, late Song dynasty) in the anthology [*Shuo fu* 說郛 ed. Tao Zongyi 陶宗儀] abbreviated [TZ:95a,page(s)]
Age-old practices: Jiang fu shou xiang yuan li zi 醬佛手香櫞梨子[TZ:95a,28]. (Buddha's hand) Fu shou 佛手, *Citrus medica* var. *sarcodactylis*; (rock fungus) Shi er 石耳, *Umbilicaria esculenta*; (yellow coat bean sauce) Shui dou chi fa 水豆豉法 [TZ:95a,34-35]
Preserved food: ('abacus sticks') Suan tiao ba zi 算條巴子[TZ:95a,21]; (eggplant) Tang zheng qie 糖蒸茄 [TZ:95a,26]
Pickles: (bamboo shoots) Shai dan sun gan 晒淡筍乾 [TZ:95a,34]; (chives) Yan yan jiu fa 醃鹽韭法[TZ:95a,32-33]; (eggplant) Zao qie zi fa 糟茄子法 [TZ:95a,28]; (ginger) Zao jiang fang 糟薑方 [TZ:95a,28]; (melons) Pan jiang gua fa 盤醬瓜法 [TZ:95a,30]; (cucumbers) Niang gua 釀瓜 [TZ:95a,26]
Slippery noodles: Shui hua mian fang 水滑面方; ('the fullness of its character') Mian xing fa de shi fen man zu 面性發得使十分滿足 [TZ:95a,38]
Techniques: (cabbage) Bao ji 暴齏 [TZ:95a,29]; (crispy-skinned chicken) Lu bei ji 爐

焙雞 [TZ:95a,21]; (seared meat) rou sheng fa 肉生法 [TZ:95a,22];(salad) Sa ban he cai 撒拌和菜 [TZ:95a,30-31]

Pastry: (thin crisps) Tang bo cui fa 糖薄脆法 [TZ:95a,38-39]; (butter biscuits) Mian he you fa 面和油法 [TZ:95a,36]

Postscript: *Yi Ya yi yi* 易牙遺意 by Han Yi 韓奕 (1328-1412?) ed. by Qiu Pangtong 邱龐同 (ZPGC, 1984) pp. 15, 22, 26-32; [Zun sheng ba jian 遵生八箋 by Gao Lian 高濂, ch. 11, pp. 43-47, 50-52; ch. 12, pp. 1-15]

CHAPTER TWENTY-FIVE

THE MONGOL DYNASTY

In Xanadu did Kubla Khan....

Following history is like looking through a kaleidoscope. At a given moment space (geography) is composed of fragments with different colours and patterns (cultures). Turn the scope (time). Some pieces tumble toward each other producing new colours and patterns while others fall free. While one's attention was drawn to the doings of gentlemen cooks and housewives, major changes were taking place elsewhere. In the twelfth century, invaders from the northeast had succeeded in dividing the Song empire into north and south, claiming the north for their own, establishing the Jin dynasty. Originally nomads, they spoke a language related to Turkish. Because they did not have a written language, the first two Jin emperors of China ordered one to be created. It was swiftly done. The new script had less than a thousand words and resembled Chinese characters. The Jin quickly accepted many Chinese ways, using the existing government structure and adopting Confucian beliefs.

Even with the loss of the north to the Jin, China was vast, a world unto itself. The proximity of a state called Western Xia lying between China and

Mongolia posed no threat. Like the Jin they spoke a different language but it was related to Tibetan. Western Xia too was strongly influenced by Chinese culture. Their royal palaces were built in the Chinese style. Their written language closely resembled Chinese, the words being modelled on the same ideograms, but incomprehensible to the Chinese.

All this changed in the beginning of the thirteenth century when an astonishing force to the west of China emerged. These were the Mongols, led by Genghis Khan. Genghis Khan had started his conquests attacking Western Xia and the Jin. Then the Mongols moved west, overwhelming central Asia, reaching Europe. Twenty years later and nearing the end of his life, Genghis Khan turned again to Asia, obliterating Western Xia and defeating the Jin. There were, then, no buffer states between Mongolia and China. The Mongols invaded lands to their east and south. It was decades before all of China fell to the Mongols. When Genghis Khan's grandson Kublai Khan ascended the throne in 1280 and established the Yuan (Mongol) dynasty, China experienced foreign rule for the first time. Kublai Khan moved the capital back to Beijing. He made a city to its north the summer capital. It was called Shangdu; that was Coleridge's Xanadu. Kublai Khan's aim was to set the Yuan dynasty firmly in the mainstream of China's history. To this end some of his successors became Chinese in many ways. So the two cultures occupied the same space in an uneasy arrangement that held for about a century.

Mongolian Food Culture

In 1258 a Chinese man of Jin descent set down what he had heard about Mongolian food and drink. Perhaps with tongue in cheek, this government official called them 'the eight delicacies, tent style.' He was referring to the Mongolian way of life: on the move with their horses, camels and transportable tents. Food was supplied along the way by 'travelling kitchens,' a term that stood for the attending cook and all matters culinary. One such cook named the delicacies.

1. Clarified butter
2. Fermented mare's milk (known as koumiss, cosmos or airag)
3. Camel hoofs soup

4. Moose lips
5. Rice gruel made with camel's milk
6. Roast swan
7. Black cosmos
8. Red (grape) wine

The government official had a few comments. 'In the deserts of the west where there are salt lakes one occasionally sees some wild camels. They are no different from our domesticated two-humped camels. Their meat is very good. Their hoofs can be made into a superb soup.

'The moose inhabits the north. Its meat has an unusual flavour, the lips are a delicacy.

'Mare's milk is placed in a leather bag and shaken periodically. The taste is sour but drinkable. It is even served on grand occasions. The more the milk is shaken or pounded, the sweeter it gets.'

Koumiss (fermented mare's milk) was weakly alcoholic. William of Rubruck, a monk who had journeyed to Mongolia before Marco Polo went to Cathay, described the taste of koumiss as pungent. A Chinese had this to say about koumiss. 'Mare's milk is too sweet — I cannot drink it. In two or three days it turns very sour. I cannot drink that. Mare's milk wine is only good for making distilled liquor. Distill it several times, until the liquor is very strong.' Black cosmos was a different, more agreeable drink. It was made by churning koumiss until it separated into white solids and clear liquor. The lords drank the liquor. The white solids were given to the slaves.

Chinese Delicacies
The eight delicacies of ancient times were composed of meat and fat. By the Song dynasty, they had been replaced with foods that were more refined in concept and execution, reflecting an elegant style of living. Among the delicacies were roast osprey, bear's paw, rabbit fetus, carp tail and orangutan lips.

The Dyke
Her family lives here in princely style.
The moon hangs behind her: an earring.

Her hair is piled high like clouds,
Tonight we shall tour the grand dyke
And gaze at the fields and river.
I shall dine on carp's tail, and
She will have lips of the orangutan.

The tail of the carp was a delicacy because it had both the fat and the lean. The skin and its underlying fat were bonded to the sweet flesh. The carp's fins were left attached to the tail so that when cooked, juices collected where flesh met the delicate bones.

Rabbit foetus soup was prepared for an empress of the Mongol dynasty; it was cooked with bamboo shoots, surely a Chinese ingredient. This choice might have reflected the Mongols' effort to become as Chinese as possible. At that time the emperor, Kublai Khan's immediate successor to the throne, was engaged in building a splendid palace. Chinese regard foetus as nutritional food. A poem written around 1200 mentions panther foetus soup thickened with rice, served in a rich man's house. The modern practice of preparing foetus in the intact placenta was handed down from those times. In modern Cantonese cuisine there is a clear soup prepared with fresh deer foetus. Only a bulge or two under the placenta's smooth form reveals the presence of the foetus within. It is steamed with dried human placenta, morinda root, lean pork, cooked Chinese foxglove root and wolfberries.

Bear paw was left whole, placed in a cloth bag to preserve its shape during cooking. The correct texture was soft but not overly so, just tender enough to cut with the edge of a spoon. It might be braised in a brown sauce, or served in the clear soup, immaculate in appearance.

Chinese chefs had extraordinary cooking skills. The Mongolian feast was the obvious choice for a rousing drinking session. These two food cultures almost merged at a moment in history.

The Imperial Palace

The year was 1330, a century after Genghis Khan's death. In the capital, the Mongolian rulers had built gorgeous palaces. Curved roofs supported by immense columns gleamed with glazed tiles. Dark interiors were richly adorned with silk, paintings and calligraphy. On the huge grounds there were ponds and lakes spanned by bridges with carved balustrade. In this setting a seventh generation descendent of Genghis Khan became emperor. He was steeped in Chinese culture, taking particular interest in calligraphy and poetry. To bring Chinese culture to the Mongol court this emperor established an academy of scholars. Its greatest achievement was publication of a compendium of laws and statutes intended to guide Mongol rulers in administration of the country.

The Essentials of Nutrition

Among other publications from the academy was a book written by the imperial physician Husihui. A Mongolian by birth, he had been trained in Chinese medicine. Husihui had been at the imperial court since 1315 when he was appointed to serve the empress dowager. Later he was appointed to serve the emperor's wife. Husihui's work was published with all the support a book of that time could get. A ranking academician and co-editor of the compendium of laws wrote an introduction. Husihui dedicated the book to the emperor. 'In antiquity there were physicians, nutritionists and specialists to supervise the emperor's food. Thanks to your indulgence, it has been my duty to oversee your food and drink.' Ironically, the compendium was lost to history while Husihui's book survived.

The Essentials of Nutrition was compact, informative and amply illustrated. Its purpose was to explain Chinese principles of nutrition to the Mongol court. Husihui's approach to this task was adroit. He introduced the subject of Chinese medicine by starting the book with something familiar to his audience — fine foods in the Mongol court. In the second chapter he discussed the principles of diet therapy with recipes handed down from practitioners of Chinese medicine.

The last chapter dealt with edible plants and animals. Here, Husihui characterized each ingredient in the traditional Chinese manner, by their nature, taste and therapeutic uses. He included Mongolian ingredients. Chickpeas (called Muslim beans) were grown in western lands, but now they could be found growing everywhere in China. They were sweet and non-toxic. Although many of the spices used in Mongolian cooking were known to Tang dynasty herbalists, they were not commonly used in Chinese food or medicine. However, these spices had been classified in the Chinese manner.

Fenugreek was named 'bitter bean'; its nature was warming and non-toxic; it relieved stomach distress and bloating. Turmeric, called yellow ginger in Chinese, was described as bitter and peppery. Asafetida was likewise bitter and peppery, its nature was warm and non-toxic; it could rid the body of worms and of noxious elements. A detoxifying tonic was made with fox meat, turmeric and asafetida, further seasoned with vinegar and pepper. This prescription was in keeping with traditional medicine that considered fox meat to be both strengthening and purifying.

In Husihui's time only two spices used by Mongolians were new to Chinese herbal medicine. They had no Chinese names, so their foreign names were rendered phonetically. Husihui described the taste of mastic (a gummy resin) as bitter and sweet; its nature non-toxic; it was detoxifying and it sweetened the breath. Mastic grows in western lands, he added. Saffron was sweet, bland and non-toxic. It was said to be from a red flower that grows in the west but this was unconfirmed, Husihui added. Saffron dispelled melancholy and its prolonged use made the heart glad. Grilled lamb heart flavoured with rose water and a little saffron relieved heart palpitations.

Diet Therapy

The 61 recipes that Husihui presented for treating specific disorders were drawn mostly from Tang and Song dynasty works that spanned seven centuries, up to the Mongol dynasty. Gruels and soups predominated, composed of animal and herbal ingredients that were considered to have therapeutic value. For example, foxglove is a flowering plant, its medicinal value found principally in its root. The juice of the raw root can be taken like a tonic. Broomrape is a plant found in the arid lands of China's northwestern provinces. It consists of a thick stem that may bloom with flowers. A parasite, broomrape draws sustenance from the roots of neighbouring trees. Benefits to the heart and kidneys are attributed to the core of the stem.

The kidneys of lamb, pig and deer were highly valued in Chinese medicine, promoting good health and benefiting the patient's kidneys in particular. Husihui instructed cooks to make the food palatable. Thus, for lamb kidneys, the soup would be seasoned with sauce, salt and scallions. The seasonings for deer kidneys, in addition to fermented black beans, were to be adjusted accordingly. Routinely, the ingredients were cooked in water or wine, the solids were strained out, and the nutrients were taken in liquid or semiliquid form. The recipes were tailored to the type of disorder. For example, the first eight foods were for general debility.

Rice gruel with the juice of *raw foxglove root*, stirred in at the last minute

Rice gruel cooked in the juice of *sour jujubes*

Rice gruel prepared with *meat stock, ground cooked lamb* and mashed *Chinese yams*

Rice gruel prepared in a concentrated stock made with *chopped lamb bones, galangal, ginger* and *cardamom*

Rice gruel prepared in stock made with a pair of *pig kidneys, tangerine peel, cardamom* and *wild Siamese cardamom*

Thick soup prepared with a pair of *lamb kidneys, lamb fat, broomrape, tangerine peel, black pepper, long pepper* and *cardamom*, that was reduced, strained and thickened with pasta

Thick soup prepared with *lamb heart, lungs, liver and kidneys*, packed into a *lamb stomach*, sewn closed and placed in a silk bag; cooked further with *butter, fermented black beans, tangerine peel, galangal, black pepper, long pepperand cardamom*

Decoction prepared with *lamb fat, lamb marrow, honey*, fresh *ginger juice* and raw *foxglove root juice;* taken dissolved in wine, soup or gruel.

Decreased wine output was treated with the following foods:

Egg yolks (up to three) taken raw or cooked

Thick soup made with *Chinese mallow*, whose leaves provided a thickener

Thick soup made with *hog badger* (a small mammal), *rice* and *cardamom*

Thick soup made with *lamb spine, broomrape, long pepper, cardamom* and *rice*

Thick soup or *gruel* made with a pair of *deer kidneys, fermented black beans* and *rice*

Thick soup or *gruel* made with *lamb, daikon, long pepper, galanga* and *rice* or *pasta*

Medicinal Wines

Food was not the only means for nourishing the body. Camel milk was warming, its taste sweet. It fortified man's core and promoted vital energy, strengthened bones and sinews and staved off hunger. Mare's milk was cooling, its taste sweet. But of the fermented drink koumiss, Husihui said not a word.

When Husihui wrote, 'Wine amplifies the effects of medicine, cleanses the body, improves the circulation, helps digestion, smooths the skin and relieves melancholy,' he was speaking about Chinese medicinal and tonic wines. Lamb wine was extremely nourishing. It was also popular and poems were written about drinking it on snowy nights. There were several different ways of making lamb wine (in one version fresh pear juice was added). A later recipe illustrates the fermentation method, carried out with yeast cake and rice, together with cooked lamb.

Lamb Wine

Soak 70 kg of glutinous rice in water and cook it until pasty. Cut four kg lamb into pieces. Boil apricot kernels to loosen the skins and remove the bitterness. Boil 600 g of the blanched kernels and the lamb in a large quantity of water until very soft. To 70 L of the liquid add 37 g of ground costus (an aromatic medicinal root). After it cools, mix in the rice and 500 g of yeast. The sweet clear wine can be consumed after ten days of fermentation.

Other medicinal wines were likewise made with yeast, rice and a medicinal ingredient. Chinese foxglove wine was made by adding an extract of the raw root to fermenting rice; pine knot wine was made with an extract of the crushed wood. Pine knot wine was made by boiling the crushed wood and adding the extract to rice and yeast cake. The mixtures underwent fermentation for five days and then filtered.

Medicinal wines were also made by simply steeping the ingredients in wine. For example, pine root wine was made by immersing the tree root in wine. It strengthened bones and tendons. Tiger bone wine was made with bones that had been buttered, roasted, and crushed. Placed in a silk bag, the bones were steeped in wine for five days. It was taken for joint pain.

To Chinese, this kind of food and drink was comforting and even attractive. To Mongolians, the idea and practice of diet therapy was new, so different was it from the cuisine of the Imperial court.

SLIPPERY NOODLES

NOTES

Opening quotation: *Xanadu – Kubla Khan* by Samuel Taylor Coleridge (1772-1834)

Eight delicacies, tent style: Xing zhang ba zhen shi 行帳八珍 詩 in [*Shuang xi zui yin ji* 雙溪醉隱集 by Yeluu Zhu 耶律鑄 (1221-1285) ch. 6, pp. 3-5]. (travelling kitchen) Xing chu 行廚

Explorer: *The journey of William of Rubruck to the eastern part of the world* (1253-1255), tr. W.W. Rockhill, V, Kumiss. http://depts.washington.edu/silkroad/texts/rubruck.html

Distilling koumiss: *Xiao Daxiang* 蕭大亨 (1532-1612) quoted in [Ge zhi jing yuan 格致鏡原 by Chen Yuanlung 陳元龍 (1652-1736), ch.22, p.15]

Eight delicacies: (osprey) E 鶚, *Pandion haliaetus*; (bear's paw) Xiong zhang 熊掌; (rabbit foetus) Tu tai 兔胎; (orangutan lips) Xing chun 猩唇; (carp's tail) Li wei 鯉尾. Unidentified: Long gan 龍肝, Feng sui 鳳髓, Su luo chan 酥酪蟬. Source: *Luu xi zhe za ji* 呂希哲雜記 [*Tian zhong ji* 天中記 by Chen Yaowen 陳耀文, ch. 46, pp. 89-90], (dating of source) [*Chan hai ji* 蠡海集, Ti yao 提要, p. 1]

The Dyke: Da ti qu 大堤曲 [*Chang gu ji* 昌谷集 by Le He 李賀(791-817), ch.1, p. 5]

Rabbit foetus soup: Yuan shi ye ting ji 元氏掖庭記 [TZ:110a, pp. 33-34]

Mongol emperor and empress: (Borjigin Temur) Chengzhong 成宗 (r 1295-1307); (empress) Jing yi huang hou 靜懿皇后

Panther foetus soup: Ci yun Feng Kongwu xue zhong jian wen ren bo qi tan 次韻馮孔武雪中簡聞人簿乞炭 by Ao Taosun 敖陶孫 (fl 1199) [*Song shi ji shi* 宋詩紀事 by Li E 厲鶚, ch. 57, p. 28]

Deer foetus soup: Shu di he che dun lu tai 熟地河車燉鹿胎 in *Guangdong liang tang: zi bu pian* 廣東靚湯:滋補篇 (2007) by He Guoliang 何國樑. Guangzhou 廣州: Guangzhou chubanshe 廣州出版社.

Other ingredients: (dried human placenta) Zhi he che 紫河車; (morinda root) Ba qi tian 巴戟天, *Morinda officinalis*; (cooked foxglove root) Shu di huang 熟地黃

Bear paw: *Jiangsu feng wei* 江蘇風味 (1986) by Sun Dening 孫德寧. Hong Kong: Wing King Tong Co. pp. 28-30

The emperor: Yuan Wenzong 元文宗 (r 1330-1332)

Academy of scholars: Kuizhang ge xue shi yuan 奎章閣學士院

The Essentials of Nutrition: Yin shan zheng yao 飲膳正要 (1330) by Husihui 忽思慧 (fl 1315-1330). Shanghai上海: Shanghai shu dian 上海書店 (1989); this is a facsimile edition of the version published in 1935 by Shang wu yin shu guan 商務印書館. Hereafter abbreviated (YSZY:page(s)

Dedication: (YSZY: p.3)

Ingredients: (chickpeas) Huihui dou zi 回回豆子, *Cicer arietinum* (YSZY: p. 119);

(turmeric) Jiang huang 薑黄, *Turcuma longa* (YSZY: p. 174). (fenugreek) Ku dou 苦豆, *Trigonella foenum-graecum;* (asafetida) Ha xi ni 哈昔泥, *Ferula assa-foetida* ; (mastic) Ma si da ji 馬思荅吉, *Pistacia lentiscus*; (saffron) Za fu lan 吉夫蘭, *Crocus sativus* (YSZY: p. 176).

Medicinal food: (fox meat, spices) Hu rou tang 狐肉湯 (YSZY: p. 85); (lamb heart, saffron) Zhi yang xin 炙羊心 (YSZY: pp.34-35)

Diet therapy: (broomrape) Rou cong rong 肉蓯蓉, *Cistanche salsa*

Lamb, pig, deer kidneys: (*Shi liao fang* 食療方, by Husihui 忽思慧, ed. by Ren Yingqiu 任應秋 and Wu Shouju 吳受琚 (ZPGC, 1985), pp. 142-151

Mallow: Kui 葵, *Malva verticillata* (*Shi liao fang* 食療方, by Husihui 忽思慧, ed. by Ren Yingqiu 任應秋 and Wu Shouju 吳受琚 (ZPGC, 1985), pp. 114-115

Hog badger: Tuan 猯, *Arctonyx collaris* (*Shi liao fang* 食療方, by Husihui 忽思慧, ed. by Ren Yingqiu 任應秋 and Wu Shouju 吳受琚 (ZPGC, 1985), pp. 164-165

General debility: Xu lao 虛勞. Foods: Sheng di huang zhou 生地黃粥; Suan zao zhou 酸棗粥; Shan yao zhou 山藥粥 (YSZY: p. 86). Yang gu zhou 羊骨粥 (YSZY: p. 82); Zhu shen zhou 豬腎粥 (YSZY: p. 83). Bai yang shen geng 白羊腎羹 (YSZY: p.82). Yang zang geng 羊髒羹; Yang mi gao 羊密膏 (YSZY: p. 81).

Decreased urine output: Xen xu 腎虛, xiao bian bu tong 小便不通. Ji zi huang 雞子黃 (YSZY: pp. 92-93). Kui cai geng 葵菜羹(YSZY: p. 93). Tuan rou geng 猯肉羹 (YSZY: p. 91). Yang ji gu geng 羊脊骨羹 (YSZY: p.82). Lu shen geng 鹿腎羹; Yang rou geng 羊肉羹 (YSZY: p.83)

Lamb wine: Yang gao jiu 羊羔酒 [*Zun sheng ba jian* 遵生八箋 by Gao Lian 高濂, ch.12, p. 36]; (with pear juice) Yang gao jiu 羊羔酒 [*Ben cao gang mu* 本草綱目 by Li Shizhen 李時珍, ch. 25, p.43]

CHAPTER TWENTY-SIX

FINE FOODS AT THE MONGOL COURT

Food for the emperor must be meticulously prepared. Who made it? What ingredients were used? Were the wine cups made of fragrant aloeswood, gold or crystal? Everything is recorded.

True to the Chinese doctor's aim, Husihui was responsible for the health of his patients. To this end, he oversaw the emperor's nutrition. A soup made with leg of lamb was his principal approach to keeping the emperor healthy. The phrase 'nourishes the core, increases vital energy' was frequently used in medicine. It meant strengthening the patient's general health and increasing his vitality. Husihui applied it to the dozens of soup recipes in the first chapter. They usually began with the same instruction: 'Boil a leg of lamb (or two) with a few cardamom seeds to make a soup.' The cooked lamb was set aside and the soup was strained. Sometimes cooked lamb, cut up or made into meatballs, was put back into the soup. Chickpeas often were added as a thickener. Different soups were made with the meat stock, as illustrated by a few selections below.

Thick Lamb Soups

Mastic - With cooked lamb, cardamom, cinnamon, chickpeas
Barley - Add cooked lamb and barley
Indian Style - Saffron, turmeric, pepper, asafetida, daikon, chickpeas
Daikon Greens -With cooked lamb added
Fenugreek - Seasoned with asafetida and salt
Quince - Meatballs, cooked chickpeas, sweetened quince juice
Deer Head - The head was first seasoned with asafetida and fried
Pine Pollen - Cooked lamb breast, ginger juice, coriander
Sugar Cane Juice -Sliced breast of lamb, chickpeas, sugar cane juice
Barley Dumplings - Dumplings made with barley flour and bean flour
Puffer Fish Dumplings - Fried dumplings made with fish, lamb and
citrus peel
Blood Noodles - Made with foxnut flour, soybean flour and lamb
blood
Mixed Soup - Lamb heart, lungs, intestine, with noodles mushrooms,
almond paste, pepper, coriander
Yellow Soup - Meatballs, carrots, turmeric, saffron, ginger
Uighur Style - Tongue, yams, mushrooms, carrots, pickled ginger,
wheat flour dumplings

Clear Broths

Lighter soups were also on the menu. Many of them called for a clear broth. To clarify lamb soup, the cooks added a mixture of chopped raw lamb liver and fermented paste made from wheat flour or soybeans. It picked up all the fine particles and was easily removed. The clear broth was the base for what might be the outstanding dish that Mongol chefs contributed to Chinese cuisine. Carp in lamb broth was an unexpectedly harmonious combination, flavoured with coriander, some ginger, a little wine and three kinds of pepper: Hu (black) pepper, long pepper, and tiny seeds of 'small pepper' ground to a powder.

Pasta was often added to clarified lamb broth.

SLIPPERY NOODLES

Lamb Skin in Broth - Cooked lamb skin, lamb kidneys, tongue, mushrooms, pickled ginger
Barley Pasta Broth - Lamb, lamb liver, pickles, pepper, galanga
Yam Noodles - Noodles made with egg white, cooked yams, wheat-flour and bean flour
Slippery Noodles - With chicken, mushrooms and sliced roast lamb

Colourful Food

The Mongols were fond of colourful food. Chefs made lamb roll with layers of dough and egg and served the tricoloured slices in clear broth together with yams, carrots, pickled ginger and pickles. 'Spring Noodles' was made with lamb broth. Fine-cut noodles were served with the meat of two legs of lamb, a pair of lungs and one lamb stomach, garnished with young ginger, eggs and mushrooms. The spring vegetables were young green cabbages; sprouts of the peppery knotweed; yellow chives whose colour was achieved by shielding the plants from sunlight; and rouge (safflower). It must have been a splendid sight. Husihui considered rouge plants to have some pharmaceutical benefits but in the Mongol court, its principal application was as a food dye.

Saffron and turmeric provided strong yellows. Marco Polo wrote of seeing a vegetable resembling saffron, which serves the (same) purpose. This was probably the fruit of the gardenia, an indigenous plant. A yellow batter was made with bean and wheat flours coloured with saffron and gardenia. Lamb ribs and tendons were fried in this batter.

'Garlanded Lamb's Head' was composed of three lamb heads and four kidneys, garnished with lamb stomach and lamb lungs both dyed with rouge, and decorated with radishes and eggs cut like flowers. 'Hibiscus Chicken' was an entrée, garnished with lamb stomach and lungs dyed yellow and red. Carrots, egg flowers and red-stemmed coriander made it even more colourful and apricot kernel paste poured over all completed the striking presentation.

Fine Foods

It was at this point in the narrative that Husihui withheld his comments on the health benefits of each dish. Facing the best foods the court chefs could produce he was wise enough to remain silent.

Lamb

Lamb Lungs, Western Style (*lungs filled with batter made with chive juice, butter*)
Lamb Tendons (*cooked, coated with yellow batter and deep-fried*)
Lamb Intestines on Skewers (*filled with lamb tail, meat, eggs, seasoning*)
Fried Lamb Patties (*seasoned with asafetida, pepper and coriander*)
Fried Lamb Intestines (*made with salted, air-dried intestines*)
Wraps of Lamb Breast (*mixed with hardboiled eggs and vegetables*)
Cooked Lamb (*mixed with spices, cattail pollen and root, served cold*)
Braised Lamb Heads (*cooked in meat stock with ginger and pepper*)
Raw Lamb Liver (*slivered, dressed with radishes, basil, knotweed and vinegar*)
Spicy Lamb Hoofs (*boiled, chopped, and cooked with spices and noodles*)
Breast of Lamb with Noodles (*braised in stock, stir-fried with noodles*)
Whole Lamb (*roasted in a stone-lined oven covered with willow branches*)

Fowl, Fish and Other Meats

Braised Chicken (*10 fat chickens cooked in chicken soup*)
Quail Stir-fried with Noodles (*with quail soup*)
Stir-fried Rabbit (*with lamb tails and noodles*)
Fried Carp Balls (*made with lamb tail fat, asafetida and tangerine peel*)
Fried Carp (*10 carp, skinned, boned, batter-coated, fried, garnished*)
Wild Geese (*chopped, braised in meat stock and stir-fried*)
Pig Heads (*stewed with tangerine peel, galangal, cinnamon, cardamom and honey*)
Beef Hoofs/Horse's Hoofs/ Bear Paws (*braised in meat stock*)
Stir-fried Carp (*with basil, mustard seeds, daikon, sprinkled with rouge*)
Roasted Wild Goose (*or duck or cormorant, stuffed with lamb tripe*)
Water Fowl (*individually wrapped in butter dough, either oven-roasted or steamed*)

Chinese-Mongolian Food

The palace kitchen was under Mongolian direction, for how would a Chinese cook know the way to season a dish with mastic or asafetida? True enough, but Chinese touches were plain to see. A few Chinese seasonings were used. Lamb was cooked with tangerine peel, whose aroma stood up well to the flavour of the meat. Ginger preserved in wine lees was another good foil for lamb. Two kinds of Chinese sauces were used; both were thick pastes. One was sauce that might have been similar to the bean paste made in Jia Sixie's day. The other, also called simply 'sauce' was probably the flour-based fermented product used as seasoning. Husihui, like other nutritionists of his time, believed these two products would neutralize any toxicity in the food.

The pasta and bread were Chinese. 'Hung' noodles (so-called because they were hung on rods for air-drying) came in varying widths; some noodle dough was strengthened by the addition of alkali or eggs. Hand-rubbed noodles were like slippery noodles except they were flattened into rounds with the palm. Hu cakes, grilled wheat cakes and steamed rolls were called by their Chinese names. Steamed buns were filled with the indisputably Chinese filling of oyster mushrooms.

In the palace setting the two food cultures came together. However, their respective elements were easily teased apart. The palace kitchen prepared the Chinese noodles called red threads, composed of lamb's blood and flour, steamed and cut into strips, and garnished in the Chinese fashion with ginger, radishes, coriander and knotweed. But it was seasoned according to Mongolian taste — vinegar, salt and mustard added with a heavy hand.

The Mongolian version of wonton soup was unfortunate. Whereas Chinese wonton was customarily served in a soup 'so clear it could have been used for grinding ink' (as clear as water), lamb wonton was cooked in lamb soup, thickened with rice, cooked chick peas, and quantities of ginger juice and quince juice.

Carp was skinned, boned and slivered and stir-fried with ginger, scallions, knotweed and radishes. All would have been well had they stopped there, but Mongolians liked colour in their food, so red dye had been sprinkled over the ingredients, giving the dish an unusual look.

The palace kitchen made a Mongolian version of dim sum. Mung bean flour wrappers were filled with a mixture of lamb, lamb's tail, mushrooms, fox nuts, pine pollen, almonds, almond paste, walnuts, pistachios, rouge (the red dye), gardenia fruit (a yellow dye), oil, ginger, yams, eggs and lamb stomach, lungs, and intestines.

As for alcoholic drinks, there was Chinese glutinous millet wine, the grape wine of which Mongolians were fond, and arak, the distilled liquor. Although arak originated in the Mediterranean or Middle East, it had become part of the Mongolian drinking scene. Celebrating a victory in the southern reaches of the Volga, another Mongol ruler 'sat on his Royal throne and presided at the banquets. Wine, koumiss, mead, date wine and arak were handed around in golden cups amidst music and singing.' Traditionally arak is flavoured with aniseed. Husihui described arak simply as a distillate of wine. It was a new item. Outside the palace its preparation involved a makeshift still which is described in the next chapter.

NOTES

Opening lines: Husihui's introduction (YSZY: p. 3). (aloeswood) Chen xiang 沉香, *Aquilaria agallocha*

Thick lamb soups: (nourishes the core, increases vital energy) Bu zhong, yi qi 補中益氣 (YSZY: pp. 19-26)

Uighur style soup: (Uighur name) Shuo luo tuo yin 搠羅脫因 (YSZY: p. 33). The Uighur are one among many Turkic-speaking peoples, located in central Asia and northwestern China.

Soup clarification with raw liver: (garlic shoot soup) Tai miao geng 薹苗羹 (YSZY: p. 28). The sauce, Jiang 醬, could have been soybean-based (dou jiang 豆醬) or wheat flour-based (mian jiang 麵醬) (YSZY: p.121)

Carp in lamb broth: Li yu tang 鯉魚湯 (YSZY: p. 29). (small pepper) seeds of Xiao jiao cao, 小椒草 *Peperomia reflexa*

Slippery noodles: Xi shui hua 細水滑 (YSZY: p. 32)

Colourful food: (lamb roll) Shui long qi zi 水龍碁子 (YSYZ: p. 32); (spring noodles) Chun pan mian 春盤麵 (yellow chives) Jiu huang 韭黃, *Allium tuberosum*; (rouge) Yan zhi 胭脂; Hong hua 紅花, florets of the safflower, *Carthamus tinctorus* (YSZY: p. 30)

Yellow dye: *The Travels of Marco Polo*, by Marco Polo (1254-1324). New York: Signet Classics (1961) ISBN 0-451-52951-0, p. 201.

(gardenia) Zhi zi 梔子, *Gardenia jasminoides*; (yellow batter): Jiang huang jian zi 薑黃腱子 (YSZY: p. 36)

Dyed foods: (lamb's head) Dai hua yang tou 帶花羊頭; (hibiscus chicken) Fu rong ji 芙蓉雞 (YSZY: pp. 36, 37)

Fine foods: (lungs) He xi fei 河西肺, (tendons) Jiang huang jian zi 薑黃腱子, (skewers) Chi er qian zi 豉兒簽子, (lamb patties) Rou bing er 肉餅兒, (lamb intestines) Yan chang 鹽腸, (wraps) Nao wa ci 腦瓦剌, (cold cooked lamb) Pu huang gua ji 浦黃瓜虀, (lamb heads) Zan yang tou 攢羊頭, (lamb liver) Gan sheng 肝生, (lamb hoofs) Ao ti er 熬蹄兒, (lamb with noodles) Ao yang xiong zi 熬羊胸子, (whole roasted lamb) Liu zheng yang 柳蒸羊, (braised chicken) Zan ji er 攢雞兒, (quail) Chao an chun 炒鵪鶉, (rabbit) Pan tu 盤兔, (fish balls) Yu tan er 魚彈兒, (fried carp) Jiang huang yu 薑黃魚, (wild geese) Zan yan , 攢鴈, (pig's head) Ju tou jiang chi 豬頭薑豉, (hoofs) Zan niu ti 攢牛蹄, (fish) Yu kuai 魚膾, (wild goose), Shao yan 燒鴈蔫, (water fowl) Shao shui ja 燒水札 (YSZY, pp. 35-41)

Chinese items: (hung noodles) Gua mian 掛麵 (YSZY: p. 30); (Hu cakes) Hu bing 胡餅 (YSZY: p. 29); (steamed rolls) Cang man tou 倉饅頭 (YSZY: p. 41); (filled buns) Tian hua bao zi 天花包子 (YSZY: p. 43); oyster mushroom 天花, *Pleuratus ostreatus*

Chinese-Mongolian food: (red threads) Hong si 紅絲 (YSZY: p. 41); (wonton soup) Ji tou fen hun tun 雞頭粉餛飩 (YSZY: p. 25); (carp) Yu kuai 魚膾(YSZY: p. 40); (dim sum) Lian he dou zi

荷蓮兜子 (YSZY: p. 43)

Soup as clear as water: (TG-ZPGC. p.32) Arak: *History of the Mongols,* part II, division I (1880) by Henry H. Howorth. London: Longmans, Green and Co., p. 248

CHAPTER TWENTY-SEVEN

OUTSIDE THE PALACE

Fill a squat jar four-fifths full with wine that is sour, sweet or too weak. Put another jar on it, upside down. Make a hole on its side and insert a bamboo tube. Seal the gaps with pieces of broken china, paper twists and a thick coat of lime. Set the whole assembly in a large pot and put hardwood embers around the lower jar. When the wine boils vapours will fill the upper jar and drip down the tube. The liquor collected is one-third the volume of wine.

One turns to *The Complete Household Manager* to learn how people outside the palace lived. This book was published in the Mongol era, author unknown. Next to chapters on education and training of children, marriage and funeral customs, all solidly based on Confucian traditions, there were sections on food and drink. The book's collection of recipes reflected cooking history. The fermentation procedures to make seasoning pastes from beans, flour, raw meat or fish, and methods for preserving vegetables, meat, fish, and eggs were all there. One will search in vain for the lamb leg and cardamom soup made in the palace kitchen. But here was something new, a way of making liquor from wine that was off. 'This is the southern foreigners' method. They call it *aliqi,*' the author added – in other words, arak.

The Complete Household Manager was a mirror of its times, reflecting the society, made up of Chinese and foreigners. It included Mongolian, Islamic and Jurchen recipes, calling attention to the ethnic groups that in its time held power. To govern China, the Mongols had introduced a four-tier caste system that was distinctly unfavourable to the Chinese. Mongols were placed at the top. Below them were Semu, literally 'coloured eyes' but best translated as 'other' in the sense that word is sometimes employed for classifying ethnicities. Semu was made up of those who were neither Mongols nor Chinese. Into this group were placed Muslims, Uighurs, Tibetans, and many others. By one count it included 31 different ethnicities. Northern Chinese (including foreign peoples who lived in north China) were the next lowest. The Jurchen had been in China longer than the Mongols, but they had been defeated by the latter. Formerly they were the highest class, now they were classified with the northern Chinese in the third tier. Southern Chinese were at the bottom.

Foreign Influences
To some extent food choices catered to the Mongols in power. Banquets featured grilled and roasted meats. Meats were skewered, dipped in a mixture of oil, salt, spices, sauces, vinegar and wine, and then grilled over a charcoal fire. They were followed by a whole roast lamb, the signature dish of the Mongolian feast.

> Sliced Lamb, Lamb Ribs, Slices of River Deer and Deer,
> Beef Shoulder, Ring-necked Pheasant, Quail,
> Water Fowl, Bitter Intestine & Hoofs, Liver,
> Kidney, Sliced Tenderloin, Lamb Ears and Tongue.,
> Ground Squirrel and Gerbil Marmot Spleen,
> Lamb Breast, Wild Duck and Wild Goose, *Tutapi* (unidentified),
> Oven-roasted Whole Lamb

The choice of meats and offal reflected Mongolian preferences. Bitter intestines were considered a delicacy. Despite its name that part was said to be the tastiest segment of the small intestine, located just before the 'blind' intestine (the appendix in man). In the palace the dish called fried lamb intestines was made of bitter intestine. Some large rodents were considered good food. Husihui spoke favourably of the marmot, 'Sweet and non-toxic; cooked, it is suitable food for man. Although it has fat, it is not oily; its soup has no taste.' Of the ground squirrel, Husihui had written, 'Its taste is sweet and mild, its nature non-toxic.' Chinese and Mongolian tastes were in several ways not too far apart.

Foreign foods were included in *The Complete Household Manager*. There were a dozen recipes under the heading 'Muslim Food' and half a dozen Jurchen recipes. Another household manual of the same period had similar foreign recipes, including one for Jurchen rice gruel, making a total of seven extant Jurchen recipes from the thirteenth to fourteenth centuries.

Muslim Food

Muslims were the largest group among the Semu — those with 'coloured eyes.' Many had settled in the cities along the Silk Road. Others had arrived on the southern coast of China by sea. From there some migrated inland, so Muslims lived in many parts of China. They continued to observe their culinary traditions, butchering animals a certain way, using lamb and beef but not pork, shunning alcoholic drinks. Muslim restaurants all over China still maintain these traditions.

Most of the Muslim food items in *The Complete Household Manager* had foreign names. In the book they were rendered phonetically into Chinese. For this discussion, the Chinese was rendered phonetically with the English alphabet. In spite of these hurdles, something can be learned from these items.

Pastry

Item 1. She-ke-er-pi-la. Mix 1.3 kg crushed walnuts with 0.63 kg each of honey and crushed qu-luu-che cakes (baked sesame seed-coated cakes) and form little balls with the mixture. Wrap them in small pieces of the same kind of cake. Bake them in the oven until they hold together.

Item 2. Gu-la-chi. Make pancakes with egg white, bean flour and sour milk. Make a filling with walnuts, pine nuts and sugar. Make a stack of 3 or 4 pancakes, with filling between them. Pour chick pea oil over all.

Item 3. Fried pastry rolls. Mix walnuts, pine nuts, peach seeds, hazelnuts, tender lotus seeds, dried persimmons, lotus root, gingko, ripe chestnuts and olives. Add honey and rock sugar. Chop them all fine, except for the chestnuts. Mix in some lamb, salt and ginger. Roll them up in pieces of dough and fry them.

Good enough, but note the inclusion of lotus seeds, lotus root and gingko in item 3. These are Chinese ingredients.

Main Dishes

Item 4. Hai-luo-si. Beat 20 eggs. Cut 1.3 kg of lamb into small pieces and mix it with spices, chopped scallions and sesame seed oil, half a dish each of vinegar and wine, and 80 g of bean flour. Add the eggs, mix well and pour the mixture into a wine jar, seal it and place it in boiling water. After it cools, crack the jar, slice the food and pour butter and honey over it.

The idea of destroying the jar in which food was cooked was impressive. It was something a Chinese cook would never do. Skinless whole grain wheat (shelled wheat) was the identifying ingredient in item 5, the Muslim meat soup resembling porridge; also called *herriseh, keshkeg* or *harissa.*

Item 5. Ha-li-che. Use one bowl of wheat grains. Remove the shells. Cut the meat into slices and cook them with the grains until very soft and thick. Douse it with fat from lamb tail or lamb head. Serve it with grilled pancakes. It is good with pine nuts.

Item 6. Tu-tu-ma-shi. This is like slippery noodles. Make small pellets and soak them in water. Flatten them between the hands and boil them. Stir-fry them, add vinegared meat, or any way you like.

Item 6 was a surprise. The trick of soaking flour dough in water described by Jia Sixie had been taken into a foreign cuisine and given a foreign name. The name tu-tu-ma-shi appears in the context of Muslim cuisine and it is derived from Turkish.

Another household manual of this time gave a fuller version of Muslim tu-tu-ma-shi. 'Mix the dough in usual fashion for slippery noodles. The dough must be smooth and springy. Soak it in water and press it between the hands to make little flat pieces. Boil them and transfer to a plate. Brown pieces of lamb in butter, adding salt, and mix it with some sour-sweet soup. Add some crushed garlic mixed with sour milk, to taste. This is best made with fat from lamb head; next best is butter, third is lamb tail fat. If none of these fats is available use ordinary lamb fat.'

Jurchen Food
The Jurchen recipes are a treasure, for not much is known about Jurchen food. Some terms (such as ta-bu-la) used in the recipes are undefined.

> Jurchen Cold Mallow Soup
> Ta-bu-la Duck
> Braised Ring-necked Pheasant
> Steamed Lamb
> Persimmon Pudding
> Korean Chestnut Pudding
> Glutinous Rice Gruel with Lamb

The cold soup was an elegant dish served in summer. Leafy green Chinese mallow, cucumbers and lamb cut in strips were presented in a deep bowl into which peppery knotweed juice and meat stock was poured. This dish was embellished by the addition of chicken, ginger, bamboo shoots, asparagus lettuce, mushrooms; duck, lamb meat, tongue, kidney, tripe, head, hoofs and skin.

Directions for cooking fowl were explicit. 'Take a large duck, remove the feathers and entrails, and cook it with elm nut paste, meat stock, slivered scallions and whole small peppers that have been stir-fried with oil and cook it until the meat is just done. Chop the duck into pieces being sure to collect its juices. Goose and wild goose are cooked the same way.' Pheasant was braised until tender and then seasoned with bean sauce, knotweed, ground mustard seed and salt. Quail was cooked in the same manner.

Unlike the Chinese the Jurchen did not always use chopsticks. Each person had his knife for cutting meat at the table. A whole lamb, with the head and hoofs removed, was cut into eight pieces. Thyme and fine spices were rubbed into the meat that was marinated overnight with wine and vinegar. Placed on a rack in a wok and steamed, the meat juices fell into the water below making a soup. The steamed lamb was brought to the table as eight large chunks of meat. Each person sliced off a slab of meat with his knife, and took it with a bowl of soup. The use of personal knives to cut meat at the table persisted to the Qing dynasty. Descendants of the Jurchen, the Manchus, tried to perpetuate the custom as part of their culture.

As for the lamb's head, it was cooked until the meat could be removed with the fingers. The soup in which the head was cooked was saved. The slivers of meat were stir-fried in lamb tail fat and sesame seed oil. Glutinous rice was added with the soup. When the gruel and meat were soft and tender pieces of lamb were placed in individual bowls and the gruel was ladled over.

Chinese Food

Mock food was still a favourite with the Chinese. There was mock conch soup (actually, river snails fed duck egg yolks). The raw fish favoured by revellers of old appeared in a new variation. Raw fish cut as thin as silk was presented on an elaborately garnished platter and was doused with hot fish stock; this step took away the rawness without losing the taste of the fish. People were fond of meat: meat to take with wine, meat dishes to take with rice, meat soups. 'Roasted Bones' was the name given to lamb ribs with the skin on, boiled three times, roasted and finally doused with good wine. Pig or lamb spine similar prepared was called by the same name, even river deer or rabbit if they were wrapped in a sheet of lamb fat.

There seemed to be no end to the ingenuity of Chinese cooks. A new kind of noodle appeared — it had holes in it. Raw diced beef or lamb was mixed with uncooked noodle dough. 'When the mixture is dropped into boiling water, the dough will expand and float, the meat will contract and sink.' The pasta that resembled lace or openwork was served in a bowl of meat soup.

The word *mian* means wheat flour or wheat flour noodles, to the exclusion of flour milled from oats, foxnut, sorghum, buckwheat, millet, mung beans, rice, and the different kinds of pasta made from those flours. The special word conveyed the notion that wheat flour was in some way different from other starchy substances (which it is, having the unique ability to form gluten). At this period some cooks added alkali to noodle dough, a practice that appears to be uniquely Chinese. The alkali was sodium carbonate. It caused dough made of wheat flour and water to be slightly gummy but also harder, stronger and more elastic. This culinary trick is still used in making some kinds of noodles.

Another trick was to pummel the dough with the fist, or beat it with a wooden bat or rolling pin. Beating the dough forced moist and drier particles to come together, firming up the texture by compressing the dough instead of kneading it. The directions for making slippery noodles that were quite unlike those before or after this particular time. 'Hit the dough with your fist, slam it 100-200 times and repeat two or three times until the dough softens. Then lay the dough on the board and hit it with a wooden bat over 100 times. If you do not have a bat, punch it with your fist a few hundred more times.' Third, noodle dough was deliberately set aside to rest for a period. Thus, ribbon noodles were made with a little alkali added, they were beaten and then were allowed to rest. 'Use 1.3 kg of the best flour and 80 g each of salt and alkali. Add enough freshly drawn water. Beat the dough 100 times with the bat, and then let it rest for two hours and beat it 100 times again. Roll it out very thin. Cut it into ribbons. Drop them into boiling water, and then into cold water. Flavour it as you wish.'

NOTES

Foreign liquor: (arak) Aliqi 阿里乞. (*The Complete Household Manager*) *Ju jia bi yong shi lei quan ji* 居家必用事類全集. Facsimile edition, Beijing 北京: Shu mu wen xian chubanshe 書目文獻出版社ISBN 7-5013-0584-6/Z.18. p. 141.
Caste system: *A History of Chinese Civilization* by Jacques Gernet, tr. J.R. Foster and C. Hartman. 2nd edition, Cambridge University Press, pp. 368-369
Coloured eyes: Semu 色目 [*Chuo geng lu* 輟耕錄 by Tao Zongyi 陶宗儀 (fl 1360-1368), ch. 1, p. 19]

SLIPPERY NOODLES

Mongolian preferences: *The Complete Household Manager*, p.153

Bitter intestine: Ku chang 苦腸 used in Yan chang 鹽腸 (YSZY: p. 37).

Rodents: (marmot) Ta-lab-u-hua 搭剌不花, genus *Marmota*; (gerbil) Sha shu 沙鼠, *Merionus unguiculatus*, (ground squirrel) Huang shu 黃鼠, family *Sciuridae*

Husihui's comments: (YSZY, pp. 134-135)

Other household manual: *Shi lin guang ji* 事林廣記 (1340) by Chen Yuanliang 陳元靚. (2011) Nanjing 南京: Jiangsu renmin chubanshe 江蘇人民出版社. ISBN 978-7-214-06902-3. (foreign recipes, pp. 343-345)

Muslim food: She-ke-er-pi-la 設克儿疋剌; Gu-la-chi古剌赤; (fried pastry rolls) Juan jian bing 捲煎餅; Hai-luo-si 海螺廝; Ha-li-che 哈里撤; Tu-tu-ma-shi禿禿麻失. *The Complete Household Manager*, pp. 157-158

Tu-tu-ma-shi, derivation: Sabban, F. 1986. Court cuisine in fourteenth century imperial China: Some culinary aspects of Hu Sihui's *Yinshan Zhengyao*. Food and Foodways 1:161-196.

Fuller description: *Hui hui tu-tu-ma-shi* 回回禿禿馬失. *Shi lin guang ji* 事林廣記 by Chen Yuanliang 陳元靚, p. 344

Jurchen food: (cold mallow soup) Si-la kui cai leng tang 廝剌葵菜冷羹; Ta-bu-la Duck 塔不剌鴨;(ring-necked pheasant) Ye ji che-sun 野雞撒孫;(steamed lamb) Zheng yang mei han 蒸羊眉罕; (persimmon pudding) Shi gao 柿糕; (Korean chestnut pudding) Gao li li gao 高麗栗糕. *The Complete Household Manager*, p. 158

Jurchen rice gruel: Nu zhen rou gao mi 女真肉糕糜. *Shi lin guang ji* 事林廣記 by Chen Yuanliang 陳元靚, pp. 343-344

Roasted bones: Gu zhi 骨炙. *The Complete Household Manager*, p. 155

Wheat flour or wheat flour noodles: Mian 面 or 麵

Alkali in noodles: Ong, Y.L., Ross, A.S., Engle, D.A. 2010. Glutenin macropolymer in salted and alkaline noodle doughs. Cereal Chem. 87:79-85.

Noodles: (lacy) Ling long bo yu 玲瓏撥魚; (beaten, slippery) Shui hua mian 水滑麵; (ribbon) Jing dai mian 經帶麵. *The Complete Household Manager*, pp. 158-159

CHAPTER TWENTY-EIGHT

THE INVENTION OF SOY SAUCE

Method for Soy Sauce
To 10 L yellow coat beans, add 6 kg salt (weighed out) and 12 kg water (weighed out). Make it during the dog days. — *Ni Zan (fourteenth century)*

Mongolian rule over China did not hold for long. In the mid-fourteenth century the country was overtaken by turmoil that lasted nearly two decades. Peasant rebellions erupted. When the Mongol emperor was forced to withdraw from Beijing he ordered that its splendid palaces be destroyed. He retreated to Xanadu, and died two years later. The leader of the rebellion was a peasant. He made himself emperor and ruthlessly consolidated his hold on the throne. Thus began the Ming dynasty that was to last 300 years.

The Artist

It was the wrong time for an artist. Caught in the havoc at the end of the Mongol dynasty was a well-known artist named Ni Zan, who was born into a rich family. Ni's style of painting was austere. The paintings of mountains, woods and landscapes were usually devoid of human figures, but they conveyed the intimacy between man and nature. Ni's art was much imitated

SLIPPERY NOODLES

and he had a following. His studio was named Pure Seclusion. According to one biography it contained several thousand books that Ni would personally arrange. Ni was a fastidious man, compulsive about keeping himself clean. 'He would wash his face and hands and shake out his clothes many times in the course of a day. There were some trees and rocks around his studio. Ni would wash and wipe them off. He avoided vulgar people, afraid that he would be contaminated.'

'All was well up to about 1341,' the biography continued. Ni was then about 40 years old. 'Abruptly Ni sold his family's things and gave away all the money. Some people laughed at him. As the soldiers were about to pillage his home, he moved into a boat and headed for the lakes and calm waters.' Although he earned enough money as an artist to support himself, he spent the next several decades without a permanent home, roaming the lakes in his houseboat. He died at the age of 74, just six years after the Ming dynasty was founded.

Ni Zan enters the narrative here, not because he was a painter. He wrote a charming cookbook. In it Ni gave a tip on cleaning the ink stones that were used to prepare ink for painting and writing. 'Use ashes from rice stalks, ordinary ashes, my homemade ashes or the ashes of burnt paper offerings at the temple — they all work well.' Some think such an item does not belong in a cookbook but after all, Ni Zan was an artist.

Ni's recipes were simple, perhaps a consequence of living on a boat. 'It is easy to open the clam if a large sewing needle is first pushed into it,' he wrote. 'Open four or five clams, and place them in a bowl. Drizzle the juices over them and then add some very hot wine. Eat! There is no need for salt, pepper, etc.' He had a light touch with food.

Mr. Conch

Crush the shell and rinse the conch meat very well. Do not use any of the liquid in the conch. Cut the meat in spirals, as if you were peeling a pear, or cut it into thin slices straight across. Blanch it in boiling chicken broth for a few moments.

To make tossed noodles with jellied perch, thin slices of fish were cooked simply by pouring over them some hot stock cooked with swim bladder.

(Swim bladder contains isinglass that like gelatin can form a jelly.) 'Mix the juice of grated ginger, ground Sichuan pepper with vinegar and some sieved bean sauce. Do not add water. Add the jellied fish, some coriander leaves or chopped chives and toss it with a pair of chopsticks. Add boiled noodles that have been rinsed in cold water. Toss everything together.' Ni's recipe for making soy sauce consisted of the 24 words that begin this chapter. As starting material he used yellow coat beans (cooked beans covered with yellow mould that had been sun-dried). He soaked the beans in brine and allowed them to ferment during the hottest days of the summer: the dog days – typically between July 19th and August 18th. Actually, *The Complete Household Manager* had a similar recipe employing freshly made yellow coat beans.

Yellow Bean Sauce

Make this during the dog days of summer. Use yellow or black-skinned soybeans, soaked overnight and then boiled. Drained and cooled, the beans are mixed with flour, spread on mats and covered with cocklebur (the spiky fruit of a wild plant). By the second day the beans are covered with yellow coat. Stir the beans and sun them for at least another day. The proportion of yellow coat beans to salt is 4:1 by weight. Add enough water to cover the beans to the depth of a closed fist. More flour makes the mouldy beans yellower and more sunning improves the flavour.

Ni was not the first to carry out fermentation of yellow coat beans in brine but he was probably the first to call soy sauce by its modern name (*jiang you*). Notably, he removed the beans before using the sauce that he called soy water.

Carp with Soy Sauce

Cut the carp into pieces. Fry ginger and peppercorns in a mixture of sesame and rendered oils, and set them aside. Fry the carp in the hot oil until golden. Remove it from heat for a short while. Add soy water, the ginger and pepper, and bring it to a boil for a second or two.

SLIPPERY NOODLES

Origins of Soy Sauce

It has been said that the origins of soy sauce go back two thousand years because the word 'sauce' goes back that far. That is more of a reach than one might care to make because sauce made with soybeans cannot be traced back that far. In antiquity condiments were made with meat or with vegetables; the soybean was not among them. If the search were limited to products made with soybeans, the history of soy sauce would be shorter. It might include Jia Sixie, who had all the elements for making soy sauce: soybeans, wheat, yellow moulds and salt. The soybean sauces of Jia's time were made by steeping fermented black beans in hot water and by thinning bean paste with wine or meat broth. They were not soy sauce. Eight centuries elapsed before Ni Zan's book appeared. In that interval Chinese Buddhist monks brought a fermented soybean condiment to Japan. The dark brown paste, like the *miso* that was developed centuries later might have been a distant precursor of soy sauce, but these pastes bore little resemblance to the yellow coat beans that Ni used as starting material for soy sauce.

Shortly after Ni Zan, another gentleman cook – a physician named Han Yi – came out with a book that included some notes on making soy sauce. Han Yi was but one among the countless individuals who tried various combinations of soybeans, moulds, wheat and brine, with innumerable adjustments of the duration and temperature of fermentation. Han's notes suggest the failures and incremental advances made over the centuries before the steps to making soy sauce finally fell into place.

Bean Sauce

I used 70 kg soy beans, sunned them, cleaned them and ground off the shells, soaked them until they were swollen and steamed them until soft. When the beans cooled to body temperature, I added about 45 kg of flour, spread them out on reed mats in a layer about 7 cm thick. Yellow coat forms in 3-5 days. I turned the the beans and after 3-4 days, mixed them with 30-35 kg salt, placing them in the jar with enough water to dissolve the salt. More salt was put on top.

If the beans are spread too thin, not enough heat is generated; if too thick, they turn black and smelly. If it rains, raise the cover

213

of the jar so gases can escape, and sprinkle more salt on top.

Han also noted, '*Use more water than usual (to dilute the salt), the beans will settle and the sauce will be on top.*' The step of separating the liquid from the beans on a large scale, instead of doing it in small batches as Ni had described, was important.

The Procedure
A possibly unforeseen advantage was to be gained by separating the fermented liquid from the beans. It enabled the beans to be re-used for further cycles of fermentation in fresh brine. The first complete directions appeared in 1504, describing two batches of soy sauce made from one portion of beans. There were four steps.

Soy Sauce

Boil 100 L of soybeans plus 30 L of red beans and drain them. Add 120 kg of wheat flour to grow the yellow coat, and sun-dry the beans.
For every 3 kg of yellow coat beans, use 1.2 kg salt and 6 kg of water boiled with purple perilla. Place them in a jar under the sun.
Ladle out the sauce and put it in another jar to ferment under the sun, to intensify the flavour.
Make more brine, let it cool and pour it over the beans. Keep the jar under the sun. (In time) more soy sauce can be ladled out.

Like wine and vinegar, soy sauce was home-made. A large quantity of yellow coat beans was made and stored for later use in the first step. A small portion of the mouldy beans was fermented in brine, to be warmed by the sun for weeks or months. In step 3, soy sauce was collected by separating the liquid from the beans. An ingeniously designed sieve was used for this purpose. It was a woven bamboo cylinder about the height of the jar, placed upright in the fermentation jar. Liquid seeped sideways into the hollow of the cylinder, from which it was ladled out and placed in another jar for further fermentation. In step 4, fresh brine was added to the used beans to initiate the second round of fermentation.

In current parlance the first collection was called new brew; it was light brown in colour and had a fresh taste. It was useful for seasoning food without colouring it dark. As the beans underwent two or more rounds of fermentation over a period of months, the sauce turned progressively darker, its taste richer. Later batches of soy sauce were called old brew.

Many Uses

Two or three centuries had passed since Lin Hong first used soy sauce to dress vegetables. Now it was used to make an array of mouth-watering foods.

A bowl of noodles: The noodles were cooked in broth made with chicken or goose (their juices were rich and fatty). To this was added a little pepper, soy sauce, a few drops of vinegar and some scallions.

Shredded beef: Lean beef was seasoned, cooked in a mixture of water, wine, soy sauce and vinegar until the liquid was all absorbed. Cooled, the meat was shredded by hand.

Lamb or goat: The meat was cooked until it fell off the bone, then wrapped in a clean cloth and weighted. The terrine was sliced and served with scallion sauce, or Sichuan pepper oil, or the slices were just placed n the cooking liquid with a little soy sauce added.

Shrimp: marinate large raw shrimp in a mixture of soy sauce and ground Sichuan peppercorn. Serve with vinegar.

Soy sauce came to be a mainstay of Chinese cooking because it was versatile. It could keep raw food tasty. A new class of pickles was created, with cucumbers and melons stored in soy sauce. A few drops of soy sauce added to slivers of raw meat improved the flavour of stir-fried dishes. Fatty meats such as pork, duck and goose were painted with soy sauce (mixed with other seasonings) before roasting and grilling. It was added to stews, lending a deep brown colour to fresh hams. A small amount could be added to fish during cooking, or after frying. The Cantonese dilute soy sauce with water, add a small amount of sugar and pour it over a perfectly steamed fish; they shower it with quantities of slivered raw scallion and fresh ginger, and douse everything with scalding oil, achieving a sublime combination.

Red and White

The vocabulary of the cuisine expanded because of soy sauce's dominant role. The word 'red' (standing for soy sauce) coupled to a second word describing the cooking method meant that soy sauce was used in the cooking. Oxtail could be *red-stewed,* and turtle meat *red-braised.* The latter might entail coating the meat with soy sauce and wheat starch, deep-frying it; then stir-frying with belly pork, and mushrooms, adding more soy sauce, garlic for stewing. *Red-cooked* bean curd was a common dish often made with slices of carrot, bamboo shoots and mushrooms, cooked with soy sauce.

The absence of soy sauce was as noteworthy as its presence. Dishes designated 'white' or 'clear' (likewise coupled to the second word) meant that no soy sauce was employed in the cooking process. *White-stewed* meat balls were delectable, made with pork, pork fat, crab meat and roe, so large only four would fit into a casserole. They were cooked with meat stock and garnished with green leafy vegetables. *White-cooked* pork might consist simply of slices of fat pork rubbed with salt, laid on top of sliced eggplant, cooked in a sealed casserole. Soups might be *clear-steamed* in order to retain the colours of a golden-skinned chicken or silvery fish. *White-boiled* duck's tongues were simply cooked in salted water, and *white-cut* chicken was prepared without a drop of soy sauce. Of course soy sauce might still be used on white dishes because it was placed on the table as a condiment.

NOTES

Opening lines: *Jiang you fa* 醬油法. *Yun lin tang yin shi zhi du ji* 雲林堂飲食制度集 by Ni Zan 倪瓚 (1301-1374) ed. by Qiu Pangtong 邱龐同 (ZPGC, 1984) hereafter abbreviated NZ-ZPGC, page(s) p. 1
Last Mongol emperor: (Togon Temur) Shundi 順帝 (r 1333-1370)
First Ming emperor: Taizhu Zu Yuanzhang 太祖朱元璋 (r 1368-1398)
Biography of Ni Zan: Ni yuan lin xian sheng xiao zhuan 倪雲林先生小傳 [Qing pi ge quan ji 清閟閣全集 by Ni Zan 倪瓚 and Cao Peilian 曹培廉, ch. 11, p. 17]
Ni's recipes: Yun lin tang yin shi zhi du ji 雲林堂飲食制度集 by Ni Zan 倪瓚 ed. by Qiu Pangtong 邱龐同 (ZPGC, 1984). (ink stones) Xiang hui 香灰, (NZ-ZPGC, p. 34); (clams) Han zi 蚶子, (NZ-ZPGC, p. 11); (conch) Xiang luo xian sheng 香螺先生, (NZ-ZPGC, p. 13); (tossed noodles) Leng tao mian fa 冷淘面法, (NZ-

ZPGC, p. 7)

Yellow coat beans: Huang zi 黃子, huang 黃 or jiang huang 醬黃

Yellow bean sauce: Sheng huang jiang 生黃醬. *The Complete Household Manager*, p. 144

Soy sauce: (modern term) Jiang you 醬油 (NZ-ZPGC, p. 1); (soy water) Jiang shui 醬水 (for carp) 煮鯉魚, 又法 (NZ-ZPGC, pp. 22, 23)

Origins: Shurtleff, W., Aoki, *A History of Soy Sauce*, Shoyu and Tamari (2007) http://soyinfocenter.com

Trials: *Yi Ya yi yi* 易牙遺意 by Han Yi 韓奕 (1328-1412?), ed. by Qiu Pangtong 邱龐同 (ZPGC, 1984), pp. 9-10

The procedure: [*Zhu yu shan fang* 竹嶼山房間 (1505) by by Song Xu 宋詡, Song Gongwang 宋公望 and Song Maocheng 宋懋澄 Yang sheng bu er 養生 部 二 , part II] hereafter abbreviated [SX:chapter,page(s)] Xiao mai jiang you 小麥醬油 [SX:1,16-17]. (red bean) Chi dou 赤豆, *Vigna angularis*

Soy sauce: (new brew) Sheng chou 生抽; (old brew) lao chou 老抽

Many uses: (noodles) Ji e fei zhi mian 雞鵝肥汁面 [SX:2,1-2]; (beef) Shu niu ba 熟牛羓 [SX:3,3-4]; (lamb or goat) Peng yang 烹羊 [SX:3,5]; (shrimp) Sheng jiang xia 生醬蝦 [SX:4,17]

Red and white (red-stewed) Hong wei 紅煨; (red-braised) hong men 紅燜; (red-cooked) hong shao 紅燒; (white-stewed) qing dun 清燉; (white-cooked) qing shao 清燒; (clear-steamed) qing zheng 清蒸 (white-boiled) bai zhu 白煮; (white cut chicken) bai qie ji 白切雞

CHAPTER TWENTY-NINE

HIGH ENDEAVOURS AND SMALL PLEASURES

The moon lies beyond the mountain, appearing so small.
So the mountain is larger than the moon.
But if I could see far into the heavens,
The moon would be larger than the mountain.

Improbable as it may seem, this poem was written by an 11-year-old (who became one of the leading thinkers of the sixteenth century). Some events in the period we are about to enter may seem as implausible. One man weighed the therapeutic value of every substance known to traditional medicine, and wrote the classic on Chinese medicinal materials. The Great Wall was rebuilt on its old foundations and extended, stretching thousands of kilometres from the seacoast east of Beijing to the desert far inland. New palaces rose in Beijing, ringed by broad terraces that faced immense open spaces. The surreal city was enclosed by massive walls. The emperor ordered a compilation of everything of value in the literature since antiquity — it was the world's largest encyclopedia. The task of making a second copy was so daunting that it was put off for more than a century.

SLIPPERY NOODLES

Expansion

The Ming emperor, one of the founder's sons, ordered a Chinese Muslim eunuch to explore the seas. Zheng He made seven such voyages over a period of 28 years, on a scale never before attempted. One would not have predicted such a career. He was born to a Muslim family; both his father and grandfather were *hajji*, meaning they had made the pilgrimage to Mecca. His father died in a rebellion. The 10 year-old boy was captured by Ming soldiers, castrated and placed in the service of a royal prince. Zheng distinguished himself in military conflicts. He was 32 years old when the prince gained the throne.

Two years later, Zheng set out on his first naval expedition with 27,800 men and a large fleet, including 62 wooden junks that were 140 meters long. Its purpose was to expand China's presence on existing trade routes. Sailing south to Vietnam, weaving its way around the islands of Indonesia, the fleet entered the vast expanse of the Indian Ocean. It sailed northwest to the Andaman Islands, west to Ceylon and up the southwestern coast of India, arriving in Calicut. The fleet was meant to impress and it did. With four more expeditions over the next decade, 19 nations sent envoys and tribute to the Ming emperor, the great trading centre of Calicut among them.

A Chinese who had converted to Islam was one of the translators on three of Zheng's seven expeditions. He compiled his observations into a book. 'With the winds behind us we left Calicut. It took only 10 days to reach Zufar.' They had reached the southern coast of the Arabian Peninsula; to its east lay the straits of Ormuz, to its west the seaport of Aden; beyond Aden, the way to Mecca. In Zufar the king presented frankincense, myrrh and other substances much valued in Chinese medicine. The Chinese saw a strange animal that lived in the mountains of Zufar. 'The camel chicken has a long neck and looks like a crane, with legs about over a metre long and only two toes on each foot. It walks like a camel. The king sent camel chickens as a gift to our emperor,' the chronicler wrote.

In the city of Aden there were more strange animals. The 'unicorn' had front legs two metres long. 'No man could ride this animal because its body sloped from head to tail. The lion had the body of a tiger, a massive head and a thunderous roar.' The ostrich, giraffe and lion were among the treasures Zheng He's fleet brought back to Beijing.

On the seventh and last expedition the Muslim translator went to Mecca as an envoy. He described arrival at the seaport of Jiddah, a day's journey to Mecca, from there another half-day's journey to the Kaaba mosque that was surrounded by 466 arches supported by 467 white stone pillars. He mentioned the Zamzam spring and the *hajji*. Zheng Ho, the expedition's Chinese Muslim leader, did not go to Mecca. He died on the return voyage.

Small Pleasures

Other aspects of life in the Ming dynasty were played on smaller scales. Literature took new directions. There was no set form for a novel. Some were lengthy epics. One author seemed to have broken new ground in the field of erotic literature. Another would make an anthology of literature that struck his fancy. Many were short pieces — even incomplete fragments, chosen with such perception that they encapsulated an era of Chinese literature.

A few would record every detail of household activities, as if to seize the small pleasures of life. Song Xu was the author of *Bamboo Islet Studio*, a work covering many topics including the raising of animals, the cultivation of trees, potting flowers, and the preparation of food and wine. Song Xu was a member of a family that traced its lineage back to the twelfth century and flourished well into the seventeenth century. Almost every one of its ten or more generations included a noted scholar, poet or official. The founder of the clan was a gentleman who followed the Song emperor to the southern capital of Hangzhou when the north was lost to the Jurchens. For this act of loyalty he was allowed to take the name of the royal house as his surname. Song Xu was four generations removed from the founder and the first to record the family history. It would be extended three more times by later descendants.

The clan had its roots in the Yangtse delta. Song Xu's home was near Shanghai. 'I now live in the southern end of the Yangtse,' Song Xu wrote, 'near sandy estuaries where there are mullet. They do not fear winter's cold and thrive at the river's bottom. Nearby are ponds that have no sand, suitable for raising black or silver carp.'

Had Song Xu not found pleasure in the activities of daily life he would not have recorded them all. 'The honey made by bees here is just as good as that from Fujian and Guangdong,' Song Xu said, referring to the southern provinces.

SLIPPERY NOODLES

Beekeeping

To make the hive, construct a square box with three or four shelves. Place two small bamboo slats at each level to support the shelf. The bottom has a panel that slides out. The back of the box is covered by a fine woven bamboo mat with holes in it just large enough for a bee to pass through. The bees begin to stir in spring, they want to leave the hive and form a swarm. The top of the box is smeared with honey. The bees gather there, but it is sealed shut. Tapers are lit to create smoke and a bundle of mugwort is used to poke them out.

By summer the honeycombs are full. A thin cleaver is inserted into the centre without disturbing the bees, and the honeycomb is wrapped in pieces of strong silk. (After the honey is separated) the comb is heated in water. The melted beeswax is collected by pouring it on to a smooth surface.

Flower Arrangement

To prepare flowers for a vase, first flame the cut end. Select branches that are twisted or winding. They must look natural and have leaves and buds. It is vulgar to put many branches in a single vase. Only plum flowers can be massed together.

Suitability

'What one seeks in drinking tea is purity of taste,' Song wrote 'Fruits and flavourings are unimportant. Lychees, longan and persimmons must never be added. They are too sweet and totally unsuitable.' Suitability was one of Song Xu's favorite words. Applied to food, suitability meant things that belonged together, like shad roe and vinegar. The idea of suitability ran through all of his recipes, even to making candy. He made caramel brittle, 'White granulated sugar is heated in a copper pan with a small amount of water. When the sugar is melted, add the other ingredients, mix them in thoroughly, remove from heat and let the caramel harden a little. Break up the clumps and finish drying the pieces on paper, near heat.' He had made a list of suitable ingredients.

Shelled walnuts, hazelnuts, watermelon seeds, calabash seeds, seeds of the black olive, seeds of the fruit called 'human face,'

the seeds of the bayberry, embryonic lotus shoot, almonds and
seeds of the Chinese parasol tree
Ground chestnuts, lotus seeds, and torreya nuts, tangerine peel
and citron peel, toasted sesame seeds, toasted ground soybeans,
ground purple perilla, three kinds of cardamom, tea leaves,
mint leaves, ginger, osmanthus flowers.

Home Life
Song Xu's book touched on some aspects of women's lives. As was the practice
in wealthy families girls had their feet bound. This practice entailed binding
the feet so that the toes were tucked under, resulting in a hoof- or lotus-like
shape. After years of painful binding, the ideal foot might be only 8 to 10 cm
long, making walking without assistance difficult. Song Xu had a preparation
for keeping bound feet healthy, and another for steadying the much-admired
'golden lotus' gaits that resulted from this practice. He also provided formulas
for dying hair black, preventing greying and stimulating hair growth. For
women, there was face cream with egg and face cream with pearl powder.
For men and women, there were bath scents, deodorants, antiperspirants and
sachets for perfuming clothes.

Song Xu's studio had the usual paraphernalia for writing and painting.
Literary gentlemen chose paper and brushes with care. Ink stones were carved
in different styles from the ornate to the seemingly unadorned. Ink sticks
had raised designs, distinctive shapes and styles that were usually sufficient
to identify the maker. Ink was made by grinding the stick on the stone with
a few drops of water. Everyone knew that black ink was made with soot, but
how many knew that red and yellow dyes went into some formulas? Song Xu
had the method of a famous ink stick maker, who had lived five centuries
earlier.

It was a complicated process, first making the soot, and then combining
it with other substances to make the ink stick

Fine Ink (made according to Li Tinggui)
20 g sappanwood (the source of a red dye)
32 g golden thread (a medicinal plant, the source of a yellow dye)
26 g apricot kernels

These three items were crushed, pounded and heated with 8.6 kg of sesame oil, filtered and mixed with 4.6 kg of plant oil. A single wick was placed in the oil with an earthen plate positioned above the flame to collect the soot.

For every 58 g of soot, 6 g of golden thread and 52 g sappanwood was boiled with 2 small cups of water and filtered. Two g of aloeswood (a resinous wood) was added to 58 g of the filtrate, heated and filtered. Next, 0.7 g camphor, 1.4 g musk and 2.5g calomel were ground with a small amount of the latter filtrate, and heated with 13 g of glue together with the rest of the earlier filtrate, mixing thoroughly. The soot was stirred in; the ink was placed in a room with no drafts. At this point the ink should have no bubbles in it and possess a mirror-like sheen. Dried, steamed and dusted with talcum powder, they were dried for five weeks. Then they were polished, scrubbed and dried again.

Culinary Matters

It was the beginning of the sixteenth century. It seemed that the preparation of each dish was a little grander than before. Ni Zan had spoken of adding meat juices (instead of eggs or water) to flour to make noodles. Song Xu used soup made with a small, plump chicken for the same purpose. 'Chop the head, feet, skin, meat, bones and marrow into a mushy paste and tie everything up in a piece of silk and boil it. Mix the fatty stock with flour to make noodles, which should be cut thin as threads. Boil the noodles in more stock, rinse them with cold water. Sprinkle spices over them, add mustard sauce or simply ladle hot stock over them.' Fresh shrimp were pounded and their juices used to prepare noodles.

Song Xu could not look at creatures in the market without thinking of how they should be prepared. Dried whitebait could simply be moistened with wine and steamed with Sichuan peppercorns and scallions. It was suitable for frying, with some chives; or cooked with wintermelon and bamboo shoots; or fried with noodles. Whitebait was suitable for soup. Dried croaker first soaked in water could be cooked with hot peppers and bamboo shoots. Fish roe was salted, placed on new tiles and dried under the hot sun. It was steamed and served with vinegar.

HSIANG JU LIN

Crabs

Many literary gentlemen were obsessed with crabs. They were the subject of several monographs and of numerous poems. Song Xu was fortunate. He lived near the mouth of the Yangtse River, where white crabs were abundant. White crabs were coastal creatures; their two bottommost legs were shaped like paddles. They hid in the mud and sand, emerging at high tide to feed.

> *Small boats set out at high tide,*
> *To bring the first crabs to market.*

Song Xu recalled, these were the crabs used in Ni Zan's recipe, where crabmeat was mixed with honey and eggs, put in the shell and steamed until the egg just set. He attempted something similar, probably with less success. He mixed crabmeat and tomalley with mung bean flour and milk curd and steamed it. The sauce poured over it was made with the crab juices, ginger, wine, vinegar, licorice, Sichuan peppercorns and scallions.

Crabs were prized for the 'paste'— a creamy semi-solid mixture of yellowish-green tomalley (the liver-pancreas) and firm orange-red roe. This mixture would fill the crab's abdomen, distending it. In the words of a poet the crab would be 'Bursting with paste as rich as marrow, heaped in the bowl of its shell.' Not too far from Song Xu's home was a large fresh water lake, home to a very different kind of crab, a species with hairy claws. Song Xu prepared them very simply, in Ni Zan's style. Ni had added ginger, perilla and salt to the water, but Song Xu did otherwise. He thought it more suitable to serve the boiled crabs with a separate dish of slivered tangerine peel and ginger, salt and vinegar.

Altogether, Song Xu compiled over 800 recipes, a rather large number for a household. To understand how this profusion of food was used, one must turn to some passages in the famously erotic novel of this period. Briefly, the central character of the novel was a corrupt, lecherous fellow who rose from poverty to become wealthy. He had several wives and concubines. The plot revolved around the scheming women around him. The novel described in detail how the wealthy ate. The next chapter begins with breakfast with the main character and two of his freeloading men friends.

SLIPPERY NOODLES

NOTES

Opening poem: *Bi yue shan fang* 蔽月山房 by Wang Shouren 王守仁 (1472-1529) [*Ming ru yan xing lu* 明儒言行錄 by Shen Jia 沈佳, ch. 8, p. 28]

The emperor: Yongledi 永樂帝 (r 1403-1424), fourth son of the Ming dynasty founder

Largest encyclopedia: *Yongle Dadian* 永樂大典 (1408)

Muslim eunuch: Zheng He 鄭和 (1371-1425)

Expeditions: [Ming shi 明史, ch. 304, pp. 2-5]

Translator: Ma Huan 馬歡 (fl 1414-1451). (book) *Ying ya sheng lan jiao zhu* 瀛涯勝覽 (1962) by Ma Huan 馬歡, annotated by Feng Chengjun 馮承鈞.Taipei 台北: Taiwan shang wu yin shu guan 台灣商務印書館

Observations: (Zufar) Zu fa er guo 祖法兒國, pp.52-54; (Aden) Ah dan guo 阿丹國, p. 55; (Ormuz) Hu lu mou si guo 忽魯謀廝國, p. 63; (Mecca) Tian fang guo 天方國, pp. 68-69

Medicinal materials: (frankincense) Ru xiang 乳香, *Boswellia carterii*, (dragon's blood) Xue jie 血竭, *Daemonorops draco*; (medicinal aloe) Lu hui 蘆薈, *Aloe barbadensis*; (myrrh) Mu yao 沒藥, *Commiphora myrrha*; (benzoin) An xi xiang 安息像, genus *Styrex*; (rose malues) Su he you 蘇合油, *Liquidambar orientalis*, pp. 53-54

Animals: (camel chicken) Tuo ji 駝雞, p. 54 ; (giraffe) Ji lin 麒麟, (lion) Shi zi 獅子, (zebra) Hua fu lu 花福鹿, p. 55. Descriptions, p. 58

Song Xu's family: A survey of Song Family's lineage in the Songjiang Prefecture and their achievements in literary creation, by Li Yueshen. J. Zhejiang Univ (Hum Soc Sci) 2006; 36, no.1, 117-125.

Bamboo Islet Studio: [*Zhu yu shan fang* 竹嶼山房間 (1505) by by Song Xu 宋詡, Song Gongwang 宋公望 and Song Maocheng 宋懋澄 Yang sheng bu er 養生 部二, part II] hereafter abbreviated [SX:chapter,page(s)] Song Xu's home: (mullet) Zi yu 鯔魚, *Mugil cephalus* [SX:12,15]; (beekeeping) Xu mi feng fa 畜蜜蜂法 [SX:12,17-18]; (flower arrangement) Cha hua fa 插花法 [SX:7,8]

Suitability: Yi, 宜; (drinking tea) Yin cha 飲茶 [SX:1,3-4]; (caramel brittle) Tang chan 餹纏, Yi ru tang wu 宜入餹物 [SX:2:25]

Additions to brittle: (embryonic lotus shoot) Lian xin 蓮心, *Nelumbo nucifera*; (parasol tree, seeds) Wu tong zi 梧桐子, *Firmiana simplex*; (lotus seed) Lian di 蓮芍, *Nelumbo nucifera*; (cardamom) Bai dou kou ren 白豆蔻仁, *Elettaria cardamomum*; (cardamom) Suo sha ren 縮砂仁 *Amomum villosum, A. xanthoides;* (cardamom) Cao guo ren 艸果仁, *Amomum tsao-ko*

Home remedies: (for bound feet) Hong yu san zhi bang jiao zhi xiu lan 紅玉散治縫腳臭爛, Jin lian wen bu fa 金蓮穩步法 [SX:8,7]; (hair dye) Ran bai fa hei 染白鬚髮黑, (preventing greying) Gao fa chang hei 膏髮常黑 [SX:8.1-2]; (stimulating hair growth) Zhi fa bu sheng 治髮不生 [SX:8,5]; (face cream with egg) Ji zi fen 雞子粉, (face cream with pearls) Zhu zi fen 珠子粉 [SX:8,3]; (bath scents) Mu yu wu xiang tang 沐浴五香湯, (deodorant) Xiang shen wan 香身丸, (anti-perspirant) Pi han xiang shen fen 辟汗相身丸[SX:8,6]; (sachet) Tou yi xiang 透衣香 [SX:8,8]

Ink: (sappanwood) Su mu 蘇木, *Caesalpinia sappan*; (golden thread) Huang lian 黃連, *Coptis chinensis*; (apricot kernels) Xing ren 杏仁, *Prunus armenica* [SX:7,1-2]

Noodles: (chicken) Ji mian 雞面 [SX:2,1]; (shrimp) Xia mian 蝦面 [SX:2,2]

Market: (whitebait) Yin yu gan 銀魚乾; (croaker) Hong yu 烘魚, refers to yellow croaker, Shi shou yu 石首魚, *Pseudosciaena polyactis*; (fish roe) Yu zi 魚子[SX:4,12]

White crabs: Bai xie 白蟹, also called You mou 蝤蛑, family *Portunidae*

Poem: *(white crabs) Qiu ri za yong* 秋日雜詠 by Lu You 陸游 [*Jian nan shi gao* 劍南詩槀 by Lu Ziju 陸子虞 and Lu You 陸游, ch. 47, pp. 15-16]

Ni Zan's recipes: (white crab) Mi niang you mou 蜜釀蝤蛑, (NZ-ZPGC, p.3); (hairy crab) Zhu xie fa 煮蟹法, (NZ-ZPGC, p.4).

Song's recipes: (white crab) Ma nao xie 瑪瑙蟹 [SX:4,19]; (hairy crab) Peng xie 烹蟹 [SX:4,18]

Bursting: Er yue qi ri Wu Zhengzhong wei huo xia 二月七日吳正中遺活蝦 [*Wan ling ji* 宛陵集 by Mei Yaochen 梅堯臣(1002-1060), ch. 43, p. 7]

Crabs with hairy claws: Pang xie 螃蟹, also called Da jia xie 大甲蟹, *Erocheir sinensis*

CHAPTER THIRTY

SCENTS AND TASTES

Two servants set up the table. There were ten small dishes and four bowls with leg of pork, squab, pickled vegetable with milk curd, and chicken soup with wonton. Silver-clad china bowls held plain rice, several kinds of nuts, and sweetened rice gruel. After breakfast, the host poured some wine for himself and the two friends, and they each had three cups.

Although the excerpt above is fictional, the food might well have come from Song Xu's kitchen, about a hundred years earlier. Many of the food items in the novel were readily matched to some recipes in Song's book. Since both works fell in the same era such concurrences come as no surprise. Bringing them together could reveal how the wealthy of that era took their three meals a day.

For breakfast, the fictional characters had leg of pork. Song Xu's recipe called for soaking a leg of pork in wine seasoned with salt, scallions and Sichuan peppercorns, then stewing it in a pot sealed with moistened paper to prevent evaporation. The novel said it was served in a bowl, so copious amounts of the cooking liquid must have been ladled over the pork.

Fledgling squabs were another breakfast item in the novel. Song Xu's recipe was as follows. 'Leave the squabs whole. Soak them in salted water, and then half-cook them. Stuff the squabs with scallions and Sichuan peppercorns and cook them in wine until done. Sprinkle oil or vinegar over them until brown and fragrant. Serve with garlic and vinegar.' This was rich, strongly seasoned food.

Milk curd steamed with pickled vegetable: the plain name of the dish was deceiving, for much expertise had gone into its creation. The pickle was made with a particular variety of cabbage. It had many names, among them 'everlasting spring' and 'snow vegetable' because this vegetable thrived in winter. It is grown principally to make the pickle, and for good reason: fresh, the cabbage was inedible, bitter and peppery. Pickling transformed it into something extraordinary. 'Ni Zan removed the leafy parts and the pickle juices, using only the stalks that he put on the bottom of a bowl,' Song Xu wrote. 'He placed slices of milk curd on top, added salt, pepper, ginger and wine and steamed it until very soft.' So this humble dish was well over two centuries old by the time the novel was written. The other ingredient, milk curd, was made by curdling cow's milk with vinegar.

If the wonton had been made according to Song Xu, each piece would have been a small pouch with a pointed bottom, sealed at the top. Uneven edges were trimmed off. The wonton was steamed, rinsed in cold water and finished in chicken soup. These main courses were sufficient for breakfast.

The wine that they took at breakfast was a common rice wine called 'golden flower,' suitable for many purposes, one that Madame Wu had used in her kitchen.

Lunch

> With business done, lunch was served. First, four dishes of fruit and vegetables, then, four appetizers were brought in: salty duck eggs with their glistening, reddish yolks; golden shrimp mixed with cucumber; delicious-smelling 'fried bones'; and waxy chicken, steamed.

Wine was taken with these refreshments. The four dishes of fruit and vegetables were almost insignificant, the next four a little more interesting.

Salty duck eggs went well with wine. Boiled but not shelled, they were cut lengthwise into quarters. Their golden red yolks were grainy in texture, with an intriguing taste. The egg white resembled fine white porcelain in colour and sheen. In Song Xu's home, salty duck eggs were made by the thousands. Fried ribs were also known as 'fried bones.' Song Xu said, 'There must be meat on the bones,' for he knew that the enjoyment of ribs lies in tearing the meat off the bones with one's teeth. 'They are boiled, seasoned and allow to stand for a while before frying in oil.'

Two items that do not appear in Song Xu's book are noteworthy. Golden shrimp taken from northern seas were salted and sun-dried; deep flavours developed, replacing the fresh taste. Dried shrimp were softened with scalding water and soaking, then mixed with fresh cucumbers. The chicken was small, its bones tender. It had been salted and sun-dried, turning the skin waxy. It was 'dry-steamed,' meaning it was placed in a covered and sealed pot without seasoning or sauce, and steamed. The chicken was chopped into eight pieces, the wings being the choicest parts.

> The main courses were served with rice: braised duck, 'crystal' leg of pork, a dish of fried pork, stir-fried kidneys. Then, shad preserved in wine lees, steamed, was brought in on a blue and white platter. It had a sweet fragrance, the flesh melting in the mouth. The scales and bones were as sweet. The host poured lotus wine into small flowered cups.

In Song Xu's kitchen there was a versatile piece of equipment: a covered wok with a removable rack, used to cook fish, meat or fowl. The braised duck was first browned in the wok (without the rack) in hot oil. Some peppercorns and scallions were placed in the body cavity. The wok was converted to a steamer by replacing the oil with water and putting the rack in position. The cooking of the duck was completed by steaming.

'Crystal' pork was merely jellied pork. In Song Xu's recipe pig's knuckles were stewed and the bones removed. The soft parts were returned to the seasoned, clarified cooking liquid, together with some bamboo shoots or cabbage.

Stir-fried kidney came toward the end of the meal; it would not wait for it was cooked in seconds. Song Xu's directions conveyed the idea. 'Toss the sliced kidney and seasoning into hot fat, drizzle soy sauce and wine over it. Stir it. It is finished.'

Shad caught during its annual migration upstream was a rare treat. In the novel shad was steamed with the fragrant wine lees in which it was preserved.

Since antiquity the very mention of shad usually included the admonition not to remove the scales. In Song Xu's recipe, this point was made twice.

Shad

(From an ancient text: Shad, a sea fish resembling bream. Its scales are large and luscious. Shad may appear in the rivers. Suitable for sun-drying and packing in wine lees. Do not remove the scales.)

Prepare the shad with its scales. Remove the innards and clean the fish. Steam it in a pewter-clad dish with a mixture of wine, vinegar and water.

The lotus wine that the host offered had little or nothing to do with the flower. It was distilled liquor. According to Song Xu's recipe, rice was mixed with six pellets of 'medicine' for every 10 L of the fermenting brew. The composition of the medicine was kept a secret, a common practice in the making of many herbal wines. The distilled liquor was collected in bottles containing pieces of sandalwood. The scents and tastes of food in that period were extremely pronounced; the liquors were likewise infused with strong aromas.

Dinner

As the guests arrived tea was served, along with 40 small dishes of fruits, nuts and sweet pastries, probably much like Song Xu's tea refreshments. The musicians, entertainers and singers arrived. The guests were present, seated according to rank, importance, and such attributes. Lesser persons were seated at neighbouring tables, and so on down the social ladder. Young girl singers hovered around the head table, where the guest(s) of honour had the privilege of choosing the songs and music. As the music began, so did the meal.

The grandest of meals might have five different meats and three soups, to start with. It was a meal, but it was also a show. In order of importance, whole cooked geese, ducks, chickens, pork and lamb were brought out for the guests to see and then returned to the kitchen to be cut up. Song Xu was explicit as to whether fowl was left whole or cut up before cooking. He had only one way of cooking whole lamb or pig and that was to employ Husihui's roasting method, in a stone-lined pit that served as an oven, covered with willow branches. The presentation of whole cooked animals was a way of honouring the guests.

The novel depicted how a lady, the guest of honour, was shown even more courtesy. 'The lady sat at a table with eight others, with two more at a side table, making a total of 11. Two hired girls sang and played music as the rest of the meal proceeded. The chef appeared, presenting the lady with a dish of crystal goose, and she gave him a tip of 7.4 g silver.' Silver was a form of currency at that time, apart from metal coins. 'Next, he brought her some soft-stewed pig's knuckles whose skin had been crisped over a flame and she tipped him 3.7 g silver. Braised duck brought him another tip of 3.7 g silver.' The main dishes were served with rice. Small plates of red plums and wild grapes provided an intermission. Then, a huge bowl of noodles cooked with slivered eel tempted the sated diners to take a little taste. In Song Xu's recipe the eel was cooked with the fat and juices of chicken and goose. The noodles were cut thin as threads. Steamed buns filled with bright green spinach and bamboo shoots came with this final course.

NOTES

Opening quotation: *Jin ping mei* 金瓶梅 (probably written between 1582-1602) by Lanling Xiaoxiao Sheng 蘭陵笑笑生 (pseudonym), chapter 22, abbreviated (LXS:22) Source: (*Food and Drink in 'Jin Ping Mei'*) *Jin ping mei yin shi pu* 金瓶梅飲食 譜 (2007) by Shao Wankuan 邵萬寬 and Zhang Guochao 章國超. Jinan 濟 南: Shandong huabao chubanshe 山東畫報出版社. ISBN 978-7-80713-399-5 (abbreviated SWZG). Because the references to food in '*Jin ping mei*' are all given in the source, they are abbreviated (LXS:chapter,SWZG:page). Different editions of '*Jin ping mei*' may differ significantly in their content, extending to the descriptions of food.
Pork: Song Xu's recipe for Yan jiu shao zhu 鹽酒燒豬 [SX:3,8] matches the stewed

pork Ti zi 蹄子 in the opening quotation (LXS:22,SWZG:273)

Squab: Song Xu's braised whole squabs Ge zhi shu 鴿之屬 [SX:3,31-32] match the fledgling squabs, Ge zi chu er 鴿子鶵兒 on the breakfast menu (LXS:22,SWZG:273)

Pickled vegetable and milk curd: Song Xu gave Ni Zan's way of preparing this dish [SX:5,5]. It is called Chun pu lao zheng ru bing 春不老蒸乳餅 in the novel (LXS:22,SWZG:273). (pickled cabbage) Chun bu lao 春不老, also called Xue cai 雪菜, *Brassica juncea,* var. *ulticeps.* (milk curd preparation) Ru bing 乳餅 [SX:6,9]

Wonton: Hun dun 餛飩 [SX:2,4-5]

Golden flower wine: Jin hua jiu 金華酒, mentioned in Jiu xiao shi 酒小史 by Song Boren 宋伯仁 (thirteenth century) [*Shuo fu* 說郛 ed. Tao Zongyi 陶宗儀, ch. 94b, p. 68]; Zhong kui lu 中饋錄 by Wu shi 吳氏 [*Shuo fu* 說郛 ed. Tao Zongyi 陶宗儀, ch. 95a, p. 34]

Lunch menu: Wu can shi dan 午餐食單 (LXS:33,SWZG:273)

Appetizers: (salty eggs) Yan dan 醃卵 [SX:3,35]; (fried ribs) You jian zhu 油煎豬 [SX:3,10]; (shrimp) Jin xia wang gua 金蝦王瓜 SWZG:23); (chicken) Pi shai ji 劈晒雞, (dry steaming) Gan zheng 乾蒸(SWZG:21)

Main dishes: (braised duck) Shao ya 燒鴨 [SX:3,30]; (wok with rack) Jia guo 架鍋; (jellied pork) Dong zhu rou 凍豬肉 [SX:3,13]; (stir-fried kidney) Zhu shen 豬腎 [SX:3,23]; (shad) Shi yu 鰣魚[SX:4,1]

Lotus wine: Zao lian hua bai jiu fa 造蓮花白酒法 [SX:15,3-4]

Song Xu's tea refreshments: Cha guo 茶果 [SX:1,2]

Dinner: (five meats, three soups) San tang wu ge 三湯五割 (SWZG:267); (braised goose) Shao e 燒鵝, (steamed goose) Zheng e 蒸鵝 [SX:3,24-25]; (braised duck) Shao ya 燒鴨, (roast duck) Zhi ya炙鴨 [SX:3.30-31] (chicken) You jian ji 油煎雞 [SX:3,27]; (pit-roasted lamb) Kang yang 炕羊 [SX3,6]; (pit-roasted pig) Kang zhu 炕豬 [SX:3,15]

Tipping: [LXS:41,SWZG,266]. A fuller version is given in Jin ping mei 金瓶梅 (1977) by Lanling Xiaoxiao Sheng 蘭陵笑笑生. Singapore: Xingzhou shijie shu ju 星州世界書局. Vol. 2, ch. 41 p. 409

Other banquet courses: [LXS:49,SWZG,274]. (eel) Hu shan 糊膳 (SX:4, 8-9], (spinach-filled buns) Man tou 饅頭, Su xian 素餡 [SX:2,6-7]

CHAPTER THIRTY-ONE

THE PLAYWRIGHT

First I talk about tea, infusions and gruel, then vegetables, meat and wine, followed by pasta and sweet cakes.

There was a Ming dynasty playwright named Gao Lian who wrote a drama about a young scholar and a nun — actually a young girl forced to take refuge in a convent. It was a romance that had a happy ending and its popularity extended to modern times. Drama was but one aspect of Gao Lian's life. In his youth he went to Beijing, working in the palace bureau that arranged state occasions, ceremonies and related social gatherings. It was probably there that he learned how 'silk nests' were made in the palace kitchen. Eventually he chose to adopt the simple life and retired to the mountains near Hangzhou. There, Gao Lian wrote a book titled *Eight Ways to Harmonious Living*. It was a success. It gave advice for living a long life in good health. There had been several books on this topic. Like the others Gao Lian's book dealt with medicine and nourishment, food and drink, directing advice to old people: even how to sit, sleep and clothe oneself. He advocated the use of massage, exercise and moxibustion ('cupping,' the practice of applying a flame to the skin to increase the blood supply).

Too much good advice can be a bore, but Gao Lian was a clever writer. Living in harmony with the seasons meant not only taking appropriate tonics and infusions at given months, he wrote, but enjoying nature. In spring one could drink tea made with freshly picked leaves; one might watch the clouds moving over a lake as a summer storm approached, or smell wild flowers and hear strange animal cries along a mountain path. He described his studio, referring to himself as Master Gao.

Master Gao says, studios must be calm and quiet, to ease one's spirits. They must not be too spacious for that would be a strain. The walls outside must be covered with climbing plants. There should be a few pine trees and bonsai, or an orchid plant or two, some grasses and a shallow pond with lively golden carp.

Inside the studio there is a long table. On it is my old ink stone, an antique pitcher, an old clay pen rest, a bamboo rack for brushes, a jug of water to wash them in and a brass paperweight. To the left of the table there is a couch, a footstool beneath and a small table beside it. I might put an old bronze vase with some flowers on the table; in winter, a small stove. I have hung a zither on the wall and placed a table directly below it. In Ni Zan's style I have a few paintings on the wall: those of mountains and waters, some trees and flowers — no animals, birds or people.

Gao Lian opened a chapter on food and drink with the words of a plain-living scholar. 'I favour practical things over the unusual. I shall leave the use of exotic spices and strange foods to the chefs who serve official circles. Let them display their grand cuisine. That would be unsuitable for me — a man living in the mountains. So I shall not write one word about it.' He assembled a collection of recipes drawn from different sources: traditional medicine, the home kitchen, the royal kitchen, the vegetable plot and the wild. They might as well have been scenes in a play.

Gao Lian was not trained as a doctor yet he wrote extensively and knowledgeably about physiology and herbal medicine. He may not have done any cooking, but he ably presented recipes for many different kinds of food and drink, including home cooking, sweets and pastries. To accomplish the latter feat, Gao Lian copied recipes from other works. He was especially taken with Madame Wu's cookbook that he reproduced almost in its entirety. Her recipes were given verbatim, often grouped in their original order, without attribution. Lin Hong also contributed a few recipes, incognito, as did Han Yi, the gentleman cook who attempted to make soy sauce.

Decoctions, Infusions and Gruel

Gao Lian began the section on food and drink with decoctions and infusions. Decoctions were boiled down herbal mixtures; for consumption a spoonful or two of the concentrate was diluted with water. For example, black plums, sandalwood, cardamom, musk and honey went into one decoction. Aromatic substances such as purple perilla, cloves, nutmeg, tangerine leaves, jasmine buds or rose buds were steeped in hot water to make various infusions. Here again, Han Yi made several anonymous contributions to Gao's book. In the Mongol dynasty Husihui had described infusions that were beneficial to health. Gao Lian took many formulas from another book from the same period, titled *Health and Longevity*. As was his style, he did not name their source.

Gruel was recommended by physicians because it was easy to digest and nourishing. There were many different kinds of rice gruel. Gruel made with sugar cane relieved coughing. Rice gruel containing milk was fortifying. Milk obtained from a plump woman was considered to be especially nourishing.

Cow's Milk Rice Gruel

Use raw, genuine cow's milk. Make gruel with white rice, stopping when the rice is half done, pour out some of the water, add the milk and continue cooking. To a bowl of gruel, add one spoonful of butter.

Rice Gruel with Milk

Use milk from a plump woman (in the same manner). To a bowl of gruel, add 5-6 g butter and stir it in. This is sweet, delicious and nourishing. The butter may be omitted.

Second Thoughts

'Master Guo says, eating for good health or eating without restraint may do good or harm. Seeking new tastes just to please your palate often leads to trouble. A vegetable, a fish, some meat and rice is enough for most people. Of course it is not like raising a golden cup at the splendid table, and quietly breaking into song when the spirit moves you, or to be offered the best foods in the world. The chefs in the royal kitchen would try to outdo themselves, preparing delicacies from far lands just to delight us. But one can get drunk from an earthenware jug as well as a jade cup. Unpolished rice will fill you up as well as bear's paw and chicken feet.'

In this passage Gao Lian advocated moderation in eating. Then he recalled moments of high living. This may have relieved some of the ennui brought about by a frugal diet. Just as he seemed to be having second thoughts about the simple life, he caught himself and declared that coarse rice was as good as chicken feet. (In Chinese cuisine, chicken feet are considered a delicacy.)

True to his intention, Gao Lian's recipes were plain and simple. The feeling that one had read much of it before was correct because Madame Wu's clever ways with food were all there. There is one item that deserves attention. It might have been included because it reminded Gao Lian of the high life that he had lived. This magnificent dish consisted of thick slices of marbled meat, coloured with red mould and overlaid with crystal clear juices redolent of spices. Han Yi's recipe was made up of five parts. Gao Lian hardly changed a word.

Stewed Pork

The pig should weigh about 24 kg. Carve the meat from a foreleg. Trim off the fat, bone and belly muscles to get a single piece of meat weighing about 3 kg. Cut it into four squares and parboil them. After the meat cools, trim it and slice it into pieces the thickness of a finger. Remove the fat from the cooking liquid and place some of the concentrated meat juice in a wok. Add the *fine spices* (see below), the meat and some sieved bean sauce. Bring everything to the boil. Add more meat juice and sprinkle more spices on top. Mix *red mould powder* with some meat juice and pour it on the meat. Add *prepared stock* and some salt. (The meat was probably set aside as the liquid was clarified.) Remove any beans that may be present in the liquid. Chopped raw shrimp is added for further *clarification* and fat removal. Correct the seasoning and immediately pour it over the meat. The meat must not be reheated.

Clarification of Liquids with Raw Shrimp

Pound raw shrimp with sauce and add it to the liquid, heating the wok on one side. As the liquid comes to the boil, the solid mass will float toward the cooler side, where it is removed. Raw pork liver chopped and mixed with water will work as well. Repeat as necessary to remove every trace of fat.

Prepared Stock

The stock is brought to the boil once a day. Let it settle as it cools. If not used that day store it in a pewter or earthenware jug and hang it in the well.

Red Mould Powder

Soak the red mould in wine, overnight. Grind it to make a paste. Thin it with some meat juice.

Fine Spices

Licorice, cinnamon, angelica, lesser galangal, osmanthus flowers, sandalwood, hyssop, wild ginger, spikenard, Sichuan peppercorns, cardamom, greater galangal, apricot kernels.

In an ordinary household a few herbs were used, but this was *haute cuisine*. The spice mixture consisted of 13 ingredients, each dried and milled to a fine powder. The spices came from the south including present-day Thailand, Vietnam, and Malaysia, and from different parts of China.

Licorice (root), from western China; a sweetener
Cinnamon (bark), from southern regions; unique aroma
Chinese angelica (root), from central China; fragrant, slightly bitter

Lesser galangal (root), from southern regions; aromatic, peppery
Osmanthus (flower), from southern China; strong fragrance
Sandalwood (bark), from southern regions; incense-like smell, bittersweet
Giant hyssop (leaves), from western China; peppery and minty
Chinese wild ginger (root), from northern China; peppery
Chinese spikenard (root), from central China; musk-like fragrance
Sichuan pepper (seed pod), from central China; complex, spicy
Cardamom (seed), from southern regions; nutty, fruity
Greater galangal (fruit), from southern regions; cardamom-like flavour
Apricot (kernel), from central, northern and western China; bitter

Wild Vegetables

Plain living meant simple food, country cooking, at times eating like peasants. With help from Madame Wu, Gao Lian laid out an impressive spread of pickles made with garden vegetables. Then he led the reader through a field of wild vegetables with unfamiliar names. Perhaps readers found them difficult to identify, but they were entranced by the names: 'eye vegetable, 'golden sparrow' and 'dog footprints.' There were over 80 recipes for wild vegetables. Why would Gao Lian devote more space to wild vegetables than to cultivated ones? They had a certain cachet. Like bracken ferns and water shield they evoked plain living and the rustic life.

The first book on wild vegetables was written by a prince, a son of the first Ming emperor (who was born a peasant). *Plants for Famine Relief* was intended to be a guide to edible vegetables when starvation threatened. Mencius the philosopher was quoted in the introduction: 'When grains are not ripe one turns to eating weeds.' The prince described over 400 edible wild plants giving the plant's habitat, describing its flowers, leaves and so on. He detailed the ways to prepare the vegetable in times of famine. There was a fine illustration of each plant. The suggested methods of cooking did not always fit the realities of famine. The royal prince recommended frying wild vegetable leaves, then soaking them in water (to remove any bitter or harsh flavours) and dressing them with oil and salt. He applied these directions to almost every kind of edible leaf. He suggested cooking some root vegetables by steaming or boiling, then dipping them in honey, as if oil and honey would be abundant in times of famine. Nonetheless the book found an audience.

Over the next two centuries several books on the same topic followed, using the same format. Wild plants were classified by their edible parts: leaves, roots, stems, flowers, and seeds or fruits. Gao Lian perused them. His interest in wild vegetables might have been inspired also by a contemporary who lived on one of China's most famous mountains and had written a book on wild plants. He had seen peasants plucking wild vegetables on the mountain for their daily fare — a kind of scene that the playwright liked. He and Gao Lian were alike in another respect. Gao Lian had plagiarized recipes from *The Book of Wild Vegetables*, written about 50 years earlier. The mountain man had lifted several dozen entries from the prince's book. Even the accompanying illustrations were strikingly similar, and he faithfully copied the prince's directions for preparing the vegetables with copious amounts of oil.

NOTES

Opening quotation: (on food and drink) Yin zhuan fu shi jian 飲饌服食牋 [*Zun sheng ba jian* 遵生八箋 by Gao Lian 高濂 (fl 1573)] ch. 11, p. 1. Hereafter abbreviated [GL:chapter,page(s)]

Further source: *Yin zhuan fu shi jian* 飲饌服食牋 (1985) by Gao Lian 高濂. Cheng du 成都: Ba Shu shu she 巴蜀書社. The food and drink sections of Gao Lian's book, annotated and translated into modern Chinese.

Early life: (the drama 'Jade Hairpin') *Yu zan ji* 玉簪記; (palace bureau) Hong lu si 鴻臚寺 [*Ming shi* 明史, ch. 74, pp. 9-10]

Enjoyment of nature: (tea) Hu pao quan shi xin cha 虎跑泉新茶 [GL:3,52-53]; (lake) Guan hu shang feng yu yu lai 觀湖上風雨欲來 [GL:4,62-63]; (mountain path) Bu shan jing ye hua you niao 步山徑野花幽鳥 [GL:4,63-64]

His studio: Gaozi shu zhai shuo 高子書齋說 [GL:7,29-30]

Plain food: Yin zhuan fu shi jian 飲饌服食牋 [GL:11,1]

Quoted without attribution: Madame Wu, Wu shi 吳氏; Lin Hong 林洪; Han Yi 韓奕; (Health and Longevity) [*Shou qin yang lao xin shu* 壽親養老新書 by Chen Zhi 陳直 and Zou Xuan 鄒鉉, ch. 3, pp.17-18]

Decoction: (black plums, etc.) Ti hu tang 醍醐湯 [GL:11,24]

Gruels: (sugar cane juice) Gan zhu zhou 甘竹粥 [GL:11,32]; (cow's milk) Niu ru zhou 牛乳粥 [GL:11,31-32]; (human milk) Ru zhou 乳粥 [GL:11,36-37]

Second thoughts: Yin shi dang zhi suo sun lun 飲食當知所損論 [GL:10,10]

Stewed pork: Da lu rou 大爐肉 (Yi Ya yi yi 易牙遺意 by Han Yi 韓奕, ed. by Qiu Pangtong 邱龐同 (ZPGC, 1984), pp. 16-19) [GL:11,42-43]

Spices: (angelica) Bai zhi 白芷, *Angelica anomala*; (lesser galangal) Gao liang jiang 高良姜, *Alpinia officinarum*; (sandalwood) Tan xiang 檀香, *Santalum album*; (hyssop) Huo xiang 藿香, *Pogostemon cablin, Agastache rugosa*; (ginger) Xi xin 細辛, *Asarum heteropoides*; (spikenard) Gan song 甘松, *Nardostachys chinensis*; (greater galangal) Hong dou kou 紅豆蔻, *Alpinia galangal*

The prince's book: *Plants for Famine Relief [Jiu huang ben cao* 救荒本草 by Zhu Su 朱橚 (d 1425)] (introduction) Yuan xu 原序, p. 1; (edible leaves) Ye ke shi 葉可食, ch. 1-8; (edible roots) Gen ke shi 根可食, ch. 3, 4, 7, 8

The Book of Wild Vegetables: Many items in [GL:12, pp. 21, 23] matched those in *Ye cai pu* 野菜譜 by Wang Pan 王磐 (fl 1521) [*Yu ding pei wen chai guang chun fang pu* 御定佩文齋廣群芳譜, ch. 17, pp. 45-47]

The mountain man: [*Ye cao bo lu* 野草博錄 by Bao Shan 鮑山 (fl 1622)] The reader may wish to compare the prince's text and illustrations vs. Bao Shan's versions. See for example ch.1, p.2 in the prince's book vs. ch.1, p. 3 in Bao Shan's book; ch.1, p. 4 in both books.

Note: Plagiarism may have been frequent but the practice of citing literary sources was upheld by others. Excerpts and illustrations from the prince's book were acknowledged in the treatise titled *Agricultural Policy* [*Nong zheng* 農政 by Xu Guangqi 徐光啟 (1562-1633), ch.46, p. 1]

CHAPTER THIRTY-TWO

THE PRESERVED EGG

Nowadays people no longer use oak bark to make salty eggs. They mix rice and water with salt and plant ashes to form a thick paste that is moulded around the eggs. But they still call them by the old name, salty oak bark eggs.

The art of curing eggs had taken a different direction at the beginning of the Ming dynasty. Instead of soaking fresh eggs in a salty bark extract as Jia Sixie had described, eggs were encased in a paste containing ashes, salt and rice. The use of ashes for this purpose was new. Ultimately it would result in a completely different kind of cured egg - one that had different colours, that was not salty and required no cooking. Some consider it to be one of the finest things in Chinese cuisine. To be sure, the new product was strange. That probably explained why it acquired names bearing words such as 'cowhide,' 'transformed,' 'different-tasting,' 'pine blossom,' and 'multicoloured.' In English, 'century' and 'thousand year-old' have been applied to this kind of egg, conveying the idea of long shelf life. I prefer calling it the preserved egg.

In appearance the preserved egg is unique. The strong alkali ultimately used in its production chemically cooks the egg and changes its colours. Egg white is transformed into a firm brown transparent jelly. There may be some blossom-like crystals in the jelly; they are to be admired. When the shelled egg is cut in quarters lengthwise, the yolk appears cradled in the brown jelly. The yolk is a mossy green and it will have expanded to twice its original size. It will be firm on the outside but creamy in the center, like that of a perfectly poached egg.

Ashes and Lime

The preserved egg is the result of the combined actions of salt, plant ashes, lime and tea. The path to success was not smooth. Advances were made incrementally over a century and half. Several choices emerged when ashes took the place of oak bark. Wood, charcoal or straw fueled the kitchen stove, producing different kinds of ash. (A famous roast goose recipe called for three large bunches of straw burned one after the other.) Song Xu used rice stalk ashes to make the traditional salty egg with an orange yolk surrounded by fluid egg white. These eggs were remained raw and required cooking. 'For every thousand eggs, use 40 L of rice stalk ash plus 9 kg of salt, pounded into wet hemp. Store the eggs in a jar or packed in a basket.'

Song Xu had another recipe for preserving eggs with ashes; he added lime.

Muddled Eggs

Boil 10 L coal ash and 1 L lime in brine, cool the mixture and soak eggs in it for 35 days. The whites and yellow yolks will run into each other.

As can be imagined, the muddled egg's appearance was not ideal. The taste must have been appealing because muddled eggs continued to be made for over a century. Further observations were made.

According to a method handed down, it takes five kinds of wood ashes to make the eggs. If buckwheat ash is used, the white and yolk will run together. But if lime and ashes are added, the yolk turns green and firm.

The Way to Success

In 1633 the food administrator of the Ming court published a voluminous work on food and drink. It contained a recipe for 'cowhide duck eggs' – actually something one would recognize today. Eventually the name was shortened to two words, 'hide' and 'egg,' the modern name for these eggs. 'Cowhide' referred to the firm jelly enveloping the yolk.

Cowhide Duck Eggs
For every 100 eggs, use 370 g salt, 1 L lime and 5 L chestnut charcoal ash. Make it in the usual way, storing them in a large jar turning them once every third day for nine days, then seal the jar. It is ready in one month.

Lime water was more alkaline than any kind of ash. The recipe published was not very different from Song Xu's formula, but the proportion of ash to lime by volume was reduced to 5:1. In five works authored between the mid - eighteenth century to the early twentieth century the proportions of ash to lime used for preserving eggs ranged from 4:1 to 2:1. Song Xu had used 10 volumes of ash to one volume of lime; that was probably the reason why his eggs came out muddled.

Shortly after the importance of using enough lime was recognized by some, another ingredient - strong tea - was added. In a book probably written in the late seventeenth century, tea was combined with ash to make a paste. 'For 100 chicken eggs, make brine with 370 g salt and strong tea and mix it with ashes derived from charcoal, buckwheat chaff and cypress wood. Coat the eggs with the paste. They will be ready in a month.'

Notably, lime was not used in the above method. It might have taken over a century for a procedure employing both lime and tea to be adopted. A coating of rice husks kept the lime paste in place and prevented breakage.

How to Make Preserved Eggs
Get the ashes from a tinsmith because he only uses chestnut wood charcoal. It makes the best-tasting eggs; the jelly is dark and not spicy. The lime must be in chunks so the solution will be strong enough. Filter the lime water and mix it with crushed salt. The proportions of salt to lime and ash are 1:2:4. Make a pot of strong tea, and mix it with the ash and lime water to form a paste. Coat the egg with the paste and roll it in rice husks. Put them in an earthen jar. They will be ready in 20 days.

Pine needles might be added, supposedly producing the blossom-like forms. By the early twentieth century, preserved eggs were factory-made. Currently manufacturers may use less ash and substitute lye and washing soda. Some might use a transparent wax to coat preserved eggs, instead of rice husks. But tea, salt and lime are still essential.

A Mystery

The eggs remain a mystery. What accounts for the colour changes? What are the blossom-like forms? How does the yolk develop its mellowness of taste? Why add strong tea instead of water? Several lifetimes could be well spent studying the chemistry of the preserved egg. Such endeavors probably will not take place, and the preserved egg will remain a mystery.

In its small way it will bring pleasure. Not meant to be eaten in quantity, the preserved egg is served as an appetizer, freshly shelled and split lengthwise into quarters. It is best taken at room temperature. It does not need any fancy garnishes; a thin slice or two of sweet ginger will do, with a splash of soy sauce and a few drops of black vinegar. The jelly and yolk should be taken together in one mouthful: stiff jelly, firm yolk, soft center. The flavour is mild like a sip of tea. A kind of fragrance floods the mouth and a certain taste appears. One cannot put a name to it. It is something far beyond the sensations of salty, sweet and sour - a kind of mellowness, an entity in itself, a mystery. Swallow, and take a sip of wine.

Footnote

The preserved egg was perfected in late Ming or early Qing dynasties. As the cuisine entered the era of overindulgence, cooks tried to improve on it. In an excess of zeal they fried it; or prepared 'red-stewed eggs' employing only the preserved egg's brown jelly (fried) with the whites of chicken eggs, pigeon eggs and bamboo shoots cooked with soy sauce, wine and chicken stock. Preserved eggs were paired with sea cucumber; or they were boiled, the yolks removed and the cavities filled with something else, steamed and served on small plates, one for each guest. Preserved eggs were also paired with spare ribs. Fortunately, that era is behind us.

NOTES

Opening quotation: [*Chuo geng lu* 輟耕錄 by Tao Zongyi 陶宗儀, ch.7. p.14]

Overview: *Pi dan jin xi* 皮蛋今昔 by Cao Yuanyu 曹元宇 in *Pengren shi hua* 烹飪史話 (1987) by editors of 'Zhongguo pengren', <中國烹飪>編輯部. Beijing 北京: Zhongguo shangye chubanshe 中國商業出版社, pp. 368 - 374

Roast goose recipe: (NZ-ZPGC pp. 39 - 40).

Song Xu: (salty eggs prepared with ashes) Yan luan 醃卵 (muddled eggs prepared with ashes and lime) Hun dun zi 混沌子[SX:3,35]

Lime and ashes: [*Wu li xiao shi* 物理小識 by Fang Yizhi 方以智 (1611 - 1671), ch. 6, p. 17]

Cowhide duck eggs: Niupi ya zi 牛皮鴨子 in *Yang yu yue ling* 養餘月令 (1633) by Dai Xi 戴羲 (modern name) Pi dan 皮蛋

Ash - lime proportions by volume: (4:1) *Xing yuan lu* 醒園錄 by Li Huanan 李化南 (mid 18th c), ed. by Hou Hanchu 候漢初, and Xiong Sizhi 熊四智 (ZPGC, 1984) p. 36; (3:1) Tiao ding ji: Q*ing dai shihpu daguan* 調鼎集: 清代食譜大觀 (2006) by Tong Yuejian 童岳薦 (18th - 19th c), edited by Zhang Yannian 張延年. Beijing 北京: Zhongguo fangzhi chubanshe 中國紡織出版社. ISBN 7 - 5064 - 3647 - 7, p. 147; (2:1) Zhong kui lu 中饋錄 by Zeng Yi 曾懿 (1852 - 1927) ed. by Chen Guangxin 陳光新 (ZPGC, 1984). (method) Zhi pidan fa 制皮蛋法, pp. 10 - 11; (7:3) Mei wei qiu zhen 美味求真 (anonymous, probably 19th c). Guangzhou 廣州: Wuguitang Press 五桂堂, p. 23; (8:2.5) Blunt, K., Wang, C.C. Chinese Preserved Eggs - Pidan. J. Biol. Chem. 1916;28:125 - 134

Addition of tea: Pidan 皮蛋 in *Shi xian hong mi* 食憲鴻秘 by Zhu Yizun 朱彝尊 (1629 - 1709), annotated by Qiu Pangtong 邱龐同 (ZPGC, 1985) p. 121

Footnote: *Tiao ding ji: Qing dai shihpu daguan* 調鼎集: 清代食譜大觀 by Tong Yuejian 童岳薦, p. 147

CHAPTER THIRTY-THREE

MEDICINES: ANIMAL, PLANT AND MINERAL

How subtle are the variations of the natural world, how difficult to know them all.

Among the great achievements of the Ming dynasty - the building of the imperial palaces in Beijing, the fortification of the Great Wall and the travels of a fleet to distant seas — there was one that took place in a very small space, the mind of one man. In the sixteenth century, Li Shizhen wrote the premier reference book for medicinal materials. It stands today as the best treatise ever written on the substances that are used in Chinese traditional medicine.

Li was the grandson of an itinerant doctor. Itinerant doctors did not have much status. They peddled pills and plied their trade at markets. They made their presence known by ringing hand-held bells. In that period the way to success lay in education - becoming a scholar, and passing the successive levels of civil service examinations. This was the way persons of humble origin could gain high office, become wealthy and move up in the world. Civil service examinations were conducted at four levels: county, provincial, metropolitan and imperial. Li Shizhen's father, the itinerant doctor's son, passed the county examination attaining the rank of licentiate. Despite several tries he failed the provincial examination. Nonetheless he gained a reputation as a fine doctor, and wrote several medical monographs on ginseng (the medicinal root) and other herbs.

Li did as well as his father, becoming a licentiate at age 16. He too failed the provincial examinations that were held every three years. Li tried at age 17 and again at age 20 (when he got married). When the third try made at age 23 also failed, he gave up. He spent the next decade reading medical books, which he loved to do, and he joined his father's practice. Like his father, he earned a reputation as a good doctor. Because he successfully treated a prince's son the prince appointed him to an official post. Li rose to a high position in Beijing's medical institute, but then he decided to give it up and returned home.

Li started writing *Outline of Medicinal Materials* when he was in his early forties, finishing it when he was over 60. Nearing the book's completion he followed the custom of asking a prominent scholar to write the preface. In the year 1580 they finally met. The scholar described their meeting.

> I asked him to stay for a few days in my home, I observed him. His face was haggard and he was thin. Words tumbled out of him. I thought he was an extraordinary person. He had brought only a few dozen chapters of his book with him. Li told me, 'In my youth I was sickly, somewhat dull and stupid. But I devoured books as if eating cane sugar. Or, I was like a hunter or fisherman seeking prey.'

This was a mind that could absorb the contents of 800 medical texts. The scholar praised Li's work in eight words: 'Learned but not tedious, detailed, to the point.' Li's book was directed at physicians and herbalists, but in time historians, naturalists and even cooks turned to it. It summarized all the knowledge of the substances that were considered to be medicine (and food). Altogether there were nearly two thousand items. More importantly, Li organized them in a logical fashion. Each section was divided into groups; under each group were the individual items. For example, the minerals section contained five groups, the first of which included 28 metals such as gold, silver and tin. Jade, crystal and quartz were among the 14 items in the next group. The third and fourth groups dealt with 73 items including cinnabar, mercury, lime and asbestos. Twenty different kinds of salt were discussed in the last group.

The items were described in the same way: name, other names, general information, preparation method, taste and nature, indications, effects and prescriptions. The total number of prescriptions in *Outline of Medicinal Materials* was 8160.

Donkey Hide Glue

Li Shizhen's scholarship and style can be appreciated by turning to almost any page of his book. His entry on donkey hide glue is a good example. It was an established article in traditional medicine. Donkey hide glue may be compared to gelatin which is likewise extracted from animal skins or bones. It is sold in Chinese pharmacies in the form of small stiff rectangular sheets wrapped in cellophane. The product was used as medicine and as glue, the adhesive. The first mention of donkey hide glue in a prescription probably appeared around the first to third century. The seventh century physician Sun Simiao had dozens of prescriptions containing donkey hide glue.

An abbreviated version of Li's entry for donkey hide glue follows. Li documented his sources of information meticulously. The numbered references are identified under Notes and Li's comments are identified by (L).

> **Section** Animal
> **Group** Domesticated Animals
> Including pig, dog, lamb; sour milk, butter, clarified butter; donkey hide glue, ox/buffalo gallstone, dog bezoar
> **Name** Donkey Hide Glue. A superior item (1)
> **Other names** Fuzhijiao (1). The glue is called '*a*-glue' (*a*jiao) after the place it is produced in, the county of Dong-*a* (2). The water comes from wells in Dong-*a* (called '*a*-wells') that are as wide as wagon wheels, two meters deep (L).
> **General information** At present Dong-*a* glue is made by boiling cowhide. There is old glue, new glue, glue made with clear or muddy water. Glue does not form unless a piece of deer horn is added. There are three kinds of glue. Painters use the thin and clear kind. The thick and clear kind is used for medicine. The black muddy kind is not suitable for medicine but you can

glue things with it (2). Now they can make the glue using well water north of Donga city. Real donkey hide glue is difficult to get, and much of it is fake. The best product is made with black donkey hide and Donga well water. Cowhide can be used but it is not as good, it is used as adhesive, not as medicine (3). Make the glue between November-December and April-May. The hides of ox, water buffalo or donkey are best. Pig, horse, mule or camel hides are inferior, and old leather shoes are the worst. Soak fresh hide in water for four or five days, and scrape it clean. Cook it, stirring often. Filter it and cook it some more until it turns into glue. Pour it into a pan to let it gel. After it sets, collect the material near the bottom of the pan. It should taste salty and bitter. In olden times cowhide was used but now donkey hide is favoured. Fake glue is made from old horse hide, saddles, boots and such. It smells bad and is unsuitable for use as medicine. The genuine article is clear and yellow as amber, or black and shiny as lacquer. It does not have a bad smell and will not soften in summer (L).

Method of preparation
According to (2), first hold the piece of glue over a fire. Master Lei says, wash it, soak it in lard overnight and hold it over a fire of willow branches until dry, then crush it (4). The current methods are: to heat it in a pan until beads form, to stir it in a hot pan with flour or clam shell powder or plant ashes, or to dissolve it wine or water. Follow the prescriptions (L).

Taste and nature Sweet, neutral, non-toxic.

Indications Internal disorders, with shivering as in malaria; back and abdominal pains; aching limbs; women experiencing bleeding, pregnant women (1); for men experiencing lower abdominal pain, weakness and exhaustion, lacking *yin* force, weak in the legs and unable to stand for long (2). In cases of vomiting of blood, nosebleeds, blood in urine; for women with irregular menstruation, infertility, vaginal discharges, various ailments before and after pregnancy; for men and women with

249

rheumatism; edema; exhaustion. This is an excellent remedy (L).

Effects All glues are effective in treating rheumatism, diarrhea and debilitation. Donkey hide glue is especially effective for rheumatism (5). The chief strength of donkey hide glue lies in its effects on blood and other bodily fluids, thus it can clear the lungs (L).

Prescriptions For rheumatism: first make 1 L of rice gruel adding scallions and fermented beans. Separately, boil 1 L of water with 200 mL mild (unsalted) fermented beans, remove the dregs and add donkey hide glue that has been slightly heated to soften it; cook it until it is thick like syrup, and drink it. Then take the warm rice-scallion-fermented beans gruel. Take three or four such doses (6).

For lung congestion, with production of phlegm and watery eyes, the remedy is donkey hide glue, perilla and black plums, cooked together with some water over a slow fire (7).

Plants

Having read every pharmacopeia, Li drew upon his knowledge and experience of herbal medicine to edit existing information. He would use a single name for each plant. For example he would use ginseng as the principal name for the plant whose roots made a powerful tonic, but he would also list and reference the plant's ten other names. He would only include those items of proven efficacy. He also named and referenced 153 plants he thought were useless.

Over a thousand items were placed in five sections: plants, grains, vegetables, fruits and trees. Li grouped plants by habitat (mountain, marshlands, wetlands, rocky plain, fresh and salt water) or kind (aromatic, poisonous or mossy). He arranged the items in each group according to their importance, placing the more useful items in front. Thus, licorice headed the group of mountain-grown plants because its root was used in countless prescriptions. It was compatible with other plants and many minerals. Soybean was placed first among 14 kinds of beans and pulses. Soybeans strengthened the muscles, improved the complexion and fortified the marrow. Li listed its uses.

Varieties are black, white, yellow, brown, green or mottled. Fermented black soybeans can be used in medicine. The yellow variety can be made into curd, crushed for its oil or made into condiments. The other kinds can be made into curd and stir- fried.

In the tradition of Chinese herbalists, culinary uses of the item were often included along with their medicinal applications.

He reduced the complex to the simple. Chrysanthemum roots and flowers were used for medicine, and the flowers also were used in pastry, in wine, and to make a hot beverage like tea. 'There are 900 varieties of chrysanthemum. The plant's stalks might be purple, red or green, the leaves large or small, thick or thin, pointed or round; its flowers could be any colour ranging in hue from dark to light, the number of petals few or many, large or small, with or without seed pods, with or without seeds. In addition there are the summer, spring and winter varieties. To put it simply (as some have done) there are just two kinds of chrysanthemums, sweet and bitter. Either one can be used for medicine, but use only the sweet kind for food.'

Li discussed the root, stem, leaf, flower and seed of each plant if they had different properties and uses. For example, distillation of Arabian jasmine flowers yielded aromatic oil that could be added to creams for the face or hair, or used to flavour tea. Jasmine root was prescribed for patients with broken bones - they would feel no pain. Three cm of the root ground and taken in wine rendered a person unconscious for one day; twice that length and he was out for two days; three times the length, and he would not wake for three days.

One wonders how one man could have undertaken this monumental task. Li's achievement is not diminished by the fact that he had two assistants: the second of his four sons and a student, also a local boy, who eventually became a noted physician in his own right. Their most important contributions lay in helping Li collect herbs and plants over a period of four years. Starting from Li's home on the banks of the Yangtse River they travelled to the north, to the south as far as Guangdong, and to the eastern end of the river.

People eat vegetables every day, Li wrote, but they are unaware of differences in their individual natures. He sorted them into fungi, seaweed, gourds and melons, mild-tasting vegetables such as spinach and bamboo shoots, and pungent vegetables. To the latter group - members of the onion family that were forbidden to vegetarians - Li added rape, cabbage, turnips, radishes, mustard and ginger. Some sources had treated turnips and radishes as the same plant while others listed them separately. (Those who dislike such technicalities may prefer the comment of a seventh century nutritionist, 'Turnips go very well with lamb,' or let their thoughts dwell on *navarin d'agneau*.)

Differences between Turnips and Radishes

Based on the study of their roots, leaves, flowers and seeds, that are all different, the turnip and radish are not the same plant. The turnip is related to rape; its roots are long and white, its taste peppery and bitter; its short stem is thick, its leaves broad. In summer it puts forth yellow flowers with four petals like those of rape; its seed-bearing branch also resembles that of rape; its seeds are purplish red.

The radish is related to cabbage. Its roots may be round or elongated, they may be red or white; its taste is peppery but sweet; its leaves are coarse; at the beginning of summer the flowers arepale purple; its seed-bearing branch is shaped like a worm, tapering to a point; the seeds are irregular in shape, yellow and brown. This is how I can tell them apart.

Li's characterizations of turnip and radish are in line with their current botanical classification. One might think the large white daikon to be related to the large white turnip, but in fact it is cousin to the little red radish.

Maize was introduced to China from Europe in the early 1500s. That was only a few decades before Li and his two assistants were scouring the country for plants and herbs. Hence the entry for maize consisted entirely of Li's observations.

Maize

Name Jade sorghum
Other names Jade gao liang
General information The plant originated in dry Western lands. Its stalk and leaves resemble those of sorghum but are

fatter and shorter like those of Job's tears.

In August-October, the stalk is 3-4 m high, its flowers form tassels. A fish-like ear grows from the stalk, bearing white silk. Soon it forms seeds as large as those of the hemp palm, white and yellow. They can be fried or stir-fried. The flowers can also be stir-fried (L)

(Grains) Taste and Nature Sweet, neutral, non-toxic

(Grains) Indications Strengthens the core, improves appetite

(Roots, leaves) Incontinence, pain from stones. Make an infusion and take it frequently (L)

Li called maize 'jade sorghum' to distinguish it from local sorghum that was used as animal feed. An illustration showed the plant's rigid stalk, long leaves and an ear of maize in its husk with rows of kernels and drooping silks.

Salt

Salt had a wide range of medicinal uses. Li gave many of the applications taken from pharmaceutical books old and new that he referenced.

Salt Remedies

For severe abdominal distension, induce vomiting with a solution of 500 ml table salt boiled with 1 L water. If this does not work, repeat.

For acute gastroenteritis, pan-dry table salt, make two paper packets with it, place one on the patient's abdomen, another against his back.

For the feet, steam 3 L table salt, divide it and bind tightly against the sides and bottom of each foot.

To avoid getting drunk, take a spoonful of table salt first and then drink.

For bright eyes and clean teeth, boil sea salt and recrystallize it, storing the snow-white crystals in a new earthenware dish. Every morning, clean your teeth with the salt and some water, and apply a drop or two as eyewash.

Li classified salt into four groups, differentiated principally by their tastes. Table salt was produced by human labour or by nature's unpredictable forces.

Table Salt

There are very many kinds of salt. Sea salt is made by simply boiling down sea water, as they do in the coastal provinces. Then there are salt water wells in Sichuan and Yunnan, producing saline that is similarly boiled down. A few salt ponds located inland are sometimes 'farmed.' First they build a trench around it and then they flood it with fresh water that in time turns reddish. At summer's end the 'salt south wind' might arrive. It will make the salt in these ponds crystallize overnight. If that wind fails to arrive, then there will be no salt.

Salt was also prepared from briny pools in some lands west of Beijing. Two salt products were obtained from these pools, Li explained, differing in their mode of preparation.

Alkaline Salt

Salt prepared from brine and alkaline salt are two different things. In autumn the pools appeared to have mounds of snow on them, but they were actually salt crusts. Local people would scoop up the contents of these pools and boil them down. As the saying goes, 'Nature makes brine, man makes salt.' The salt so formed was yellowish-green and bitter. All raw mixtures of brine and salt from the pools are bitter and inedible. When the brine is allowed to drip off (instead of being evaporated) hard crystals are left behind. This is alkaline salt.

Unfit for the table, alkaline salt was used in a tincture for eye inflammations. Alkaline mud from the pools was cooked down and made into a paste to treat tooth decay.

Foreign salt (also called Hu salt) was naturally formed crystalline salt that was mostly found at sites along the Silk Road. A wide variety of products were included under foreign salts.

SLIPPERY NOODLES

Foreign Salts
Black salt forms in the northern lake; red salt in the southern
one. Foreign salt is bitter and foul-smelling. It formed when sea
water washed over the mountains, and over time salt crystallized.

There are nine kinds of salt in these northern lands, including
the white variety for the table. Black salt is for treating abdominal
symptoms; Hu salt is for treating deafness and treating the eyes.
Hu salt comes via Dunhuang, in white or purple pieces shaped
like eggs; they do not taste salty but they smell like infertile
eggs.

They say there are nine kinds of salt, but no one knows them
all. Doctors use black salt, foreign salt.

Li commented, 'If the northern and southern lakes produce black and red
salts, and they still use white salt, it does not make sense. The black and red
salts are foreign salts used as medicine. As for the white variety, it is crystal salt.'

Crystal Salt
Unquestionably white Hu salt tasted the best. Li placed it in a group by
itself. The white salt had acquired flattering names: crystal salt, brilliant
salt, monarch's salt, jade salt. Hu tribes had presented crystal salt to the
royal kitchen, Li noted. Indeed, crystal salt continued to be held in high
regard down the centuries. To illustrate this point I have taken the liberty of
including a few selections from the literature.

Salt and Wine
A hundred years before Jia Sixie, an emperor wished to reward one of his
ministers. 'We have talked late into the night,' the emperor said, 'Our thoughts
complement each other like salt and wine. So I shall give you something in
kind.' The emperor presented him an ounce of crystal salt and ten jars of
wine. (This minister was the man who wrote 'The Food Classic' that Jia cited
many times. The good will did not last; the next emperor had the minister
and his whole clan executed.)

HSIANG JU LIN

A Tang dynasty scholar wrote, '*Crystal salt (from Samarkand) is so hard it can be carved into a plate. To have with meat, all you do is moisten the plate. Furthermore, only this salt has the flavour can stand up to the taste of wine.*'

In that period it was a sign of hospitality to provide guests with crystal salt and wine. Li Bo wrote a thank-you poem to a friend with whom he had been staying near Xian.

> *A house on this spot, with the willows in front —*
> *I lingered here as if in the company of long-gone poets.*
> *For your guest there was plentiful wine and crystal salt.*
> *Cup in hand, I watched blossoms blown against the eaves.*

Crystal salt was part of the Mongolian feast called Zhama, which features whole roast lamb. A poem written in the Mongol dynasty described gorgeously robed guests arriving on horseback for the festivities.

> *Summoned, the guests crossed the sandy deserts,*
> *The walls of the tents were richly covered.*
> *Goblets of fine Lu wine appeared endlessly*
> *As fragrant smells came from roasting birds.*
> *The guests wore silk, brocade and pearls*
> *Exotic meats were served day and night,*
> *Always with crystal salt on golden plates.*

NOTES

Opening lines: (on salt) Zao hua sheng wu zhi miao cheng nan dan zhi ye 造化生物之妙誠難殫知也 in
Outline of Medicinal Materials [Ben cao gang mu 本草綱目 by Li Shizhen 李時珍, ch. 11. p. 2] Hereafter abbreviated [LS:chapter, page(s)]
Chinese-English Dictionary: *Classified Dictionary of Traditional Chinese Medicine* 新編漢英中藥分類詞典 (2002) by Zhu-fan Xie 謝竹藩. Beijing: Foreign Languages Press. ISBN 7-119-03216-0
Biography: *Li Shizhen ping zhuan* 李時珍評傳 (1991) by Tang Mingbang 唐明邦.

SLIPPERY NOODLES

Nanjing 南京: Nanjing daxue chubanshe 南京大學出版社. ISBN 730500846X, ch. 3, 4, pp. 338-380

Preface to Li's book: by Wang Shizhen 王世貞 (1526-1590) [LS:Yuan xu 原序]

Donkey hide glue (first mention): (licorice soup) Gan cao tang fang 甘草湯方 [*Shang han lun* 傷寒論注釋 by Wang Shuhe 王叔和 (third-fourth century), Cheng Wuji 成無己 (twelfth-thirteenth century) and Zhang Ji 張機 (first-third century) ch. 4, p. 26]

Donkey hide glue prescriptions: (master recipe) A jiao tang zhu zhi zhi fa 阿膠湯主之之法 [*Bei ji qian jin yao fang* 備急千金要方 by Sun Simiao 孫思邈, ed. by Lin Yi 林億 and Gao Baoheng 高保衡, ch. 2, p. 25]

Name (Donkey hide glue) A jiao 阿膠, made in Dong-*a* 東阿 [LS:50b,39]

Other names Shi ming 釋名: Fuzijiao 傅致膠 [LS:50b:39]; (illustration of *a*-well) A jing 阿井 [LS:Illustrations ch. 3c, p. 41)]

General information Ji jie 集解 [LS:50b:39-40], based on refs (2) (3) and Li's comments (L).

Method of preparation Xiu zhi 修治;

Taste and nature Wei xing 味性 [LS:50b:40]

Indications Zu zhi 主治[LS:50b,40-41]

Effects Fa ming 發明[LS:50b; 41]

Prescriptions Fu fang 附方 [LS:50b:41-42]

References and abbreviations for the above:

(1) *Shennong ben cao jing* 神農本草經 [LS:1a,1], the pharmacopoeia ascribed to the mythical figure of Shennong 神農. Li abbreviated the title of Shennong's book to *Shennong Ben jing* 神農本經 or *Ben jing* 本經. Posterior versions of Shennong's work, exemplified by ref. (2) usually had different titles.

(2) *Ming yi bie lu* 名醫別錄 [LS:1a,1] by Tao Hongjing 陶弘景 (456-536). Abbreviated Bie *lu* 別錄.Tao expanded Shennong's work with additions from medical literature from Han and later dynasties. He also increased the categories of medicinal materials including jade and stones, plants,trees, fruits and leaves, and rice and grains.

(3) *Tu jing bencao* 圖經本草 [LS:1a,9] by Su Song 蘇頌 (1020-1101), about the production of medicinal materials, commissioned by the emperor (r 1023 -1063)

(4) *Lei gong pao zhi lun* 雷公炮炙論 [LS:1a,3] by Lei Xiao 雷斅 (5th c), about the taste, nature of medicines and their methods of preparation

(5) *Ben cao shi yi* 本草拾遺 by Chen Cangqi 陳藏器 (8th c) [LS:1a,5-6]

(6) *Tang Xuanzong kai yuan guang ji fang* 唐玄宗開元廣濟方 (8th c) [LS:1a,14]

(7) *Yang Shiying ren zhai zhi zhi fang* 楊士瀛仁齋直指方 (1264) [LS:1a,19]

Ginseng: Ren shen 人參, Panax ginseng [LS:12a,12]

Useless plants: You ming wei yong 有名未用 [LS:21,13-28]

Licorice: Gan cao 甘草, *Glycyrrhiza uralensis* [LS:12a,1-7]

Soybean: Da dou 大豆, *Glycine max* [LS:24,1-8]; (Li, on its uses) [LS:24,1]

Chrysanthemum: Ju 菊, *chrysanthemum monifolium* [LS: 15,1]; (Li's comments) [LS:15,2]

Jasmine: Mo li 茉莉, *Jasminum sambac* [LS:14,71-72]

Assistants: (son) Li Jianyuan 李建元; (student) Pang Xian 龐憲

Turnips and lamb: Jiu ying song he yang rou shen mei 九英菘和羊肉甚美 in *Shi liao ben cao* 食療本草 (1984) by Meng Shen 孟詵 and Zhang Dingzhuan 張鼎撰.

Beijing北京: Ren min wei sheng chubanshe 人民衛生出版社, p. 104

Turnip: Man jing 蔓菁 (other names: Wu jing 蕪菁, Jiu ying song 九英菘), *Brassica rapa* [LS:26,39]; (differences between turnip and radish) [LS:26, 40-41]

Radish: Lai fu 萊菔 (other name: luo bo 蘿蔔), *Raphanus sativus* [LS:26:44-50]

Maize: Yu shu shu 玉蜀黍 (other name: Yu gao liang 玉高粱*), Zea mays* [LS:23:7]

Animal feed: Shu shu 蜀黍 (other name: Gao liang 高粱), genus *Sorghum* [LS:23,67]

Illustration: (maize) Yu shu shu 玉蜀黍 [LS:Illustrations ch. 2b, p. 21]

Salt remedies: (abdominal distension) Xin fu zhang jian 心腹脹堅; Huo luan fu tong 霍亂腹痛; Yi qie jiao qi 一切腳氣 [LS:11,5]; Yin jiu bu zui 飲酒不醉 Ming mu jian chi 明目堅齒[LS:11,6]

Table salt: Shi yan 食鹽; (sea salt) Hai yan 海鹽 [LS:11,2]

Alkaline salt: Lu jian 鹵鹹 [LS:11,11-121

Foreign salt: Rong yan 戎鹽 or Hu yan 胡鹽 [LS:11,8-9]

Crystal salt: Guang ming yan 光明鹽 (other names, Hu salt 胡鹽, Shui jing yan 水晶鹽) [LS:11,10-11]

Salt and wine: (minister) Cui Hao 崔浩 [Wei Shu 魏書 by Wei Shou 魏收 (506-572), ch. 35, p. 7]; (emperors) Mingyuandi (北)魏明元帝 (r 409-423), Taiwudi (北)魏太武帝 (r 424 452)

Samarkand salt: *Bei hu lu* 北戶錄 by Duan Gonglu 段公路, cited in two sources [*Shuo lue* 說略 by Gu Qiyuan 顧起元, ch. 25, p. 21] [*Yi lin hui kao, yin shi bu* 藝林彙考 飲食部 by Shen Zinan 沈自南] The SKQS version of Duan's book is incomplete and does not contain the quotation.

Thank-you poem: Ti dong xi gong you ju 題東谿公幽居 by Li Bo 李白 (701-762) [*Li Taibo ji zhu* 李太白集注 by Wang Qi 王琦 and Li Bo 李白ch. 25, p. 9]

Zhama banquet in Xanadu: Shangdu zhama da yan 上都詐馬大燕 by Gong Shiqin 貢師秦 (Yuan dynasty 1260-1368) [*Yuan shi xuan*元詩選 ed. Gu Sili 顧嗣立 (1665-1722) I, ch. 40, p. 30]

CHAPTER THIRTY-FOUR

THE GRAND TABLEAU

The gourmet seeks flavour in everything – whether rich and fatty, fresh and crisp, raw or cooked. He will eat anything exotic from land or sea. The glutton just wants to fill his belly. The healthy man insists on the best water, the finest rice, fresh vegetables, fish and meat. Seek real flavour, never mind the exotic.

Early in the seventeenth century, northern tribes were once again on the move seeking to conquer China. The Jurchen had ruled northern China before they were unseated by the Mongols. Now, one leader took Jurchen tribes to the Great Wall, threatening Beijing. At the same time China was torn by a peasant revolt and loyalties were tested in a three-way conflict. The turn of events was swift and unpredictable. The Great Wall was breached, but not by military power. The Chinese officer in command of a post northeast of Beijing switched his allegiance to the Jurchens. The rebel peasant having reached Beijing declared himself the emperor; upon finding his situation untenable he fled south. Two years later, after much conflict and bloodshed, the Jurchen were supreme.

The second attempt of the Jurchen at governing China was different from the first. This time they styled themselves Manchus, and named the dynasty

Qing. At times it seemed as if it were the Manchus who had capitulated. Although the Qing emperors were Manchus they adopted China's culture without reservations. Breaking the precedent of excluding Chinese from government posts, many former officials of the Ming dynasty were taken into the administration. Starting in the second half of the seventeenth century, three successive emperors reigned over a peaceful and prosperous China. The first of these three was on the throne for 61 years, his son reigned for 13 years and his grandson abdicated after a reign of 60 years (out of deference to the grandfather).

Zhu Yizun was in a way a fortunate man. He was 33 years old when the first of these three emperors ascended the throne; he would be the only emperor Zhu would know for the rest of his life (he lived to be 81). Zhu was a learned man, a member of the prestigious academy that undertook literary tasks for the emperor. He collected books. He was pleased as punch to have 80,000 volumes in his personal library. When in 1682 his wife joined him on the occasion of his taking up a post in Beijing, she brought no furniture, only two big baskets of books.

Zhu was also a gentleman cook, author of a book titled *Secrets of Gastronomy*. Zhu may have seen himself as one of the few in a culinary world that was rapidly taking on the aspect of a grand tableau. He ate for good health, in contrast to the gluttons, gourmets and others. Zhu declared a preference for simple meals. In reality, his tastes were anything but simple.

Water and Rice

Zhu's home lay at the southern end of the Grand Canal in a region renowned for its scenery. Actually it was not far from Song Xu's family seat. The region had its own style of cooking, derived from the produce of the fertile land and waters. It was known for its wine, the vinegars and ham that were often identified by the places where they were made. Their names were evocative, just as Beaujolais, Dijon and Bresse call up the gastronomy of Burgundy.

But gastronomy must take second place to basics. In Zhu's opinion, this meant the best water and finest rice. Zhu was fond of rice. He hardly mentioned wheat flour noodles.

SLIPPERY NOODLES

Rice and Grains

Rice grows under the sun's fierce rays; it nourishes man's vital force and fortifies the blood. One might tire of other foods, but rice and grains are endowed with nature's forces, in perfect balance. Rice is bland and sweet. One does not tire of it. It is the key to good health.

Some people have storerooms full of coarse rice containing chaff, grit and assorted grains. They treat their stomachs as grindstones. These rich people may be nobility or just loudmouths. Could they spend less money on self-promotion, and a little more on rice?

Northerners steam rice, losing its juices and flavour. Southerners boil rice, retaining its full flavour. But it is difficult to use just the right with the amount of water and the right amount of heat. Boiled rice is often too soft or too hard — hardly ever just right. Perhaps steaming is the best compromise.

River and Lake Waters

Mountain spring water is suitable for making tea or brewing wine. River and lake waters are best for cooking food and rice because they are earthy, they lack the essence of mountain springs. For health, water must be drawn from sunny and free-flowing rivers located far from human habitation. Do not use freshly collected water, nor water just after a rainstorm. Water is collected at night when there was no boat traffic on the river. It is hauled into earthenware jars on a boat positioned midstream to take advantage of the swifter current.

Back on land, pour the water into a large jar, stir it about 100 times with a bamboo stick, cover it and let it stand undisturbed. An empty jar is held in reserve. In three days about 70% of the water is ladled from the top and transferred to the empty jar, stirred, covered and left for another three days. The used jar with its sediment was washed. The transfer step was repeated twice.

It is best to use a large pot reserved specially for boiling water. Bring the water to a vigorous boil. Transfer it to a large jar containing about 10 g of rock sugar. It will be ready for use in a month or two. The longer the water ages, the better. This water is used for cooking rice. In fact, one can even make tea with it.

Specialities of the Region

The stem of the wild rice plant was a favourite local vegetable. This plant grew wild in shallow waters. Its stiff outer leaves were stripped off, revealing the edible cream-coloured stem, 'so fat, so thick.' (It could be compared to European white asparagus.) Yet the stem was so tender it would cook in the time it took to stir-fry pork, with which it was often paired.

Lotus root and lotus seeds were summer favourites. 'The root was crisp and fragrant, the seeds sweet and tender, pleasing to eat and good for one. The locals say lotus grown elsewhere could not compare. They like to prepare the root sliced thin, cooked with vinegar and sugar.'

It is hard to believe that this tuber grows in the mud beneath murky waters. The root consists of linearly joined segments each about the size of a large potato, with air-filled cavities. When the root is sliced crosswise the cavities appeared as large and small holes. The sweet-sour sauce would pool in the holes.

Lotus seeds were made into soup or taken raw. 'Well do I remember being in a boat, eating lotus seeds and discussing painting with a monk,' a writer reminisced.

The principal meat was pork, not lamb. The ham from Jinhua (a town close to Zhu's home) was famous, prepared from a distinctive variety of pig. Its torso and legs were white, its head and rump black. Salt and pepper were the only seasonings used for preparing ham. Crude salt was recrystallized to remove the bitter taste, and then pan-dried. 'Unless the salt is fresh and clean, all the cooking skills in the world will not be of any use,' Zhu said.

Jinhua Ham
(Insert a silver probe into the ham and withdraw it. If the probe smells fragrant, it is a real Jinhua ham.)

SLIPPERY NOODLES

To salt the pork: Use 30-37 g pan-dried salt for every 600 g of fresh pork. Slip your hand into a soft straw slipper (warm hands make the meat spoil). Rub saltinto the pork skin until it is as soft as cotton, and pearly beads of water appear. Rub it with ground pepper and put the pork in a large jar. Put a straw mat on top and weight down the meat with a heavy stone. Turn the ham every 10 days, four or five times. Smear it with rice stalk ashes, air-dry it and then hang it near a fire. Pine branches are best for smoking.

Local cooks might sandwich a slice or two of this ham between two slices of bamboo shoots, tying them together with a strand of seaweed. A number of these bundles were steamed with some water, slowly, for many hours. The flavours blossomed and the small amount of soup that was formed was superb.

Autumn might see the arrival of some migratory birds. One species was called yellow sparrow, although it was actually a kind of finch with yellow markings. These small birds summered in the northeast. Unpredictably, in some years they would migrate in the autumn to the southern coast of China, passing over the area in which Zhu lived. Three centuries earlier, the artist Ni Zan had prepared yellow sparrows by stuffing the skinned birds with their finely chopped heads and wings and cooking them with sweet wine.

Zhu's recipe likewise called for a touch of sweetness. One wonders how many autumns it took to perfect his recipe. Alive, the yellow sparrow weighed less than 20 grams.

Yellow Sparrows

The birds must be plump. Remove their feathers. Get a dozen of the servants' children to remove the insides with their fingers. (Collect the lungs in a bowl, soak them in wine and cook them with tender ginger, bamboo shoots and spices; fermented black beans can be added) Use a little salt and wine to wash out the body cavity. Chop leaf lard (the delicate fat near the pig's kidneys), mix it with some sugar, Sichuan pepper, cardamom and salt and fill the cavities.

Pack the birds tightly in an earthen dish in two layers, breasts down. Mix sweet soy sauce (containing maltose and brown sugar), scallions, pepper, fennel, cardamom and wine and stir it into near-boiling vegetable oil. Shower the scalding mixture over the birds, immediately covering the dish. After the birds cool, transferthem to a second dish like the first, with the topmost layer of birds now placed on the bottom, the bottom layer at the top. Douse them again with hot seasoned oil. Altogether the birds are doused with oil three times. In this manner they became thoroughly cooked without losing any flavour.

Winter melon was a delight, growing to the size of large pumpkins. The waxy white coating on its green peel enabled storage over ensuing months. The cook liked to use an 'old' melon (last year's melon) that had lost its sweetness yet retained the juices in the pulp. He would slice the melon several centimetres below the stem to make a lid. The seeds and spongy tissue were removed, leaving a large cavity to fill. He might put in it diced pork, duck, chicken or lamb, and then fill it with good wine, soy sauce and seasonings. He would fasten the lid in position with bamboo skewers. The melon was packed all around with rice chaff, and entirely buried in hot embers. In about a week, a certain fragrance appeared in the air. Brought to the table with the lid removed and the peel around the rim trimmed off, the pulp had a jade-like translucence and colour.

The Cooking Style

Zhu said, 'The ingredients must be fresh, clean, thoroughly cooked and prepared in a suitable manner.' The Cantonese way of poaching chicken just to the point where the juices ran pink was not appreciated, nor was the northerners' taste for dipping raw meat into hotpots. Here, beef, lamb and pork were all thoroughly cooked. In fact, Song Xu had recommended that pork be boiled first and then stir-fried.

Many different flavours and textures often would be combined in a single dish. Ham trimmed of bone and skin was sliced, cooked together with bamboo shoots, chives, wild rice stems, and clam stock, seasoned with a little wine and soy sauce; in this manner tender, smooth and crunchy textures were added to complement the ham. Or, a Jinhua ham (with the lower leg removed) was split in half and boiled (to remove some of the fat). Then, it was stewed in a fresh portion of water until tender. At the last minute, shrimp and bamboo shoots were added for sweetness.

The food was dainty and easy to eat, with no bones in the way. Chicken breast was difficult to cook well. The cook stripped the skin, silver skin and membranes from the raw meat. He sliced the chicken breast against the grain and then lightly pounded and seasoned the slices. They were scalded in boiling stock for a few seconds and then finished in a fine sauce. 'Some call this 'pounded chicken.' That is wrong for something so nice to eat,' Zhu wrote. Instead he called it 'delicate chicken' to convey the impression of something soft and smooth.

Local freshwater fish were usually small and bony. The cook made them into dumplings. He stripped 600 g of fish of its skin and bones and chopped the flesh. He separately chopped 150 g of pork fat with a little salt. Then he chopped the fish and fat together, gradually adding 12 egg whites. The next step was performed without pause. He made a crater in the mixture, adding a cup of water bit by bit, chopping quickly and continuously and until the paste no longer stuck to the cleaver. He spread the paste on the chopping board and scored it. The paste could now be treated like dough. He cut it into slices, scooped them up on the flat of the cleaver and dropped them into simmering water. Poaching was followed by chilling in cold water. The dumplings were served in a clear soup.

NOTES

Opening lines: (*Shi xian hong mi* 食憲鴻密 by Zhu Yizun 朱彝尊 (1629-1709), annotated by Qiu Pangtong 邱龐同 (ZPGC, 1985), pp. 4-5
Jurchen leader: Nurhachi 努爾哈赤 (1559-1626)
Chinese officer: Wu Sangui 吳三桂 (1612-1678)
Rebel peasant: Li Zicheng 李自成 (1606-1645?)
Three emperors: Kangxidi 康熙帝(r 1662-1722); Yongzhengdi 雍正帝 (r 1723-1735); Qianlongdi 乾隆帝 (r 1736-1795)
Zhu's library: (80,000 books) [*Bao shu ting ji* 曝書亭集 by Zhu Yizun 朱彝尊, ch. 35, p. 24]
Biography: (events by year) *Zhu Yizun* 朱彝尊 in Baidu baike 百度百科
http://baike.baidu.com/view/80170.html

Secrets of Gastronomy: Shi xian hong mi 食憲鴻密 by Zhu Yizun 朱彝尊 (ZPGC, 1985). (rice and grains) Lun mi gu 論米谷, pp. 18-19; (steamed rice) Zheng fan 蒸飯, p. 19: (river and lake waters) Jiang hu chang liu su shui 江湖長流宿水, pp. 8-9; (recrystallized salt) Fei yan 飛鹽, p. 48; (Jinhua ham) Jinhua huo tui 金華火腿, p. 122; ('yellow sparrow') Zhi huang qiao fa 制黃雀法, p.117; (slow-cooked winter melon) Wei dong gua 煨冬瓜, pp. 117-118; (cooking style) Peng ren he yi 烹飪合宜, p. 6;

(boiled ham, two methods) Zhu huo tui 煮火腿, p. 143; (delicate chicken) Fen ji 粉雞, p. 115; (fish dumplings) Yu bing 魚餅, p. 97

Local flavours: *Bai men shi pu* 白門食譜 by Zhang Tongzhi 張通之 Nanjing 南京: Nanjing chubanshe 南京出版社. ISBN 9788-7-80718-474-4. (wild rice stem) Hou hu jiao bai 後湖茭白 p. 118; (lotus root and seeds) Mo chou ou yu lian zi 莫愁藕與蓮子, p. 119; (Jinhua ham -bamboo shoots soup) Yu ban tang 玉板湯, p. 126

Migratory bird: (Eurasian siskin, a kind of finch Zhu called 'yellow sparrow') Huang qiao 黃雀, *Carduelis spinis*. (Ni Zan's recipe) Huang qiao 黃雀 (NZ-ZPGC) pp. 36-37.

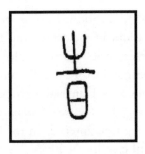

CHAPTER THIRTY-FIVE

A KITCHEN TIMER

The animals are back in their pens.
The girls have left the looms for today.
Yet the moon pauses, unsure that it is evening.
I have to decline your invitation to dinner,
For I shall be here tinkering all night,
Watching incense burn as the water clock drips,
Checking scored candles against the drum tower's beats.
— *(Sixth century)*

This poem mentions four time-keeping devices. Its author was attempting to use burning incense and candles to keep time. For centuries the water clock was the standard time-keeping device in China. Larger water clocks consisted of a series of containers that functioned as reservoirs intended to keep water dripping at a constant rate into the last container. A floating marker in the latter indicated the water level and the time of day. One calendar day was divided into twelve intervals, signalled by striking bells or drums. The drum tower broadcast the time to the city's inhabitants and it sounded five times every night.

Although the poem's author was a contemporary of Jia Sixie, none of these four time-keeping devices was mentioned in *Essentials Skills for Common Folk*. The *duration of a meal* was one of the expressions to denote a time interval, a standard term used for centuries. For example, the artist Ni Zan mixed snail meat with a little sugar and let it stand for *the duration of a meal* before cooking it. The playwright Gao Lian had a recipe where sugar syrup and crude sugar were cooked together for *the duration of a meal*.

A new way of expressing time intervals in the kitchen appeared around the end of the seventeenth century, in Zhu's *Secrets of Gastronomy*. He was discussing ways of preparing eggs. The flavour of Jinhua ham was superb; he did not waste it. He boiled eggs in the water used for cooking the ham. After lightly cracking their shells all over he put them back in the stock to cook for the *time required to burn one or two incense sticks*, allowing the ham juices to seep through the cracks into the eggs. A dainty dish was made by rubbing seasoning into a chicken and steaming it for the *time required to burn one incense stick*. Its meat was then pulled from the bones and steamed again for *one incense stick*. A wondrous mixture of dried mussels, glutinous rice wine lees, soy sauce and pork fat seasoned with ground pepper required cooking for *three incense sticks*.

Other gentleman cooks soon followed, employing incense sticks as kitchen timers. By the eighteenth century it had become the way to express cooking times. 'Use a large turtle, and with it a young chicken. Kill and prepare them for cooking in the usual ways. (The turtle is blanched, skinned, eviscerated and cut into quarters.) In the bottom of a large earthenware pot place an onion, garlic, star anise and Sichuan peppercorn. Place the pieces of turtle and chicken on top of them, some scallions and enough sweet wine and soy sauce to cover the bottom of the pot. Place the covered pot in a steamer and steam it for *the time required to burn two incense sticks*.'

Yuan Mei spoke admiringly of the way duck was prepared in the Ho family of Hangzhou. A fat duck was cut into eight pieces, placed in an earthenware pot with soy sauce and enough sweet wine to immerse it. The sealed pot was steamed over a charcoal fire for *the time required to burn two incense sticks*. (This method was called 'dry steaming' because no water had been added to the ingredients.)

Incense Culture

Incense was composed of flammable tree resins or gums mixed with wood, aloeswood or sandalwood. Aloeswood came from mould-infected trees; it was so heavy with resin that it sank in water. Sandalwood had a strong, natural fragrance. The wood was milled to powder and mixed with frankincense, camphor or spices such as cinnamon, cloves and Chinese spikenard for their distinctive aromas. Perfume fixatives might be added, such as musk, secreted from the navel gland of the Indian musk deer. Another fixative, ambergris, a waxy product from the whale's digestive system, was used less often because it was expensive. Saltpeter was added to some kinds of incense to achieve more uniform combustion. In *Master Chen's Incense Book*, written in the eleventh century, incense was prepared as a powder, or with honey as a binder to make pellets or cakes of incense.

Traditionally, incense burning was a form of religious worship in temples. It was also used in ancestor worship. In the house, smouldering incense lent atmosphere to the scholar's studio; it refreshed the air. It was added to coal, lending fragrance to heat. The word for incense also stood for fragrance so incense and perfume were closely linked. Master Chen gave many formulas for fragrances to be added to laundry, perfumed sachets and deodorants; these formulas were of course non-flammable.

Incense Timers

There was no obvious connection between the burning of incense to time-keeping. The fragrant woods and resins in incense were consumed incompletely and slowly. Incense did not actually burn like a candle; it smouldered. Incense became a time-keeping device because of advances in technology. A steady rate of burning was achieved by milling the components into fine powders. In addition the burn times could be controlled by adjusting the thickness and length of the incense.

Incense timers took several forms. The most sophisticated was the incense seal timer, first used in the eleventh century to determine the five night-time intervals. The 'seal' was a square or round block in which narrow channels were precisely carved, incised in maze-like patterns. Incense powder was pressed into the grooves. Time was told by the position of the smouldering edge. Incense seal timers were highly sophisticated devices, their dimensions and designs precise to the millimeter, tailored to the time of year to reflect changing durations of day and night. It is interesting that in China this sophisticated incense timer was in use before the simplest of its kind - the slender incense stick - appeared. In 1369 the latter was among tribute items to the Chinese emperor offered by Annam (present-day Vietnam); in 1675, eight thousand incense sticks were presented as tribute.

By the mid-seventeenth century incense sticks were made in China. A dozen formulas for preparing stick incense can be found in the voluminous work titled *History of Incense*. They were of course made by manual labour, a practice that continued well into the twentieth century. In brief, an incense stick consists of a thin core of split bamboo coated with incense powder. It was made in batches. A worker would take several dozen sticks in one hand, splay them out and dip them in water. He plunged the sticks into a pile of sticky incense powder, tapping them to produce an even coating of powder, and they dried under the sun. This process was repeated several times, until the desired thickness of coating was attained.

Monks burned incense sticks to keep track of time. Song Xu's directions for colouring hair called for applying black dye *for the time required to burn one incense stick*. According to Li Shizhen, pearl powder for use as a cosmetic was prepared by first placing pearls in a silk bag tucked into a piece of bean curd and boiling the curd for the duration of *one incense stick* before grinding it. Following the pharmacists' lead, cooks brought the incense stick into the kitchen. Given the method of manufacture, it is doubtful that the burn times of the sticks would be uniform. Nonetheless, incense sticks must have been a boon to cooks. Inexpensive, a burning stick occupied almost no space in the kitchen. A cook could keep track of time with a mere glance at its length.

The Burn Time

I think the kitchen incense stick was meant to burn for about 30 minutes. This is based on the frequency of occurrence of the term '*burning (number) incense sticks*' where the number ranged from 0.5 to 12. A search in an electronic library uncovered over a dozen entries for *half an incense stick*; over 200 entries for *one incense stick*; over 80 for *two sticks*; over 40 for *three sticks* and only one for *four sticks*. The frequencies for higher numbers were mostly nil or close to that.

SLIPPERY NOODLES

Why did almost no one use the term 'burning four incense sticks'? The reason may be: there was an existing term for the two-hour interval, 12 of which formed a calendar day. The notion of the 30-minute burn time was put to a practical test. I scrupulously followed a nineteenth-century recipe for sponge cake that called for steaming the batter in a copper vessel for *the time required to burn half a stick of incense*. The cake turned out perfectly after 15 minutes of steaming.

Another Kitchen Timer

The incense stick timer was used until the early twentieth century. A Jesuit priest from Italy had introduced the Western clock to China at the end of the sixteenth century. It would take over three centuries to make its way into the Chinese kitchen. This occurred around the time the Qing dynasty fell, ushering in the republican era. The Western clock enabled cooking times to be measured in even shorter intervals. A lengthy informal history of the Qing dynasty was compiled by a journalist with excerpts from many sources. It had a few recipes with cooking times given in *minutes* and *hours* as measured by the Western clock. The following recipe was among them.

Soft-boiled Egg

Put 600 to 700 mL boiling water in a pot, and gently lower an egg into it. Leave it for barely *6 minutes*. If the egg is small, *5 minutes* will do. For those who prefer a firmer white, use *7 minutes*. This egg is excellent - the white will be set but not hard.

NOTES

Opening poem: Feng he chun ye ying ling 奉和春夜應令 by Yu Jianwu 庾肩吾 (487-551) [*Han Wei liuchao bai san jia ji* 漢魏六朝百三家集 by Zhang Bo 張薄, ch. 99, pp. 37-38]

Incense timing in cooking: (1/2/3 sticks of incense) Yi/er/san zhu xiang 一/二/三 炷香. *Shih xian hong mi* 食憲鴻密 by Zhu Yizun 朱彝尊 (ZPGC, 1985). (ham-flavoured eggs) Wei dan 煨蛋 p. 120; (steamed chicken) Zheng ji 蒸雞, p. 115; (dried mussels) Dan cai 淡菜, p. 105

Turtle: Bie 鱉 or Jiao yu 腳魚, *Trionyx sinensis*; (recipe) Dun jiao yu fa 燉腳魚法 in:

Xing yuan lu 醒園錄 by Li Huanan 李化南, ed. by Hou Hanchu 候漢初 and Xiong Sizhi 熊四智 (ZPGC, 1984) p. 32

Dry steamed duck: *Suiyuan shi dan* 随園食單(2006) by Yuan Mei 袁枚. Bei jing 北京: Zhongguo fang zhi chubanshe中國紡織出版社. ISBN 7-5064-4028-8. Gan zheng ya 乾蒸鴨, p. 85

Incense ingredients: (camphor) Long nao 龍腦, (musk) Xie xiang 麝香; (ambergris) Long yan xiang 龍涎香; (saltpeter) Xiao shi 硝石

Master Chen's Incense Book: [Chen shi xiang pu 陳氏香譜 (fourteenth century) by Chen Jing 陳敬] (scented coal) Xiang mei香煤, ch. 3, pp. 52-53; (laundry) Xi yi xiang 洗衣香, ch. 3, 33-34; (sachets) Yi xiang 衣香, ch. 3, pp. 34-37; (deodorant) Gui ren jue han xiang 貴人絕汗香, ch. 3, p. 38 (nighttime intervals) Wu xiang ye ke 五香夜刻, ch. 2, pp. 1-3

Incense timers: (incense seal timers) Yin xiang 印香, or Yin zhuan 印篆; (incense sticks) Xian xiang 線香

Tribute item: [*Ling hai yu tu* 嶺海輿圖by Yao Yu 姚虞] (1369) Nan yi tu ji 南夷圖紀, p. 57; [*Guangxi tong zhi* 廣西通志 by Jin Hong 金鉷 and Qian Yanchang錢元昌] (1675) Chao gong fang wu 朝貢方物, ch. 96, p. 25

History of Incense: [Xiang sheng 香乘 (1619) by Zhou Jiazhou 周嘉冑 (b1582)] (incense sticks) Xian xiang 線香 ch. 23, pp. 7-10

Manufacture: Chen Kayan. Joss stick manufacturing: a study of a traditional industry in Hong Kong. J. Roy. Asiatic Soc. Hong Kong Branch 1989;29:94-120.

Colouring hair: Ran bei xu fa hei 染白鬚髮黑 [SX:8,1-2]

Pearls: Zhen zhu 珍珠[LS:46, 9-10]

Electronic library: *The Electronic Version of Wenyuange Siku Quanshu* (SKQS) 淵閣四庫全書電子版. Portable hard disk version 1.0 (2010). Hong Kong: Digital Heritage Publishing Ltd.

Two-hour interval: Shi chen 時辰

Sponge cake: Ji dan gao 雞蛋糕 in: *Mei wei qiu zhen* 美味求真. Guangzhou 廣州: Wuguitang Press五桂堂, p. 20

Jesuit priest: Matteo Ricci (1552-1610)

Soft-boiled egg: Bai zhu ji dan 白煮雞蛋 in: *Qing bai lei chao* 清稗類鈔 (1984) by Xu Ke 徐珂 (1869-1928). Beijing 北京: Zhonghua shu ju 中華書局. p. 2253

CHAPTER THIRTY-SIX

BIRD'S NEST

Unlike vegetables, oyster mushrooms, morels, bird's nest and straw mushrooms are not planted from seed. – Song Xu

Seafood was not among the eight delicacies of ancient times. Now people love seafood and I must go with the current trend. (First on my seafood menu is bird's nest.) – Yuan Mei

Some confusion about bird's nest is evident in these statements. Song Xu thought of bird's nest as a vegetable despite differences in the manner of propagation. This is not surprising; initially the full name of this item was 'bird's nest vegetable.' Of course, some might question the idea that bird's nest was a vegetable because feathers or down were often found in it. Nonetheless the idea persisted. Over two centuries later a Manchurian-Chinese dictionary listed bird's nest among vegetables, after coriander and celery, and before mushrooms.

The gourmet Yuan Mei considered bird's nest to be seafood (after all, most of it came from the South Seas). Still, no one was quite sure what bird's nests were. 'If you ask the local people, each person will tell you something different.'

'I simply don't know what it is,' one person confessed.

Some thought they knew. 'When they are about to nest swallows peck at a kind of snail to eat them. There are two firm ribs in the snail's back. The bird eats it all, digesting everything but the ribs which it spits out, making nests that attach to the rocks.'

A fourth account told of swallows building nests with small fish. 'The bird is the size of a turtledove. It builds its nest on the sea walls by laying down soft strands resembling white seaweed.'

One person gave an account of collecting bird's nest on Hainan Island in the South China Sea.

Bird's Nest Vegetable

There are some rocky islands in the seas around Hainan Island, with caves containing many swallow's nests; the swallows are as large as crows. They eat fish and then spit out some foamy saliva, usually in winter, before they shed their feathers. Island men in leather garments and leather hats enter these caves bearing torches. The birds shriek. Island people collect the nests with spades tied to bamboo poles. This is bird's nest vegetable. Older and weaker men might fall off the precipices and perish. Some collect many nests while others return empty-handed.

Others say these birds eat the eggs of the sea hare that resemble seaweed. They spit it out to make nests on the walls of the cave. Sea hare eggs are salty, but what the bird spits out is sweet. It reduces phlegm and improves the appetite. Bird's nest comes in three colours: white, dark and rarely, red.

The Birds

The birds that build edible nests are not swallows and they are smaller than crows or turtledoves. Called cave swiftlets, these birds have more in common with hummingbirds. With wing spans longer than their bodies, they can remain airborne for long periods. Their food consists mostly of airborne insects. Their legs are short, ideal for clinging to cave walls. In spring they build their nests on the walls high above the floors of some sea caves. Nests may be white, tan, or red depending on the species and on the time of year.

SLIPPERY NOODLES

The birds may construct nests up to three times per year, the first being the whitest and considered to be the best. Unlike some birds that make their nests with twigs and saliva, cave swiftlets make their first nests of the year entirely with their saliva. It sticks to cave walls and it dries and hardens to form a light strong shell roughly the shape and size of a cupped hand.

The Nests: A Luxury Food

Although collecting the nests was a hazardous occupation, the islanders would not give it up. The product fetched high prices. From the beginning bird's nest was intended for the rich man's table, a place from which it has never budged. Typically, bird's nests were collected from islands in the South Seas such as Borneo and shipped to ports in southern China. They were an important source of revenue for the provincial governments. Taxes on bird's nest imported from the South Seas around 1590 were comparable to those levied on ivory.

Item Tax	(g silver per 60 kg)
Betel Nut	0.8
Scented Rosewood	1
Mother-of-Pearl Shells	2
Long Pepper	2
Nutmeg	2
Beeswax	7
Cloves	7
Asafetida	7
Frankincense	7
Pepper	9
Myrrh	12
Sandalwood (top grade)	19
Ivory (top grade)	37
Bird's Nest (white, top grade)	37
Aloeswood	59
Camphor (top grade)	118
Rhinoceros Horn (top grade)	126

Market prices were much higher. 'In my youth,' a commentator wrote, 'one catty (about 0.6 kg) of bird's nest cost 30 g silver. In the first years of this emperor's reign (in the 1640s) the price did not change much, and then it rose. Now it costs 150 g silver for the same amount. One does not use bird's nest carelessly. It is only for banquets for very important guests.'

Bird's nest was wildly expensive. Yet there was a place for it in the grand tableau of Chinese cuisine. 'At banquets the food is judged by cost, not taste. Bird's nest is ten times more expensive than anything else, so it is placed at the head of the menu. To a guest a bowl of bird's nest soup tastes like chicken noodle soup. To his host, the guest might as well have consumed a silver ingot. Does one fry pearls, cook jade, boil gold and braise silver? Why spend a fortune on something that tastes like wax?'

Nonetheless the demand for bird's nest did not abate. Two centuries later the naturalist and explorer Alfred Russel Wallace (who had published on natural selection before Darwin) wrote of the resources found in the Malay archipelago. 'Pearls, mother-of-pearl and tortoise shell find their way to Europe while edible bird's nests and sea-slug (sea cucumber) are obtained by shiploads for the gastronomic enjoyment of the Chinese.'

Gastronomy
Did bird's nest have a special flavour? None that was noticeable. It had no fat. It had no smell. Song Xu used it like mushrooms but it possessed neither the fragrance of the shiitake nor the intriguing textures of other mushrooms. 'Don't people know that bean curd tastes better than bird's nest?' Yuan Mei had said, referring to the poor man's sustenance.

Painstaking care went into its preparation prior to cooking. The dry nest was soaked in several changes of cold water for about a day. In this process the gelatinous strands would swell, gaining from four to seven times its weight (the better qualities absorbed more water). It was then boiled until the correct degree of softness was attained. Successful cooking of bird's nest was wholly dependent on using good stock. The strands absorbed the broth; they mingled with the liquid; the solid and liquid parts of the soup would be almost indistinguishable.

Yuan Mei was fastidious about the preparation and presentation of bird's nest. To his mind, portion size was important. Too much was as bad as too little. He thought it ridiculous when on one occasion each guest was served 150 g of bird's nest. 'The soup came in a tub,' he grumbled. Yuan Mei had definite ideas on how bird's nest should be prepared.

Bird's Nest

Bird's nest is expensive, and should not be used casually. If you must use it, allow 75 g (about a third of a cup) per person. First soak it in boiled spring water, and pick out the feathers with a silver needle.

Combine three different stocks - chicken, ham and mushroom - and boil the bird's nest in it. When the substance acquires the colour of jade, stop. This substance is pure and clear, no fat or oil must touch it. It is delicate; do not treat it roughly.

People often add chicken or meat slivers to it; this is eating meat, not bird's nest! Some people might lay 10 g of bird's nest over a bowl of noodles, like strands of thinning hair. They are beggars pretending to be rich men. If you must add other ingredients, use mushrooms cut in slivers, bamboo shoots, slices of carp belly or the meat of the ring-necked pheasant (that is very lean).

I was once in east Guangdong, and tasted bird's nest cooked with winter melon, a perfect match of the clean and the pure. The soup was the colour of jade. Some people have made bird's nest into noodles or balls. That is intolerable.

Not everyone was so fastidious. There was a gentleman cook, a contemporary of Yuan Mei, whose bird's nest recipes would have caused the connoisseur much distress. He made meat balls and coated them with bird's nest. Bird's nest can also be put *inside* the meat balls, he added.

In the grand setting of a salt merchant's home, bird's nests were prepared in more elaborate ways. Bird's nest balls were simmered in fine stock with other balls made of minced shrimp or chicken breast stuffed with pieces of carp. The dish named 'Gold and Silver Bird's Nest' had bicolour strands of bird's nest made by dipping one end of each strand of bird's nest in egg yolk; they were cooked with chicken skin. The dish was completed by the addition of pigeon and goose eggs beaten together and fried to form small golden balls.

Nutrition

Bird's nest was first mentioned in a fourteenth century book on nutrition titled *Knowledge of Food and Drink*. It was grouped with other table delicacies - frog's legs, sea cucumber and oyster. The author lived to be 106 years old. Summoned by the first Ming emperor when he was already over 100, he was asked how to keep fit. 'Beware of what you eat!' he said, and presented the emperor with a copy of his book. It dealt with the toxicity of different foods. Almost every entry was followed by a dire warning. The comment on bird's nest was, 'If there is a black or yellow mould on it, it is spoiled and poisonous. Do not eat it.'

Physicians began to extol bird's nest's health benefits well after it had gained popularity at the banquet table. An eighteenth century work said bird's nest would reduce phlegm, clear the lungs, stop any coughing and fortify the body. 'Some make rice gruel with bird's nest or cook it in chicken broth. Although that is tasty it is at cross purposes with the purpose of bird's nest which is to stop the production of phlegm. Bird's nest can be added to medicine, or simply boiled.' That was not at all appealing.

Another physician prescribed bird's nest steamed with a fresh pear and rock sugar, to be taken every morning. This recipe took hold, for in the physician's lifetime, the Qing emperor was known to take a bowl of bird's nest prepared with rock sugar every morning.

NOTES

Opening quotations: Qing ke cai fa 頃刻菜法 [SX:11,22]; Hai xian dan 海鮮單 in: *Suiyuan shi dan* 随園食單(2006) by Yuan Mei袁枚. Bei jing 北京: Zhongguo fang zhi chubanshe中國紡織出版社. ISBN 7-5064-4028-8 p. 30

Manchurian dictionary: *[Yu zhi zeng ding Qing wen jian* 御製增訂清文鑑 (1771) by Fu Heng 傅恒] Yan wo 燕窩, ch. 27, pp. 20-21

Ask the local people: *[Min zhong hai cu shu* 閩中海錯疏 by Tu Benjun 屠本畯 (Ming dynasty 1368-1644)] (appendix) Fu lu 附錄, p. 1

Simply don't know: *[Min bu shi* 閩部疏 by Wang Shimao 王世懋 (1535-1588), ch. 175, pp. 10-11]

Snail ribs: *Quan nan za zhi* 泉南雜志 by Chen Maoren 陳懋仁, quoted in [*Wu li xiao shi* 物理小識 by Fang Yizhi 方以智(1611-1671), ch. 10, p. 5]; also quoted in [*Ge zhi jing yuan* 格致鏡原 by Chen Yuanlong 陳元龍 (1652-1736) ch. 26, p. 11]

Small fish: [*Xiang zu bi ji* 香祖筆記 by Wang Shizhen 王士禎 (1634-1711), ch.5, p. 16]

Turtledove: [*Hai* yu 海語 by Huang Zhong 黃衷(1474-1553), ch. 2, p. 7]

Bird's nest vegetable: Yan wo cai, 燕窩菜. *Guangdong xin yu* 廣東新語 (1933) by Qu Dajun 屈大均 (1630-1696). Yangzhou 揚州市: Jiangsu Guangling gu ji ke yin she 江蘇廣陵古籍刻印社. ch. 14, pp. 22-23

Sea hare: Hai tu 海兔, *Notarchus leachii*, a sea slug whose eggs are called Hai fen 海粉

Taxes: (land revenues) Lu xiang 陸餉.*Dong xi yang kao* 東西洋考 by Zhang Xie 張燮 (1574-1640), ch. 7, pp. 12-14]

Market prices: *(Shun zhi* 順治, r 1644-1661) *Yue shi bian* 閱世編 by Ye Mengzhu 葉夢珠 (b 1624), ch. 7

Foods judged by cost: *Jing hua yuan* 鏡花緣 by Li Ruzhen 李汝珍 (1763), ch. 12

Edible bird's nests: *The Malay Archipelago* (2000) by Alfred Russel Wallace (1823-1913). Hong Kong: Periplus (HK) Ltd. ISBN 962-593-645-9. ch.28, p. 309

Yuan Mei's remarks on bird's nest: *Suiyuan shi dan* 随園食單 (2006) by Yuan Mei 袁枚. Beijing 北京: Zhongguo fang zhi chubanshe中國紡織出版社. ISBN 7-5064-4028-8 (compared to bean curd; portion size) Jie er can 戒耳餐, p. 19; (preparation, presentation) Yan wo 燕窩, pp. 30-31

Bird's nest meat balls: Zhu yan wo fa 煮燕窩法 in: *Xing yuan* lu 醒園錄 by Li Huanan 李化南, ed. by Hou Hanchu 候漢初, and Xiong Sizhi 熊四智 (ZPGC, 1984) pp.29-30

Salt merchant: *Tiao ding ji: Qing dai shihpu daguan* 調鼎集: 清代食譜大觀 (2006) by Tong Yuejian (18th-19th c)童岳荐, edited by Zhang Yannian 張延年. Beijing: Zhongguo fangzhi chubanshe 中國紡織出版社 ISBN 7-5064-3647-7. (bird's nest balls) Yan wo qiu chen yu bao ji yu 燕窩球襯荷包鯽魚, p. 71, p.164; (gold and silver bird's nest) Jin yin yan wo 金銀燕窩, p. 71, p. 152

Knowledge of Food and Drink: *Yin shi xu zhi* 飲食須知 (14th c) by Jia Ming 賈銘 (1966) Taipei 台北: Taiwan shang wu yin shu guan yin hang 台灣商務印書館印行. (bird's nest, etc.) p. 44

'Beware!': Ming dynasty emperor, Hongwudi 洪武帝 (r 1368-1398) [*Qin ding shu wen xian tong kao* 欽定續文獻通考 by Cao Renhu 曹仁虎 and Ji Huang 嵇璜, ch. 181, p. 11]

Nutritional benefits: *Ben cao cong xin* 本草從新 by Wu Yiluo 吳儀洛 (1704?-1766). (facsimile edition) Xu xiu siku quanshu 續修四庫全書, ch. 16, p. 366

Steamed with pear: *Bencao gangmu shi yi* 本草綱目拾遺 by Zhao Xuemin 趙學敏 (1719?-1805) (facsimile edition) *Xu xiu siku quanshu* 續修四庫全書, ch. 9, p. 109

Qing dynasty emperor: Qianlongdi 乾隆帝 (r 1736-1795)

CHAPTER THIRTY-SEVEN

THE SALT MERCHANT

Light rain in spring: in the city
Every crack is choked with growing weeds.
On the river, only a few huts,
Beyond the bridge is a sharp bend.
There is the wine boat following us —
Emerging from the clump of willow trees.

The city of Yangzhou, crisscrossed with natural and man-made waterways, lay at the junction of the Grand Canal and the Yangtse River. Temples and pagodas bordered the lakes and inlets. Bridges of different design spanned the waterways. A sweeping arch and a semicircle defined one bridge; its design was completed by the mirror image in the waters below. Another bridge had five small pavilions built upon it, resembling an island more than a bridge. Yet another spanned a narrow inlet, its thick supports permitting only the slenderest of boats to pass under it. In Yangzhou there was the custom of touring the waterways in painted boats, from which one could comfortably enjoy the scenery. The boats were one- or two-tiered vessels. Some were converted old salt barges or coal barges. Others were built to order as pleasure boats. Many were owned by people from different walks of life: famous people including famous courtesans, monks and Taoist priests. Those who were in the business of providing entertainment for officials and important people had their own luxurious boats. There were also boats especially designed for ladies. With screened windows and even toilets on board, the latter provided privacy for ladies on occasions such as watching the Dragon Boat races that took place in spring.

Generally speaking there were two styles of boating. 'Cultured' meant the sole purpose was to view the scenery, or it could be 'common' where a group of friends would hire one of the many boats provided by brothels.

To spare the passengers the unpleasantness of kitchen smoke and clatter, a pleasure boat would be followed by a smaller wine boat where food and drink were prepared. Wine boats were specially built with an upright support and equipped with a stove. Everything needed was on board: stove, utensils, china, sauces, spices, meat and other provisions. Guests could order what they wished. Full meals could be provided, with a hired cook. He had only to bring his knives, rolled up in a cloth.

Culture

Painted pleasure boats were but one expression of Yangzhou culture.

It was based on the wealth of its citizens, mainly derived from the salt trade. The Grand Canal was a navigable north-south highway set back from the seacoast. It merged with some rivers and lakes in its path and crossed the salt-producing Huai River region. The proximity of salt production to canal transportation enabled Huai salt to be traded in eastern and central China. It made a number of salt manufacturers and distributors immensely wealthy.

Many of these merchants settled in Yangzhou, their fortunes allowing them to indulge in many pleasures, among them the adornment of house and garden. Bonsai graced the courtyards and interiors of the homes. An artfully stunted plant could evoke the vision of an immense tree; a small arrangement of moss and rockery could suggest a landscape. Different varieties of goldfish were bred. They might be golden, red, black, white or variegated. The fish swam slowly in shallow, rock-lined garden ponds, their veil-like tails billowing, moving to a separate rhythm.

'Money was flung around like dung and dirt.' One example was Rong

Garden, owned by a Mr. Zhang.

> Mr. Zhang's home 'Rong Garden' was outstanding. There were 38 salons, each one different. In summer silks and fine woven bamboo screens kept them cool. In winter brocades and furs kept out the cold. These rooms were filled with fragrant incense, books and paintings, precious jades and rare ink stones. On birthdays and holidays, the whole place was lit with innumerable lanterns and candles. Colours reflected in the glass shimmered; the gold and jade glinted. The people, the flowering branches, each of them cast shadows that made a dazzling blur.
>
> Immaculate landscapes lay outside. In the morning one was free to move about. Around noon the host appeared with a dozen ladies, perhaps to admire the flowers, fish, play music or sing verses. Whatever he ordered was done. His attendants were all pretty, their speech quick and easy. At meals they waited upon him. At his word the music and singing began. The host remained ignorant of the fact that these girls were from an actors' troupe.

Yangzhou was known for its stylized gardens. In the latter part of the Ming dynasty, gardens were given modest names such as *Mon Repos*, The Retreat, and Shadow Garden (suggesting the shadows of willow leaves, water or the hills). At the beginning of the Qing dynasty, it became fashionable to use the previous owner's name such as (Mr.) Ka's Garden, Yuan Garden, and probably Rong Garden. Yuan Mei's cookbook was titled *Menus from Sui Garden* (his home in nearby Nanjing formerly belonged to a gentleman named Sui). More sophisticated names were used toward the end of the eighteenth century, often highlighting a feature of the garden such as 'A Crooked Stream on the West', 'Mulberry Trees by an Ancient River' or 'Lotus Breezes at River's End.'

Yangzhou's society was perhaps the most sophisticated of its time. Some salt merchants became patrons of the arts; sponsoring music, theatre, libraries and literary societies. The appreciation of the arts was not trivial. A few poetry societies held games where their members would draw ivory chips bearing different words; they were to compose poems using those words. One might draw words that did not belong in a poem   a disaster. Or else, hope for a thought to come to mind that would link the random words. It was a difficult game, indeed.

Imperial Patronage

During his reign of 60 years, the emperor made six tours to the south, travelling on the Grand Canal. He stopped at Yangzhou every time, visiting the old temples, the gardens and the scenic spots in the vicinity. He lived in his lodge or on his boats and he dined rather well. Aside from his chefs, a few home cooks were recruited to prepare food for the emperor. Some of the best cooks in the region worked in private homes.

Daily records of the emperor's meals were kept. The record for March 6, 1765 was typical. Upon awakening he took a bowl of sweetened bird's nest. The emperor dined principally on Chinese food, but he preferred Manchu bobo over noodles or rice. Bobo was bread or pastry; it could made with millet, sorghum, wheat, rice, bean or corn flour; unleavened, leavened or fermented; plain or filled; unflavoured, sweet, sour or savory; steamed, boiled, fried or baked.

> Upon Arising (5:00 a.m.)
> Bird's Nest Soup Prepared with Rock Sugar
>
> Breakfast (6:00 a.m.)
> Stir-fried Chicken in Casserole, Bird's Nest with Fine-cut Duck
> Slices of Lamb, Platter of Steamed Duck Eggs and Pork
> Spring Bamboo Shoots Stir-fried with Meat
> Bobo, Steamed Bread

Pu Fu, a high official, sent three of his own cooks to prepare food for the emperor. Each of them made one dish: a mixture of smoked ham and duck eggs encased in a coat of glutinous rice and fried; spinach stir-fried with chicken slivers; bean curd soup.

> Mid-morning Meal
> (In addition to the three items prepared by Pu Fu's cooks)

Duck with Glutinous Rice, A Clear Meat Soup
Bird's Nest with Chicken Slivers
Bamboo Shoots and Chicken Prepared with Wine Lees
Assorted Vegetables Served in Silver Dishes

On the emperor's order, the three cooks were tipped; they each received two small silver ingots. The cooks prepared more of their specialties for the emperor's lunch: bean curd cooked with a fat chicken; the spring bamboo shoots prepared with meat preserved in wine lees; and a fruit pastry. There were other dishes including those named in the last few lines, sent by the governor-general.

Lunch (2:00 p.m.)
Rich Chicken Soup, Smoked Ham Fried in Thin Egg Batter
Pheasant with Steamed Chicken Fat on Skewers
Meat Buns, Steamed Buns

Meat Slivers, Duck Eggs
Bamboo Shoots, Smoked Ham and Cabbage
Gluten Stir-fried with Pickled Vegetables, Ham
Rice, Chicken Soup, Bobo, etc.

(The emperor could not eat everything presented to him.) He sent one dish to each of the consorts who had accompanied him on this trip: to the Empress, chicken with bean curd; to the highest-ranking concubine, fruit pastry; and to the two concubines of lesser rank, the duck eggs, and pheasant on skewers.

For supper, sour and peppery lamb tripe plus two more dishes prepared by Pu Fu's cooks: bamboo shoots stir-fried with pickled vegetables; bird's nest stir-fried with duck. The governor-general (who had supplemented the emperor's lunch) now sent him some ham and sweet-sour preserved turnips. The emperor presented the empress with the lamb tripe, the high-ranking concubine with stir-fried bamboo shoots, and for the other concubines, stir-fried duck and sweet-sour turnips.

SLIPPERY NOODLES

Eight Delicacies, Times Four
Compared to the food of the Mongol period five centuries earlier, the cuisine had grown immensely complex. At its most elaborate, there were four groups of eight delicacies.

From the sea: bird's nest, shark's fins, sea cucumber, fish swim bladder, fish bones, abalone, seal, giant salamander

From the mountains: camel hump, bear's paw, monkey brain, orangutan lips, elephant trunk, panther foetus, rhinoceros tail, deer tendons

Fowl: Chinese grouse, quail, swan, partridge, peacock, turtledove, red-headed hawk, red bird's nest

Plants: lion's mane mushroom, silver fungus, veiled lady fungus, morel, shiitake, daylily and two other kinds of mushrooms

Granted, some of these delicacies were fads. 'Fish bones' was soft cartilage from the shark's head and cheeks: snow-white, crisp and tender. It never gained the popularity of some other delicacies such as the veiled lady fungus, one of nature's oddities — the mesh-like skirt of a mushroom, perfect for encasing delectable tidbits.

Although the composition of each group of eight might vary from one region to another, bird's nest and shark's fins were considered the finest of foods. These were relatively recent discoveries. Song Xu had seen shark's dorsal fin for sale in the market. All he said about it was, 'Steam it and serve it with vinegar.' But that was at the beginning of the sixteenth century; by its end shark's fin was an established food item. Of the shark, Li Shizhen wrote, 'There are fins on its back and on its belly. Their taste is rich and pleasing. Southerners regard them highly.'

Southerners were taken by this wondrous creature. 'Fish reproduce by laying eggs. Only the shark is a live-bearer. Cut open the shark's belly to obtain the foetus. Its eyes are not even open! The meat (of the foetus) is very tender and should be prepared in a thick soup. The (full-grown shark's) meat is coarse and bland. The best part of the shark is the fins.'

The Salt Merchant's Manuscript
It was against this background that *Classic Cooking* was written by a salt merchant named Tong Yuejian. He is one of the hundreds of people mentioned

in the full text of *The Painted Boats of Yangzhou*. 'Tong was from Shaoxing (on the Yangtse delta). He was a salt merchant, a shrewd man, and he lived on Dyke Street.' This street was still there at the end of the last century, although his residence was gone. *Classic Cooking* was never published in the author's lifetime. In 1988 the work was set in print for the first time, based on the only extant (handwritten) manuscript. With over 2200 entries, Tong described the *haute cuisine* of his time. It was a reflection of the society in which he moved.

In this milieu, novel ways to prepare banquet food were constantly called for (even if there were only a handful of excellent ways to cook each kind of delicacy). The sea cucumber is a creature that lives in warm salt seas; its spineless, tubular body is composed of gelatinous tissue. It was best paired with ingredients with like textures — cockscomb, tendons, pig's knuckles and tree fungus. Tong listed a total of 24 ways in which to serve this delicacy.

Pairings with Sea Cucumber

Butterflied sea cucumber: Cut a large sea cucumber into thin slices. Combine it with strips of fat ham, the skin of a sturgeon's head, and cook them together with the flesh of the sturgeon's belly. Butterfly a second large sea cucumber and cook it with the sturgeon.

Cook sea cucumber with cockscomb.

Pair sea cucumber with fried shrimp balls.

Stir-fry sea cucumber with ham slivers.

Cook sea cucumber until it is very soft, and combine it with tiny fish balls or shrimp balls.

Stew sea cucumbers with tendons or knuckles.

Cook them until very tender with aged rice wine lees.

Combine slivered sea cucumber with shredded crab claw meat.

Make sea cucumber balls adding ham, chicken skin and bamboo shoots. and braise them with or without soy sauce.

Stuff a sea cucumber with pine nuts and pounded shrimp and use it to make soft rice gruel with meat stock.

Mock eel: coat sea cucumber with egg white and wrap it in caul fat. The flavour of this surpasses that of real eel.

Mock eel: cut sea cucumber into about 1.7 cm dice, cook it until very soft.

Sea cucumber cut fine can be made into a soup.

SLIPPERY NOODLES

Cut a sea cucumber into three pieces. Add some diced ham, and cook them in chicken stock. Reassemble the pieces in their original positions.

Cook sea cucumbers with cockscomb, and then add more sea cucumber, cartilage from pig's trotters, pork loin and bamboo shoots.

Remove the bones from a fish head, and cook the soft parts with sea cucumber.

Stir-fry sea cucumbers with duck tongues, ham and bamboo shoots.

Cook sea cucumber with pig tongue.

Mix minced shrimp paste with pork and shape it into a roll. Wrap it in caul fat and stuff a sea cucumber with it. Wrap another piece of caul fat around the sea cucumber.

Make a soup with pheasant and sea cucumbers, and garnish it with ham and sweetbreads.

Prepare sea cucumber with fish liver.

Deep-fry pig brains mixed with egg yolks, and combine them with sea cucumber.

Cook sea cucumbers with chicken livers and pork loin.

Pair sea cucumber with tree fungus.

The Banquets

Upon arrival guests might be served tea: sesame seeds or almond cream, with walnuts or pine nuts, flavoured with half an olive, a few peanuts, tangerines, dates, or dried longan from the South.

Depending on the preferences of the important guests, appetizers might include eight kinds of cold cooked meats, different cuts of lamb or even lamb hotpot. Typically, banquets began with 16 *hors d'oeuvres*. Aside from the usual assortment of fruits and nuts, a few items of interest.

> Garnished Ham, Drunken Crab
> Pig's Feet Sausage, Three-layered Duck

Slivers of ham had been mixed with slivered jellyfish, a surprising but successful combination. Tong had described eight ways of preparing drunken crab: with and without soy sauce or vinegar, using dry wine, sweet wine or distilled liquor. The two halves of pig's feet sausage looked curiously different. The cook had split salt-cured and fresh pig's feet lengthwise, boned and reassembled them in a novel way. One salt-cured duck and two fresh ducks were required to make layered duck. To ensure that ducks for the table would be meaty and tender they had been fattened for two weeks on cooked unhusked glutinous rice. Salt-cured duck was prepared by air-drying. All three ducks were boned. One fresh duck was stuffed into the salt-cured one that in turn was stuffed into the third duck. Steamed, cooled to room temperature and then sliced, it displayed a mosaic of meat, skin and fat.

Menus could be described in a kind of shorthand such as 16-4-4-4 or 16-8-10-4-4. Appetizers were followed by the main courses – typically groups of four dishes cooked in the same manner: fried, stir-fried, braised and so forth. These were presented on warming dishes consisting of the plate or bowl set on a lower compartment containing hot water. Soups were usually served between different stages of a meal. After the hors d'oeuvres a 16-4-4-4 might take the following form.

Four *Fried Foods*
(Fried Chicks, Fried Pig's Liver in Caul Fat, Fried Shrimp Cakes, Fried Ham Rind)
Bird's Nest Soup

Four *Stir-Fries*
(Stir-fried Shark's Fins and Crabmeat, Chicken Stir-fried with Clams and Bamboo Shoots,
Stir-fried Duck Tongues, Stir-fried Mallard Duck with Abalone)
Bamboo Shoot Soup

Four *Braised Dishes*
(Braised Soft-shelled Turtle, Duck Feet Braised with Ham, Braised Mushrooms, Braised Eel)
Carp Soup

Dim Sum and Rice
(Chives Pastry, Glutinous Rice and Millet Gruel,
Rice Gruel Cooked with Chicken Soup, Red Rice)

SLIPPERY NOODLES

Every item in the banquet had been designed to impress, from the combination of colours in a given dish to the shapes in which the ingredients were cut. The rice gruel cooked with chicken soup was embellished with bird's nest, diced ham and duck tongues, and plain rice had been dyed red to make it more attractive. The palate been assaulted in every conceivable way. Nonetheless, some guests like Yuan Mei were disapproving.

> Tang poetry was elegant. These days poets do not use words and rhymes with economy because that style is no longer fashionable. So it is with styles in food. In official circles they talk about '16 appetizers, eight entrees, four kinds of dim sum,' 'the Manchu-Chinese feast,' 'the eight little dishes,' and 'the 10 grand courses.' This is the vile work of common cooks. It is only suitable for weddings and official receptions, together with the seat and table coverings, ornamental screens, incense burner table and the bowing and scraping. When there is a family celebration in my home, or friends come here for a civilized drink, what need is there for those trappings? Hired cooks may practice such vulgarities, but I have trained my servants to do otherwise.

NOTES

Opening poem: Hong qiao 紅橋 [*Bao shu ting zi* 曝書亭集 by Zhu Yizun 朱彝尊, ch. 8, p. 6]

The Painted Boats of Yangzhou: (selections and commentary) *Yangzhou hua fang lu* 揚州畫肪錄 by Li Dou 李斗 (2007), commentary by Wang Jun 王軍. *Beijing: Zhonghua shuju* 中華書局 ISBN 978-7-101-05835-2. (painted boats) ch. 18, p. 261; Fan zhou hu shang 泛舟湖上, Tang ke chuan 堂客船, ch. 11, pp. 165-167; (wine boats) Sha fei 沙飛 ch.11, pp. 167-168, Hang bian da guan 航扁大觀, ch. 18, p. 257; (bonsai) Yangzhou pen jing 揚州盆景 ch.2 , pp. 22-23; (goldfish) Jin yu 金魚, ch. 3, p. 46; (garden names) Ba jia hua yuan 八家花園, ch. 1, pp. 13-14; (poetry societies) *Shi wen zhi hui* 詩文之會, ch. 8, pp. 113-114

Dung and dirt: (Rong garden) *Zhang shi rong yuan* 張氏容園 in: J*in hu qi mo quan ji* 金壺七墨全集 (1929) by Huang Junzai 黃鈞宰 (fl 1856). (facsimile edition) pp. 21-22

Sui garden: (origin of name) Suiyuan zi su yuan 隨園之溯源. *Suiyuan yi shi* 隨園

軼事 (1935) by Yuan Mei 袁枚. Shanghai 上海: Da da tushu gong ying she 大達圖書供應社. p. 77

The Qing emperor: Qianlongdi 乾隆帝 (r 1736-1795) visited Yangzhou at intervals between 1751 and 1784

Daily records of meals: Er yue shi wu ri 二月十五日 in: *Qianlong san shi nian jiang nan jie ci shan di dang* 乾隆三十年江南節次膳底檔 http://tieba.baidu.com.cn/p/1109826151

Bobo: Man zhu shi shu yu Qing gong yu shan 滿族食俗與清宮御膳 (1988) by Wu Zhengge 吳正格. Shenyang 沈陽: Liaoning kexue jishu chubanshe 遼寧科學技術出版社. ISBN 7-5381-0009-1. pp. 162-164

Calendar date conversion: *Zhongguo shi li ri he zhong xi li ri dui zhao biao* 中國歷日和中西歷日對照表 (2007) by Fang Shiming 方詩銘 and Fang Xiaofen 方小芬. Shanghai: Renmin chubanshe 人民出版社. ISBN 978-7-208-07016-5

Time of day: *Chinese History, A Manual* (2000) by Endymion Wilkinson, Cambridge (Massachusetts): Harvard-Yenching monograph series; 52. ISBN 978-0-674-00249-4. pp. 209-213

Delicacies from the sea: (bird's nest) Yan wo 燕窩; (shark's fin) Yu ci 魚翅; (sea cucumber) Da wu shen 大烏參, class *Holothuroidea* ; (swim bladder) Yu du 魚肚; (fish bones) Yu gu 魚骨; (abalone) Bao yu 鮑魚, genus *Haliotis*; (seal) Hai bao 海豹, family *Phocidae*; (giant salamander) Wawa yu 娃娃魚, *Andrias davidianus*

From the mountains: (camel hump) Tuo feng 駝峰; (bear's paw) Xiong zhang 熊掌; (monkey brain) Hou tou猴頭; (orangutan lips) Xing chun 猩唇; (elephant trunk) Xiang bi 象鼻; (panther foetus) Bao tai豹胎; (rhinoceros tail) Xi wei 犀尾; (deer tendon) Lu jin 鹿筋

Fowl: (grouse) Zhen ji 榛雞, *Tetrastes sewerzowi*; (quail) An chun 鵪鶉, *Coturnix coturnix*; (swan) Tian e 天鵝, genus *Cygnus*; (partridge) Zhe gu 鷓鴣, *Francolinus pintadeanus*; (peacock) Kong que 孔雀, family *Phasianidae* ; (turtledove) Ban jiu 班鳩, genus *Streptopelia*; (red-headed hawk) Hong tou ying 紅頭鷹. Hong yan 紅燕 usually refers to red bird's nest.

Plants: (lion's mane mushroom) Hou tou jun 猴頭菌, *Hericeum erinaceus*; (silver fungus) Yin er 銀耳, *Tremella fuciformis*; (veiled lady fungus) Zhu sheng 竹笙, *Phallus indusiatus*;(morel) Yang du jun 羊肚菌, genus *Morchella*; (shiitake) Hua gu 花菇 *Lentinula edodes;* (daylily) Huang hua cai黃花菜, *Hemerocallis citrina*; (unidentified) Luu wo jun 驢窩菌,Yun xiang xin 雲香信

Shark's fins: (Song Xu's comments) Sha yu qi gan 鯊魚鬐乾 [SX:4,12-13]; (Li Shizhen's comments) Jiao yu 鮫魚 [LS: 44,42-44]

Sharks: [*Guangdong tong zhi* 廣東通志 by Shi Yulin 郝玉麟 (d 1745) and Lu Zengyu 魯曾煜 (fl 1736), ch. 52, pp.106-107]

The Painted Boats of Yangzhou: (full text) Yangzhou hua fang lu 揚州畫肪錄 by Li Dou 李斗 (d 1817)

<http://zh.wikisource.org/wiki/%E6%8F%9A%E5%B7%9E%E7%95%AB%E8%88% AB%E9%8C%84>

Printout of the full text (introduction and 12 chapters) is 142 pages. (Tong Yuejian) ch. 9, p. 65.

Classic Cooking: Tiao ding ji: Qing dai shihpu daguan 調鼎集: 清代食譜大觀 (2006) by Tong Yuejian 童岳薦, edited by Zhang Yannian 張延年. Beijing 北京: Zhongguo fangzhi chubanshe 中國紡織出版社. ISBN 7-5064-3647-7. (sea cucumber pairings) Hai shen chen cai 海參襯菜, p. 189; (tea upon arrival) Ke chu zhi xian cha 客初至 獻茶, pp. 35-36; (fruits and nuts) Xian guo 鮮果, p. 62; (garnished ham) Ban huo tui si 拌火腿絲, p. 114; (drunken crab) Zui xie 醉蟹, p. 181; (pig's feet) Dui ti 對蹄, p. 103; (fattening ducks) p. 128; (layered duck) Tao ya 套鴨, p.140, calls for one salted duck, Feng pan ya 風板鴨, p.143. (fried chicks) Sheng zha ji 生炸雞, p. 132; (fried pig's liver) You zha gan 油炸肝, p. 107; (shrimp cakes) Zha xia yuan 炸蝦圓, p. 183; (fried ham rind) Zha huo tui pi 炸火腿皮, p. 113; (bird's nest soup) Zhi yan wo 制 燕窩, p. 36; (shark's fins stir-fried with crabmeat) Xie rou chao yu chi 蟹肉炒魚翅, p. 37; (chicken stir-fried with clams) Chao san si 炒三絲, p. 131; (stir-fried mallard duck) Chao ye ya pian 炒野鴨片, p. 149; (stir-fried duck tongues) Chao ya she 炒鴨舌, p. 144; (bamboo shoot soup) Ya sun tang 芽筍湯 , p. 209; (soft-shelled turtle) Su wei jia yu 酥煨甲魚, p.187; (eel) Hong wei man 紅煨鰻, p.174; (duck feet) Wei ya zhang 煨鴨掌, p. 144; (mushrooms) Wei kou mo 煨口蘑, p. 65; (carp soup) Li yu geng 鯉魚羹, p.157; (chives pastry) Jiu cai bing 韭菜餅, p. 313; (rice-millet gruel) Xiao mi zhou 小米粥, p. 332; (chicken rice gruel) Ji tang zhou 雞湯粥, p. 331; (red rice) 紅米飯, p. 327

Vulgarities: Jie luo tao 戒落套. *Suiyuan shi dan* 隨園食單 (2006) by Yuan Mei 袁 枚. Beijing 北京: Zhongguo fang zhi chubanshe 中國紡織出版社. ISBN 7-5064- 4028-8 pp. 26-27

CHAPTER THIRTY-EIGHT

THE POLITICS OF FOOD

Two ministers headed the administration, one Manchu and one Chinese. They had two assistants, a Manchu and a Chinese. Palace banquets and receptions were managed by two officials — one Manchu and one Chinese, assisted by two Manchus. One Manchu and one Chinese were in charge of fine foods, assisted by two Manchus. The same arrangement was applied to fine wines and preserved meat. Oxen, sheep and pigs, fowl, salt, fruits and vegetables were managed by one Manchu and one Chinese.

— Records of the Qing Dynasty

Dual representation was one way in which the Manchu rulers were able to govern China in the first two centuries of their rule. In that period Chinese and Manchus did not intermarry and ethnic identities were preserved. Ethnicity was a paramount factor in filling official posts. Dual representation was in a way an admission of the cultural differences. Many branches of government including food administration encountered the language problem. Chinese had to cope with two foreign languages because government affairs were conducted in Manchu, Mongolian and Chinese. The foreigners must have found the Chinese language baffling — its words were formed with symbols and phonetic elements, whereas Manchu and Mongolian used alphabets that had much in common.

In 1779 the emperor commissioned the compilation of a three-way dictionary that was directed primarily at Chinese who had to converse in Manchu or Mongolian. It included a section on food and drink. Each item required 11 entries.

(1) Chinese word for *bobo* (Manchurian bread and pastry)
(2) Phonetic translation of (1) into Mongolian
(3) Phonetic translation of (1) into Manchurian
(4) Mongolian word for *bobo*
(5) Phonetic translation of (4) into Chinese
(6) Phonetic translation of (4) into Manchurian
(7) Phonetic translation of (6) into Chinese
(8) Manchurian word for *bobo*
(9) Phonetic translation of (8) into Chinese
(10) Phonetic translation of (8) into Mongolian
(11) Phonetic translation of (10) into Chinese

Many conversational phrases in the three languages were given in the dictionary. Understandably they tended to be brusque: 'Taste this,' 'Dice the meat,' 'This food has spoiled,' 'Inedible, I cannot swallow this,' 'He is a little drunk.'

Dining Protocols at Court

In the palace there was no attempt to bridge the food cultures. Although Manchu and Chinese cooking never appeared on the same occasion, food service was based on similar ranking systems. The principle was to give each person food appropriate to his official rank or position. There were six classes of Manchu banquets. Class one was reserved for marking the deaths of the emperor or empress; classes two and three were used, respectively, on the occasion of the death of an imperial concubine of the highest rank, and of a lesser rank. Class four banquets were held on major holidays, important weddings or birthdays, or to celebrate military victories.

The government made an effort to establish the Manchu presence by holding Manchu banquets for visiting dignitaries. Envoys bearing tribute from Korea, religious leaders such as Tibet's Dalai Lama and Panchen Lama, Mongolian princes or married Manchu princesses were accorded class five banquets. The palace was keen on impressing foreign visitors. Class six banquets were given typically for envoys from Viet Nam, the Ryukyu Islands, Thailand, Burma, the Philippines and Laos.

Individuals accorded titles of Crown Prince, Prince, or imperial concubine attended first class banquets, just once, to acknowledge their advancement. Thereafter, they were respectively relegated to class two, three or four, depending on the individual's rank.

The administration strictly regulated the amount of money, the weight of flour and other expenditures for each of these classes. For example, first class Manchu banquets were allotted 120 measures of flour. It was reduced by 20 measures for the rank below it, and so on, leaving class six with an allotment of only 20 measures of flour.

Chinese banquets were divided into five tiers: classes one to three, followed by superior and medium. At a banquet to mark the imperial examinations, presiding officials were seated at 50 tables, 10 of the first class, 24 of the second class and 16 of third class. Principal and assistant examiners were given a superior banquet; lesser examiners and proctors had a medium grade meal. Here too, the amount and quality of food was specified. Goose was served only at first class banquets. Ducks were not served at banquets of class three and below.

Politics

The two food cultures were always kept apart in the palace, but circumstances in Yangzhou were different. There were reasons for Manchus and Chinese to share a meal. 'The Chinese and the Manchu are trying to curry favor with each other,' Yuan Mei noted. Yangzhou was the hub of the salt trade in eastern China, a stop on inspection tours of the salt administration bureau. The thirty Chinese merchants who owned the salt production facilities ran the business — a monopoly — and had become very rich. About 200 other Chinese merchants made smaller fortunes in trading and distribution. The rosters of the Huai River salt administration showed that in the first 20 years of Manchu rule, all of the salt inspectors were Chinese. Over the next 140 years 60% of the inspectors were Manchus. In effect they had control over the salt trade without seizing the business from the Chinese. Salt taxes brought in substantial revenues; by the mid-eighteenth century they were second only to land taxes. The Manchus wanted to promote the lucrative salt trade and the Chinese had to have the inspectors' backing.

The Manchu-Chinese Banquet

Compared to Chinese cuisine, Manchu food was limited. The meat was called 'red' if it was roasted or cooked with soy sauce or other coloured flavourings. Meat boiled or steamed without any sauce was 'white.' (The modifier indicating the cooking method was often omitted.) Although Manchu cooks excelled at preparing roasts, one might say they lacked culinary finesse. The disparity between the two cuisines can be seen in the section on Manchu food in Tong's book. It is given below in entirety.

Manchu Banquet Dishes
Whole pig, red or white, Whole lamb
Roasted piglet, Pair of oven-roasted ducks
White steamed piglet, Pair of white steamed ducks
Braised piglet, Spiced duck with sausages
Pig steamed with wine condiment, White pork shoulder
Roast chicken or butterfly chicken, Roast pork shoulder
White steamed chicken, White boiled boneless pork shoulder
Chicken with pine nuts, Red and white breast meat
Roasted ribs, Boiled white ribs
Red and white spine, Red and white liver, large intestine
Pig marrow, Lamb marrow
Lamb brain or pig brain with meat balls, ham and sea cucumber
Stir-fried lamb omasum with garlic, bamboo shoots and meat slivers
Lamb tail with wine condiment

To have both Manchus and Chinese dining at the same table, the banquet menu would have to incorporate items from both food cultures. The first description of the Manchu-Chinese banquet appeared in *The Painted Boats of Yangzhou*. Fusion of the two cuisines was not attempted. The banquet simply combined the styles of cooking in one lengthy menu. It was composed of five parts, the first three and the fifth were Chinese, the fourth Manchu.

Part One

Bird's Nest Soup, Sea Cucumber Stewed with Pig Tendons
Razor Clam and Daikon Soup, Pig Tripe and Seaweed Soup
Abalone with Pearl Vegetable, Soup of Dried Mussels and Shrimp Roe
Shark's Fin and Crab Soup, Chicken Braised with Mushrooms
(Unidentified) Fish Swim Bladder with Ham
Shark Skin in Chicken Juices, Blood Noodles Soup
Superior Soup

Many of Chinese menu items in the banquet were detailed in Tong's *Classic Cooking*. Sea cucumber braised with pig tendons, a pairing recommended by Tong, was a dish so fragrant one would linger over it. Pearl vegetable was a medicinal herb known as gripeweed. Razor clams and strips of daikon made an exquisite soup, as did the pairing of dried mussels with shrimp roe in another soup. Shark's fins were combined with crabmeat. Shark skin was another edible part of the shark, although it never attained the popularity of the fins. The 'chicken juices' in which it was cooked were, according to Tong, were prepared by cooking a young chicken in a soup made with an old (more flavourful) chicken. Six of the 32 delicacies had been served at the beginning of the banquet. Lest no one forget the importance of the occasion, more delicacies appeared in the second part.

Part Two

Carp Tongues with Bear's Paw.
Pig Brain with Orangutan Lips Preserved in Wine Lees
Mock Panther, Foetus Steamed Camel Hump
Palm Civet with Pear Slices, Steamed Deer Tail, Pheasant Soup
Air- Dried Pork, Air-Dried Lamb, Rabbit Meat
Meat Skewers, Superior Soup

If Tong's suggestions were heeded, the camel hump would have been cooked with a whole walnut (in its shell) to make it tender, and sliced very thin, to be dipped in honey. There was also masked palm civet combined with pear slices, an excellent pairing since these cats mostly ate fruit.

Part Three
Rice Gruel Prepared with Chicken Soup and Bamboo Shoots
Pig Brain Soup, Hibiscus Eggs, Goose Giblet Soup
Carp Steamed with Wine Lees, Mock Fish Liver
Dolphin Testicles, he Monk's Bean Curd Soup
Soft-shelled Turtle Soup, Pupa Soup, Superior Soup

Hibiscus eggs was a beautiful dish of cooked egg white cut in the shape of flower petals, bathed in chicken juices. Surely, this must have been one of the best parts of the feast. The monk's bean curd soup was a fine example of Yangzhou cuisine. The monk Wen Si lived in Yangzhou, near the emperor's travelling lodge. The soup named after him was composed of slivered bean curd (first blanched in chicken soup and then cut into vermicelli-thin strips) and mushrooms, bamboo shoots, ham and chicken (all cut into fine matchsticks). They were combined in clear chicken soup. Expert knife skills were required to prepare this soup. The ingredients had to be combined with a delicate touch, the flavours perfectly balanced. This was the Yangzhou style of cooking.

The Manchu guests must have welcomed the 20 plates of roasted meats and Manchu breads.

Part Four
Roast Suckling Pig, Fried Pork, Fried Lamb
Roast Chicken, Roast Goose, Roast Duck, Pigeon Soup
Assorted Pig Offal, Assorted Lamb Offal, Singe-roasted Pork
Singe-roasted Lamb, Boiled Lamb, Steamed Suckling Pig,
Steamed Young Lam
Steamed Young Chicken, Steamed Duck Steamed Goose
Bobo, Baked Buns, Filled Buns

There were two styles of roasting in the Manchu kitchen. One was called 'dark' because the meat was roasted in an enclosed space. Suspended by means of a metal hook or skewer over the fire, the meat hung free, ensuring even and intense heating. This method was usually applied to suckling pig and to fowl. The other style was 'bright' because an open-mouthed jar or tank was used to contain the fire. The meat was placed on a rack above it and turned from time to time. Such a mode of roasting would be applied to offal, and to chunks of meat roasted with the coat of hair still attached; the hair would burn off as the skin was singed.

The fifth part of the banquet was designed to encourage more drinking. Twenty kinds of refreshments were served, followed by 20 small dishes of hot food (the 40 items were not named). Ten platters of dried or glazed fruit and 10 platters of fresh fruit finally brought the Chinese-Manchu banquet to an end.

Feeding the Staff

The Painted Boats of Yangzhou sometimes took the reader into the odd corners of the city that were not part of its attractions. In the eighteenth century, when the Manchu-Chinese banquet was first held, the vast kitchens of the salt administration not only served up feasts for the hundreds of officials, they routinely fed the visitors' entourage and all of the lesser staff.

At the back of the building were the pens for horses and oxen. There were tents set up for the lesser Manchu officials, guards and others. They were served food appropriate for their rank.

Class 1: Butter-sesame tea, jellyfish, raw fish and noodles, red and white pork, roast suckling pig, roast goose, hard bobo

Class 2: Almond cream soup, roasted tripe and omasum, stir-fried chicken, fried bread, red and white pork, roast lamb

Class 3: Milk, bread, soup, red and white lamb, roast beef, mixed grill

Class 4: Blood soup, grilled beef and lamb, pig and lamb offal, wheat cakes

Class 5: Biscuits, singe-roasted pork and lamb braised with wine and vinegar, sliced meat, meat patties

Later History

The Manchu-Chinese banquet evolved over the centuries that followed, becoming longer and more elaborate. Several regions in China would develop their own versions of the banquet, including their local specialties in the feast. The Manchu-Chinese banquet acquired the aspect of an elaborate Chinese feast, an occasion to feature many of food oddities beloved by the gourmets. But even as time passed the oven-roasted fowl with their crisp brown skins and the adorable roasted suckling pigs would regularly appear at these feasts. At one banquet held in the twentieth century, after the Manchu dynasty had been overthrown, eight suckling pigs were presented, each one prepared in a different style. Some of the guests might have recognized their Manchu origins; it was more likely they had been forgotten.

NOTES

Records of the Qing dynasty: Guang lu si 光錄寺 [*Qin ding da Qing hui dian* 欽定大清會典 (1694) by Ai Xin Jue Luo Yun Tao 愛新覺羅允陶, ch. 85, p. 1]

Three-way dictionary: [*Yu zhi Manju Menggu Han zi san he qie yin qing wen jian* 御製滿珠蒙古漢字三合 切音清文鑑 by A Gui 阿桂 (1717-1797); commissioned by Qianlongdi 乾隆帝] (*bobo*) Bobo 餑餑 ch. 26, p. 39; (conversational phrases) ch. 26, pp. 49, 54, 62; ch. 27, pp. 25, 30

Manchu and Chinese banquets: *Man zhu shi shu yu Qing gong yu shan* 滿族食俗與清宮御膳 (1988) by Wu Zhengge 吳正格. Shenyang 沈陽: Liaoning kexue jishu chubanshe 遼寧科學技術出版社. ISBN 7-5381-0009-1. pp. 230 -231

Primary source for the above item: [*Qin ding da Qing hui dian ze li* 欽定大清會典則例 (1694), by Ai Xin Jue Luo Hong Li 愛新覺羅弘曆] (Manchu banquets) Man xi 滿席, ch. 154, pp. 2-4; (Chinese banquets) Han xi 漢席, ch. 154, pp. 4-6

Currying favour: Ben fen xu zhi 本分須知 In: *Suiyuan shi dan* 隨園食單 (2006) by Yuan Mei袁枚. Beijing 北京: Zhongguo fang zhi chubanshe 中國紡織出版社. ISBN 7-5064-4028-8. p. 16

Salt merchants: *The salt merchants of Yang-chou: A study of commercial capitalism in eighteenth century China* by Ho, Ping-ti. Harvard J. Asiatic Studies (1954) 17:130-168

Huai River salt administration rosters: *Chong xiu Huai yan fa zhi* 重修淮鹽法志 (Chapter 131, 1368-1891) http://www.archive.org/details/02089449.cn

Salt taxes: The significance of the salt industry in Ch'ing China 清代鹽業的重要性 by Chiang Tao-chang 姜道章. Inst. Geography C.C.U. Reports中國文化大學 地學研究所研究報告, No.7 (1994) 52-92 (in English)

Banquet dishes: Man xi 滿席 in *Tiao ding ji: Qing dai shihpu daguan* 調鼎集: 清代食譜大觀 (2006) by Tong Yuejian童岳薦, edited by Zhang Yannian 張延年.

Beijing 北京: Zhongguo fangzhi chubanshe 中國紡織出版社. ISBN 7-5064-3647-7. (Manchu banquet dishes) Man xi 滿席, p. 73. ('chicken juices') Ji zhi 雞汁, p. 39; (camel hump) Tuo feng 駝峰, p. 190; (hibiscus eggs) Furong dan 芙蓉蛋, p. 40
Manchu roasting methods: *Man zhu shi shu yu Qing gong yu shan* 滿族食俗與清宮御膳 (1988) by Wu Zhengge 吳正格. Shenyang 沈陽: Liaoning kexue jishu chubanshe 遼寧科學技術出版社. ISBN 7-5381-0009-1. pp. 206-207
The Painted Boats of Yangzhou: (full text) *Yangzhou hua fang lu* 揚州畫肪錄 by Li Dou 李斗 (d 1817)
Printout of the full text (introduction and 12 chapters) is 142 pages. (Manchu-Chinese Banquet) Man Han xi 滿漢席, (feeding the staff) ch. 4, p. 35. (the monk) Seng Wen Si 僧文思, ch. 4, p. 29. Little is known about (dolphin testicles) Xi shi ru 西施乳 and (pupa soup) Jian er tang 蠒兒湯, ch. 4, p. 35, beyond their chief ingredients.
Later history: *Zhongguo yin shi tan gu* 中國飲食談古 (1985) by Wang Renxing 王仁興 . Beijing 北京: Qing gong yeh chubanshe 輕工業出版社. pp. 81-85

CHAPTER THIRTY-NINE

MORE VEGETARIANS

Vegetables have no flavour.

This opinion was held by many people, although some might not have had Tong's audacity to voice it. This chapter is about how vegetarianism was regarded by the gourmets and by a true vegetarian, and how the art of vegetarian cooking was practiced. One might begin by listening to what Tong had to say.

The Occasional Vegetarian

Usually one cannot keep to a vegetarian diet for any length of time. Start by eating 'clean' meats from animals that you have not seen or heard being killed or those not expressly killed for you. Take ham, salted or dried fish, and eggs. Be an occasional vegetarian: have a vegetarian breakfast, a regular lunch and a vegetarian supper, or be a vegetarian just six days a month. Some suggestions:

Gelatin slices: Use 6 parts deer antler glue to 4 parts tiger bone glue. (Deer antlers obtained in August-September are the best; bone from the tiger's head or the shinbone are best.) Dissolve them in aged wine, mix thoroughly with peach and watermelon seed kernels and some crushed rock candy. Cut it into slices.

Pine mushrooms: Boil the mushrooms and mix the liquid with noodles. Or braise chicken with pine mushrooms.

Duck tongues: Braised with oyster mushrooms and daikon; or simply cooked with greens.

Watermelon: Chill a 6 kg watermelon in water. Cut off the cap. To make a drink, crush the pulp with 150 g of sugar and add 0.6 kg liquor.

Black tree fungus: Stir-fry it with silvery mung bean sprouts (stems only, both ends pinched off).

Chili peppers: Stir-fry them with sesame oil, sweet sauce and a little sugar.

Tong recommended Su Dongpo's soup, a simple vegetable soup. Typically cabbage, daikon, and a few slices of ginger were placed in the boiling pot of a steamer and covered with an inverted oiled bowl to prevent foaming. Rice was placed in the steamer. When the rice was cooked, the soup was also ready. The poet had named the soup after himself, and it was widely copied as his fame spread. He wrote a poem about this soup when he was age 65.

> My host surprised me with his Dongpo soup.
> The daikon tasted of morning dew.
> It has been years since I tasted it,
> Almost as if in another life!
> When I was poor I cooked this soup
> In the pot with a broken leg.

Tong approached the meatless diet in a circumspect manner because he had reservations about vegetables in general. 'Serve vegetarian food in small dishes, and be sure to include some dim sum.' He meant that seeing too much vegetarian food was off-putting; the dim sum would be some kind of rice or noodle. 'Use good soy sauce for vegetables. Some vegetables are cooked with soy sauce; soy sauce is added to other vegetables when they are half-cooked, or at the last second.'

SLIPPERY NOODLES

'To give vegetables some taste, borrow flavours from other ingredients,' Tong advised. Yuan Mei would stir-fry hyacinth beans in their pods with pork, adding some meat stock. The meat was removed before plating. He cooked morels in chicken soup or ham stock. 'When the mushrooms are ready, you must remove the chicken or ham,' Yuan advised. 'They should not be seen.' This was what Tong meant by borrowing flavours.

The Goal

One of the goals of Buddhist dietary restrictions was to keep the food bland, in order to suppress man's internal heat and to keep his temperament on an even keel. 'Things bitter, spicy, salty and sweet are not allowed as food. They can be taken as medicine but only in exceptional circumstances.' Dietary restrictions forbade the use of alcohol and the use of scallions, garlic, onions, coriander and mustard. Of course, these restrictions deprived food of much flavour. In the tenth century, a Buddhist monk made a sauce for boiled noodles with only pickles, crushed sesame seeds and ginger. He drew this taunting remark, 'Add some stir-fried scallions and chives for flavour — *if you are not a Buddhist.*'

Buddhist food was plain by intention. To make the vegetarian dish called Buddha's Delight the recommendation was, 'Do not use fermented bean curd or any thick fermented flour- or soy-based sauce in this dish. It would not be correct. It has a strong Buddhist flavour. It was meant to be plain.'

A True Vegetarian

But man's omnivorous nature is difficult to overcome. 'It is natural and normal for man to love meat,' Xue Baochen acknowledged. Xue was a Buddhist, the author of an excellent vegetarian cookbook and eloquent advocate of the vegetarian diet.

> The vegetarian kitchen is a decent place with foods cooked for human consumption. Why do people insist on cooking fatty ingredients and large chunks of meat, seeking momentary pleasures for the palate while inflicting cruel death on creatures of the land and sea? Just think how the living things were as they flew, swam, jumped and ran. How did they feel when captured?

303

Beasts brought to the slaughter tremble with fear. They are terror-stricken when about to be thrown into the cooking pot. Men and beasts differ in intelligence, but they are alike when it comes to the fear of death. How sad! The butcher neverlays down his knife, and animal cries from the slaughterhouse never cease. How pitiful! The wagons keep rolling to the slaughterhouse. A few hundred quail have to die to make quail soup for the minister. Life should be nurtured, and slaughter should be forbidden. How can we endure this, and let it go on? Hosts love to see beautiful fish and the great meats brought to the table, displaying the best food and finest delicacies. Stewed turtle and steamed lamb follow in succession, bringing new flavours to the feast. Guests see all this glorious food, they fill their cheeks and chew continuously, but they seem unsatisfied, wanting some more food but having no place to put it.

If we did not eat meat, so much suffering could be evaded. If people despised eating meat, and refrained from doing so, they would realize that vegetarianism is fitting. Famous men of old have cooked gourd so well they tasted like steamed duck; bean curd could taste like lamb.

Vegetarian Cooking

But why would committed vegetarians try to make vegetables taste like meat? It is because man has an innate craving for meat even as he rejects it on principle. The earlier chapter on vegetarians discussed how vegetarian food was made to look like meat. To make vegetables taste like meat, or as tasty as meat was a test for any cook. Chief among the requirements was the umami taste, which is found in many dried seafoods (such as dried bonito, dried shrimps and some vegetables including tomatoes). Dried mussels and dried oysters were allowed in the Buddhist diet; the proffered reason was that oysters and mussels have no blood. By extension oyster sauce was allowed; it was a by-product in the preparation of dried oysters and it was a strong flavour-enhancer. Soy sauce also possesses the umami taste. Used together, they strongly enhanced the taste of bland food.

Just as good meat stock was essential in many kitchens, vegetarian cooks made meatless stocks, typically prepared with soybean sprouts, soybeans or broad beans, and a variety of mushrooms.

Superior Vegetarian Stock

Combine 3 kg bean sprouts that have been heated to evaporate some of their moisture, 500 g shiitake mushroom stems, 100 g red dates and 10 L water. Simmer the soup for 3 hours and then strain it, removing the solids. Monosodium glutamate can be added to the stock.

It is debatable how well these stocks worked. When vegetarian restaurants were suspected of violating Buddhist dietary restrictions, the most common accusation was substitution of meat stock for vegetarian stock.

Another device was to introduce different textures by adding deep-fried nuts, fried gluten and different kinds of mushrooms and fungus. Liberal amounts of oil were used (as suggested by Tong) to make the taste richer.

The Disciples' Feast was a Buddhist dish that complied with the dietary rules, yet made certain concessions to man's instinctive love of food. It pleased the eye by combining vegetables with different colours and it employed all the wiles that vegetarian cooks used to make food tasty. The 18 principal ingredients represented Buddha's 18 disciples.

The Disciples' Feast

Shell the *walnuts,* and blanch the *black olive seed kernels* and *almonds.* Deep-fry them separately and set aside. Use *elm fungus, veiled lady fungus, black fungus* and *orange fungus.* Soften them by soaking, then blanch them and plunge them in cold water. Rinse well and cut into appropriate sizes. Set aside. Remove the stems of *shiitake mushrooms* and *straw mushrooms.* Dust *common mushrooms* with flour, blanch them and remove the stems. Wash them thoroughly to remove sand and grit. Set aside. Shell the *gingko.* Boil *fresh lily bulbs* for a few minutes and plunge them into cold water. Boil *gluten,* rinse it in cold water and soak it in vegetable oil. Strip the membranes off fresh *lotus seeds.* Peel and slice: *bamboo shoots, carrots* and young *ginger.* Stir-fry them with quite a lot of oil, adding soy sauce and oyster sauce. Set aside. Stir-fry the ingredients, adding vegetarian stock and braise them until done. Add the tender *hearts of vegetables* — any kind will do. Add thickener, mix gently and plate it. Scatter the fried walnuts, olive kernels and almonds on top.

Ostentation

In China, cuisine was constantly being pushed or pulled in different directions, however gently, by some individuals. So it was that in one instance vegetarian food, originally meant to be plain and bland, was made into luxury food. There had long been a custom in Buddhist temples of serving food to its visitors, and Ding Hu (Tripod Lake) temple, located at a scenic mountain site near Canton, was no exception. For its wealthy, pleasure-seeking guests, an old monk at the temple devised a spectacular vegetarian dish. The monk probably had the mindset of many lay hosts who favour ostentatious displays of food. Like the host who gave his guests too much bird's nest, the old monk gave the visitors food meant to impress, with a dish called Ding Hu Vegan Supreme.

Ding Hu Vegan Supreme was a 12-ringed mound topped with what appeared to be a cluster of orange flowers. The mound was made of various kinds of fungus and mushrooms. Straw mushroom was the only mushroom used fresh and whole; it was harvested before it matured, its stem still hidden under the smooth cap. The other mushrooms were dried and dehydrated; they had to be soaked in cold water to soften. Among these was the white mushroom from the high grasslands inland; the flower mushroom from northern Guangdong (so-called because of floral pattern on its black cap); and the veiled lady fungus. In Vegan Supreme, only the mesh-like skirt of this strange mushroom and only the caps of wild meadow mushrooms and the mushroom-like elm fungus were used.

The other kinds of dried fungus were, after soaking in water, jelly-like and crunchy. The leaves of snow fungus had rippled edges, yellow brain fungus had tightly curled leaves; and the astonishing jelly fungus called osmanthus ear actually resembled the yellow-orange flowers of the cinnamon tree.

To make all these ingredients pleasing to eat, they were variously soaked, steamed or blanched and then cooked with vegetarian stock, wine, vegetable oil, sesame oil, and judicious amounts of sugar, salt, monosodium glutamate, light and dark soy sauce. Then the cook began constructing the mound. First, he made nine rings inside a large bowl, one above the other, in contrasting colours.

Ding Hu Vegan Supreme

1 White mushroom (at the bottom of bowl)
2 (black) Flower mushroom
3 (cream) Veiled lady mushroom
4 (brown) Straw mushroom
5 Yellow brain fungus
6 (white) Fresh lotus seeds, blanched
7 (white) Meadow mushrooms
8 (cream) Bamboo shoots cut into fancy shapes, blanched
9 (brown) Elm fungus

The hollow within the rings was packed to the brim with the remainder of the nine ingredients. The cook put a plate over the bowl, inverted it and removed the bowl, revealing the nine-ringed mound, with the white mushrooms on top. He made a thick sauce and poured some of the hot liquid over the mound. Smaller portions of sauce were mixed with the remaining four ingredients. Around the base of the mound, the cook made three concentric rings.

10 (white) Snow fungus
11 (green) Tender vegetables, blanched
12 (white) Bean sprout stems, blanched

He placed the 13th ingredient, osmanthus ear fungus, on top of the mound, and it was done.

In time a few vegetarian restaurants in the area would copy this dish, drawing visitors from around the world. Eventually, Ding Hu Vegan Supreme was included in Manchu-Chinese banquets held in Guangdong province.

NOTES

Opening line: *Classic Cooking* by Tong Yuejian, p. 71

Tong's suggestions: *Tiao ding ji: Qing dai shihpu daguan* 調鼎集: 清代食譜大觀 (2006) by Tong Yuejian童岳薦, edited by Zhang Yannian 張延年. Beijing 北京: Zhongguo fangzhi chubanshe 中國紡織出版社. ISBN 7-5064-3647-7. (occasional vegetarian) Hua zhai花齋, pp. 56-57. (deer antler glue) Lu jiao gao 鹿角膠; (pine mushroom) Song jun 松菌, *Tricholoma matsutake;* (oyster mushroom) Tian hua gu 天花菇, *Pleurotus ostreatus;* (watermelon) Xi gua西瓜 , p. 57. (black tree fungus) Mu er 木耳, *Auricularia auricula- judae* ; (chili pepper) Ta jiao 大椒, *Capsicum frutescens,* p. 59. (vegetarian food) Su cai dan 素菜單, p. 65; (borrowing flavours) Jie wei 借味 , p. 71 Dongpo soup (poem): Excerpts from Di Shaozhou zhu man jing lu fu geng 狄韶 州煮蔓菁蘆菔羹: [*Dongpo quan ji*東坡全集 by Su Dongpo 蘇東坡, ch. 25, p. 13] Borrowing flavours: *Suiyuan shi dan* 随園食單(2006) by Yuan Mei袁枚. Beijing 北京: Zhongguo fang zhi chubanshe中國紡織出版社. ISBN 7-5064-4028-8 . (hyacinth bean) Bian dou, *Lablab purpureus*, pp. 124-125: (morel) Yang du cai羊肚 菜, that is cooked in the same manner as Gexian mi 葛仙米 *Nostic commune var. sphaeroides,* an edible form of algae, pp. 116-117.
Things bitter: [Fa yuan zhu lin 法苑珠林 by Shi Daoshi 釋道世 (7th c), ch. 55, p. 13]
Monk's noodles: Hu ma zhi ran zhi 胡麻自然汁 (TG-ZPGC, pp.37-38)
Buddha's Delight: Luo han zhai 羅漢齋. *Mei wei qiu zhen* 美味求真 (anonymous, probably 19th c). Guangzhou 廣州: Wuguitang Press五桂堂. p.22
Vegetarian cookbook: (introduction) Zi xu自序 in: *Su shi shuo lue* 素食說略 by Xue Baochen 薛寶辰 (1850-1926) ed. by Wang Zihui 王之輝 (ZPGC, 1984) pp.1-6
Vegetarian stocks: Zhai shang tang 齋上湯 in: *Su cai shi pu da quan* 素菜食譜大 全 (1970) by Zhao Zhenxian 趙振羨. Hong Kong香港: Wei Tung Book Store 匯 通書店, p.5
The Disciples' Feast: Shi ba luo han hui 十八羅漢會 in: *Lingnan shih pu* 嶺南食 譜 by Gao Laoliang 高佬梁 (Republic, 1912-1948) (in volume 1 of two handwritten volumes without pagination)
Ding Hu vegan supreme: Ding hu shang su 鼎湖上素. *Zhongguo ming cai Lingnan feng wei* 中國名菜嶺南風味 (1997) by Ran Xiande 冉先德 and Qu Xianyin 瞿 弦音 ISBN 7800971678. pp. 235-238. (1, white mushroom) Bai jun 白菌; (2, flower mushroom) Hua gu 花菇; (3,veiled lady fungus) Zhu sheng 竹笙;(4, straw mushrooms) Cao gu lei 草菇蕾, *Volvariella volvacea;* (5, yellow brain fungus) Huang er 黃耳, *Tremella mesenterica;* (6, lotus seeds) Lian zi 蓮子, *Nelumbo nucifera;* (7, meadow mushrooms) Mo gu 蘑菇, *Agaricus campestris* ; (8, bamboo shoots) Sun hua 筍花; (9, elm fungus) Yu er 榆耳, *Gloeosterium incarnatum* ; (10, snow fungus) Xue er 雪耳, *Tremella fuciformis;* (11, fresh vegetables) Cai yun 菜運; (12, bean sprout stems) Yin zhen 銀針; (13, osmanthus ear) Gui hua er 桂花耳, *Dacryspinax spathularia*

CHAPTER FORTY

NOODLES, PRESSED AND PULLED

When I was a boy my mother worked at the noodle factory. At the gate was a glass-enclosed cubicle with a bench and a long thick bamboo pole on it (with one end stuck into the wall). The noodle-maker placed a piece of dough under the pole and sat on the end of the pole, bouncing up and down. The dough was pressed and folded repeatedly. He might do this for hours on end to make a stack of compressed noodle dough. The noodles were never dried so they were tender. They would keep only a day or two and they tasted best when very fresh. Everyone has indelible childhood memories of food. I remember the bamboo pole noodles.

This chapter is about two kinds of noodles that are unique to China. Bamboo pole noodles, made of compressed egg noodle dough, are found in southern China; they are made only in a small region that includes Canton and Hong Kong. Pulled noodles are made over a vast area in northern China stretching from the old cities along the Silk Road to points east.

Bamboo pole noodles were invented about a century ago. The art has been passed from one generation to the next. It is time-consuming, labour-intensive work. The number of people who still choose to make it their livelihood is diminishing so it is worthwhile to record (or view) how it is done. The work bench is placed flush against a wall. The bamboo pole is about two metres long and 8-10 cm in diameter. It is straight and strong, relatively light and springy, the kind of bamboo pole that was used in shipbuilding. A hole is cut into a sturdy (brick or cement) wall, about 15 cm above the bench, 2-3 cm wider than the diameter of the pole. One end of the pole is wrapped in several folds of cloth and inserted into the hole. A thick wad of cloth that is placed on the bench about 20 cm from the wall supports the pole. The block of dough is placed under it. The free end of the pole extends about a metre beyond the edge of the bench, allowing the operator to sit astride it (women sit sidesaddle). His feet reach a long footstool. The pole pivots as he steps from one end of the stool to the other, bouncing up and down. In this manner he can apply the full weight of his body to the pole, compressing the dough at 16-20 cm intervals, applying more force than would be possible than kneading by hand.

The dough is made with wheat flour and duck eggs. A crater is made in the heap of flour. Eggs are broken into the crater and mixed in by hand to form rather dry dough. As the dough is pressed under the pole it becomes a long rectangle; it is folded several times and pressed again. Pressing and folding are repeated over the course of one and a half to two hours. Then, the dough can be fed into machines for rolling and cutting noodles.

A Special Texture

Although pressed noodles might be compared to pasta cooked *al dente* because they retain a degree of firmness, there is a difference: the texture of pressed noodles results principally from the way the noodle is made, not the duration of cooking. Cut fine as angel hair pasta, pressed noodles are delicate but chewy; they are elastic and they do not break. Characteristically, they form of tangle of strands when they are boiled.

Although the procedure for making these noodles does not sound difficult, merely time-consuming, there are caveats. First, no water must be added to the dough at any time. Water interferes with the interaction between flour and egg. Second, allow 1.5 to 2 hours for the pressing step. This allows enough time for the dough to achieve the correct degree of firmness. Third, the bamboo pole must not be too thin. A pole with too small a diameter produces a soft noodle that is not worth eating.

Additionally, the raw noodles must be cut thin, about 1 mm wide for the correct mouth-feel. They must be dropped in a large quantity of rapidly boiling water, so that it quickly returns to boiling. They are cooked in less than two minutes, and transferred with a wire scoop to bowl or plate.

What accounts for the special texture of pressed noodles? My guess is that it results from close interlinking of nascent gluten strands as the dough is pressed. The dough is initially dry and flaky because the flour has not had the chance to combine with the water present in the eggs. Because of its high fat and protein content, the egg releases its water slowly; thus, the strands of gluten form gradually. The dough is compressed as this process takes place and the resulting noodle acquires a firmness and elasticity that other noodles do not possess.

Eating Pressed Noodles

It takes several hours to make the noodles and a just a few minutes to eat them. There are those who like the noodles served in a bowl of clear pale broth, such as the wonton noodles prepared in Canton and Hong Kong. The wonton wrapper is smooth, the shrimp inside is sweet and tender; the wonton complements the chewiness of the noodle.

Purists prefer to have noodles served on a small plate, separate from the soup. Traditionally a little rendered lard is splashed over the noodles followed by a sprinkling of dried shrimp roe. The roe will cling to the noodles, adding a little saltiness and flavour. A bowl of tasty broth accompanies the noodles. Together, they make a small meal that can be taken mid-morning, at lunch or mid-afternoon.

An equally delicious combination is suitable for vegetarians. Boiled noodles are simply topped with long thin slivers of scallions and ginger, showered with some rendered lard (or vegetable oil) and a little light soy sauce. The ginger and scallions are caught in the tangle of noodles — as they should be — when lifted to the mouth.

Others might prefer something heartier, like a bowl of noodles in a rich beef soup, topped with slices of beef tongue. The noodles could also be served in a soup made with a variety of pig offal, with pieces of intestine, spleen (or whatever) on top, rich, spicy and filling. This is typically served in a large bowl, garnished with fresh coriander and scallions.

Pulled Noodles

Pulled noodles have acquired at least six different names, probably a result of their long history. Pull, drag, stretch, draw, swing and toss are words associated with this particular kind of noodle. Song Xu may have been one of the first to describe how pulled noodles were made. 'Make a dough with say, 600 g flour, water and a little salt. Smear the dough with sesame oil, and cover it with oiled paper; in summer, leave it for two hours; in winter, overnight. Cut it into pieces the size of a big thumb. Slowly pull it with both hands, holding the ends around the forefinger, middle and third fingers, until fine strands are formed. Have boiling water ready and drop noodles in as they are pulled. They are done when they float.'

The vegetarian Xue Baochen was born in Xian but he was reluctant to try his hand at pulling noodles.

> Here in the north everyone here knows how to make noodles, except me. They make 'pulled' noodles with flour and water, salt, alkali and oil, knead the dough, cover it with a damp cloth, and wait for the dough to blend. Then they pull it into fine strands and boil it. The noodles can be made thin as chives, three-sided or hollow. They can be fried after boiling, and reheated in good broth. There is nothing a cook in a rich man's house cannot do. I have tasted these noodles but I do not dare to try making them.

The process of pulling noodles was indeed daunting. Whether in a roadside stall or a restaurant, the noodle-maker would give a riveting performance. A thin log-shaped piece of dough is held at both ends and swung in the air. It stretches, forms a loop that twists into a coil; with one hand the cook slips his fingers into the loop and brings it up, transferring it to the fingers of his other hand. He grabs the free end of the dough, and stretches both arms. Every time he pulls the noodles, the number of strands doubles. After the eighth pull he will have 256 strands.

SLIPPERY NOODLES

Eating Pulled Noodles

Northern Chinese devised several sauces that went perfectly with pulled noodles. There was a sauce made of sliced pork, stir-fried with chopped scallions, minced garlic and minced ginger. More flavouring was added: wine, fermented bean paste and some soy sauce; water was added together with salt and pepper and the sauce was thickened with wheat starch. It could be set aside, and ladled over steaming bowls of boiled noodles as needed.

A different sauce was made with belly pork, first browned with mixed spices, and then boiled and sliced. Daylily flowers and black fungus, native products that stretched many a dish, were added. With some seasoning and thickening added, a beaten egg was stirred into the boiling sauce. It was finished with a sprinkling of sesame oil. This was a brilliant combination of ingredients. The spices deepened the flavour of the meat and the daylilies and fungus were perfect foils for the belly pork. The airy pieces of egg brought everything into balance.

Tomatoes were not native to China, as could be guessed from a few of its names: foreign eggplant, Western red persimmon, imported persimmon. To make a sauce for pulled noodles — actually it was almost a soup — tomatoes were stir-fried over high heat until they released all their juices. Large puffy chunks of egg (scrambled separately in another pan, in near-smoking oil) were added. A generous amount sauce was ladled over the noodles. In a minute or two, drops of red pepper oil and sesame oil in the sauce would float to the surface.

Pulled Noodles, Chinese Muslim Style

Pulled noodles prepared by Chinese Muslims tasted completely different from the above, because of different dietary traditions. In the Tang dynasty, many Muslims had come from the west via the Silk Road and settled in northern China in cities such as Xian and Lanzhou. There and elsewhere, they held to their traditions, continuing to employ the old ways of slaughtering animals, cooking and baking. They ate oxen and lamb but not pork; wheat flour, not rice, was the principal source of sustenance. The city of Lanzhou, situated on the banks of the Yellow River, acquired a signature dish when a vendor combined pulled noodles with a Muslim-style beef soup. This event is said to have occurred in 1915.

Over the years this particular way of serving of pulled noodles spread far beyond Lanzhou. Unavoidably, it was altered by changes of locale. A Chinese food critic recently went back to its city of origin to taste the noodles. Of course what he tasted was not the simple bowl of noodles that a street vendor would put together. But he was not disappointed.

Lanzhou Pulled Noodles
Our host brought us to a Muslim restaurant. It was packed. Wonderful aromas wafted by, seeming to penetrate my very being, to sharpen my senses. Waitresses circulated, bearing large bowls of snow-white noodles covered with slabs of beef, almost translucent slices of daikon, bright green coriander in a soup brightened by the sheen of red pepper oil.

We were given a private dining room. On the table were 'pure and clean' Muslim dishes, meaning all the food had been prepared according to Muslim dietary rules: beef, beef heart, tripe, and some vegetables. Pulled noodles were served, but they did not resemble the big bowls I saw outside. We were given small bowls. Although the noodles were fine but strong it was the soup that impressed me. No sooner had we finished the small bowls than the waitress brought us fresh bowls that looked exactly like the first, except that the noodles were broad. I came to realize how subtly the width of the noodles affected their taste and feel. The waitress explained that they would pull the noodles to the guests' preference: extra wide, wide, as fine as chives, and four varieties of even thinner strands.

The beef soup contained 10 kinds of spices and herbs, many used in traditional medicine. It was clear as glass, full-bodied without a trace of rankness. Each of us drank the soup to the last drop.

Although the recipe for the soup was kept secret by the restaurant some things were known about its method of preparation. The meat was from cattle that fed in the grasslands, or from yak, a large long-haired bovine native to the mountains of western China. The bones of the animal were also used. A chicken was added for better flavour. A soup was prepared separately with beef liver, clarified and added to the stock.

Beef noodle establishments generally do not disclose their spice formulas either. Many spices were used, the most important being Sichuan pepper, cardamom, ginger peel and cassia buds. Star anise, fennel, cinnamon, cloves, tangerine peel, galangal, nutmeg and pepper are among other spices known to be used by Chinese Muslims.

The principal difference between the different styles of pulled noodles lay not in the way the noodles were made, but how they were presented. Chinese sauces for pulled noodles tended to be thick, heavy and rich. The outstanding attributes of Lanzhou noodles were the clarity of the broth and its delicate flavour. One would not have expected that, knowing it was prepared from oxen. Such are the surprises one may encounter in eating just one kind of noodle.

NOTES

Opening excerpt: Zhu sheng mian shi wo yi ji tong nian 竹升面使我憶記童年 from Zhongshan meishi shenghuo wang 中山美食生活網 http://www.zspoco.com/news/2/2585.shtml

Video (in Cantonese): (Master Liu's bamboo pole noodles) Liu shi fu de zu sheng mian 劉師傅的竹升面 http://yueyu.cntv.cn/lanmu/20110823/115370.shtml

Bamboo pole noodles: Zhu sheng mian 竹升面. Hudong baike 互動百科 <http://www.hudong.com/wiki/%E7%AB%B9%E5%8D%87%E9%9D%A2>

Song Xu's directions: (pulled noodles) Che mian 撦麪 [SX:2,3]

Pulled noodles: Mian tiao 面條. *Su shi shuo lue* 素食説略 by Xue Baochen 薛寶辰, ed. by Wang Zihui 王之輝 (ZPGC, 1984) p. 49

Sauces for pulled noodles: *Shanxi mian shi* 山西面食 (2009) by Sun Xiufen 孫秀芬. Beijing 北京: Huaxue gongye chubanshe 化學工業出版社 ISBN 978-7-122-02134-2 (pork sauce) Rou pian zha jiang lu 肉片炸醬鹵, p. 5; (belly pork sauce) Rou pian mu er huang hua lu 肉片木耳黃花鹵, p. 6; (tomato sauce) Xi hong shi ji dan lu 西紅柿雞蛋鹵 p. 7

Chinese Muslim food: *Hui zhu qingzhen meishi wenhua* 回教清真美食文化 (2010) by Hong Meixiang 洪梅香 and Liu Wei 劉偉. Yinchuan 銀川: Ningxia renmin chubanshe 寧夏人民出版社 ISBN 978-7-227-04561-8. (beef noodles) Niu rou la mian 牛肉拉麵, pp. 179-180

Lanzhou noodles: *Tan chi* 談吃 (2006) by Zhang Zhenmei 張振楣 . Harbin 哈爾

濱: Beifang wenyi chubanshe 北方文藝出版社 ISBN 7-5317-2020-5 pp. 195-196
Soup ingredients: Lanzhou niu rou mian ru he zuo 蘭州牛肉面如何做. Mei ri
Gansu 每日甘肅 http://eat.gansudaily.com.cn/system/2007/07/23/010420310.shtml
Cassia buds: Gui zi 桂子, *Cinnamomum loureiroi*

CHAPTER FORTY-ONE

DOMESTIC DUTIES

The New Bride
Third day: she went to the kitchen,
Washed her hands and made a soup.
Not knowing her mother-in-law's tastes
She asked the little sister to try it.

'Every girl must learn how to cook before she gets married,' Zeng Yi wrote in the introduction to her cookbook, *Domestic Duties.* Zeng Yi was born in 1852, married at age 20, and died in 1927. Her life spanned momentous political events in China: the ceding of coastal ports to European powers, several internal rebellions, the fall of the Manchu dynasty and the establishment of a republic. Zeng Yi was a physician. Compared to the medical books that she wrote, the cookbook was one of her lesser works. Yet with only 20 recipes, it gave a capsule view of home cooking in the nineteenth century.

Zeng Yi must have undertaken domestic duties as a traditional daughter-in-law. In her time, after marriage a woman would be responsible for making sure every member of the household was properly fed. That would consist of dozens of people, young and old, able-bodied and infirm. It was a source of pride to have three or even four generations living under one roof. The rules for managing a household were strict. In some households, they were set out in black and white.

Women's Duties

All women will take turns being manager, ten days at a time. Women over 60 years of age are excused. A new bride is excluded; but after three months she will take her turn as manager. Domestic duties included maintaining the ancestral hall and attending to the needs of all. If a woman could not manage all this, her husband would be punished, and she would have to hand over the locks and keys to the food larders to the next manager.

The duties included making wine and condiments and preserving meat, fish and vegetables. There were set tasks in every household. 'She must personally cook the food, measure out the rice and salt, and never leave the stove,' a Ming dynasty scholar wrote. The salt merchant said that 'one must make one's own soy sauce, salt, vinegar, wine and pickled vegetables.'

At first glance Zeng Yi's book gives the impression that home food preparation had not changed since Jia Sixie's time. Making white wine in winter, Jia mixed yeast cake with steamed glutinous rice, covering the jar with a piece of felt. Making sweet wine in winter, Zeng Yi mixed hot glutinous rice with yeast cake in a jar; straw was packed around the jar, and she covered it with thick cotton bedding. Making fermented black beans, Zeng Yi (like Jia) saw coats of fuzzy mould appear and felt the heat generated. Yet, there were significant differences. A few brush strokes of culinary history might fill some blanks, patch the bare spots and show how some of the changes came about.

Spices

There were very few spices in Jia's culinary world except for a few kinds of pepper and ginger. Pepper wine was made with Hu pepper (black pepper) and pomegranate juice. Another spice wine called for cloves and the tiny black seeds of long pepper. Jia mentioned nutmeg in a chapter on foods found outside China. (Tea was similarly listed because in his time China did not extend south of the Yellow River.)

Spices were used in medicine in the seventh century. The physician Sun Simiao gave countless prescriptions that included licorice, a native plant. Cinnamon, cloves and fennel were used in other prescriptions. Cloves were imported from Indonesia, India or central Asia.

The eight-pointed star anise, the fruit of a tree found in Vietnam, arrived in China later, by sea. Up to the end of the eleventh century, it was called 'ship fennel' an inappropriate name because star anise was much different in taste and appearance from fennel. The name was then changed to the equally inappropriate 'large fennel,' a step that required renaming fennel 'small fennel.' Madame Wu used the terms 'small' and 'large' only when she used both fennel and star anise in the same recipe; most of the time she just used the word fennel. By the end of the twelfth century star anise acquired the descriptive name it now bears, 'eight points.' 'Eight-pointed fennel has a strong taste, peppery and sharp. It can only be used in cooking, not for medicine. Adding a little of it to wine imparts a fine aroma.'

Star anise became a key ingredient in mixtures often called 'five spices.' Pre-mixed spices might number five or not and their composition varied from place to place; typically it might contain fennel, star anise, cinnamon, cloves and Sichuan pepper. The 'smoked fish with five spices' that Zeng Yi made meant simply that it was spiced. She stuffed raw fish with salt, pepper, star anise and fennel; smoked it over smouldering embers with tea and rice and then hung it up in a breezy place to air-dry. One thinks she might have chosen a spot in the shade — under the eaves on the northern side of the house — as Jia did for air-drying meat.

Soy Sauce
It was not until the beginning of the twentieth century that factories for soy sauce production were started in China. Before that era soy sauce was usually home-made. Zeng Yi's directions were explicit.

Making Soy Sauce
Cook soybeans, and then cook them all night over low heat.
The next morning, transfer the cooked beans to a crock, and
mix them thoroughly with wheat flour. Spread them out in a

319

bamboo basket, and cover it with a reed mat. If the weather is hot, let the beans cool before covering them. Three or four days later, there will be a layer of yellow mould. Sun-dry them and leave them out all night. When the beans are dry (and caked), break them up.

To make soy sauce: for every kg of soybeans use one kg of salt and seven kg of water. (To make the brine) pour boiling water over salt and let it cool overnight so the impurities can settle. (Put the beans in a large jar.) Add brine and leave the jar in the sun. In the early morning, before sunrise, stir it. Leave the jar outdoors for about 20 days. If you do not want flies, cover the jar with a piece of gauze. When it rains, cover the jar with a cone-shaped mat. If the jar gets too hot standing in the summer sun, just covering it will not do. Instead, keep a mat suspended over the mouth of the jar by means of four poles, so that air can circulate.

Soy sauce was the ubiquitous seasoning. Zeng Yi used it for sausages, for smoking fish, preserving and stewing meats. To preserve cabbages over the winter, she salted them and partially sun-dried them. Soy sauce and wine were rubbed into the cabbage before packing them into a jar. A few days later, the cabbage was sun-dried again. She would repeat the steps of seasoning and drying the cabbage. It would last not only through the winter but through summer, turning reddish. 'In summer, it is delicious steamed with meat,' she wrote.

Preserving Eggs with Wine Lees
Since Jia's time wine lees were known to keep many foods fresh, even raw meat. However, it was not until the seventeenth century that attempts were made to preserve raw eggs in wine dregs. Zhu Yizun gave two such methods. The first method called for pickling no more than two goose eggs for three years; the white and yolk ran together, as in Song Xu's attempt to preserve eggs with ashes. The second method was shorter.

100-Day Preserved Goose Eggs
Make a vat of freshly fermenting wine. Suspend goose eggs in

it by means of hemp fibres hung from a bamboo pole placed across the mouth of the vat. The next day, the egg shells will resemble crackle ware (kiln-fired ceramic with distinctive cracks). Remove the shells without breaking the underlying membrane. Totally immerse the eggs in wine lees mixed with salt, 20 to a jar. After two months, a taste of it will burn your tongue and make it swell up! The heat will diminish. When the eggs are ripe they taste almost sweet.

Zeng Yi's method for preserving duck eggs was similar. 'Lightly tap duck eggs, cracking the shell without piercing the membrane. Immerse them in salted distilled liquor for 50 days. Then pack them in a second jar alternating the eggs with layers of sweet wine dregs (previously mixed with distilled spirits and salt). Fill the jar in this manner, seal it with mud, cover it with a plate and place it in the sun, leaving it outdoors at night. It is ready in 100 days.'

In the course of pickling, the egg shells came loose and were removed before serving. One merely had to pierce the membrane and spread it apart, revealing the chemically cooked egg. It was as firm as a 4-minute egg and the colours of the white and yolk were unchanged.

Moon Cakes
'At the mid-autumn festival, the 15th day of the 8th lunar month, families would present each other with moon cakes. In the evening families feasted and viewed the moon. Others, wine cups in hand, would tour the lake by boat. On the dyke they sang and danced until dawn, each person holding his neighbour's sleeve.' Such were the ways the mid-autumn festival was celebrated in the sixteenth century. The giving of moon cakes was a popular custom; their round shapes symbolized the moon and the family circle.

By Zeng Yi's time, each region in China developed its own kind of moon cake. Northern style cakes were light in colour, made with sweet lard crusts stamped with a red design, with fillings made from rock sugar, seed kernels and a multicoloured mix of preserved fruits and vegetables.

In central China some moon cakes were made with flour that had been heated (and then cooled). Zeng Yi's recipe is reminiscent of Song Xu's baked pastry made with dry-steamed flour with a filling of chopped walnuts, chestnuts, dates and honey. It is now known that heating flour reduces gluten formation and makes pastry tender.

Flaky Moon Cakes
Put good quality flour in a jar, and dry-steam it (do not expose the flour to steam). Meanwhile, make dough with regular flour, lard and water. Then make dry dough with dry-steamed flour and lard. Make a filling with dry-steamed flour, sugar and walnuts, adding sesame oil to hold everything together.
Take of small ball of regular dough and place a smaller ball of dry dough inside it. Roll it out to a small circle, fold the sides toward the center to make a square and repeat this step. Place the filling in the wrapper, press each cake into a mould and bake them.

Southern style moon cakes were very different: they were a rich golden brown and shiny with egg glaze. They were made in fancy carved moulds about 6 cm in diameter and half as high, lined with dough, often larger. The fillings might be sweet lotus seed or bean paste, in which one, two or four salted duck egg yolks were embedded, the more the better. Both crust and filling were rich with lard. The dough casing was sealed and the cakes unmoulded. They were baked twice, first to firm up the crust and again after glazing the cake with egg.

Red Hot Peppers
Since antiquity, the five basic flavours were salty, sweet, sour, bitter and peppery hot. Sichuan pepper and ginger had provided heat, although neither was particularly strong. Hot red pepper (chili) was grown on the other side of the world. It was brought across the Atlantic to Europe before reaching Asia at the end of the Ming dynasty. Although it would alter the taste spectrum, chilli pepper was introduced to China as an ornamental plant. The sixteenth century playwright Gao Lian mentioned it in his book. 'Foreign pepper: It bears white flowers. Its fruit resembles the tip of a writing brush, its taste is hot and its colour red.'

The plant grew well in the inland provinces of Sichuan and Hunan and this was where the full force of red peppers came to be enjoyed. In other provinces fried smelly bean curd might be dipped into garlic-flavoured soy sauce; in Hunan they were dipped in chopped red hot peppers. The local people said, 'Red peppers are really marvelous. Put a few peppers in your mouth and your tongue goes numb. Open your mouth so you can breathe in its vapours. Eat a few more and you will break into a sweat. Your pulse will race and your spirits will soar.'

Such heat was unbearable for some people. Red peppers were more tolerable if combined with some other substance. For those who liked its inimitable taste, sun-dried red pepper flakes could be added to fermented black beans or fermented bean curd, or prepared as an oil to flavour soups or dumplings. Zeng Yi made a condiment with fresh red peppers and fermented broad beans (fava beans). Cooked with meat, it made a wonderful sauce for noodles. 'Shell the beans, and blanch them. Coat them lightly with flour, cover them with rice stalks or reed mats and leave them in the dark until yellow mould forms in 6-7 days. Place the mouldy beans outdoors to get the sun during the day and dew at night. In August-September (when red peppers are about to ripen) place the beans in a vat of brine and leave it under the sun. When the peppers ripen, chop and mix them into the beans at dawn; and let them stand outdoors for 2-3 days. Place the mixture in jars, adding some sweet wine. This condiment will keep for a year.'

Saltpeter
Zeng Yi used saltpeter to cure meat. This would come as no surprise to Westerners who know that corned beef, hams and sausages are prepared with saltpeter. In China's culinary history it was noteworthy. In English saltpeter has only one meaning: potassium nitrate. In Chinese, saltpeter had two definitions. In a seventeenth-century Chinese book, the word for saltpeter was employed in descriptions of making gunpowder: 'Do not grind it with an iron pestle in a stone mortar or you will have a fire and an unimaginable catastrophe.' In another part of the book, the same word referred to a substance used for tanning animal hides. The first definition was the common mineral eventually used for gunpowder. (In certain parts of China these crystals could be collected simply by scraping the walls or sweeping the floors of a house.)

The other definition was: either the salt used for tanning leather or a salt used in medicine as a cathartic.

Li Shizhen recognized the ambiguity. 'The terminology is mixed up. The two substances may have the same appearance but their natures are radically different. One is fire, the other is water.' The fiery substance was potassium nitrate; the other was sodium sulfate. Nonetheless, confusion reigned. The salt merchant added saltpeter to many recipes for preserving pork by means of salting, air-drying and smoking. One might think that he used the nitrate for curing meat but his recipe for making Jinhua ham diminished that possibility. 'For every 6 kg of ham, use 440 g of salt and some tanner's saltpeter.' Zeng Yi was the first to record the culinary use of saltpeter (potassium nitrate).

Curing and Storing Ham

Start the ham during the winter solstice. (With the hoofs attached and the leg bones intact) the hind legs of the pig each weigh about six kg. For each leg use 220 g of pan-dried salt, 40 g of white sugar and 7 g of toasted pepper. Pierce the skin all over. Rub the pork with saltpeter dissolved in water, and then with sugar and finally a mixture of salt and pepper. Put the leg in an earthen jar and sprinkle the rest of the salt on top. Brine will form as the salt drew liquid out of the raw meat. Turn the ham every few days for about six weeks, until spring.

Hang the hams to air-dry. When the *meat turns red*, bundle the ham in rice stalks, coat it with hemp mixed with mud, and cover it with a smooth coat of mud. Air-dried, the ham will keep for a year.

In nineteenth century England, Mrs. Beeton used saltpeter to cure beef and pork, noting that it 'reddens white meats.' Zeng Yi had rubbed saltpeter solution into raw pork. In the second paragraph of the recipe she noted that the meat turned red. So it was the saltpeter used by Mrs. Beeton, namely, potassium nitrate.

SLIPPERY NOODLES

NOTES

Opening poem: Xin jia niang san shou 新嫁娘三首 [*Wang Sima ji* 王司馬集 by Wang Jian 王建 (767-830), ed. Hu Jiezhi 胡介祉, ch. 7, p. 2]

Domestic Duties: Zhong kui lu 中饋錄 by Zeng Yi曾懿, ed. by Chen Guangxin 陳光新 (ZPGC, 1984). (introduction) pp. 1-2; (sweet wine) Zhi tian lao jiu fa 制甜醪酒法, pp. 17-18; (fermenting beans) Zhi dou chi fa 制豆豉法, pp. 12-13; (five spices smoked fish) Zhi wu xiang xun yu fa 制五香薰魚法, p. 7; (soy sauce) Zhi jiang you fa 制醬油法, pp. 14-15; (cabbage pickled with soy sauce) Zhi dong cai fa 制冬菜法, pp. 16-17; (eggs pickled with wine lees) Zhi zaodan fa 制糟蛋法, p. 11; (moon cakes) Zhi su yue bing fa, p.18; (pepper flakes) Zhidou chi fa 制豆豉法, Zhi fu ru fa 制腐乳法, pp.12-14; (fermented beans with chili peppers) Zhi la douban fa 制辣豆瓣法, made with broad beans, Can dou 蠶豆, *Vicia faba*, p. 12; (ham) Zhi Xuanwei huo tui fa 制宣威火腿法, pp. 3-4. Xuanwei is a district in the province of Yunnan.

Household management: *Wang gu de zhi wei* 往古的滋味 (2006) by Wang Renxiang 王仁湘. Jinan 濟南: Shandong huabao chubanshe 山東畫報出版社. ISBN 7-80713-254 Quotations: (women's duties) Zheng shi jia fan 鄭氏家范; Xu Yuncun yi mou 許雲邨貽謀 by Xu Yuncun 許雲邨 (Ming dynasty), pp. 10-11

Salt merchant's remarks: *Tiao ding ji* 調鼎集 by Tong Yuejian 童岳荐, edited by Zhang Yannian 張延年. Beijing: Zhongguo fangzhi chubanshe 中國紡織出版社 ISBN 7-5064-3647-7. p. 64

Jia Sixie: (sweet wine) Niang bai lao fa 釀白醪法 [7:65,16]; (fermenting beans) Zuo chi fa 作豉法 [8:72,13]; (pepper wine) Hu jiao jiu fa 胡椒酒法 [7:66,26]; (spice wine) Zuo he jiu fa 作和酒法[7:66, 28]; (nutmeg) Dou guan荳蔲 [10:pp .22-23]; (tea) Cha 茶 [10:p.42]

Spices in seventh century medicine: (cinnamon) Rou gui 肉桂, *Cinnamomum loureiroi* [SS:21,20]; (cloves) Ding xiang 丁香, *Eugenia caryophyllata*, [SS:51,2]; (fennel) Hui xiang 茴香,or (small fennel) Xiao hui xiang 小茴香, *Foeniculum vulgare* [SS:69,4]

Star anise nomenclature: (ship fennel) Bo shang hui xiang 舶上茴香, (large fennel) Da hui xiang 大茴香, (eight points) Ba jiao 八角, *Illicium verum*. Usage of nomenclature: (ship fennel) *Su Shen liang fang*蘇沈良方 by Shen Kuo 沈括 (1031-1095) and Su Shi 蘇軾(1037-1101); (eight pointed fennel) *Gui hai guo zhi* 桂海果志 by Fan Chengda 范成大(1126-1193) [Shuo fu 說郛 ed. by Tao Zongyi 陶宗儀, ch. 62a, p. 45]; Ba jiao hui xiang 八角茴香 [Ling wai dai da 嶺外代答 by Zhou Qufei 周去非(fl 1163), ch. 8, pp. 6-7]

Zhu's preserved eggs: *Shih xian hong mi* 食憲鴻密 by Zhu Yizun 朱彝尊 (ZPGC, 1985). Zao e dan 糟鵝蛋; bai ri nei zao e dan 百日內糟鵝蛋, p. 119

Mid-autumn festival: *[Xi hu you lan zhi yu* 西湖遊覽志餘 by Tian Rucheng 田汝成 (1503-1557), ch. 20, p. 11]

Song Xu's pastry: Su mi bing 蜜酥餅 [SX:2,12]

Steaming flour: Prakesh, M., and Haridas Rao, H. Effect of steaming on the rheological characteristics of wheat flour dough. Eur. Food Res. Technol. 209:122-125 (1999).

Foreign pepper: Fan jiao 番椒 [Zun sheng ba jian 遵生八箋 by Gao Lian 高濂, ch. 16, p. 27]

Hunan red peppers: *Hunan ming xiao chi* 湖南名小吃 (2006) by Fan Minghui 范命輝. Changsha: Hunan renmin wenyi chubanshe 湖南人民文藝出版社 ISBN 7-5438-4510-5 p. 80

Ambiguity: *Tian gong kai wu* 天工開物 (2009) by Song Yingxing 宋應星 (1587-1666). Harbin 哈爾濱: Harbin Publishing House 哈爾濱出版社. ISBN 978-7-80753-233-0. Xiao 硝, meaning gunpowder, pp. 334-335; Xiao 硝, for tanning leather, pp. 91-93.

Fire and water: *Xiao shi* 消石 [Ben cao gang mu 本草綱目 by Li Shizhen 李時珍, ch. 11, p. 29]

On the ambiguities: *Science and Civilisation in China* Vol. 5, part 7: Military technology: the gunpowder epic (1986) by J. Needham. Cambridge: Cambridge University Press, pp. 96, 100-101

Tanner's saltpeter: Pi xiao 皮硝 in: *Tiao ding ji* 調鼎集 by Tong Yuejian 童岳荐, edited by Zhang Yannian 張延年. Beijing: Zhongguo fangzhi chubanshe 中國紡織出版社 ISBN 7-5064-3647-7. p. 112

Saltpeter: *Mrs. Beeton's Book of Household Management* (1861) by Isabella Mary Mayson (1836-1865). Ch. 17, No. 828

CHAPTER FORTY-TWO

THE NEW VOGUE

At the Jesuit mission in Beijing, the German scholar Johann Adam Schall von Bell made Western style pancakes for his Chinese friends. Composed of honey, flour and eggs, they were cooked between iron plates, and as thin as paper.

Aside from his scholarly contributions to mathematics and astronomy, the thin cakes that Schall von Bell introduced in the mid-seventeenth century enjoyed a popularity that persists to the present day. The crisp finger-width cylinders packed in large tins are sold in many places. Schall's pancakes were gaufrettes, thin cakes cooked in a metal press. Yuan Mei's friend gave him a recipe.

Mr. Yang's Western Cakes
Beat egg whites with flour and water. Use a hinged copper press with the space between the plates less than 3 mm. Heat the press, add a spoonful of batter, squeeze the press together, and dry it out. The cake is the size of a plate, snow-white and thin as tissue paper. Add some ground rock sugar and pine nuts.

The salt merchant made gaufrettes. His method called for resting the batter as in some Belgian and French recipes — 'for two to four hours in the summer (or 6 to 8 hours in winter). Use an iron griddle to cook the cake and roll it up while it is still hot.'

Schall was among the earliest Jesuit missionaries who settled in China. It was not until the nineteenth century that a larger influx of European and American missionaries as well as traders and diplomats came to live in China, often in cities that had been secured by Western powers as a result of the Opium War. Western things became the new vogue. Shanghai and Hong Kong soon had hotels and restaurants catering to foreigners. Some of these establishments attracted Chinese clientele as well. In Shanghai, tea dances at the Astor House Hotel (near the Bund) were especially popular. To have tea at one of these places, with sandwiches and cream cakes, to dance and be seen, was to be both spectator and participant in a new world. Just as the passages through China of the Jurchen, Mongolians and Manchus were reflected in some cookbooks of their times, European and American recipes written in Chinese began to appear.

The Missionary's Cookbook

In 1851 Martha Foster of Alabama married Tartleton Perry Crawford, a Baptist minister from Tennessee. T. P. Crawford was posted to China the following year. The couple moved into the Southern Baptist Mission in Shanghai, one of the five treaty ports that had been established after the Opium War. It was considered the best place for missionaries and traders. In the foreign settlements within those cities, Americans and Europeans of various nationalities could live virtually separate from the native population, if they chose to do so.

Martha Crawford assembled a cookbook composed of American recipes written in Chinese for the use of Chinese cooks. Given how American and Europeans lived in Chinese cities at that time, this kind of cookbook must have been a necessity. Foreigners hired Chinese cooks who had to prepare western food. Westerners ate meat served in large slabs on plates, with vegetables cooked separately. Above all Westerners liked sweets: cakes, pies, puddings, custards, jams and preserved fruits. *Foreign Cookery in Chinese* was first published by the Presbyterian Mission Press in Shanghai in 1866. It was reprinted 20 years later, and again in 1909. Martha Crawford's name did not appear on the book in the last edition, and the translator (if there was one) was not named. She must have been the one who selected the recipes, given in English in the index. Virtually every item among the 200-odd recipes could be found in American cookbooks of the mid-nineteenth century. Her book explained in Chinese how to prepare doughnuts, Indian meal bread, flannel cakes, beef steak pie and charlotte Russe. Pound cake was called Catty Cake because at that time the catty (590 g) was the Chinese unit of weight closest to the pound.

Catty Cake

1 catty flour
9 eggs (weight, about 1 catty)
1 catty sugar
Nutmeg, ground
Half catty of butter
1 large spoonful strong liquor
Beat the butter with the sugar until the mixture turns white. Add the beaten egg yolks. Add some of the flour, the nutmeg and beaten egg whites. Mix in the remaining flour and add the liquor. Pour it into a Western metal dish and bake it in a slow oven. When done, sprinkle sugar over the top.

Mr. Huang's book
Fifty years after Martha Crawford first published *Foreign Cookery in Chinese*, a collection of European and American recipes translated into Chinese was published by a man named Huang Zhenzhang. Huang was born in Taishan, Guangdong, the birthplace of many Chinese immigrants to the United States. Some time before the Manchu dynasty fell in 1911 he went abroad, like many of his contemporaries. He opened a Chinese-American medicine shop in San Francisco. Huang returned several years later with the cachet of being 'American-educated' and was in the import-export business in Hong Kong. As his American-educated friend wrote in the introduction, 'He spent many years in America, collecting cookbooks of various nations, diligently

studying and translating them into Chinese.'

American and European Cookbook was published in 1914, the first of four editions. In 1925 its title was changed to *Chinese and European Cookbook.* (There were only a handful of Chinese dishes among the 1700-odd items, although later editions included traditional Chinese recipes.) Huang's cookbook was an impressive feat of rendition. He successfully translated American and European recipes into Chinese. Each recipe (typically no more than three lines) conveyed the meaning and sense of the original. All ingredients were as given in the original; no Chinese ingredients were substituted. For example, the recipe for meat stock called for starting fresh beef shin and veal in cold water, skimming off the foam, and further cooking with celery, onion, parsley and carrots. To make mayonnaise, Huang wrote, the oil had to be added very slowly with constant beating of the seasoned egg yolks. He used the cup as a measure of ingredients such as flour and sugar. He defined one cup of flour as weighing 4.8 oz, a figure that falls within current estimates. He defined the tablespoon as three teaspoons and specified that these must be level measurements (as the American cook Fannie Farmer said).

The names of the Western recipes were given in English — Huang's English and some of them were atrocious (German Brains, Italian Tongue and Mint of Lamb). His book was intended for Chinese servants in the employ of Westerners as could be seen in the conversational English sentences at the end of the book. To enable Chinese to converse, the foreign language was translated phonetically as in the Manchu-Mongol-Chinese dictionary. Of course, the actual sounds produced depended on which dialect the speaker used: that of Canton, Shanghai or some other part of China.

Asking for a Cook

'Good evening, Mrs. T. Do you want a servant?'

'Yes, I wish I could get a good cook. Who did you cook for before?'

'Mr. P. the City Postmaster, for the last two years.'

'What is your name?'

'My name is Ah Quong.'

'I will call you Charley.'

SLIPPERY NOODLES

Western Menus

Huang enabled Chinese cooks to produce Western meals in the homes of foreigners or in a restaurant. The heavy soups favored by the British were intended to provide warmth and sustenance in a cold damp climate. With the spread of British colonialism these thick soups came to be served where temperatures were often scorching: Egypt, Kenya and Hong Kong. Meat and seafood were roasted or boiled but also made into patties, timbales, balls and croquettes in the European fashion. They were often accompanied by different sauces, made separately. Huang gave 65 ways of preparing potatoes. Puddings and their accompanying sauces, pies, breads, biscuits, cookies and cakes, jams and jellies took up a third of the book. The bills of fare reflected Anglo-American tastes of the early twentieth century.

Breakfast
Canned Apricots with Cream, Quaker Oats Mush
Sausages with Fried Bananas, Peas and Potatoes
Coffee, Bread and Pancakes

Lunch
Chicken Bouillon, Fried Oysters
Mutton Curry Darjeeling, Rice, New Potatoes
Raspberry Soufflé

Dinner
Oyster Cocktail, Cream of Clam Soup
Steamed Sand Dabs, Chicken Tartlets
Saddle of Lamb, Beet Salad
Cherry Sherbet, Layer Cake

Huang's Sources

How did Mr. Huang assemble the recipes for the various editions of his book? One might expect that cookbooks that would furnish Huang with many recipes but obvious choices such as *The Boston Cooking School Cookbook* were ruled out. Only one source of multiple recipes has been identified: *May Byron's Vegetable Book* (London, 1916). Huang used five of her salad recipes. Huang seems to have taken recipes piecemeal from American books, magazines and newspapers. Perfect or near-perfect matches to a few of Huang's recipes could be found in different sources.

(Walnut Wafers) *365 Cakes and Cookies* (Philadelphia, 1904); the *Castelar Creche Cook Book* (Los Angeles, 1922)

(Yankee Puffs, with sweet sauce) 'Par Excellence' St. Agnes Guild of the Church of the Epiphany (Chicago, 1888)

(Irish Moss Jelly made with sherry) *Mrs. Rorer's Diet for the Sick* by Sarah Tyson Rorer (Philadelphia, 1914)

(Bisque of Hard Crabs, with croutons) *The Post-graduate Cookery Book by* Adolphe Meyer (New York, 1903)

There was no clearer proof of his sojourn in the United States that the inclusion of 'chopsue' (his spelling) recipes in his book. He might have been curious about this American version of Chinese food. It was so firmly rooted in American cooking that by 1910 the United States government's Manual for Army Cooks had a 'chop suey hash' made with bacon, cooked beef, onions, tomatoes, turnips and corn.

Huang's recipe was in its way no less exotic, calling for what he called Western soy sauce (Worcestershire sauce), Western ketchup, soup powder and other foreign products.

Chop Beef Chop Sue

Stir-fry two teaspoons of chopped onion in butter, adding chopped tomatoes, a cup of stock, and 1.5 tablespoon soup powder dissolved in water. Add half a cup of stuffed olives, two teaspoons of Worcestershire sauce, Western ketchup, and two cups of cooked macaroni. Add a cup of chopped beef jerky stir-fried in butter, and some salt and pepper.

In the Chinese Kitchen

Western food items appeared in a three-volume series titled *Home Cooking* that was directed principally at Chinese housewives. In the first volume (1923) the only foreign item was foreign peppermint candy made with peppermint extract (obtainable from Western pharmacies in Shanghai). In the third

SLIPPERY NOODLES

volume (1926) there was a recipe for brandy, made to be sold. 'Filter 6 kg of grape wine through 20 sheets of paper. Distill it to concentrate the alcohol. Distribute it into glass bottles and stick on the labels. It is good enough to compete with the foreign product.'

Ten kinds of Western desserts and baked goods also were included in the third volume. 'This book includes some Western-style food to suit a new kind of household.' The recipes called for new equipment and tools for the kitchen: refrigerator, hand-cranked ice cream machine, cookie press and double-boiler.

Ice cream

Chill 1.8 L of milk in the refrigerator until it becomes thick, and put it in the inner container of the ice cream maker. Mix some lotus root starch (a thickener) with a little milk to make a paste, and mix it with 50 eggs, 1 cup cocoa and 1.8 kg sugar and 10 drops flavouring. Add all this to the container, and close it tightly. Put ice around the outside, and salt on top of it. Turn the crank slowly for 7 to 8 minutes and then quickly for 6 to 7 min until ice cream solidifies. If you do not use cocoa, flavour it with banana, almond, coffee, lemon, rose water, cherry or jackfruit. This ice cream is better than the kind sold in the city.

S-shaped Cookies

Mix together, 600 g flour, 5 eggs, 230 g lard, 230 g sugar, and one spoonful each of lemon extract and grape wine. Pack the dough into the cookie press with the plunger. Use a fancy tip to extrude the dough into the shape of the English letter S, and bake the cookies.

White Pudding

Mix 0.5 cup of lard with 2 cups sugar and heat the mixture until itnearly boils. Mix in 1.5 cups flour and some grape wine, and then add 1 cup corn meal. Beat 5 egg whites until an inserted chopstick will stand upright in it; mix half of it into the flour mixture. Add the remaining half to which a spoonful of lemon extract has been added. Steam the pudding in a Western-style double boiler, and decorate it with glazed fruit.

Western foods were taken up in Chinese households mainly in the form of baked goods (cookies, jelly roll and cream cakes) and sweet desserts. They introduced a few previously unknown techniques. The beating of egg whites until they were stiff was one such technique. Whipping cream until it would hold its shape was another. Doubtless, European and American and cooks surpassed their Chinese colleagues in the arts of baking and confectionery. So Mr. Huang eventually rounded out his career as cookbook writer by publishing *European and American Cookies and Bread Book* in 1939.

NOTES

Opening lines: *Zhongguo yin shi tan gu* 中國飲食談古 by Wang Renxing 王仁興. Beijing 北京: Qing gong yeh chubanshe 輕工業出版社. pp. 114-115. Schall von Bell's Chinese name was Tang Ruowang 湯若望

Yuan Mei's recipe: Yang Zhongcheng xi yang bing 楊中丞西洋餅 in: *Suiyuan shi dan* 随園食單 (2006) by Yuan Mei 袁枚. Bei jing 北京: Zhongguo fang zhi chubanshe 中國紡織出版社. ISBN 7-5064-4028-8. p. 161

Tong's recipe: Xi yang dan juan 西洋蛋卷 in: *Tiao ding ji* 調鼎集 (2006) by Tong Yuejian 童岳薦 edited by Zhang Yannian 張延年. Beijing 北京: Zhongguo fangzhi chubanshe 中國紡織出版社. ISBN 7-5064-3647-7. p. 309

Astor House Hotel: *The Bund Shanghai* (2008) by Peter Hibbard. Hong Kong: Odyssey Books. ISBN 978-962-217-772-7. pp. 224-225

T.P. Crawford: *Fifty Years in China* by L.S. Foster. http://baptisthistoryhomepage.com/crawford.t.p.50.china.ndx.html

Making Western Food: Zao yang fan shu 造洋飯書 ed. by Deng Li 鄧立 and Li Xiusong 李秀松(ZPGC, 1987). A facsimile edition based on the 1909 edition published by the American Presbyterian Mission Press: *Hai mei hua shu guan* 海美華書館. (pound cake) Jin gao 斤糕, p. 45

Chinese and European Cookbook: Hua ou mei chu shu da quan 華歐美廚書大全 (4th edition, 1936) by Huang Zhenzhang 黃軫章. Hong Kong: Ju zhen yin wu shu lou 聚珍印物書樓. (meat stock) Bao tang 煲湯, p. 1; (mayonnaise) Mi mi 米弭, p. 39; (German Brains) Zhe wen niu nao 者文牛腦, p. 111; (Italian Tongue) Yi da li yang li 意大利羊脷,p. 110; (Mint of Lamb) Bo he yang rou 薄荷羊肉 p. 106; (asking for

SLIPPERY NOODLES

a cook) Zuo chu wen da 做廚問答, following p. 418

Hash, chop suey: *Manual for Army Cooks* (1910) Office of the Commisary General. War Dept. Doc. 379, Washington. Recipe No. 283, p. 83

Chop beef chop sue: Niu rou gan shi sui 牛肉干什碎. *Hua ou mei chu shu da quan* 華歐美廚書大全 (4ᵗʰ edition, 1936) by Huang Zhenzhang 黃軫章, p. 81. (dried soup powder) Geng fen 羹粉, (stuffed olives) Hongxin gan lan 紅心攬牛, (Worcestershire sauce) Fan chi you 番豉油, (ketchup) Fan qiechi 番茄汁, (macaroni) Fu zhu 付竹, (pepper) Gu yue fen 古月粉

Home Cooking: *Vol. I: Jia ting shi pu xu bian* 家庭食譜續編 (1923); *vol. II: Jia ting shi pu san bian* 家庭食譜三編 (1925); *vol. III: Jia ting shi pu* 家庭食譜 (1926) by Shi Xisheng 時希聖 (Facsimile editions. Original publisher: Zhonghua shuju yin hang 中華書局印行). (peppermint candy) Yang bo he tang 洋薄荷糖 , vol. I, p.137; (brandy) Bai lan di 白蘭地, vol. III, p. 305; (ice cream) Xue gao 雪糕, vol. III, pp. 32-33; (S-shaped cookies) Ai si bing 愛司餅, vol. III, pp. 45-46; (white pudding) Qing dan gao 清蛋糕, vol. III, pp. 51-52

CHAPTER FORTY-THREE

REPRISE

(Twentieth century)

About dim sum, it is said that a Tang dynasty official named Zheng Can was away on an inspection tour. The servants had prepared breakfast for the lady of the house. She said to her younger brother, 'I have not finished my makeup. I am not ready for breakfast yet. You can take some dim sum first.' This shows that dim sum originally meant breakfast.

Dim sum should not be taken in a hurry. But these days, poor people, even labourers have dim sum.

(Yuan Mei, about his cook Wang Xiaoyu, eighteenth century)

I asked him why, when he could easily have got a job in some affluent household he had preferred to stay all these years with me.

'To find an employer who appreciates one is not easy,' he said. 'But to find one who understands anything about cookery is harder still. True appreciation consists as much in detecting faults as in discovering merits. You, on the contrary, continually criticize me, abuse me, fly into a rage with me, but on every such occasion make me aware of some real defect; so that I would a thousand times rather listen to your bitter admonitions than to the sweetest praise.'

But when he had been with me not quite ten years, he died; and now I never sit down to a meal without thinking of him and shedding a tear.

(Tenth century)
The emperor asked the young scholar, 'What is the best food?' 'There's no such thing as the best. It is simply what your palate craves. For me, it is pickle juice.' The emperor laughed. 'How can that be?' 'I recall one night it was very cold. I built a fire. I was in high spirits, and then I got very drunk and fell asleep. Waking up at the fourth watch, my throat was parched. With the quilt wrapped around me, I looked out at the snowy courtyard in the moonlight. I saw a large jar of pickled vegetables. Immediately I told the boy to throw on some clothes, go outside, scoop snow into an empty wine jar and drop a handful of pickles in it. Drinking the melted snow and pickle juice, I ate the pickles. How crisp they were! A gift from heaven! I thought.'

(Ninth century)
> On the road at Qingming (in early spring),
> Drenched by many showers, and weary,
> I inquired, 'Is there a wine shop nearby?'
> The boy on a buffalo pointed.
> 'Over there, in Apricot Blossom Village.'

(Eighth century)
> I have brought you this far. Here is where we part.
> Tonight, I shall shut the gate tight.
> Next year when the grass turns green,
> Perhaps you will return?

HSIANG JU LIN

NOTES

Dim sum: Dian xin 點心 in: *Qing bai lei chao* 清稗類鈔 (1984) by Xu Ke 徐珂 (1869-1928). Beijing 北京: Zhonghua shu ju 中華書局. p. 2235. (anecdote) [Neng gai zhai man lu 能改齋漫錄 by Wu Zeng 吳曾, ch. 2, pp. 21-22]

Yuan Mei's Cook: (translation by Arthur Waley) *Yuan Mei: Eighteen Century Chinese Poet* (1956) by Arthur Waley. George Allen and Unwin, London. p. 53 (text in Chinese) Chu zhe Wang Xiaoyu zhuan 廚者王小余傳 in: *Yuan Mei quan ji* 袁枚全集 (1993) ed. Wang Yingzhi 王英志. Nanjing 南京: Jiangsu gu ji chubanshe 江蘇古籍出版社. ISBN 7805194963 *Vol. 2: Xiao cang shan fang wen ji* 小倉山房文集, ch. 7, pp. 144-145

The best food: [*He shi yu lin* 何氏語林 by He Liangjun 何良俊, ch. 11, p. 18]

The emperor, the scholar: Song Taizong 宋太宗 (r 976-992), Su Yijian 蘇易簡 (958-996)

Apricot blossom village: *Qingming* 清明 by Du Mu 杜牧 (803-852?) [*Yu xuan Tang shi* 御選唐詩by Chen Tingjing 陳廷敬 and Ai Xin Jue Luo Xuan hua 愛新覺羅玄燁, ch. 30, p. 11]

Parting: Song bie 送別 [*Wang Youcheng ji jian zhu* 王右丞集箋注 by Wang Wei 王維, ed. Zhao Diancheng 趙殿成, ch.13, p. 12]

TIMELINE

(b, born; BCE, Before Common Era; c, century; d, died; fl, flourished; r, reigned)

Zhou Dynasty 周   1122-255 BCE
     Confucius, philosopher (551-479 BCE)

Qin Dynasty 秦   255-209 BCE
     Lu Buwei, minister (3rd c BCE)

Han Dynasty 漢   206 BCE-220
     Zhang Qian, explorer (b 195 BCE)

Northern Wei Dynasty 北魏   386-534
     Cui Hao, minister (d 450)
     Jia Sixie, civil servant (6th c)

Liang Dynasty 梁   502-557
     Wudi, emperor (r 502-549)

Sui Dynasty 隋   581-618
     Wendi, emperor (r 581-604)
     Yangdi, emperor (r 605-617)
     Xie Feng, food administrator (fl 605-616)

Tang Dynasty 唐   618-906
     Sun Simiao, physician (581-682)
     Meng Shen, nutritionist (621?-713?)
     Wang Wei, poet (699-759)
     Du Fu, poet (712-770)
     Lu Yu, tea connoisseur (733-804)
     Liu Xun, civil servant (9th-10th c)

Northern Song Dynasty 北宋   960-1126
     Tao Gu, scholar (902?-970)
     Su Dongpo, poet (1036-1101)

TIMELINE

Southern Song Dynasty 南宋   **1127-1279**

Jin Dynasty 金   **1115-1234**
        Meng Yuanlao, writer (fl 1126-1147)
        Zhang Jun, general (1086-1154)
        Wang Zhuo, sugar cane farmer (fl 1161)
        Lin Hong, gentleman cook (13th c)
        Madame Wu, housewife (late Song)

Yuan Dynasty 元   **1260-1368**
        Genghis Khan, conqueror (1162?-1227)
        Husihui, physician (fl 1315-1330)
        Ni Zan, artist (1301-1374)

Ming Dynasty 明   **1368-1644**
        Tao Zongyi, editor (fl 1360-1368)
        Han Yi, physician (1328-1412?)
        Zheng He, explorer (1371-1425)
        Ma Huan, chronicler (fl 1414-1451)
        Song Xu, scholar (fl 1504)
        Gao Lian, playwright (fl 1573)
        Li Shizhen, pharmacologist (1518-1593)

Qing Dynasty 清   **1644-1911**
        ZhuYizun, academician (1629-1709)
        Li Huanan, civil servant (mid-18th c)
        Yuan Mei, scholar (1716-1798)
        Tong Yuejian, salt merchant (18th-19th c)
        Martha Foster Crawford, missionary (1830-1909)
        Xue Baochen, academician (1850-1926)
        Zeng Yi, physician (1852-1927)
        Xu Ke, journalist (1869-1928)

Republic 民國   **1912-1948**
        Shi Xisheng, journalist (fl 1920s)
        Huang Zhenzhang, business man (fl 1920s-1930s)

TABLE OF UNITS OF WEIGHT, CAPACITY AND LENGTH

Table of Units of Weight, Capacity and Length

Unit		Dynasty							Current Definition of Unit	
		Han 221 BCE-220	Northern Wei 386-534	Sui 581-618 / Tang 618-906	Song 960-1279	Yuan 1260-1368	Ming 1368-1643	Qing 1644-1911	Metric System	Other Systems +
Weight										
hu/dan	斛/石*	26 kg	53 kg @	L: 79 kg S: 26 kg	76 kg	76 kg	71 kg	71 kg	50 kg	110 lb
jin	斤**	220 g	440 g	L: 660 g S: 220 g	633 g	633 g	590 g	590 g	500 g	1.1 lb
liang	兩#	14 g	27.5 g	L: 41 g S: 13 g	40 g	40 g	37 g	37 g	50 g	1.76 oz
qian	錢##	-	-	L: 4.1 g S: 1.4 g	4 g	4 g	3.7 g	3.7 g	5 g	0.18 oz
Capacity										
hu/ dan	斛/石*	20 L	40 L	L: 60 L S: 20 L	67 L	95 L	100 L	100 L	100 L	23 gallons
dou	斗	2 L	4 L	L: 6 L S: 2 L	6.7 L	9.5 L	10 L	10 L	10 L	2.3 gallons
sheng	升	200 mL	400 mL	L: 600 mL S: 200 mL	670 mL	950 mL	1 L	1 L	1 L	1.8 pints
ge	合	20 mL	40 mL	L: 60 mL S: 20 mL	67 mL	95 mL	100 mL	100 mL	100 mL	0.18 pints
Length										
zhang	丈	230 cm	300 cm	L: 360 cm S: 300 cm	310 cm	310 cm	B: 320 cm V: 327 cm T: 340 cm	B: 320 cm V: 345 cm T: 355 cm	3.33 m	3.65 yd
chi	尺	23 cm	30 cm	L: 36 cm S: 30 cm	31 cm	31 cm	B: 32 cm V: 32.7 cm T: 34 cm	B: 32 cm V: 34.5 cm T: 35.5 cm	33.3 cm	1.1 ft
cun	寸	2.3 cm	3 cm	L: 3.6 cm S: 3 cm	3.1 cm	3.1 cm	B: 3.2 cm V: 3.3 cm T: 3.4 cm	B: 3.2 cm V: 3.45cm T: 3.55 cm	3.33 cm	1.3 in
fen	分	2.3 mm	3 mm	L: 3.6 mm S: 3 mm	3.1 mm	3.1 mm	B: 3.2 mm V: 3.3 mm T: 3.4 mm	B: 3.2 mm V: 3.45 mm T: 3.55 mm	3.3 mm	0.13 in

* In the Song dynasty *dan* totally replaced *hu* which was redefined as 0.5 *dan*   ** Catty   # Tael or Chinese ounce   ## Mace   @ Values near the end of this dynasty

L: Large scale, for general use   S: Small scale, applied to weighing medicine, gold and silver, and to linear measurements in time-reckoning and musical temperament

B, V, T: Length units for builders, surveyors and tailors   + Weight: avoirdupois system; capacity: SI equivalent; length: international measure

TABLE REFERENCES

Reference 1: Zhongguo li dai du liang heng zhi yan bean jian biao - Hong Peixin bo ke 中國歷代度量衡演變簡表 - 洪培欣博客
http://eblog.cersp.com/userlog/11802/archives/2009/1231390.shtml

Reference 2: *Qi min yao shu* 齊民要術 (1982) by Jia Sixie 賈思勰, annotated by Miao Qiyu 繆啟愉. Beijing 北京: Nong ye chubanshe 農業出版社 p. 3

Units:

The table is based on reference 1. As stated in Chapter One, the values for capacity during the Northern Wei dynasty were fluid. Therefore to employ a single value (such as 300 mL given in reference 1) for the capacity of one sheng 升 over the entire Northern Wei period may be misleading. I have instead used the value of 400 mL for one sheng 升 as given in reference 2 that deals specifically with Jia's book.

INDEX OF RECIPES

INDEX OF RECIPES